Dying and Deliverance

Dying and Deliverance

Searching Paul's Law–Gospel Tension

Gary E. Gilthvedt

Foreword by
Arland J. Hultgren

WIPF & STOCK · Eugene, Oregon

DYING AND DELIVERANCE
Searching Paul's Law–Gospel Tension

Copyright © 2016 Gary E. Gilthvedt. All rights reserved. Except for brief quotations in critical publications or reviews, no part of this book may be reproduced in any manner without prior written permission from the publisher. Write: Permissions. Wipf and Stock Publishers, 199 W. 8th Ave., Suite 3, Eugene, OR 97401.

Wipf & Stock
An Imprint of Wipf and Stock Publishers
199 W. 8th Ave., Suite 3
Eugene, OR 97401

www.wipfandstock.com

ISBN 13: 978-1-4982-2918-0

Manufactured in the U.S.A. 12/23/2015

The Scripture quotations contained herein are from the New Revised Standard Version Bible, copyright © 1989 by the Division of Christian Education of the National Council of the Churches of Christ in the U.S.A., and are used by permission. All rights reserved.

To Mary

He said to Simon, "Go and Preach."

"To the men who crucified thee, Lord?"

"Yes."

"To those who brought the crown of thorns?"

"Yes. To them say that I still have my crown,
and to him who came with the reed
say that I have a scepter too."

"Preach, Lord, to the men who drove the nails?"

"Yes. And to those who cursed me say that I have a song for them;
and to the soldier who pierced my side
say that there is a nearer way to my heart
than that."

—Paul Scherer, *Love Is A Spendthrift*

Contents

Foreword by Arland J. Hultgren | ix
Preface | xiii
Abbreviations | xv
Introduction | xxi

1. The Cross and the Law in Paul | 1
    1.1 Paul and the Cross | 1
    1.2 The Cross in Galatians | 9
    1.3 Paul and the Law | 14
    1.4 The Law in Galatians | 22
    1.5 The Cross and the Law | 26

2. Galatians 2:19 | 33
    2.1 Dying to, Living to | 33
    2.2 Crucified-with | 40
    2.3 Through Law | 44
    2.4 Comparison to Romans 7:1–6 | 53

3. Galatians 2–3 | 63
    3.1 Works of the Law | 63
    3.2 Curse of the Law | 88

4. End of the Law | 126
    4.1 Sons, not Slaves, Galatians 4:1–7 | 126
    4.2 Paul's Summation, Galatians 6:14–15 | 134

5. Sacrifice and Deliverance in Galatians 1:4 | 144
    5.1   He Gave Himself, Galatians 1:4a | 144
    5.2   To Deliver Us, Galatians 1:4b | 153
    5.3   According to the Will of God, Galatians 1:4c | 164

Conclusion | 168

Bibliography | 171
Subject Index | 189
Index of Scriptural References | 213

Foreword

PAUL'S LETTER TO THE Galatians is one of his most significant writings. It is counted as one of the four *main letters* (*Hauptbriefe*, in German) of Paul, the other three being Romans and 1 and 2 Corinthians. There can be no surprise that Galatians would be so highly regarded. In that letter of only six chapters, as in no other, Paul puts forth a concise and penetrating case for freedom from the law for his Gentile Christian converts, a robust case for the gospel that he had received and proclaimed, and a clarion call to live out the life that flows from faith.

Galatians has too often been read in light of Romans and the other letters of Paul without a hearing by itself. That is not all bad, for there is considerable consistency in the theology of the apostle expressed in his letters. But each letter has its own distinctive character, addressing issues important to Paul and his readers on specific occasions, and that is no less the case with Galatians. Moreover, not only can Galatians get submerged in other letters of Paul, and indeed other books of the New Testament, but also by the history of doctrine.

Gary Gilthvedt takes up various matters in Galatians, among them issues concerning Paul and the law, and Paul's view concerning the atoning work of Christ. Both have to do explicitly with the death of Christ within the context of the letter. These matters are probed and discussed in ways that are refreshing and certainly helpful for the interpreter of Galatians and of Paul's thought more generally.

In regard to Paul and the law, there is a long-standing tradition, especially among Protestants, to think of the law in Judaism as a burden, from which Christ has freed his followers—thanks to the great insights of Paul. But Paul does not actually speak that way in his letters, even though he has a lot to say about freedom from the law in Galatians and Romans. On the contrary, as a starting point, Paul's own Jewish heritage must be taken into account. Anyone who has read the Psalms, especially the very first of them, should know that to the Jew the law is a delight, not a burden to be carried. Paul too can speak of the law in positive terms, especially at Romans 7:12.

The immediate issue for Paul—the one that prompts his comments about the law in Galatians—arose in a specific context, and that was the attempt to impose the law upon his Gentile converts in Galatia by other Christian leaders. That is sufficient to explain Paul's polemical remarks about the law in this letter.

But Gilthvedt takes us further. In regard to Paul and the law—meaning the law of Moses, as interpreted by Second Temple Judaism (the Judaism that existed prior to, during, and after the time of Paul)—the author delineates the various meanings of the term *law* in Galatians, and then goes on to show in this letter that the death of Jesus, which occurred under the law, meant not only Jesus' death under the law, but also that of all who share his destiny by faith. The believer, like the crucified and resurrected Jesus, is therefore no longer under its power. Living in union with the risen Christ, the believer lives in a new era; the old has passed away. While this claim was advanced by Paul to his believers in Galatia, it is also a way for subsequent theological reflection to take up and advance.

In regard to the atoning work of Christ, Christian theologians and others have had difficulties to make a clear statement concerning it. Although the church has defined the *person* of Christ in the ancient ecumenical creeds and councils, it has never come to a specific, sole definition of the *work* of Christ. The result is that various theories have been advanced. The most well-known is the so-called satisfaction theory, in which the death of Christ was a necessary sacrifice to appease the wrath—or to satisfy the justice—of God. But such thinking is not to be found in the letters of Paul. Even though the death of Christ, in Paul's understanding, was *for us* and was atoning, he expresses its meaning in a different way.

Gilthvedt shows that it is *deliverance*, not *sacrifice*, that is at the forefront of Paul's thinking. The fundamental human problem is enslavement to the power of sin, which leads to cultural exclusivism, religious institutionalism, and political authoritarianism. The remedy is deliverance from that power. The atoning work of Christ in his death was thus to deliver believers, in union with him, from the old era of enslavement and consequently bringing them into the new era of life. Further, the atoning work of Christ was in accord with the will of God. This view of Paul stands over against any that would pit the Son over against the Father in the work of reconciliation. As Paul says elsewhere, "In Christ, God was reconciling the world unto himself" (2 Cor 5:19). The same way of thinking, if not that particular sentence, is shown by the author to be operative in Galatians. It is also a salutary way of thinking for believers after Paul.

Other issues and themes within Galatians are dealt with by the author, but the two touched upon here stand out in particular, and the author's treatment of them is carried on with special care. He engages the work of other scholars along the way, as amply demonstrated by his references and quotations from their writings. The book is a fine guide to Galatians, written by a scholar who has pondered the nuances of Galatians for many years, and with skill.

—Arland J. Hultgren

Asher O. and Carrie Nasby Professor Emeritus
of New Testament, Luther Seminary

Preface

PAUL'S LETTER TO THE Galatians is the *Magna Carta* of Christian Liberty. Martin Luther spoke of Galatians respecting its pure doctrine of faith, saying that it must continually be read and heard in public. Luther believed that Galatians can never be discussed and taught enough. It will always be involved with new beginnings:

> If it is lost and perishes, the whole knowledge of truth, life, and salvation is lost and perishes at the same time. But if it flourishes, everything good flourishes — religion, true worship, the glory of God, and the right knowledge of all things and of all social conditions . . . "When human beings have finished, they are just beginning."[1]

In Galatians Paul speaks of new beginning in terms of *new creation* (6:15); *freedom* (5:1); status as *children, crying,"Abba! Father!"* (4:6); *heirs according to the promise* (3:29); *redeemed from the curse of the law* (2:13); and *set free from the present evil age* (1:4). In every chapter and throughout the whole, the letter announces freedom from enslavement, accomplished for all sides of every boundary that once divided, distinguished, and identified those who *now* are *one in Christ Jesus* (3:29). The new beginning was inaugurated when Christ *gave himself for our sins* (1:4a). Paul advances this tradition to a new level with his news of *deliverance* (1:4b).

How are we to comprehend this message? Perhaps we understand it best from the far side of its happening, with a view backwards from the future it has secured, opened to us today in confidence of its coming. The believer remembers a purposeful past, but lives under the power of a promised future. The meaning of Christ's death on the cross has cosmic dimensions:

> The death of Jesus was either a tragic incident, which meant that his kind of life was futile and impotent and would be broken

---

1. LW 26, front. Luther agreed with and quoted Ecclesiasticus 18:7.

at last by a world that was too much for it, or it meant that mercy and justice and peace are so closely akin to the Eternal God himself that they can be nailed to wooden beams and still win!—wiped out, and they'll come back!—buried, only to break death itself wide open.[2]

Thus, when God did act *to break death itself wide open* it established the most powerful and poignant of affirmations that the *mercy and justice and peace* lived in Jesus Christ are according to God's own heart, anchored in God's own intention, and in service of the whole long purpose of God's cosmic redemption. Such facts of redemption are not conquered, but conquer, through the energetic truths tested and told by persons such as the Apostle Paul.

The first four parts of the present study were a doctoral dissertation for the University of St. Andrews, under the title, "Dying 'Through the Law to the Law' (Galatians 2:19)." That work was done under the careful eye and salutary direction of Dr. A. J. M. Wedderburn. I appreciate the lasting gift of his scholarly and supportive supervision. I am fortunate to have been one of his students at a fine university.

But some of what it means to keep the faith is to continue our studies of the *Word-in-search-of-words*. Consequently, it is right to update, revise, and amend the original document before publication. The time since St. Andrews has brought resources both new and important that have voiced new challenges for parish and classroom ministries, have added their perspectives to this project, and have taken significant place also in the addition of part 5.

Dr. Arland Hultgren has given generously of his time and attention to studying the manuscript and offering helpful suggestions. He has given special consideration to the final part, *Sacrifice and Deliverance*, in relation to the tenor of this whole project, to the knowledge of faith that we seek, and to Paul's evangelical proclamation as we find it in the epistles.

There is both advantage and relief in having a publisher, editor, and staff who handle a project with competence, professionalism, and civility. I am grateful to Wipf and Stock for their work and support in seeing the project through to completion in such manner.

Mary, my wife-pastor-conversation partner, is a committed and competent student of the Scriptures. We have returned often to the theological issues of Galatians generally and 1:4 in particular. These times have had much to do with the direction of this work. I hope that testimony to her encouraging presence and lively witness bears reflection of my esteem and the joy with which this volume is dedicated to her.

—GEG, Easter, 2015

---

2. Scherer, *Love Is A Spendthrift*, 30.

Abbreviations

Old Testament

Gen	Genesis	Eccl	Ecclesiastes
Exod	Exodus	Song	Song of Solomon
Lev	Leviticus	Isa	Isaiah
Num	Numbers	Jer	Jeremiah
Deut	Deuteronomy	Lam	Lamentations
Josh	Joshua	Ezek	Ezekiel
Judg	Judges	Dan	Daniel
Ruth	Ruth	Hos	Hosea
1 Sam	1 Samuel	Joel	Joel
2 Sam	2 Samuel	Am	Amos
1 Kgs	1 Kings	Ob	Obadiah
2 Kgs	2 Kings	Jon	Jonah
1 Chr	1 Chronicles	Mic	Micah
2 Chr	2 Chronicles	Nah	Nahum
Ezra	Ezra	Hab	Habakkuk
Neh	Nehemiah	Zeph	Zephaniah
Esth	Esther	Hag	Haggai
Job	Job	Zech	Zechariah
Ps	Psalms	Mal	Malachi
Prov	Proverbs		

New Testament

Mt	Matthew	1 Tim	1 Timothy
Mk	Mark	2 Tim	2 Timothy
Lk	Luke	Titus	Titus
Jn	John	Philem	Philemon
Acts	Acts of the Apostles	Heb	Hebrews
Rom	Romans	Jas	James
1 Cor	1 Corinthians	1 Pet	1 Peter
2 Cor	2 Corinthians	2 Pet	2 Peter
Gal	Galatians	1 Jn	1 John
Eph	Ephesians	2 Jn	2 John
Phil	Philippians	3 Jn	3 John
Col	Colossians	Jude	Jude
1 Thes	1 Thessalonians	Rev	Revelation
2 Thes	2 Thessalonians		

Dead Sea Scrolls

1QH	Thanksgiving Hymns
1QM	War Scroll
1QpHab	Pesher Habakkuk
1QS	Manual of Discipline
4QEn	Book of Enoch, Cave 4
4QFlor	Florilegium, Cave 4
4Q174	Text 174, Cave 4
4Q246	Text 246, Cave 4
4Q504	Words of the Illuminaries
11QPs	Psalter, Cave 11
11QtgJob	Targum of Job, Cave 11
CD	Damascus Document

Josephus

Ag. Ap.	Against Apion
Ant.	Jewish Antiquities
J. W.	The Jewish Wars

Philo

Abr.	De Abrahamo
Jos.	De Josepho
Mos.	De Vita Mosis

Apocryphal/Deuterocanonical Books

Tob	Tobit	Song of Thr	Prayer of Azariah and Song of the Three Holy Children
Jdt	Judith		
Add Esth	Additions to Esther		
Wis	Wisdom		
Sir	Sirach (Ecclesiasticus)	Sus	Susanna
Bar	Baruch	Bel	Bel and the Dragon
1 Esd	1 Esdras	1 Macc	1 Maccabees
2 Esd	2 Esdras	2 Macc	2 Maccabees
Let Jer	Letter of Jeremiah	3 Macc	3 Maccabees
		4 Macc	4 Maccabees
		Pr Man	Prayer of Manasseh

Reference Abbreviations

AS	Abbott-Smith Manual Greek Lexicon of the New Testament
ASV	American Standard Version
BDAG	Bauer, Danker, Arndt, Gingrich Greek–English Lexicon
BDF	Blass, Debrunner, Funk Greek Grammar
BTB	Biblical Theology Bulletin
BZ	Biblische Zeitschrift
BJRL	Bulletin of the John Rylands Library
BWANT	Beiträge zur Wissenschaft vom Alten und Neuen Testament
BZNW	Beihefte zur Zeitschrft für die neutestamentliche Wissenschaft
BDB	Brown, Driver, Briggs Hebrew–English Lexicon
CBQ	Catholic Biblical Quarterly
CJT	Canadian Journal of Theology
EST	English Standard Version
ET	Evangelische Theologie
EQ	Evangelical Quarterly
ExpTim	Expository Times
HCSB	HarperCollins Study Bible
HDB	Harvard Divinity Bulletin
HTR	Harvard Theological Review
HR	History of Religions
HBT	Horizons in Biblical Theology

Reference Abbreviations (continued)

IDB	*Interpreter's Dictionary of the Bible*
Int	*Interpretation*
IBS	*Irish Biblical Studies*
ITQ	*Irish Theological Quarterly*
IEJ	*Israel Exploration Journal*
JB	*Jerome Bible*
JBC	*Jerome Bible Commentary*
JSB	*Jewish Study Bible*
JAAR	*Journal of the American Academy of Religion*
JTC	*Journal for Theology and Church*
JBL	*Journal of Biblical Literature*
JNES	*Journal of Near Eastern Studies*
JR	*Journal of Religion*
JSNT	*Journal for the Study of the New Testament*
JSNTSup	*Journal for the Study of the New Testament—Supplement Series*
JTS	*Journal of Theological Studies*
KD	*Kerygma und Dogma*
KEK	*Kritische-evangelischer Kommentar über das Neue Testament*
KJV	*King James Version*
KNT	*Kommentar zum Neuen Testament*
LS	Liddell and Scott, *A Greek–English Lexicon*
LNTS	*Library of New Testament Studies*
LPS	*Library of Pauline Studies*
LCL	*Loeb Classical Library*
LN	Louw and Nida, *Greek–English Lexicon of the NT Based on Semantic Domains*
LW	*Luther's Works*
LXX	*Septuagint*
MT	*Masoretic Text*
NAB	*New American Bible*
NEB	*New English Bible*
NET	*New English Translation*
NIB	*The New Interpreter's Bible*
NIBCNT	*New International Biblical Commentary, New Testament*
NICNT	*New International Commentary on the New Testament*

NIDB	New Interpreter's Dictionary of the Bible
NIGTC	New International Greek Testament Commentary
NRS	New Revised Standard (Version)
NT	New Testament
NTK	Neues Testament und Kirche
NTS	New Testament Studies
NTT	Norsk teologisk tidsskrift
NovT	Novum Testamentum
NovTSup	Novum Testamentum Supplements
OT	Old Testament
OTL	Old Testament Library
RGG4	Religion in Geschichte und Gegenwart, 4th ed.
RQ	Restoration Quarterly
REB	Revised English Bible
RSV	Revised Standard Version
SNT	Die Schriften des Neuen Testaments
SJT	Scottish Journal of Theology
SBLAB	Society of Biblical Literature Academia Biblica
SBLDS	Society of Biblical Literature Dissertation Series
SBLRBS	Society of Biblical Literature Resources for Biblical Study
SBLSBS	Society of Biblical Literature Sources for Biblical Study
SBLSP	Society of Biblical Literature Seminar Papers
SBLSS	Society of Biblical Literature Semeia Series
SBLSymS	Society of Biblical Literature Symposium Series
SBLTT	Society of Biblical Literature Texts and Translations
Str–B	Strack–Billerbeck, *Kommentar zum Neuen Testament aus Talmud und Midrasch*
SB	Studia Biblica
SP	Studia Paulina
ST	Studia Theologica
STK	Svensk Teologisk Kvartelskrift
TDNT	Theological Dictionary of the New Testament
TDOT	Theological Dictionary of the Old Testament
TEH	Theologische Existenz Heute
TW	Theologische Wissenschaft
TB	Tyndale Bulletin
TNTC	Tyndale New Testament Commentaries

Reference Abbreviations (continued)

TZ	*Theologische Zeitschrift*
VT	*Vetus Testamentum*
WW	*Word and World*
WUNT	*Wissenschaftliche Untersuchungen zum Neuen Testament*
ZAW	*Zeitschrift für die altestesamentliche und Wissenschaft*
ZEE	*Zeitschrift für evangelische Ethik*
ZNT	*Zeitschrift für Neues Testament*
ZNW	*Zeitschrift für die neutestamentliche Wissenschaft*
ZTK	*Zeitschrift für Theologie und Kirche*

Introduction

THE PRESENT STUDY BEGAN with the observation that although Paul frequently refers to the death of Christ, he refers to the cross or crucifixion of Christ in relatively few places. Why is this the case? Indeed, Paul does not mention the cross or crucifixion in every epistle. Why does he do so in the few letters where the cross is an explicit part of his message? Why, on many occasions, does Paul speak of the death of Christ, but only few times speak of the manner or means of that death? Does the answer lie within certain aspects of the context that Paul addressed? Was there a development in Paul's own thought and proclamation that led him either to or away from language about the cross? Did he come to understand his own experience by way of Jesus' death on the cross? Was there a combination of these or other reasons? What purpose within the letters do his references to cross and crucifixion serve? Pursuing these questions leads to texts in which Paul responds to the problem of the law. It is particularly in Galatians that the cross and the law together occupy center stage in Paul's argument. It is specifically in Gal 2:19 alone that Paul refers both to the law and to crucifixion. What is the connection here between the cross and the law? This study is an exegesis of Gal 2:19, *For through the law I died to the law, so that I might live to God. I have been crucified with Christ.*[1] The purpose of the study is to investigate what Paul means by dying *through the law, to the law*, and what this means in relation to being *crucified with Christ*. The relation of Paul to first century Judaism is implicit in these questions. A synopsis of an investigation into that problem will introduce our method and procedure.

Beverly Roberts Gaventa's insightful analysis of E. P. Sanders' *Paul and Palestinian Judaism* surveys the methods by which the Paul–Judaism relationship has been studied. She examines Sanders' proposal for a new

---

1. The Greek text reads, ἐγὼ γὰρ διὰ νόμου νόμῳ ἀπέθανον ἵνα θεῷ ζήσω· Χριστῷ συνεσταύρωμαι (*ego gar dia nomou nomo apethanon hina theo zēso; Christo sunestaupomai*).

method, and offers an altered form of that method.[2] Her proposal serves as a point of departure for our study of Gal 2:19, and so we commence with reference to her review.

Comparison of essences is one of the major approaches that scholarship has used to deal with the question of Paul and Judaism.[3] The tendency in this method is to reduce the thought of Paul and the thought of Judaism to a few key phrases, with the resultant essences set in sharp contrast to each other. The tendency has been to characterize the thought of Paul as justification by faith, and Judaism as a religion of works. But there are several problems in doing so, and they compound one another. No religion can be reduced to a phrase or set of phrases. The polemic of Paul's letters has often been used to produce a description of Judaism, and that description has been used in the comparison or contrast to Paul. Finally, the literature that represents two religions may be so different in kind as to make comparison difficult or unfair.

Comparison of motifs is another approach to the problem. It sets the themes of one religion over against the themes of another.[4] This method, however, fails to take a religion on its own merits, and tends to neglect the whole of that religion for the sake of certain parts.

Comparison of patterns is Sanders' proposal for overcoming the deficiencies of these methods.[5] The whole of one religion must be compared to the whole of another, with each defined and described on its own terms. By *pattern* Sanders means the movement from logical starting point to the logical conclusion of a religion, hence, how *getting in* and *staying in* are understood. The pattern that Sanders sees in Judaism is what he calls *covenantal nomism*: in divine mercy God chose Israel, provided atonement in the law, and those who live in obedience to the law remain in the covenant.[6] The pattern that Sanders sees in Paul is what he calls *participationist eschatology*: those who believe in Christ have already become one with him, and upon his return will be fully transformed.[7] Sanders' conclusion is that these are two different types of religion, and Paul's critique of Judaism is that it is *not* Christianity.

One problem that Gaventa sees with Sanders' proposal is that we in fact do not have wholes to compare. In Paul's letters, for example, the Apostle

---

2. Gaventa, "Comparing Paul and Judaism: Rethinking Our Methods," 37–44.
3. Sanders, *Paul and Palestinian Judaism*, 2–6.
4. Ibid., 7–12.
5. Ibid., 12–18.
6. Ibid., 75, 236, 422–23.
7. Ibid., 549.

does not set out to establish the entire scheme of his thought and teaching, but rather intends to respond to very specific situations in particular places that involve certain problems and persons. In addition to that, we have in the letters only one side of the conversation or, to put it another way, we have Paul's answers to questions that at best we can often only infer. Again, the agenda of Paul's letters is frequently set by others to whom he is responding, and even texts to which he relates may have been chosen for him by his opponents' previous use of those texts. A further problem that Gaventa sees with Sanders' proposal is that he has presumed in advance what questions are important. Thus, Sanders' treatment of Palestinian Judaism is selective, as he has confined it to issues that have been deemed relevant to Pauline scholarship. Sanders' account of Paul is also selective: what we have in his discussion of Paul *is a compendium of Pauline thought* on a selection of topics determined by aspects of the history of Pauline interpretation.[8]

The method that Gaventa proposes may be described in three stages. First, the use of vocabulary with which Paul addresses his topics is one place to begin ascertaining what was important to him. We begin with the texts themselves rather than allowing Paul to be controlled by earlier discussion. Regarding the law, we can first note where Paul refers to *law* and where he does not.[9] That is the place to start: "What is important is that an investigation into the pattern of Paul's religion should begin, not where others have left off, but where the texts themselves begin."[10]

Second, Paul's conversation partners can be allowed to speak, and the context of Paul's communities be allowed to emerge. This involves examination of each letter in its own right, with a view to discovering what questions each letter itself wishes to ask or answer. Paul's viewpoints may become distorted if attention is not given to the perspectives of his addressees and the sociology of ancient Christianity. N. A. Dahl, speaking of 1 Cor 1:10—4:21, has made four suggestions that may be paradigmatic for every epistle; (1) the controversy can be studied as such, with Paul's answers and perspectives, and the Corinthians' questions and problems inferred from Paul's answers; (2) a reconstruction of the background can be pursued on the basis of information within the section of text being studied; (3) the contextual exegesis ought not be prejudiced by similarity to Gnostic material, Acts, or other Pauline epistles; (4) a reconstruction of historical background will be only a *reasonable hypothesis* at best.[11]

---

8. Gaventa, 40.
9. The Greek word for *law* is νόμος (*nomos*).
10. Gaventa, 42.
11. Dahl, "Corinth," 45; "Pauline Epistles," 266, Dahl says that Paul's letters, having

Third, given Paul's terminology, his opponents' issues, and the situation of the church that he addresses, can we see a pattern in each particular letter, or a number of patterns, to his response? Does he consistently present certain convictions or opinions? Do these emerge in more than one letter, or in all the letters, and can we ascertain from them the pattern of Paul's religion? It would be a difficult task to apply this procedure to the literature of two religions such as Judaism and Paul's Christianity. The literature of each religion is greatly different in kind from that of the other. Paul's literature is occasional. It tends to be problem-oriented and it is intended for the life of a specific community of faith. The literature represented by many Jewish texts is not generally as conversational in that same sense. The direction of our search is indicated by the outline of Gaventa's proposal. The basic aspects of the method inform our approach to Galatians and to the relation of the cross and the law in 2:19. It is in the tension of that relationship and in the Galatians' situation that the meaning of Paul's understanding of law and gospel comes to light and informs our understanding of what occasioned the letter.

Part 1 surveys the epistles for occurrences and contexts of the terms, *law* and *cross/crucify*.[12] Chapter 1 concentrates on cross/crucify throughout the letters. Chapter 2 narrows the survey to Galatians. Chapter 3 focuses on the *law* throughout the letters. Chapter 4 is about the law in Galatians. Chapter 5 summarizes the place of the law and the cross in Paul's epistles, and particularly in the Galatians argument. The presupposition here is *not* that an understanding of Paul's message is to be derived on the basis of statistical evidence.[13] But the point remains: if Paul is *not* talking about a particular topic, there must be very good reasons for the interpreter to import that topic into the text. Conversely, if the topic and terminology *are* present, the question why they are present should be asked and the meaning of the words examined. This is true of individual words and words in combination

---

been written for particular destinations may have been the reason why the author of Luke–Acts ignored them, even though he surely knew of their existence. The tendency of the church was for *catholic* epistles, and with it came a tendency for generalizing interpretation. And yet, 271, "To the apostle himself, letters to particular churches written on special occasions were the proper literary form for making theological statements. Of this fact both exegesis and theology, not to mention preaching, have to take account. The particularity of the Pauline epistles points to the historicalness of all theology, even that of the apostle." Cullmann, "Plurality of the Gospels," 39–58; Beker, *Paul* (1980), ch. 1.

12. The Greek noun is σταυρός (*stauros*); the verb (1st person singular) is σταυρόω (stauro-ō).

13. Barr, 233, critical of Kittel's *TDNT*, sees as flawed a method *organized under words*: "Theological thought of the type found in the NT has its characteristic expression not in the word individually but in the word-combination or sentence." Well-taken, *if* individual words were left in isolation as inflexible measures of thought.

with other words, in the context of the theological argument of the epistle. The place to begin is with the exact speech of the text itself.[14]

Part 2 targets the specific parts of Gal 2:19 and its setting in the epistle. Chapter 1 relates 2:19 to its immediate context as it commences in 2:14b, and then examines the *dying to, living to* concept. Chapter 2 explores the compound verb, *crucified-with*. Chapter 3 concentrates on Paul's phrase, *through the law*. Chapter 4 compares Gal 2:19 to Rom 7:1–6, and especially 7:4, where Paul speaks of dying *through the body of Christ*. Galatians 2:19 is part of Paul's response to the Galatians' situation of law-imposition. To illustrate and strengthen his position, Paul reports the Antioch incident with Peter. Galatians 2:19 is either part of the rebuke that Paul reports having delivered to Peter, or it is his extension of that conversation now applied to the Galatians. Peter's actions at Antioch can therefore be taken as representative of the position with which Paul contends in Galatia. Paul's answer to this position is that he has *died to and through the law*. He speaks of his participation with Christ in terms of being *crucified with Christ*. These statements express Paul's antithesis to Peter's vacillating behavior and the Galatians' problem with the law. Does the *dying to and through* and *crucified with* terminology of 2:19 indicate a particular way of thinking about the event of Christ's death on the cross? What does the epistle itself teach us about what Paul meant by this language? And what might be the significance of such a way of thinking for believers in Christ, relative to law-keeping as a way of keeping faith?

Part 3 further examines the textual context of Gal 2:19. Chapter 1 examines the phrase *works of the law* in Galatians 2 and 3. Chapter 2 examines the *curse of the law* in Galatians 3. Part 4 relates to the liberation of life from under the law, as Paul speaks of it in Gal 4:1–11 and Gal 6:14–15. Part 5 focuses on Gal 1:4, where Paul refers in 1:4a to *Christ's self-giving*, thus connecting us to 2:20, *he gave himself*.[15] Paul then adds his proclamation of *deliverance* in 1:4b, and in 1:4c attributes the liberating work of Christ to *the will of our God and Father*. The conclusion summarizes how best we may understand dying *through the law*, in light of what Paul means by *crucified with Christ*.

It can become the practice in theological pursuit to support with selected Pauline texts the dogmatic bias of an ecclesiastical tradition.[16] Paul's

---

14. Funk, 277, 304, wants the text to speak for itself, within and over against its frame of reference, and thus lexical or comparative investigations must not be disparaged out of hand.

15. *The one who gave himself* (*tou dontos hēauton*); *having given himself* (*paradontos hēauton*).

16. Gordon, 32–43, offers a re-evaluation that questions the Lutheran and other

epistles are then treated as though any one of them could have been written to any of his churches. The particularity and peculiar logic of each letter is then obscured. It may have obscured the teaching of Paul himself by making of him much more a rigid dogmatician than he in fact was. Paul used a special vocabulary in the service of his central conviction. His responses to the teaching of those whom he thought would undermine his gospel were sometimes reasoned and sometimes visceral. He relied on patterns of speech and thought that characterize his faith and his proclamation as thoroughly theological, despite his being *not a theologian but a missionary*.[17] We may regard Paul's whole mission as *a doctrine of Christ and his work*.[18] For Paul, Christ is "the supreme mighty act of God, the decisive factor in the unfolding and realization of the divine purpose."[19]

How did the cross of Christ represent that act and purpose, and why does Paul speak so explicitly of the cross in Galatians? What did it mean for Paul to be crucified with Christ? Did Paul see the law impinging on the central teaching of the cross? And what does it mean for Paul to say that he *died through the law*? In order to investigate these questions it will be helpful to locate the places throughout his letters where Paul speaks of the cross and the law, and the tension between the two. The tension is present from the outset of this letter, and clear through to the letter's end. But the tension comes especially to light in Gal 2:19 and its context in Paul's mission.

---

traditional schemes of Paul.

17. Manson, *On Paul and John*, 11. Sanders, *Paul* (1977), 433, Paul was not a *systematic* theologian.

18. Wrede, 86.

19. Manson, 16.

1

The Cross and the Law in Paul

1.1. Paul and the Cross

GALATIANS 2:19 HAS TWO central aspects of Paul's theology occurring in juxtaposition. These two aspects are the law and the cross.[1] And yet when we describe these as central aspects we encounter a problem, for in some of Paul's letters neither of them is mentioned and in other letters the mention of either is indeed scanty. We begin with Paul's use of *cross*, and *crucify*. A survey of his epistles shows the relative infrequency with which he mentions the terms.[2] First and Second Thessalonians, 1–2 Timothy, Titus, and Philemon use neither the noun nor the verb in any form.

1. In 1 Corinthians the problem of *schismata* (*dissensions*, 1:10), and *quarreling* (1:11), manifest in the *Ego* slogans of various parties (1:12), is the issue that Paul immediately addresses.[3] He reminds his hearers that it was Christ, and not Paul (and by implication no other party hero, either) who was crucified for them (1:13). Paul introduces the cross on the personal

---

1. The RSV places *I have been crucified with Christ* in v. 20. The NRS along with the Nestle and UBS editions of the Greek text place it at the end of v. 19. This latter arrangement is followed in this study.

2. Moulton and Geden, *Concordance*; Aland, *Konkordanz*; Kubo, *Lexicon*; *BibleWorks5*. What are commonly accepted as genuine letters of Paul include Romans, 1–2 Corinthians, Galatians, Philippians, 1 Thessalonians, Philemon. They are distinguished from those probably of deutero-Pauline authorship. For the sake of inclusiveness all letters bearing Paul's name in our common versions of the canon are in this survey.

3. Munck, *Salvation*, 136–39, is not convincing in his denial that factions existed in Corinth. *Bickerings*, 139, seems weak for describing a problem that Paul saw fit to address straightaway in his letter. The basis and mark of the cleavages was attachment to individual leaders, making common thought difficult and jeopardizing the common meal. Dahl, *Corinth*, 42–3; Maurer, *TDNT* 7:964; Robertson and Plummer, *1 Corinthians*, 10. The split into groups has not led to the dissolution of the community; Conzelmann, *1 Corinthians*, 32; Barrett, *1 Corinthians*, 41–2.

level, in connection with his own name, speaking of it for the first time before he begins his argument from scripture in 1:19. But having named the problem of dissensions (1:10) and quarreling (1:11) Paul moves forward immediately to his extended argument against wisdom. This suggests that the divisions (or threat of them) were an effect of a larger cause, namely the Corinthians' involvement with worldly wisdom. The movement from the party problem to the wisdom argument is clear and concise in 1:13-17. Paul makes several assertions. He baptized only a few of them, so none ought to say that they were baptized in his name (1:13-15).[4] He was not sent to baptize but to preach (1:17).[5] His preaching of the gospel was not with words of wisdom, lest the cross of Christ (1:17b) be emptied (of its power).[6] This second reference to the *cross* shows Paul's concern that the manner of his preaching should not be out of harmony with its content.[7] His references to baptism do not devalue baptism. He indicates that his call is to preach the word of the cross, which will check the developments in Corinth and bring the Corinthians to common persuasion about Christ crucified.[8]

The third reference is Paul's characterization of his own preaching as the *word of the cross* (1:18), in contrast to *wisdom* talk (1:17). The theme and contrast are continued into chapter 2, as Paul speaks of the rulers of this age with their wisdom of this age (2:6-8). In 2:2 he relates his *deliberate decision* to know nothing among the Corinthians except Jesus Christ, and him crucified.[9] This again is in contrast to *wisdom* (2:1). The *deliberate decision* refers to Paul's first visit among the Corinthians, a visit that would have come after Athens, Luke's recounting of which (Acts 17) shows no mention of the cross in the Areopagus sermon.[10] Paul recalls the decision about the

---

4. Lohse, *Canon*, 63, notes the relationship between the initiate and the mystagogue in the mystery religions, and how for the baptized in the Christian community a significant relationship was also a factor.

5. Conzelmann, *1 Corinthians*, 36-7, points out that only the preaching of the cross can check the developments in Corinth, and this preaching characterizes Paul's call to be an apostle.

6. Barrett, *1 Corinthians*, 49, speaks of preaching as the proclamation of the cross, the cross as the source of power in preaching, and the message of Christ crucified as the persuading element.

7. Weiß, *Korintherbrief*, 22-3, sees a concern in 1:17; 2:1, 4, taken together, for both form and content.

8. Munck, 154.

9. BDAG, 568, the word *decide* (*ekrina*) indicates a conscientious and intentional decision about what ought be said. Conzelmann, *1 Corinthians*, 54, speaks of it as *resolve*.

10. Haenchen, 468. We note that 1 Thes 1:9-10 may summarize Paul's message to the Thessalonians, as Paul speaks of the living God and the resurrection of the Son, but

content of his preaching as having been made upon coming to Corinth. Although the deliberateness of his word of the cross may have seemed clearer for Paul while writing than it was for his hearers when he visited and preached among them, he speaks of it here so to suggest that the decision, then having been made, is one from which he has not departed. He is now not writing as though introducing new material, but reminding his hearers of what had been there from the start, as an established part, indeed the center, of Paul's message. The references in 1:18 and 2:2 emphasize the decisive content of Paul's preaching, and 1:12 conforms to this same concern for content.[11] Paul is reacting against two aspects of wisdom, *sophia*: (1) wisdom as speech (1:17; 2:1–5; 4:20), and, (2) wisdom as a means of knowing God (1:21; 2:6—3:4).[12] It is speech as *sophia*, and it is *sophia* as salvation. It is not simply special wisdom, but saving wisdom. To counter such claims the cross is upheld by Paul as the very ground of salvation, and the content of his proclamation.

The contrast in 1 Corinthians 1 is not between wisdom and no wisdom, but between wisdom and cross, or between worldly wisdom and God's wisdom.[13] Paul's argument focuses on *the wisdom of the wise* (1:19) and *the wisdom of the world* (1:20).[14] Essential to the argument is wisdom's opposite, *foolishness, folly* (1:18, 21, 24, 25).[15] This description of the cross would have been particularly meaningful to a Greek-speaking Gentile community, to whom the *slave's death* on the *barren tree* was a well-known form of *folly*

---

not the death or cross of Christ.

11. Käsemann, *Besinnungen*, 268, maintains that *sophia* ought to be translated as *theology* throughout the wisdom argument in 2:6–16, meaning not theology in the sense of a scientific pursuit, but as doctrine of salvation.

12. Horsley, "Wisdom," 224, 229. Barrett, "Corinth," 6–14, for shades of meaning for *wisdom* in Paul.

13. Weder, *Das Kreuz*, 165, says that Paul takes over the keyword, *wisdom*, at the beginning of 2:6, and forms his own wisdom with it, thus usurping a term that had been misused in Corinth. God's coming into the world has its correspondence in just such a usurpation of worldly speech, and suffuses not only the wisdom of the world but the world's speech, with the word of the cross. Conzelmann, *1 Corinthians*, 58, Paul seizes back for his own use a traditional *revelation schema* of God's decreed mystery *now* revealed. It is critical to note that this schema is interpreted by the history of the cross, not vice versa. God is known historically only in the death and resurrection of Christ. This is the sense of the new turn given to *wisdom*.

14. The wisdom of the wise (1:19), the debater of this age, and the wisdom of the world (1:20) are not to be understood generically, but through what is happening in Corinth. Schlatter, *Theologie*, 72, notes how dissimilar are this time and the coming time: the wisdom of this time is not God's gift, but the emergence of human strengths.

15. Robertson & Plummer, 21, μωρία (*folly*) is peculiar to 1 Corinthians in the NT (1:18, 23; 2:14; 3:19).

and *madness*.[16] Such descriptions of Christianity abounded in the pagan judgments on Christians, and the term serves Paul's **bold oxymoron** as he speaks of the foolishness of the *kerygma* in contrast to wisdom of the world.[17] The inability to perceive this fundamental distinction led the rulers of this age (2:8) to crucify the Lord of Glory.[18]

This sixth reference to *cross* terminology leads on to the contrast between the spirit of the world and the Spirit which is from God (2:12), the unspiritual (2:14) and spiritual man (2:15), and the mention again of the party heroes, Paul and Apollos (3:4), allegiance to whom has been evidence that the Corinthians are *of the flesh* (3:1). With this term Paul places the Corinthians in the realm of the old *aeon*, the category also for sin, death, and law.[19] The Corinthians' problem could be understood in terms of an *over-realized eschatology* whereby "they already live on the far side of eschatological judgment in the perfection of the new aeon (4:7)."[20] Or their trouble could be stated in terms of their failure to comprehend the discontinuity between the new aeon and the old.[21] Paul, in any case, counters their position with his word of the cross. The cross is the antithesis to the Corinthian tendency.[22] It is the cross with which Paul would overturn their values: what is great in the eyes of the world in fact runs contrary to God's purpose, and God's saving purpose is established in what seems weak and foolish to the world.[23]

2. The noun, *cross*, is not mentioned in 2 Corinthians or Romans, and the verb, *crucify*, occurs only once in each of those letters.

2.1. Second Corinthians 13:4 speaks of the crucifixion of Christ *in weakness*, in contrast to Christ living presently *by (the) power of God*. Paul's own sufferings and weakness correspond to the weakness of Christ, and are the paradoxical signs and vehicles of God's power (12:9-10). Strength in weakness (12:10) is in contrast to the superlative apostles' reliance on outward signs and commendation (12:11-13), about which they have

---

16. Hengel, *Crucifixion*, 2: "The folly and madness of the crucifixion can be illustrated from the earliest pagan judgment on Christians." Gibb, 6-10; Bertram, *TDNT* 4:845-47.

17. Robertson & Plummer, *1 Corinthians*, 21.

18. Weder, *Kreuz*, 167.

19. See 2.1; 2.4; 3.1 of the present study.

20. Thiselton, 510. Wilckens, *TDNT* 7:520.

21. K. Barth, *Resurrection*, 116-21.

22. Conzelmann, *1 Corinthians*, 54 n. 16: "The Corinthians have gone on from the cross to the exaltation. Paul reverses the direction of thought: from exaltation to the cross. The result of the resurrection is not that the cross is superseded, but rather that it becomes possible to speak of it."

23. Hooker, "Interchange," 352-3.

apparently boasted (11:12, 21; 10:18).[24] Paul clearly speaks in two-aeon language, and attributes his opponents and their ministry, along with Moses (3:13) and the law (3:6), to the old aeon. In this context Paul spoke of weakness, and pointed to his own *affliction* (1:4, 8; 2:4; 4:17; 6:4; 7:4; 8:2, 13) as over against human strength, in order to defend his apostolicity against the superlative apostles (11:5) to whom he had unwillingly been compared. The cross in 2 Corinthians represents the paradoxical *when I am weak, then I am strong*, as Paul sees in his thorn in the flesh a correspondence between his own condition and the death of Christ.[25] Christ died in weakness and Paul will glory only in what corresponds to Christ's death.

Second Corinthians uses various forms of the word for *glorying* or *boasting* a total of twenty-nine times.[26] But the one use of a form of *cross/crucify* (13:4) comes in Paul's warning about his impending third visit, in which he expects to deal with the Corinthians according to God's power. This power manifests itself in Paul's weakness, which for him was the sign of true apostolicity (11:30; 12:9-12). Here *crucify* is not used with *glory* but with *weakness*.[27] Christ crucified in weakness is the paradigm for apostolicity. The theme of weakness in 2 Corinthians 10–13 indicates the letter's implicit *theologia crucis*.[28] Second Corinthians and Galatians have certain ideas in common. Second Corinthians is like Galatians in its view of the law as negative and inferior (2 Cor 3:6-11). Second Corinthians 5:21 is similar in thought and structure to Gal 3:13.[29] A similar problem of extraneous interlopers is represented by 2 Cor 11:4 and Gal 2:4. The *all* of 2 Cor 5:14

24. Lohse, *Formation*, 71; Giallanza, 1572-77; Thrall, "Super Apostles"; Kee, "Super Apostles"; Barrett, "Opponents"; "ΨΕΥΔΑΠΟΣΤΟΛΟΙ"; *Second Corinthians*, 28-30; Dibelius, *Paul*, 106.

25. Park, "*Skolops Tae Sarki*"; Giallanza.

26. καύχησις, καύχημα, καυχάομαι are the various forms for *glory/boast*. Bultmann, *TDNT* 3:645-53. The term is used almost exclusively by Paul, and can indicate human self-confidence as over against faith in God, which *implies the surrender of all self-glorying* (649). Dunn, "Works," speaks of boasting in national privilege and identity. The possibility of appropriate boasting is opened for Christians whose boast is in Christ and his work; 2 Cor 1:12; 7:4; 8:24; 11:10; 7:14; 9:2; 10:8, 13, 17; 11:30; 12:1; Gal 6:14.

27. Bultmann, *Second Corinthians*, 243: "ἐξ ἀσθενείας is scarcely meant in a causal sense—*as a result of his weakness* . . ." instead ἐκ is chosen for rhetorical correspondence with ἐκ δυνάμεως θεοῦ, *by the power of God*, and means, "as one who is weak." One who would share the risen life will also share the suffering and death, as Paul's own life is witness.

28. *Implicit* in as much as the cross terminology is for the most part absent, but also implicit in another sense. Beker, *Apostle*, 201-2, points out that in contrast to John's gospel, in which the cross is glorified as the gateway to heaven, in 2 Corinthians the cross is the hour of Jesus' weakness.

29. Hooker, "Interchange," 352-53.

reminds us of the *all* in Gal 3:26, as the new creation in 2 Cor 5:17 reminds us of the same theme in Gal 6:15. But despite these similarities the total absence of the word *law* in 2 Corinthians indicates that law *as such* was not the problem in that situation, although Paul does refer to it in terms of *the written code* in 3:6-11. The problem was the self-sufficiency of superlative apostles (12:11) who gloried in written letters of recommendation (3:1), which, like the *written code* (3:6) on *tablets of stone* (3:3), are contrasted to the new covenant, the life-giving Spirit (3:6) and the surpassing splendor (3:11) of the dispensation of righteousness (3:9).

2.2. Romans 6:6 has the compound verb, *crucified-with*, referring to the believer's incorporation into the death of Christ on the cross.[30] Paul's only other use of this compound verb is in Gal 2:19, where it refers to Paul's relation to the law. The only other NT uses of the compound form are Matt 27:44, Mark 15:32, and John 19:32. The robbers were crucified on their crosses alongside Jesus at Golgotha. The passive voice shows something done *to* a person, an action neither initiated nor completed by the person.[31] Did Paul know the tradition of the robbers crucified with Jesus and shape it to his own interpretation? The origin of Paul's idea probably lies elsewhere.[32]

3. Philippians mentions *cross* twice, Ephesians once, and Colossians refers to it twice.[33]

3.1. Philippians 2:8b, *even death on a cross*, is part of the Christ-hymn that Paul quotes, is probably a gloss, and may have been added by Paul to the

---

30. The verb (3rd person passive) for *crucified—with* is συνεσταυρώθη (*sunestaurothē*). Keck, "Post-Pauline Interpretation," 237, has noticed that in Romans Paul never expressly mentions the cross, but only alludes to it at 6:6. Keck concludes that, "Clearly, the importance of the cross for Paul is not disclosed by statistical evidence..."

31. Dana and Mantey, 161-63.

32. On the speculation that the verb in Gal 2:19 is rooted in the scene on Calvary see Duncan, 71. The explanation of Wedderburn, *Baptism*, 346-47, is more likely. He sees Paul's adaptation of an old idea (solidarity of the many with a founder) for a new purpose (dying with Jesus as one for whom Jesus died). The idea of being *with Christ* would have had to undergo a considerable shift in meaning from the idea of two fellow-victims who were with him at his crucifixion to the idea of being with Christ in Paul's sense.

33. All epistles attached to Paul's name in many English versions are in this survey, with cognizance that most scholars would include only seven as authentically Pauline. One interesting exception is proposed by Morton and McLeman, 110, who, on the basis of computer analysis of material that bears the imprint of one mind, derive a five-epistle Paul (Romans, 1-2 Corinthians, Galatians, Philemon). With respect to Ephesians, two ways of understanding certain characteristics of the letter are represented by M. Barth and Käsemann. Barth, *Ephesians*, 1:48-50, sees a mature Paul behind the ecclesiology of Ephesians. Käsemann, "Early Catholicism," 243, sees a catholicizing of Paul by the church, as his apocalyptic is replaced by a sacramental presence of Christ in the church.

hymn to bring more emphasis to the text than is carried simply by speaking of *death*.[34] The emphatic word, *even*, modifies *cross*, not *death*, and focuses on the completeness of Christ's self-emptying and obedience.[35] The gloss indicates Paul's shaping of pre-Pauline material to serve his *theologia crucis*.[36] With this word of the cross, he encourages the Philippians in their suffering for Christ's sake (1:29), to strive for the faith of the gospel (1:27), and not to fear their opponents (1:28). As in 2 Corinthians 10–13, suffering is viewed from the perspective of personal identification with the cross.

3.2. Philippians 3:18 speaks of the enemies of the cross whose minds are fixed on earthly things. The oblique reference to circumcision (*shame*)[37] and earthly mind-set in 3:19 remind of the circumcision conflict in Galatians (5:2) and the cross-wisdom contrast in 1 Corinthians (1:18–20).

3.3. Ephesians 2:16 speaks of reconciliation of Jew and Gentile *through the cross*, as the means by which Christ ends the hostility between them, making *both one* (v. 14). This *one* is a new entity, since it is neither of the former sides that were divided by the *wall of hostility*. There is *one new person* (v. 15). The theme is similar to the *new creation* of Gal 6:15, where Paul shows a third alternative to the two communities represented by *circumcision* and *uncircumcision*.[38] These two communities were indicative of

---

34. M. Barth, *Ephesians*, 1:6–8, lists characteristics of hymnic material; Kümmel, 335. Fuller, 204–7; Käsemann, "Philippians 2:5–11," 46. Wengst, 87 n. 87, refers to Hofius, who denies the gloss theory.

35. Käsemann, "Death of Jesus," 36; Lightfoot, *Philippians*, 113.

36. Weder, *Kreuz*, 209, speaks of this text as *the end of mythological speech*. He says, 213, that the question of who Christ is can no longer be answered on the grounds of mythological dramas about a Redeemer who descends and ascends again to heaven. The question of who Christ is, is inseparably connected to another question, that of who Jesus was. The insertion in the hymn of *death on a cross* has an important result for the understanding of the entire hymn. It becomes the interpretive center, by which the other statements appear in a new light.

37. Kümmel, *Introduction*, 328, calls the term (i.e. *shame*) a euphemism for genitals. But Michael, *Philippians*, 176, sees it as a reference to debased liberty; Bruce, *Philippians*, 107, does not think the sexual sense is well attested by the word itself; Loh and Nida, *Philippians*, 117, judge by the context (*bodily desires, things that belong to this world*) that it refers to immoral conduct. With Kümmel, Vincent, *Philippians*, 117, agrees with Bengel, who refers it to v. 2 and explains it as *pudenda*; K. Barth, *Philippians*, 113, understands it in terms of the biting polemic of v. 2, with v. 19 "a further allusion to circumcision which for concreteness leaves nothing to be desired." See Bultmann, *TDNT* 1:190, who recognizes here the usual meaning of *disgrace*, although the word is used in this verse in such a way as to play on its sexual meaning. Hawthorne, *Philippians*, 166, regarding the structure of the sentence, is convincing: he would read, *they have made their stomach and their glory in their shame their god*. Paul's accusation, then, would be that what has become god to them is food laws and the rite of circumcision.

38. Minear, "Crucified World."

the old cosmos. A new entity, people of faith in Christ, indicating the new creation, follows from the cross of Christ.

3.4. Colossians 1:20 strikes the same theme of reconciliation, thence of *all things* to God, making peace *through the blood of his cross*.[39] Forms of the verb, *reconcile*, are used both here and in the Ephesians text. This reconciliation is another way of speaking of the deliverance from the dominion of darkness and transfer to the kingdom of the Son (1:13).

3.5. Colossians 2:14 speaks of nailing to the cross the legal bond that stood against us. The act of nailing reminds us of the nails (John 20:25), marks of which were proof of Jesus' identity as the Crucified One.[40] The *legal demands* of the (handwritten) bond were blotted out. The terminology points to the law as what was nailed to the cross. Taken together the two thoughts about the antagonistic law and the blotting out of the written record remind us of Gal 2:19–20: Paul is dead to the condemning law that was instrumental in the curse and death of Christ.

The most uses of *cross/crucify* are in Galatians and 1 Corinthians. First Corinthians refers to the *cross* twice (1:17, 18) and *crucify* four times (1:13, 23; 2:2, 8). Galatians uses the noun three times (5:11; 6:12, 14) and the verb four times (2:19; 3:1; 5:24; 6:14). The compound form of the verb in 2:19 is the same compound as the sole instance in Romans, at 6:6. Given that these are all the texts in which *cross* and *crucify* occur in the Pauline (and deutero-Pauline) epistles, it is clear that the uses are few indeed compared to the theological weight assigned Paul's *theologia crucis*.[41]

And yet Christ's redeeming death on the cross is a message so central to Paul's message (*kerygma*) that news of the One *who gave himself for our sins* is pivotal in every letter Paul wrote. If we accept the most common consensus about the chronology of the letters we see that Paul did not refer to the cross in his earlier writings and did so infrequently in his later writings.[42] The chronologically middle epistles have the most references.[43] Why this is

---

39. *The blood of his cross* is likely an addition. Käsemann, *Essays*, 154–59; Lohse, *Colossians*, 43.

40. Hewitt, "Nails."

41. Käsemann, *Perspectives*, 34, quotes Luther's exposition of Psalm 5:12, *crux sola est nostra theologia*, (*the cross alone is our theology*) regarding the cross in Paul's theology. Luz, "Theologia Crucis," 122, recognizes that Paul's theology of the cross is not that he interprets the cross, but that the cross interprets him, and he interprets the world, the church, and humankind by the cross.

42. First Thessalonians was likely Paul's first letter, then Galatians or 1 Corinthians, then Romans and Philippians. Jewett, *Chronology*; Hurd, "Chronology"; *1 Corinthians*, 3–41; Kümmel, 179–81.

43. Benoit, "The Law," observes the same phenomenon in Paul's use of law.

so stems from Paul's own theological development,[44] the specific nature of each situation he addressed,[45] and/or the ways in which those situations influenced his message.[46] Our survey of Paul's crucifixion terminology refutes the notion of a fixed Pauline schema and attendant vocabulary with which he encountered every situation. And yet, there is a firm, consistent center to Paul's message. We have seen that center expressed in terms of cross and crucifixion the most explicitly in 1 Corinthians. The references there occur mainly within Paul's argument from Scripture, as he emphasized the cross as the overturning of worldly values. These two factors, scriptural argument and antithesis of his opponents' values and theology, are also central in Galatians, where Paul's references to cross/crucifixion are relatively frequent. We concentrate next on these references to the cross in Galatians.

1.2 The Cross in Galatians

Paul refers to *cross* or *crucify* eight times in Galatians. Four of these references have some form of the verb: 2:19; 3:1; 5:24; 6:14. Three times he uses the noun: 5:11; 6:12, 14. Galatians 3:13 does not explicitly mention either cross or crucify, but *hanging on a tree* indicates crucifixion.

1. In Gal 2:19 Paul uses the phrase *I have been crucified with Christ* to speak of his relation to the law.[47] The perfect passive in 2:19 refers to an event that has taken place at a definite time and that is still in effect. There is nothing in the context to warrant ascribing this death to the time of Paul's conversion or call. In 1:15–16 Paul has spoken of that call in terms of revelation and apostolicity. In 2:19 Paul may be referring to the event and time of Christ's death on the cross, which, when it happened, included Paul in its meaning and effect. Paul uses this phrase in conjunction with *through law to law I died*. This putting together of crucifixion and death to and through

---

44. Marshall, "Pauline Theology," 182 n. 2, lists writers who trace the stages of development in Paul's thought, as stages are reflected in the epistles, once the epistles are placed in chronological order.

45. Jewett, *Terms*, 4–8, cites the danger of abstracting a biblical term from its historical situation. His contextual analysis would: (a) take account of the literary context of sentence, paragraph, and letter as a whole; (b) analyze (anthropological) terms in relation to historical situation, theological argument, and chronological framework; (c) relate the term to the *linguistic horizon* of the first century, to discover the assumptions of Paul's conversation partners and the impact and alteration of his arguments.

46. Grant, *Introduction*, 175, has pointed out that, "there are very wide variations in Paul's use of words. His usage depends primarily on subject matter, not on some ideal norm." The subject matter would in turn depend on the contingency of the situation. Beker, *Paul* (1980), 23–36.

47. Benoit, 11–39.

the law may correspond to 3:10-13, where Christ's death under the curse of law could offer a clue to understanding 2:19.

2. The reference to (*having been*) *crucified* in Galatians 3:1 represents a point of close similarity to 1 Corinthians.[48] The same word is used at 1 Cor 1:23 and 2:2, modifying *Christ*, the object of Paul's preaching (1:23), and the content of what Paul had deliberately decided to know among the Corinthians. Paul identifies his gospel with Christ crucified. In Gal 3:1 the participle also modifies Jesus Christ as the message that was *placarded* before the eyes of the Galatians.[49]

In the context of this argument from experience (3:1-5), and taken together with *did you receive the Spirit* (3:2) and *having begun with the Spirit* (3:3), the verb points to preaching about *the one who has been crucified* (3:1) that marked the beginning of the Galatians' faith. The Crucified One was their message of salvation. These three texts in 1 Cor 1:23; 2:2, and Gal 3:1 speak of Christ crucified as the content of Paul's *kerygma*. It is only the Galatians text, however, in which *having been crucified* is implicitly in contrast to *by works of law* (3:2). In 3:2, hearing with faith and reception of the Spirit are placed on the same side as *having been crucified* (3:1), against the impossibility of faith having begun with *works of law*. Then in 3:3 Spirit and flesh are placed in opposition, and in 3:5 Spirit and miracles are placed on the same side, along with faith, against works of the law. The law is thus opposed by Spirit, faith, miracles, and the Crucified One.

3. Paul uses *stumbling block* (*scandal*) once in Galatians and 1 Corinthians, both times in proximity with *cross*.[50] In Gal 5:11 Paul says that if he had preached circumcision (of which he apparently had been accused) then the *scandal* that is the cross would be removed.[51] The scandal of the cross

---

48. Burton, 145, notes that the perfect participle "expresses an existing (in this case permanent) result of the past fact of crucifixion." The thought here is not of Jesus having been affixed to the cross and still hanging there, but of Jesus who was put to death on the cross and thereafter, although risen, is yet the Crucified One. On crucifixion as a means of death see Burton's bibliographical references, 146-7; Schneider, *TDNT* 7:572-84; Hengel, *Crucifixion*.

49. Burton, 144-45; Lightfoot, *Galatians*, 134; Betz, 131; Schrenk, *TDNT* 1:771; Bultmann, *Theology* 1:292-94; Käsemann, *Perspectives*, 49; Weder, *Kreuz*, 182.

50. The word also occurs in Romans (9:33; 11:9; 14:13; 16:17) but never in proximity to the cross. The verb occurs at Rom 14:21; 1 Cor 8:13; 2 Cor 11:29. Stählin, *TDNT* 7:339-58.

51. Betz, 269, identifies the phrase, used only here, as an *ad hoc* formulation, put in contrast to *I preach Christ*. Borgen, "Circumcision," 44, suggests that Paul reacts to the misunderstanding of his position by Judaizers, who thought, "Paul continued to preach (and practice) circumcision after he received his call to be an apostle . . . In his letter Paul objects to this misunderstanding . . . " Watson, 200 n. 99, does not speak to Borgen's thesis and says, 69, "Paul opposes circumcision because it is the rite of entry into

as the way of salvation would be nullified (5:2), they would be severed from Christ (5:4), and they would be obligated, following circumcision, to keep the whole law (5:3). This obligation amounts to slavery (5:1). In 1 Cor 1:23 the cross is *scandal* to Jews and *foolishness* to Gentiles. The general scandal is that of the crucified man, and especially in Galatians a crucified Messiah. This is expressed by Paul in his use of Deut 21:23 at Gal 3:13. The scandal in Gal 5:11 points to God's way of establishing justification and granting grace. Galatians 3:13 is the only text in which Paul explicitly refers to Deut 21:23, with hanging on a tree interpreted to mean crucifixion, although in Gal 3:13 he does so not in connection with scandal but with curse. The same thought seems near to 1 Cor 1:23, although there the Deuteronomy text is not cited and curse is not mentioned. In Gal 5:11 the use is part of the argument contrasting works of the law and hearing with faith (5:2–6), a contrast introduced in 2:15 and running throughout the letter. In 1 Corinthians the *cross* is anti-wisdom and part of Paul's defense of his own apostolicity, and it is in the context of that argument that scandal is used in combination with the cross.[52] Only in Galatians are cross and scandal used together in the argument against circumcision and the law (5:11).

    4. Galatians 5:24 is the sole declaration in terms of crucifixion that the flesh has been overcome. The reference to *crucified-with* in Rom 6:6 is part of Paul's argument against sin, not against flesh, and is passive, whereas Gal 5:24 uses the aorist active. This indicates a past activity on the part of the believer in crucifying the flesh.[53] In Rom 6:6 the *old self* is put to death. *Flesh* in Gal 5:24 refers to the sinful nature, while in texts like 6:13, where it is used with *your*, it clearly refers to the physical flesh that was cut in circumcision.[54] Flesh in 5:24 is in contrast to Spirit. Works of the flesh are opposed to fruits

---

the Jewish people, *and for that reason alone* . . . (and) because Paul has already decided that the church is only the church when it is separate from the Jewish community." But Paul's argument is that the church is the church by faith in Christ, not that the church is the church by separation from the Jewish community. Watson's view presumes an earlier split between church and synagogue than is usually attested. Davies, "Pitfalls," 6; Betz, 323. Galatians does not speak of separation from Judaism.

    52. Paul's apostolicity is at stake in Galatians as an issue that is parallel to the attack on the truth of his gospel, the law-free salvation of Gentiles, and Paul's understanding of his mission. The question was whether it would be Paul's apostolicity or that of others that was authoritative for the Galatians. The question recurs in 1–2 Corinthians. The literature on apostolicity is immense, but a place to begin is with Barrett's *Signs*.

    53. Betz, 289, argues against a sacramental interpretation of this text, stating that it refers neither to baptism nor to a moral-religious decision made by Christians after their baptism. It is rather a statement of "Christian ethical existence with specific reference to the 'flesh.'" That is, being in Christ enables the Christian to neutralize the power of the flesh to produce its passions and desires.

    54. Jewett, *Terms*, 96, 453.

of the Spirit. To be led by the Spirit is to be free from the law (5:18). In 5:24 Paul's reference to *crucified* is part of the law–Christ (or law–faith) contrast, with the phrase *belonging to Christ* serving to exclude works of the flesh and life under law.

5. The anti–circumcision statement in Gal 6:12 contrasts *good showing in the flesh* with *persecuted for the cross*, and is the only place where Paul speaks of the cross as that for which one might be persecuted. It is this persecution that the promoters of circumcision wanted to avoid, although they are not really interested in keeping the whole law.[55]

6. By contrast to his opponents, Paul glories only in the cross (6:14a). This is similar to Phil 3:18, where Paul speaks of the enemies of the cross whose *glory* is in their *shame* (3:19).[56] The good showing in the flesh corresponds to glorying in their shame (Gal 6:12; Phil 3:18), and what is negatively implied in Phil 3:18–19 is positively stated in Gal 6:14a: Paul glories only in the cross. Only in Galatians are *persecution* (6:12) and *cross* used together, and Gal 6:14 is the only text that uses *cross* with *boast*. Paul equates a return to life under the law with glorying in the flesh, as flesh takes on the double sense of *both* life in the power of the old aeon *and* the flesh that was cut in circumcision.[57] As such, flesh is opposed to life in the Spirit, faith, and the cross. The Galatians text alone places cross and glorying together, and does so as part of the contrast between the law and the cross, between works and faith.

7. In Gal 6:14b Paul says that by the cross in which he glories he is also crucified to the world. He does not glory *in flesh* (6:13), and so is in contrast to those whose lives are measured by the worldly standards that are characteristic of the two communities of *circumcision* and *uncircumcision* (6:15a). Here alone Paul speaks of crucifixion in a three-fold sense: (1) that of *Christ*, 6:12, 14; (2) that of the *world*; (3) that of *Paul* towards the world. That *the world has been crucified to me* leads to *new creation*, the third alternative to the two communities of 6:15. Where this crucifixion happens there is a total devaluation of the *world* and the world is finished as a cause of glorying or triumph. Where the world ends the new creation begins.[58]

---

55. Jewett, "Agitators," 202–3. The term in 6:13 depicts the advocacy of circumcision. Reicke, *Era*, 212–20, traces the historical events, beginning with the martyrdom of James 1, about 42 A. D., through the 50's and the increasing pressure against the church from the Judaizing and Zealot movements. As the Hellenistic mission grew so did the pressure. Galatians 6:12 may reflect this pressure.

56. *Glory* in Phil 3:19 is *doxa*, not *kauchēsis*; one could say, *doxology*, not *triumphalism*.

57. Jewett, *Terms*, 101.

58. Minear, "World," 397–98.

This ending and beginning is accomplished by the cross of Christ, in which the believer has been included.

8. Galatians 3:13 is a significant crucifixion text, although it is one in which *cross* is not explicitly mentioned. The mention of the tree in Gal 3:13 plays on the word *tree* in the quotation from Deut 21:23. Certain malefactors whose crime was punishable by death (stoning) were hung on a tree *after* execution.[59] In some interpretations this hanging was, by NT times, associated with curse. Only criminals guilty of certain crimes were subjected to this ignominy, and the body was not to be left hanging overnight, lest it defile the land given to God's people. Even before the death of Christ some Jews applied this Deuteronomy text to crucifixion, although in the OT the hanging was not a means of execution but of announcement.[60] Later the text was likely used by some Jews against Christians in pointing out that Jesus could not have been the Messiah.[61] Paul himself could have used this argument against Christians prior to his conversion.[62] But the exegesis in 3:13 that equates hanging with crucifixion is an exegesis that did not originate with Paul, and the application of that exegesis to the death of Jesus did not originally come from Paul either.[63] But Paul uses both exegesis and application in his argument against the law, to show that Christ became a curse *for us* so that the blessing of Abraham might fall upon the Gentiles. Paul's contribution to the history of interpretation of Deut 21:23 was to see the *accursed* death of Jesus on the cross as God's divine event of salvation, done so as to free believers from the curse of the law.[64] The use of *tree* in reference to the *cross* is central to this argument about blessing and curse.[65] This tree-cross identification comes within Paul's argument from Scripture in ch. 3 in which a number of OT texts are woven together with his exposition and application. The purpose of both quotation and exposition is to serve Paul's christological starting point: faith, not law (2:15). Galatians 3 becomes a focal point of the letter's *theologia crucis*, as Christ's hanging on the tree of the cross turns the law's curse into blessing for the Gentiles.[66] In Galatians Paul

---

59. Wilcox, "Deut 21:22–23," 85–99. See 3.2 below.

60. Fitzmyer, "Crucifixion," 504–10; Kim, 46.

61. Hengel, *Atonement*, 40.

62. 1:15–16, Paul is called via revelation. Stendahl, *Paul*, 78–96, emphasizes *call* over *conversion*.

63. Kertelge, "Autorität," 7, notes early Jewish polemic against early Messiah-faith. Kim, *Origin*, 47 n. 3.

64. Barrett, "Allegory," 160.

65. Acts 5:30; 10:39; 13:29; 1 Pet 2:24.

66. Donaldson, "Inclusion of the Gentiles." Elliot, *Nations*, 15–16, 190 n. 130, makes a case for usually translating *ethnae* as *nations* rather than as *gentiles*.

consistently used references to the cross and crucifixion in his argument against the law. Without exception in Galatians it is the law–faith contrast that is served by *cross/crucify* terminology. It is to the other side of this contrast to which we now go, examining first the place of the law throughout Paul's letters, and then its place in Galatians.

1.3 Paul and the Law

Examination of Paul's letters shows that his references to the law are, like those to the cross, widely varied in number, purpose, and frequency. There are no mentions of the term *law* in 2 Corinthians, Colossians, or 1–2 Thessalonians, one reference in Ephesians and three in Philippians. The term, *law*, occurs thirty-two times in Galatians, seventy-four times in Romans, and nine times in 1 Corinthians. These references to the law are of a marked difference in kind from one letter to another. Galatians and Romans often speak of the negative role of the law, and its inadequacy for bringing righteousness.[67] In 1 Corinthians, however, the polemic against the law is not only absent, but Paul freely refers to the law in support of his own position.

1. In 1 Cor 9:8–9 Paul cites the Deut 25:4 text about the right of an ox to feed upon the grain it treads, as support for the divinely decreed apostolic right of material benefits from the church. Paul has renounced this right (9:15) so that he might be free from all in the material sense (9:19) even though he is a slave to all in such ways as being *as one under the law* to appeal to those under the law.[68] In 1 Cor 9:22 this *all things to all men* attitude overrides commitment to or freedom from the law, and points to an allegiance greater than law as the motivating force in Paul's ministry.[69] It is *for the sake of the gospel* (9:23). Here, law supports Paul's case for ministry to all people.

2. In 1 Cor 14:21 Paul cites law and prophetic texts from Deut 28:49 and Isa 28:11–12, in support of his argument that *tongues* be used in a limited way and orderliness in worship be maintained (14:40). In 14:34 Paul appeals to what *the law says* without citing a particular text, to support his statement

---

67. Gal 5:14 has a positive sense and Rom 7:7–20 counters what negative reports about Paul's attitude towards the law may have preceded him in Rome. Sanders, *Paul*, (1983), 17–27, 105–13, says that *not by works of law* is Paul's consistent answer to the question of entrance; in 1 Corinthians the question of right conduct in the church leaves room for Paul to refer to the law in support of his position.

68. Hock, "Tentmaking," 559–62, sees the slavery as referring to Paul's choice of an occupation.

69. Longenecker, *Paul*, 230–44; Chadwick, "All Things."

about subordination and silence of women in the churches.[70] Genesis 3:16 may be in mind at that point. In 15:56 the only negative statement in 1 Corinthians about the law occurs. The law is *the power of sin*. This connection of sin with the law is similar to that made by Romans 7:13, and is an exception to the generally neutral or positive references to the law in 1 Corinthians. The law references in 1 Corinthians indicate that the problem there was not law vs. gospel (or faith), but *cosmos* vs. gospel, *wisdom* vs. cross, and the question of apostolic authority.[71] In speaking about the grounds of faith and behavior for those who belong to the body of Christ, Paul is free to cite the law in his own support and in service of his gospel.

3. In Phil 3:5-6 Paul speaks of his Pharisaic attitude towards the law (3:5) and his blamelessness under the law (pertaining to righteousness, 3:6) as part of the *gain* that he forsook *for the sake of Christ* (3:7) and so that he *might gain Christ* (3:8). Law is contrasted to life in Christ, similar to the either/or of Galatians (3:2, 5). Righteousness by law is contrasted to righteousness by faith (3:9). In Philippians the polemic returns, with negative (*loss*, 3:7), and stinging (*dung*, 3:8) comments about Paul's former life as a law-abiding Pharisaic Jew.

4. In Eph 2:15 the *new self* (or *person*) who has replaced the division and hostility between Jew and Gentile was the end (*the new creation*) to which the means was the abolition of the law. The law here indicates what had previously made Israel unique and separate. This is similar to Gal 6:15, where Paul says that what counts (i.e. for glorying, 6:14) is the new creation, and not *circumcision* or *uncircumcision*.

5. The law vs. faith contrast is also evident in Romans, where *law* occurs in each of the chapters 2-10, and again in 13:8, 10. The most references to the law are in ch. 2; 3:19-31; and ch. 7. Romans 3:21 represents the law–faith contrast, and so does 4:13-25, which, like Galatians 3, uses the Abraham story. In Galatians, law and curse are lumped together in contrast to faith and blessing, while in Romans, law (or works of law; see 3:20-26) and faith are the two sides of the contrast, with law as the instrument of sin and the agent of death. The cross is not part of Paul's argument against the law in Romans, but is used in his argument against sin (6:6). Sin has seized the law, found opportunity in it (7:8), and so brought death (7:10, 12).[72] So

---

70. But is it *his* statement? Conzelmann, *1 Corinthians*, 246, regards it as an interpolation.

71. Thiselton, "Eschatology," 513: "From the eschatological vision in Corinth one can see no need for apostles." That is, no need for apostles in the Pauline sense; they had reduced the apostles to party leaders, 1:12.

72. Räisänen, "Gesetz," 103; Käsemann, *Romans*, 216: the law is the instrument of sin and death.

in Romans sin uses the law to bring death (7:13), and sin, death, and law therefore belong together (7:9–11; with flesh, 8:3). The polemic is softened as it focuses on sin's use of the law, rather than the law's curse on Christ and on those who wish to adhere to the law (Gal 3:10, 13). Sanders notes one distinct difference between Galatians and Romans regarding the law:

> In Galatians the polemic had to do with the entry of Gentiles into the people of God, and the status of Jews and Gentiles prior to or without faith was referred to in a confusing way (e.g. Gal. 3:23–4:10). In Romans, on the other hand, Paul strives to state what he perceives to be the plight of Jews and Gentiles without faith in a way that distinguishes between them, while still concluding that their status, whether prior to faith or in the Christian community, is the same (Rom 1:18–3:9; 4:11f.). This change of focus leads him to discuss in detail, for the only time in his extant correspondence, the situation of "Israel according to the flesh" (Romans 9–11), and he also attempts a much fuller account of the role of the law in God's plan than appears in Galatians.[73]

It is clear that Paul's references to *law*, like his references to *cross/crucify*, is not consistent from one letter to another. His break with the law, to which Gal 2:19 refers, was by no means a finished subject, although in the Galatian context his argument against the law is the most sharply defined.

6. The variety indicates need for a kind of categorization, although this ought not be imposed on the various epistles for the sake of reducing them to systematic consistency. Fitzmyer has summarized four distinctions by which Paul's references to the law may be categorized.[74]

6.1. Paul can speak of *law* in a generic sense, not specifically designating any particular law. Texts such as Gal 5:23; Rom 4:15b; 5:13 are representative of this type. It must be added, however, that this category is not clearly distinct from category 4, the law of Moses. Although the references cited refer to no particular law they seem clearly to mean the law of Moses. Even Gal 5:23 can well be understood this way: the law of Moses has nothing against such spiritual gifts.

6.2. Paul can use a figurative sense for law, as a kind of principle (Rom 3:27a; 7:21, 23a). As such it can refer to the principle of sin (Rom 7:23c, 25b), of sin and death (Rom 8:2b), of human nature (Rom 2:14d), or of faith (Rom 3:27b), Christ (Gal 6:2), or Spirit (Rom 8:2a). In Gal 6:2 the term is

---

73. Sanders, *Paul* (1983), 31, 58–9.
74. Fitzmyer, *Theology*, 75–6.

not to be understood as synonymous with the law of Moses. Paul uses the term in a loose, almost metaphorical sense, to speak of life in Christ.[75]

6.3. Paul can speak of *law* in quoting the OT, referring either to Psalms (Rom 3:19a), Prophets (1 Cor 14:21), or Torah (Gal 3:10b; 1 Cor 9:9; Rom 14:34; 3:31b).[76]

6.4. Mostly, "about 97 times in all," Paul refers to *law* (with or without the article) to refer to the law of Moses. Representative texts include Gal 2:16, 19, 21; 3:2, 5, 10a, 11, 12, 13, 17, 18, 19, 21, 23, 24; Rom 2:12, 13, 14; 3:19b, 20, 21; 5:13, 20; 6:14, 15; 7:1–9.[77]

Fitzmyer distinguishes between Paul's use of the law in Galatians and his use in Romans, as he suggests that Paul is proposing two different explanations for the law. First, "In Galatians Paul sets forth an extrinsic explanation, ascribing to the law of Moses a temporary role in salvation history . . . (Gal 3:23–4)."[78] The law here is temporary and provisional (3:17), inferior to the promises (3:19), having been given through a mediator (3:20). Second, in writing Romans, Paul had to deal with the inability of humankind to observe God's law:

> In composing Rom 7:13—8:4, then, Paul abandoned the extrinsic explanation and used a more intrinsic one, that is, a philosophical explanation of the human predicament. In Rom he shows that the difficulty is not with the law, but with humanity in its this–worldly condition of *sarx*, "flesh," alienated from God and hostile to him.[79]

Thus, Paul says that he is carnal and sold under sin (7:14), sin dwells in him, captivates him, and wars with God's law (7:17). In Galatians Paul describes humanity as having come to the last stage of salvation history, in which freedom from law has been granted.[80] The date set by the Father

---

75. Räisänen, *Paul*, 77–80; 50–2.

76. Rom 3:21 refers to *law* in two ways: God's righteousness has been manifested apart from law (as such), although the law and the prophets (the Scriptures) witness to it. Käsemann, *Romans*, 93.

77. Fitzmyer, *Theology*, 76; Bultmann, *Theology* 1:259–60.

78. Fitzmyer, 78.

79. Ibid., 78.

80. Ibid., 30–1, 44–5, 79, describes 3 stages of Paul's salvation history, based on rabbinic thinking: (1) The period from Adam to Moses was law–less (Rom 5:13–14; Gal 3:17); (2) the period after the law was added (Gal 3:19; Rom 5:20) had humanity imprisoned or in custody (Gal 3:23) from Moses to Christ; (3) the time of the Messiah when persons are justified by faith. Fitzmyer, 19 n. 34, attributes this three–fold scheme to later rather than early rabbis, but sees Paul viewing human history "through solely Jewish spectacles." But it is Paul's own interpretation of this scheme that sees the end of

(Gal 4:2) has been reached with the fullness of time. In Romans, on the other hand, God has done in Christ Jesus what the law could not do (8:3). Acquittal has been brought about through Christ's death and resurrection. This justifies and brings about the status before God that the law did not achieve, since the law was weakened by the flesh. Sin had to be condemned in the flesh for this justification to happen. Fitzmyer's analysis is helpful in two ways. First, it takes seriously that there is a difference between Romans and Galatians regarding Paul's treatment of the law. Second, it warns us that the uniqueness of each epistle's view of the law is lost if harmonizing or generalizing is attempted.[81]

7. These references to *law* in the epistles have shown a variety of ways in which Paul speaks of the law. The either/or of Philippians, the general support for his arguments that Paul finds in the law in 1 Corinthians, the inadequacy of the law and its captivity to sin and flesh in Romans, the inferiority and termination of law, historically considered, in Galatians, and the absence of the subject in other letters, show that there was no fixed doctrine of law with which Paul approached every situation.[82]

7.1. Räisänen rightly concludes that there are contradictions and tensions that are constant features of Paul's statements about the law.[83] The only suitable approach is to accept these as indications of Paul's theological and personal struggles.[84] Räisänen uses the term *oscillation* to describe Paul's view and use of the law, and this is an appropriate word if into it we do

---

the law in the time of the Messiah, and the new status as that of faith in Christ.

81. Beker, *Paul* (1980), chs. 4–5; 104–8, describes the differences between Galatians and Romans. But on his notion that Romans is a *dialogue with Jews* see Sanders, *Paul* (1983), 58–9 n. 75. Gager, *Reinventing Paul*, 51, says: "Certainly the audience addressed in the letters is always Gentile." He references Gaston, *Torah*. Relative to the Galatians' churches, Gager, 79, says, "And they consisted entirely of Gentiles. When Paul writes to these congregations, he always addresses them as Gentiles."

82. Paul does not seem to deal with the law until it became a problem for his churches. Then, the law is relative to the central christological convictions that Paul preached. Sanders, *Paul* (1983), 4–5.

83. Räisänen, *Paul* (1983), 11.

84. Ibid., 12, rejects three other approaches to Paul that he thinks are inadequate: (1) existentialist interpretations, as that of Conzelmann, because they fail to (a) distinguish the exegetical and theological tasks, and (b) take psychological or sociological considerations into account; (2) contextual criticism begins with a logical Paul and posits someone else's hand commenting on and enlarging the text as a way of explaining Pauline obscurities, but Räisänen thinks it was personal power, not logic, that made Paul's impact; (3) development theories tend to rest on an early date for Galatians and on the South Galatian hypothesis, neither of which have been conclusively proved; so also a short time-span between Galatians and Romans makes a dramatic theological development seem unlikely, and internal inconsistencies within a given letter are not rendered explicable by this theory.

not read *wishy-washy*.⁸⁵ There is no consistently systematic whole of Paul's thought on the law, and we therefore need to understand his statements as something other than parts of a systematic scheme.⁸⁶ Each epistle has a logic of its own.

7.2. On the personal level Paul struggled to understand his Jewish past on the basis of his Christian present. As a Jew he had found his Jewish identity in his faithfulness to the law and in being anchored in its traditions. Then the revelation of Jesus Christ (Gal 1:12) shook apart the former foundations and established a new foundation for his life. So Paul could speak of his *former* life. This new foundation was faith in Jesus Christ. This had to mean for Paul, "einen tiefen Einschnitt in sein Leben."⁸⁷ Its consequences were on a theological and biographical level. In his letters we see him struggling to understand and apply what had happened to him.⁸⁸ He sees that Christian existence is based on the foundation of faith in Jesus Christ. Seeing that, he is not free *from* having to deal with the question of the law, but he is free *for* that struggle.⁸⁹

7.3. This tension is further brought to light by the diverse situations of the churches, and the demands that church problems placed upon Paul. To a certain extent, the different things Paul said depended on the questions that were raised or the problems that were posed. In that light, each answer has its own logic, comprehensible only when viewed through the context of the particular situation. Each epistle is a unique historical composition that is directed to specific circumstances and the argument of a letter needs accordingly to be understood first of all on that basis.⁹⁰ With respect to the law the oscillation of which Räisänen speaks is partly attributable to the needs of

---

85. Räisänen, *Paul* (1983), 16. *OCD*, 1236, explicates *wishy-washy* as: "weak, sloppy, feeble, or poor in quality or character." Paul was none of these.

86. That Paul was not a systematic theologian is noticed by Gardner, *Experience*, 16, 139; Wrede, *Paul*, 74-7, 80; Manson, *On Paul*, 11-12. Manson describes Paul and his theology: not ideas but events, not theologian but missionary, not theory but conversion.

87. Kertelge, "Autorität," 1. Cf. Phil 3:4-11.

88. Schoeps, *Paul*, 54, refers to Paul's language of theophany to understand the event of his call: *apocalypse* (Gal 1:16); *light of the knowledge of the glory of God* (2 Cor 4:6). Was there psychological preparation in Paul? Schoeps, 55, "It is difficult to get anywhere in this way." Kertelge, "Autorität," 3; Davies, *Paul*, 93. Theißen, *Aspects*, 234-43, suggests "a long retrospective bringing to consciousness of a conflict that had once been unconscious," of which Romans 7 is the result.

89. Kertelge, "Autorität," 1-2, acknowledges that although Paul sees the foundation of Christian existence to be based on faith in Christ he does not fully come away from (dealing with) the law.

90. Räisänen, *Paul* (1983), 9; Stendahl, *Paul*, 48; Sanders, *Paul* (1983), 4.

each situation, and variations within Paul's statements about the law, from one letter to another, can accordingly be understood.

7.4. But there are also variations or oscillations within a given letter. In view of such inconsistencies Fitzmyer's analysis of categories does not go far enough. Most of Paul's statements about the law mean the Mosaic law. And yet, certain distinctions that he could have made even within that body of material are largely ignored or are inconsistently applied by Paul. Paul never alludes to distinctions within his concept of law, and neither definitional distinctions nor differentiations arrived at on linguistic grounds provide adequate explanation of his views.[91] Paul never clearly defines the content of the law. But Räisänen says of the law and Paul, "... *nomos* in Paul refers to the authoritative tradition of Israel, anchored in the revelation on Sinai, which separates the Jews from the rest of mankind."[92] The whole sacred tradition of Israel seems to be included, with an emphasis on the Mosaic center, and its role of identifying Israel. And yet this Mosaic center could be viewed from different angles, although they are angles that Paul himself does not emphasize, but rather oscillates between them as though they did not always exist. Räisänen points to two principal ways in which Paul's reference to law oscillates.

7.4.1. Paul often makes a clear distinction between Jews who are under the law and Gentiles who are without the law (Rom 2:12-29; 1 Cor 7:17-20; 9:20-23; Gal 2:14-15). In this way Paul speaks of the law as the decisive separating factor between Jews and Gentiles, so separating Jews from the rest of humankind.[93] At other times Paul includes Gentiles among those who are under the curse of the law or who have been redeemed from the curse of the law (Gal 3:13-14, 23-6; 4:5-6; 5:1). In Gal 3:13-14 Paul does not explicitly deal with the difference between Jews and Gentiles. The *us* who are redeemed from the curse of the law (3:13c) would seemingly refer to Jewish Christians who were under the Torah before becoming Christians. The *we* (3:14) who received the Spirit seemingly refers to Galatian Gentile Christians. And yet Paul gives no indication of a contrast between *us* and *we* (3:14), or between Jews and Gentiles. And so Räisänen concludes, "Strange as it may appear, the conclusion is hard to avoid that even Gentiles were, in Paul's mind when dictating this passage, *under the curse of the law*. This is in tension with Paul's assumption in 1 Cor 9:21 or Rom 2:12, or even Gal

---

91. Räisänen, *Paul* (1983), 18 ns. 13-19.

92. Ibid., 16.

93. Does the Sinaitic law, if denoted by *nomos*, by definition concern only the Jews? Räisänen, *Paul* (1983), 18 n. 20; Herntrich, *TDNT* 3:933: The law was given *to* Israel to manifest God's love and justice *for* the nations.

2:14."⁹⁴ Paul's oscillation is thus between "a historical and particularist Torah and that of a general universal force."⁹⁵ While Paul seems to be speaking of the Mosaic law of Sinai, the situations of Jew and Gentile melt together, as law assumes wider dimensions in his thinking and works as something that concerns all people.⁹⁶ So Paul tacitly operates with a double sense of law, on the one hand speaking of the Sinaitic Torah, and on the other hand giving the law a wider application than only to Jews. In Gal 3:21-24 *law* carries the judgment of pre-Christian existence for both Jews and Gentiles.⁹⁷ While dating the law from the time of Moses (3:17-20) Paul speaks of the law as covering all humankind. It is a universally enslaving power.⁹⁸

7.4.2. The second main area in which Paul oscillates on the law is that he makes no explicit distinctions between the *cultic* (or ritual) and *moral* aspects of the Torah. It was generally the ritual laws such as circumcision, Sabbath, and food laws, that brought about the social distinction between Israel and other people.⁹⁹ In Galatians it is this cultic side of the law that is in the forefront of Paul's discussion, for he deals with, (1) circumcision (2:1-10; 5:2-12); (2) food laws (2:11-12); and (3) calendar (4:10).¹⁰⁰ And yet Paul makes no explicit distinction between these ritual codes and the whole law by which righteousness is not available. Law *as such* is set in opposition to gospel, faith, cross, and Spirit. Had Paul made such a distinction, pointing out to the Galatians that it was ritual requirement about which he differed, and thus taught his converts that ritual law and that alone has been replaced, "his task would have been very much easier."¹⁰¹ But silence on that point must be taken as symptomatic rather than accidental. In other words it is simply incredible that Paul, a Pharisee who was rabbinically trained,

---

94. Räisänen, *Paul* (1983), 20; Bruce, *Galatians*, 167, says that the inclusion of Gentiles under the curse of law is not strange, because: (1) an innate sense of right and wrong (Rom 2:12-16), and activity of conscience make Gentiles liable to the curse of the law, and (2) the blessing that replaces the curse is intended for all people.

95. Räisänen, *Paul* (1983), 21.

96. For the reverse of this situation see Räisänen, *Paul* (1983), 22, on Gal 4:1-11.

97. Räisänen, *Paul* (1983), 21 n. 37, sees this universalist application of law to be in some tension with the particularist sense of law as having arrived late on the scene (Gal 3:15-20).

98. Räisänen, *Paul* (1983), 22 n. 42, citing Vielhauer, 553.

99. Räisänen, *Paul* (1983), 24 n. 47; cf. Sanders, *Paul* (1983), 102. See 3.1 below.

100. Bousset, "Galater," 50, says that in Galatians Paul seems to have the ceremonial (i.e. cultic, ritual) law in mind, and (59) Paul does *not* make any fundamental distinction between ceremonial and moral law. In spite of this lack of distinction, Bousset says that the emphasis on ceremonial in Galatians is the original sense of Paul's teaching about the law, that righteousness is not by works of law.

101. Räisänen, *Paul* (1983), 25.

would either not have known the distinction or would have unknowingly oscillated from one aspect of the law to another without realizing his *looseness of speech*, or that he was doing so in *many confused senses*.[102] Much less could he have expected those who were similarly trained to let him get away with it. It is more plausible that,

> What interests Paul is the "lawness of law," whatever that particular law or obligation might be. Paul thinks phenomenologically about law. This is why he shows no concern to salvage law by distinguishing one law from another, the cultic from the moral law . . .[103]

Paul works inductively, as he generalizes from specific aspects of law to the law as a whole. But despite the inconsistencies and oscillation in Paul's dealing with the law, he remains, as Bruce and Sanders have rightly pointed out, a *coherent* (but not systematic) thinker.[104] That is, certain central convictions inform Paul's theology. The Christ event had become central for him. Everything else in his perspective, including law, had its place in relation to the center.[105]

1.4 The Law in Galatians

The relation of central and secondary aspects of his theology is likely where Paul's inconsistency is best explained. In Galatians the cross represents what is central. The law is an impinging secondary factor. In that situation the aspects of the law that were promoted as unwitting competitors to God's redemptive act on Christ's cross led to Paul's polemic against the law. It may

---

102. Räisänen, *Paul* (1983), 28, uses these phrases, in agreement with Grant, Sanders, and Gardner; see his n. 74. However, to use the law in *many* senses does not necessarily indicate confusion.

103. Keck, *Letters*, 86; Sanders, *Paul* (1983). What Paul rejects in Galatians is law as an entrance requirement for Gentiles; the *getting in* question he consistently answers, *not by works of law*. Sanders, 158–59, disagrees with the analysis by Keck about the *lawness* of law, as a substitute for trust in grace, and yet he fails to show that his position and Keck's exclude one another. Bornkamm, "Röm 2:14–16."

104. Bruce, "Research," 124. Sanders, *Paul* (1977), 433, and *Paul* (1983), 147–48.

105. Bruce, "Research," 124, rightly sees this fact pointing to the "the logic of Paul's Damascus-road experience—the experience which brought home to him in a flash the 'powerlessness' of the law to accomplish what it was designed to do." But this does not imply that a fully worked out view of the law was a sudden revelation on the Damascus Road, for the experience and the understanding of it may be separate. Bruce recognizes this, as he says, "Certainly the implications of this sudden insight had to be worked out in the conflict with Judaisers and in other controversies." Davies, "Interpretation," 6–7.

be argued that to attack any part of the law is to discredit law as such. This is exactly the opposition that Paul sets up in his response to the Galatian situation, as he juxtaposes the law and the cross. The wider dimensions that Paul gives to the law as that which concerns all people, and the inexactness of failing to differentiate ritual law from moral code, are logical conclusions of Paul's gospel, as he proclaimed the death of Christ to be the supreme liberating event for all people, who henceforth are free from all enslaving powers and impotent codes. In Galatians this view of law as enslaving and impotent is related to the motif of dying and living, and the transfer from one state to the other. But before turning to those themes in Part 2, we will examine more fully the place of the law in Galatians.

1. In Galatians Paul argues against the imposition of the law on Gentile converts to faith in Christ. He speaks against the whole law. He does not distinguish moral, cultic, or ritual law. Although in 2:1–18 Paul refers to specific works of the law, namely circumcision and table laws, he generalizes in 2:19 to the law as such.[106] He mentions *works of the law* again in 3:2, 5, 10, but aside from that his argument is directed against *law*. In 3:17, 19 it is the law of Moses to which he refers, as that given 430 years after the covenant with Abraham and that was ordained by angels through an intermediary. This points to Sinai and the Mosaic Law. The reference in 5:23 may be generic. The law of Christ in 6:2 is likely a play on the word *law*, with no attempt to say that Christ or faith in Christ re-establishes the law.[107] The other references to law in Galatians may be classified in four general categories.

---

106. Cranfield, "Law," distinguishes Paul's view of the good law from his view of the abused law; in Galatians the phrase *works of the law* indicates legalism; once his argument is established by this phrase, *then* Paul speaks simply of the law. Räisänen, *Paul* (1983), 43, rightly thinks this view is inadequate.

107. Räisänen, *Paul* (1983), 16, 50, points out that terms like *law of Christ* in Gal 6:2, the *law of faith* in Rom 3:27, and the *law of the Spirit* in Rom 8:2, are used in a "patently metaphorical sense." They are "metaphorical ways of speaking of the new order of things," and cannot be used to support a notion like that of Hübner, *Gesetz*, 119–20: "The 'law of faith' designates 'the right attitude to God's will . . . as it finds its expression in the Torah.'" Two problems with Hübner's view relate to grammar and syntax: (1) in Rom 3:27 the active role of law (NRS: principle) in destroying boasting (of Jew as regarding Gentile) can hardly be construed as a function of Torah. Paul speaks of what happened to *boasting* through the (principle) *law of faith*, not what happened to the law because of faith. Furthermore, if the *law of faith* in 3:27 referred to the Torah, then the question of 3:31, *do we then overthrow the law by this faith?* would never arise; (2) in Rom 8:2 Paul speaks of the (new) *order* of the Spirit. The law of the Spirit has *liberated me* from the law of sin and death. Here *law* (of the Spirit) is the subject, not the object, of liberation. The subject is not human understanding or attitude (i.e. toward the Torah). So also in Gal 6:2 there is no sense of a renewed Torah. These instances show Paul's metaphorical use with polemical nuances. Räisänen, "Gesetz," 113, comments that Paul plays with words, and actually not without a polemical purpose: he calls the

1.1. The law is opposed to Christ, faith, promise, Spirit, righteousness (justification), and life: 2:16, 19, 21; 3:2, 5, 11, 12, 18, 21; 4:21; 5:4, 18. Galatians 5:14 figures in the contrast of which 5:3 is also a part. The contrast introduced in 5:13, between freedom and flesh, connects freedom with love. In 5:14 love is connected with law (as its fulfillment), and the contrast proceeds in 5:16-26 between Spirit and flesh. Thus, 5:14 implicitly belongs to this first category. Galatians 5:3 and 6:13 connect law with circumcision, which in turn is contrasted to faith in Christ.

1.2. The law is connected with curse, transgressions, and death, using such cause and effect language as *for, because, therefore*: 2:19; 3:10, 13, 19; cf. 3:17-18.

1.3. The law is part of a means to an end, not an end in itself, as shown by purpose (means to an end) clauses: 3:24; 4:4, 5; cf. 2:19; 3:14, 22.

1.4. The law is a temporary and late addition to God's plan of salvation: 3:17, 23.

2. In the light of these references to the law in Galatians, four observations are indicated.

2.1. The role that Paul assigns to the law in this epistle is essentially negative, and is manifest in two ways. First, that the law is not an entrance requirement means that when Paul is faced with the question of entry into the church, Paul's answer is consistently, *not by works of law*. Second, Paul assigns the law a negative role in God's plan of salvation.[108] The explicit contrast established in 2:15 also answers the justification question: *not by works of law*. This contrast is implied earlier by the recounting of the Antioch episode (2:11-17), wherein Paul connects lack of straightforwardness about the gospel to Peter's fear of the circumcision party and representatives from James.[109] Circumcision and gospel are thus placed in opposition.[110] In Galatians Paul does *not* distinguish between the questions of getting in and staying in. The problem represented by Gal 2:1-10 reflects the same concern as that of Acts 15: entrance into the church. The problem represented by Gal 2:11-17 reflects the concern of behavior within the church, particularly as

---

one order (of reality) a *law* which actually is opposite the law of Moses. Thus, Räisänen, *Paul* (1983), 52: "There is no reason to abandon the until recently almost universally accepted view that in these two passages Paul is playing with words and using *nomos*— this time consciously, to be sure!— in different senses." Räisänen, "Gesetz," 117; "Spiel."

108. Sanders, *Paul* (1983), 17-64; Räisänen, *Paul* (1983), 140-54.

109. Weiß, *History*, 1:273, says that *from James* in Gal 2:12 could mean either, (1) some men had been sent and authorized by James, or (2) these men belonged to the group that followed James' opinions. Both options point to law observant Christianity.

110. Ibid., 1:258-76, for discussion of the events in Acts 15 and Galatians 2, the relation of Acts and Galatians, Jerusalem conferences and Antioch quarrels, and Paul and the churches of Jerusalem and Antioch. Barrett, *Freedom*, 10, 111 n. 11; 3.1 below.

it affected church unity. And yet Paul moves from one problem to the other, with the continuity between the two episodes being the place of the law as such. He thus indicates that the law plays no positive part in either the getting in or staying in question. Paul is uncompromising in the either/or nature of this argument.[111] The greatest positive thing Paul can say of the law is that, having been added late and ruling for only a fixed time (3:17, 23), it has made ready for the *Offspring* (Christ, 3:16) and the status of justification by faith in Christ (3:24).

2.2. Paul refuses to compromise the divine origin and ownership of the law.[112] He quotes freely from the law as an authority. He uses standard introductory formulae that indicate divine authority. Paul finds a place for the law in God's plan of salvation, but it is an essentially negative place. Only if the law *could* make alive (3:21) would it truly be a competitor with Christ's death, and render that death purposeless (2:21). These two uncompromising convictions are simply in tension in this letter, as the law that is placed in opposition to gospel, cross, Christ, faith, Spirit, and promise, yet remains God's law. When these two factors are left unharmonized and in tension, a negative role for the law is the necessary theological consequence.[113]

2.3. The function of the law is derived from its relation to the gospel that has superseded it and to which it is in opposition. The gospel assigns meaning to the law. That Paul locates the law's meaning and purpose outside of the law itself, parallels his refusal to speak of the law in terms of revelation. The language of apocalyptic is reserved for the gospel of the Son of God (1:12, 16; 2:2), revealed to Paul that he might preach to the nations. The ways in which Paul speaks of the law clearly indicate that it is not an end in itself. Not only by contrast to the terminology of the gospel, but also by the forms of speech and the law's connection to curse, transgressions, and death, the law is shown to have a subservient role. The law is no longer the ultimate priority for Paul. This is shown by purpose clauses and cause and effect phraseology. Purpose clauses using *so that* (*hina*) show that the law serves an end other than itself: *Therefore the law was our disciplinarian until*

---

111. Eichholz, 248, notes that the entire Letter to the Galatians shows that Paul argues equipped with the center of the gospel, and from that center there is for him no compromise possible. Stuhlmacher, "Ende," 24-9, sees the diametric opposition of law and gospel for Paul.

112. Against Hübner, *Gesetz*, 27-8, who maintains that the angels in 3:19 are demonic beings who authored the law with the evil intention of causing sin in humankind, and the phrase *ordained by angels* indicates God's lack of involvement in the giving of the law. But see Räisänen, *Paul* (1983), 131-33.

113. Sanders, *Paul* (1983), 68, sees tension between it being God's law and yet not saving, and how a consequently negative place had to be found for the law so as to account for its presence.

Christ came, so that we might be justified by faith (3:24; cf. 4:4-5). The means to an end constructions imply that the desired end has priority over the means in its service.[114] Cause and effect phrases indicate a causative role of law. This may be the case in regarding the law in 3:19: *it was added because of transgressions*. Rather than checking transgressions the law has increased them. The clauses in 3:10 also show cause and effect: "*Because* it is written, 'Cursed be every one who does not abide by all things written in the book of the law, and do them', *therefore* all who rely on works of law are under a curse." The *for* in the beginning of 2:19 may also reflect this causal relationship.[115] These forms of speech show the demotion through which the law has gone for Paul because of the revelation of Jesus Christ.

2.4. Paul moves from the problem of single aspects of the law, such as food, calendar, and circumcision, to speaking about the law as a whole.[116] It is the law *as such* against which he speaks. It is *the law* that does not justify. The movement is more sweeping than if Paul had generalized to include all aspects of ritual or cultic law. He includes the entire Mosaic law as that which is antithetically opposed to the gospel. This makes sense when we understand him to have thought two things about the law: (1) it is the law-ness of law that is involved, not simply the meaning of a certain ritual aspect; (2) in an obverse way, just as circumcision binds one to *do* the whole law, so also to negate an aspect of the law such as circumcision is to speak against the whole law. So it is the law itself against which Paul militates in Galatians. This precludes that the problem he addressed was misinterpretations of the law and shows that the tradition of law-keeping was a life from which Paul had separated himself.[117]

1.5 The Cross and the Law

First Corinthians and Galatians show Paul's explicit references to *cross/crucify* more than any of his other epistles. In 1 Corinthians the cross is central

---

114. Dana and Mantey, 283: "*Pure Final Clauses* . . . express a distinct purpose conceived as the aim of the action indicated in the principal verb." BDF, §369.

115. The *for* in 2:19 is related to 2:18; Bruce, *Galatians*, 142; Mußner, 177; Lambrecht, "Line of Thought."

116. Jeremias, "Paulus als Hilleit."

117. Räisänen, *Paul* (1983), 42-50; 73-77; Gal 5:12 like Phil 3:2, 8, indicates Paul's alienation from Torah piety. Manson, "Jesus," 141: "There is thus no place of final authority left for the Law in the New Testament." He gives 3 reasons: (1) as a means of salvation the law is ineffective and a stop-gap; (2) as moral demand the law is superseded by the life and teaching of Jesus; (3) but what can be said of law is stated by Paul in Gal 3:24: *the law was our pedagogue until Christ came*.

in Paul's argument against wisdom. In Galatians the cross is central in his argument against the law. In both Galatians and 1 Corinthians the arguments relate to the question of salvation. In Galatians the argument centers on the relationship with or righteousness before God, and the righteousness terminology is used frequently throughout the discussion (2:16, 17, 21; 3:6, 8, 11, 21, 24; 5:4, 5). In 1 Corinthians the righteousness terms are scarce, occurring only in three places (1:30; 4:4; 6:11). With the exception of 1:30 the justification language is absent from the anti-wisdom argument of 1 Cor 1:19—3:23, and yet the saving content of Paul's message is emphasized in a fundamental way. The salvation emphasis is seen in Paul's references to *save* (1:18, 21; 3:15; 5:5; 7:16; 9:22; 10:33; 15:2), the noun *faith* (2:5; 12:9; 13:22, 13; 15:14, 17; 16:13), and the verb *believe* or *have faith* (1:21; 3:5; 9:17; 11:18; 13:7; 14:22; 15:2, 11). This indicates that in 1 Corinthians the matter at hand is not simply that of differing christologies nor standards of behavior within the body, but the very ground of salvation and faith.[118] Paul can and does address the question of salvation without relying on righteousness terminology, and thus, justification ought not too quickly be singled out as the sum and substance of his proclamation.

In 1 Corinthians Paul's antithesis to *wisdom* is *foolishness* or *folly*, which he identifies with the cross. The Greco-Roman world, familiar with the madness of crucifixion and charged with the quest for wisdom, identified the cross with *folly*.[119] The greater *folly* would assert that a cross was God's world-saving event. But Paul contrasts God's *foolishness* with worldly *wisdom*.

In Gal 2:19 Paul uses the compound verb, *crucified-with*, to speak of an accomplished past event that yet has a present effect in his own life, particularly regarding the law. *Living to God* and having been *crucified with Christ* indicate Paul's placing life and cross together, against the law. He again aligns *Christ crucified* with the gospel, Spirit, faith, and miracles in 3:1–5, opposite which are placed works of the law and flesh. The reference to hanging and curse, in 3:13, may reflect Paul's answer to a problem that existed even before the Galatian controversy. This problem was the Jewish polemic against the idea of a crucified messiah. Paul may have responded to this scandal on previous occasions, and incorporated that previously worked-out response into the present argument. Here he indicates his break with the current Jewish view of the law and of Christ crucified, and tacitly places

---

118. Funk, 248, Paul's is a kerygmatic concern, "an attempt to refer the Corinthians to the ground of faith, Jesus." Grant, 181. Weber, 86, sees the cross as the standard of true faith in 1 Corinthians: ". . . the faithful must interpret themselves and the entire world through the crucifixion."

119. Horsley, 224, n. 1.

his opponents in Galatia on the (Jewish) side, to whose view he is opposed. These opponents, whoever they were, were committed to imposing the law upon faith in Christ and membership in the church.[120]

Paul opposes the position of the opponents by speaking of the revelation to him of the gospel and of God's Son and his call to preach to the Gentiles (Gal 1:12, 16). This serves to break the continuity between the gospel and Sinai, and between Paul's previous life under law and present life with Christ. In 1:13-14 Paul characterizes his former life in Judaism under law as persecution of the church, advancement beyond his peers, and zeal for the traditions of his fathers. In 1:15-16, by contrast, Paul sets four components of his changed life. He was set apart before birth, called through grace, given a revelation of God's Son, and intended to preach Christ to the nations. The change is signified abruptly, *But when he who had set me apart*, at the beginning of 1:15.

In Gal 1:12 and 1:16 Paul uses the language of theophany (*apocalypse, revelation; revealed*) to speak of what he perceived as divine intervention.[121] In speaking this way Paul says two things. First, his gospel is of divine and not human origin (1:11), an origin later to be contrasted to that of the law, that in 3:19-20 Paul will distance from God. Second, his apostleship is of divine institution (1:1), an institution that Paul will emphasize in 1:17-18 by distancing himself from Jerusalem. *Revelation* is the means, direct from

---

120. Sanders, *Paul* (1983), 49-51, says that the position of the opponents is more critical than an answer to who they were, and that they were Christians is borne out by three things: (1) Paul refers to their message as a *different gospel* (1:6); (2) he accuses them of wishing to avoid persecution for the cross of Christ (6:12); (3) he appeals for defeat of the false brethren and to agreement with Peter and James, factors that have significance only for an inner-Church struggle. For attempts to identify the opponents, Munck, *Paul*, 87; Schoeps, *Paul*, 65; Richardson, *Israel*, 84-97; Bonnard, *Galates*, 2-5; Howard, *Crisis*, 17-19; Jewett, "Agitators"; Davies, *Paul*, 103-4. Räisänen, (1983), 183, refers to them as "... Jewish Christians with a rather normal Jewish identity." Barrett, *Freedom*, 6, speaks of "a convinced and organized anti-Pauline party, prepared to go to any lengths to destroy the apostle's work." Nanos, *Irony*, 193-205, argues that the *influencers* who are troubling Paul's churches are not Christ-believers, but standard adherents to the Jewish assembly who want the Galatian Christ-group to be minimally conforming to what the influencers represent. Martyn, *Galatians*, 117-126, refers to the opponents as *Teachers* and says, 119: "From Galatians itself, we can also see that the Teachers are in touch with—indeed, understand themselves to represent—a powerful circle of Christian Jews in the Jerusalem church, a group utterly zealous for the observance of the Law."

121. Weiß, *Korintherbrief*, 60, says of *revealed* in 1 Cor 2:10 that revelations cannot be attained as natural tendencies, but only through a supernatural, wonderful message. Paul does not speak of mysteries in Gal 1:12, 16, but is careful to place his gospel in a realm not available to natural man. It is not *from* men (1:1), nor *through* men, nor *belonging* to men (1:11), nor pleasing to men (1:10), just as in 1 Cor 2:10-13 it is a gospel not taught by human wisdom.

God, by which Paul received his gospel, his apostleship, and his conviction about God's Son.[122] Similarly, the change in Paul has been due to this divine intervention, and not to a psychological process.[123]

Paul nowhere asserts that the toilsome demands of the law caused him to languish in guilt, nor, for that matter, does he say that the law was impossible to do. His point of departure, both theologically and autobiographically, is in "the Son of God who loved me and gave himself for me" (2:20), and who "gave himself for our sins, to deliver us from the present evil age" (1:4). Sole dependence on faith in Christ is, for Paul, the mark of the new age. The old age would be marked by life under the law. The cross of Christ marks the transition from old to new.

Beker notes that *the cross* becomes a kind of *shorthand* for God's blessings in Christ. It tears us away from the dominion of the world (Gal 6:14), the law (2:19), and the old life (5:24). The cross epitomizes apocalyptic interpretation in Paul, and occurs exclusively in three contexts: (1) cross and wisdom, 1 Cor 1:17-18, 23; 2:2, 8; (2) cross and law, Gal 2:20; 3:1; 5:11; 6:14; (3) cross and new creation, Gal 5:24; 6:14; Rom 6:6.[124] Understanding the cross as *shorthand* for the blessings of God in Christ, for the gospel or Christ-event, complements the paucity of *cross/crucify* and certain other terms in particular contexts. Resurrection, for example, is barely alluded to in Galatians, as it is mentioned only in 1:1 as part of Paul's greeting. Stanley provides four reasons why even this one time Christ's resurrection occurs in the Galatian letter:

1. it constitutes the basic testimony of an apostle;
2. it was the risen Christ who called Paul;
3. that Paul had seen the risen Christ refutes any denial of Paul's apostolic authority that may have been based on Paul's not having known Jesus during Jesus' mortal life;

---

122. Oepke, *TDNT* 3:583-84. Barrett, *Freedom*, 10: "Perhaps the negative aspect of this is what he wants to draw out here: he did not go because he was sent for."

123. Kertelge, "Autorität," 3: Paul's new orientation was through a revelation of Jesus Christ. Räisänen, *Paul* (1983), 57, 229, 231-36, dismisses the usual psychological interpretations of Paul's view of the law but does posit certain psychological commonplaces that are probably applicable to Paul's situation. This involves the dynamic struggle between what one consciously thinks and what is struggling to be born, and leads Räisänen to a discussion of the Hellenists as a possible source of Paul's practice (later to become his theological position: practice precedes theology) as he came to identify with those whom he once persecuted. Theißen, *Aspects*, 234-43.

124. Beker, *Paul* (1980), 205.

4. the letter's dominant theme is the gospel of promise, fulfilled in resurrection.

Moreover, there is a wholeness or inseparability to what can be called the *Christ-event*. This is reflected in the way that Stanley and others speak of Christ's death and resurrection. The two aspects of Jesus' life and mission are inseparable from one another, even as Christ is present in all his works and all his works are represented in him: "In the Pauline kerygma, the thought of the risen Christ includes redemptive death, just as the mention of the Cross includes his resurrection."[125] The wholeness is expressed also by Friedrich, "Whether one speaks of the crucified (1 Cor 1:23) or the risen Lord (1 Cor 15:12), the reference is always to the total Christ who has become Lord by death and resurrection, and who is proclaimed as such, 2 Cor 4:5."[126]

And yet Stanley's argument does not answer the question of why Paul speaks of the cross so explicitly on some occasions, and in other letters does so very little or not at all. If the resurrection became the basic testimony of an apostle, why is Paul not more explicit about that in Galatians? Although it was the risen Christ who called Paul, it is witness to the crucified Christ that he establishes as the central aspect of his proclamation to the Corinthians (2:2) and Galatians (3:1). And in Galatians, where the theme of promise is basic to the argument in ch. 3, fulfillment is not spoken of in terms of resurrection, but in terms of full unity and inclusiveness in Christ. The fact remains, when in Galatians Paul wants to speak of Christ's redemptive death, he does so with specific references to the cross, not to resurrection, nor even to the death of Christ.

The cross in Galatians can best be understood as representing the firm center from which Paul speaks of the transfer from the old to the new life.[127] Beker's terms, *coherence* and *contingency*, are helpful theological categories for understanding the tension between what is central, uncompromising, and firm in Paul's message, and what is conditional, secondary, and flexible. Paul relates the universal truth claim of the gospel directly to the particular situation to which it is addressed: "His hermeneutic consists in the constant interaction between the coherent center of the gospel and its contingent interpretation."[128] Paul makes the gospel *a word on target* for the particular needs of his churches, without compromising either the gospel's center or reducing the message of the cross to petrified conceptuality.[129] Cognizance

---

125. Stanley, 148-49.
126. Friedrich, *TDNT* 3:711.
127. Sanders, *Paul* (1983), 4-10.
128. Beker, *Paul* (1980), 11.
129. Beker, *Paul* (1980), 12. Childs, 301-10, notes that the canonical significance of

of the tension between the firm center of Paul's kerygma, and the contingency to which each letter was addressed, helps the interpreter understand each epistle on its own terms and recognize its impact on the present.

Galatians, therefore, can be studied on the basis of its own content, and the conclusions drawn from a study can, in the first instance, be conclusions only about Galatians. The terminology, words in combination, and theological motifs in the epistle witness to the particular address of Paul's gospel to the peculiar exigencies of the Galatian situation.[130] As we see first where Paul does or does not use certain words, or combinations of words, we are helped to determine whether a thing was a problem for Paul and the churches that he served. We can further determine what consistent theological patterns emerge in Paul's responses. It is essential to begin with the biblical texts themselves, and not with the history of interpretation, pre-determined motifs, or even the doctrinal traditions of ecclesial bodies.[131]

Paul, the church's apostle, battled for the church's *kerygma*. He speaks assertively about the cross in Galatians in order to represent God's saving work in Christ, and in order to preserve and promote the message that issues from Christ's work. The cross is the break with the old age. It stands over against the law, which in the situation in Galatia Paul's opponents promoted as a condition for faith, for entry into the church, and as a standard for belonging to the faith community.

In Galatians it is the whole law (not only one or more aspects of it), and it is the law as such (not misinterpreted or misunderstood law) against which Paul struggles.[132] His references to the cross and his strident statements about the law are not *exactly* replicated in Romans. But in both epistles Paul's position regarding the law is *essentially* the same: he has died in relation to the law, through the law's own death-bringing power, so that he might live in relation to God (Gal 2:19; Rom 7:4).[133] Furthermore, in

---

Galatians is dependent *only* on Paul's theological construal of the situation as a witness to the *kerygma*.

130. Funk, 277, 304; Barr, 233.

131. Gaventa, "Methods," 37–44.

132. Cranfield, "Law," 56, says that Christians are discharged from legalistic misunderstanding of the law. Barth, *Shorter Commentary*, 47, says that our relationship with God is one of law, regulated by Christ. Both men presuppose continuity between law and gospel, and generalize about Paul's doctrine of law on the basis of certain Romans texts.

133. Marxsen, 58, on development of ideas from Galatians to Romans; Betz, 11; Borse, *Standort*, 120–22; *Galater*, 9–10, 25–6. Wilckens, *Rechtfertigung*, 110–70, on Romans as a near repetition of the Galatian argument. But regarding an over-all change from Galatians to Romans, with respect to the law, see Eichholz, 247. Hübner, *Law*, also addresses the differences between the law in Galatians (15–50) and in Romans

both Romans and Galatians Paul speaks of this death to the law as having occurred in Christ's death on the cross. It is this aspect of his message to which we now turn.

(51–100). Beker, *Paul* (1980), speaks of *contextual interpretation* regarding Galatians (37–58) and Romans (59–93).

2

Galatians 2:19

2.1. Dying to, Living to

GALATIANS 2:19 IS EITHER included in or follows after Paul's report of his rebuke to Peter in Antioch. It is not clear whether Paul's account of that episode ends with 2:14 or includes 2:15-21 (or part thereof) as a summary of the speech he made at Antioch.[1] Only the first sentence (v. 14b) indicates direct address to Peter, and yet it seems improbable that Paul would limit his report of that episode to a single sentence.[2] Therefore Paul likely passes imperceptibly from his report of the past episode to his present argument, addressing Peter formally (at least in v. 14b) and the Galatians materially.[3] In 2:15-16 Paul states the common ground or *point of agreement* about the self-definition of Jewish Christians who are Jews by birth[4] and Christians by faith in Jesus Christ.[5] The phrase *Gentile sinners* is in reference to Gentiles

---

1. Betz, 113, and Burton, 111, says of this question, "Only the first sentence (v. 14b) contains unmistakable evidence of having been addressed to Peter, and the absence of any direct address in the remainder of the chapter makes it unlikely that through the whole of it Paul is still quoting what he said to Peter." But see Lambrecht, 484, who in agreement with Mußner, 178, sees the whole section as a speech delivered to Peter at Antioch.

2. Burton, 111.

3. Betz, *Galatians*, 114; Burton, Lightfoot, Martyn (*Galatians*), Oepke, and Schlier.

4. Betz, *Galatians*, 115.

5. Ibid., 117-18, notes that whether this is an objective genitive (faith *in* Jesus Christ as the object of belief) or a subjective genitive (the faith *of* or which Jesus Christ himself had) is not indicated by the grammatical ambiguity of the phrase, and so it must be decided on the basis of context (cf. his n. 43). Betz, 117, sees the phrase, *we have come to believe in Christ Jesus*, interpreting (the genitive in) the previous phrase, *the faith of Christ Jesus*. Hultgren, 248-63, supports the obj. gen. on the basis of syntactical observations. Bruce, *Galatians*, 138-39, has excellent bibliographical citations for both views of the genitive, but his preference is for the obj. gen. because Paul's expression with the

who are sinners in the Jewish sense because they do not have the Torah and therefore they cannot achieve righteousness: they are outside the realm of God's grace.[6] In Gal 2:17-18 Paul moves on to the disagreement regarding the implications for Gentile Christians. In 2:17a Paul uses a *correct presupposition* as he picks up the idea of justification by faith in Christ that was stated in v. 16.[7] In 2:17a.2 Paul uses the *false presupposition* that those who are justified by faith in Christ are sinners in the Jewish sense of the word.[8] Christians who were not law-observant would be sinners from the Jewish perspective. But for Paul the law no longer distinguishes who is a sinner and who is righteous. Therefore the charge about being sinners is false, from Paul's perspective, and so also is its logical conclusion that Christ is an agent or servant of sin (v. 17c). The accusation would have been made because Paul and the Gentiles who believed in Christ had forsaken the law and it was faith in Christ that led them to do so. It is to the accusation in v. 17c that Paul responds in 2:18-19. In v. 18 he offers a legal critique of the false argument of v. 17. The word *for* in v. 18 shows a close connection between this

---

verb (*believe*), rather than with the noun (*faith*) undoubtedly signifies Christ as the object of believing. This determines the sense of the other clauses in the immediate context. Fitzmyer, *JBC*, 240; Borse, *Galater*, 113-14; Schlier, *Galater*, 92-93; Duncan, 65; Mußner, 170; Burton, 121-23. But otherwise Martyn, 251, 259, 270-75; Williams, 444: "Christ is both domain and means, for when persons live in the power field created by the death and resurrection of Christ, they are beneficiaries of Christ-faith . . . faith which was first his and has now become theirs . . . With the phrase *pistis Christou*, Christ-faith, he points to eschatological faith as introduced into the world by Christ as a new possibility of human existence . . . (Paul) points to the personal act of taking up that mode of personal existence which Christ pioneered."

6. Betz, 115 n. 25, 120. Lambrecht, 485, notes two alternative interpretations. The Christians may be found to be sinners because of post-conversional acts (starting to live like Gentiles, not observing the law) or because of pre-conversional acts (prior to becoming Christians they too needed redemption, like the Gentiles). While Paul moves from solution to problem (all are saved by Christ, therefore all are sinful) in this letter, his thought here seems to relate to the idea of sinfulness in the Jewish sense. This is the problem with which the letter deals, namely whether Gentile converts to Christ need to keep the law as a condition for justification and membership in the church.

7. Betz, 119. Lambrecht, 490, calls v. 17a a simple condition, a *realis* with which Paul agrees, while v. 17b is a wrong conclusion drawn from that right premise. It is this wrong conclusion in v. 17b (not the premise in v. 17a) with which Paul disagrees. Lambrecht's view, however, necessitates taking *sinners* in v. 17 in a different sense than in v. 15, for in v. 17 the word would have to indicate Christians who in their faith saw that their previous life had in fact been sinful just as the Gentiles were sinful. But this understanding of *sinners* in v. 17 is erroneous, since the ideas of being considered sinners and Christ being the agent or servant of that sin are inseparable. It makes more sense to understand the charge to have been that faith in Christ led people outside the law, and this makes them sinners.

8. Betz, 120. *Sinners* here means the same as in 2:15. Martyn, 254-55.

and the preceding statements, as v. 18 explains and motivates the objection at the end of v. 17.[9] The critique says that if the law were re-established then *he* would be considered a transgressor (v. 18). This *building up again* is likely an allusion to Peter's conduct at Antioch. Paul is therefore saying that if he were again to build up the law, as Peter was promoting, then it is not Christ who is an agent of sin but the one who builds up the law who is found to be a transgressor. Here Paul could mean either (1) to restore the law again will prove that he had sinned in the first place by tearing it down; or (2) by restoring the law he will set himself up for a life of transgressions as marked by law.[10] But in either case his point is that it is not Christ but the one who would re-establish the law who becomes the agent of sin. But if the law were re-established (presumably for justification) then the whole belief about justification through faith in Christ collapses, and Christ died to no purpose (2:21). In v. 19 Paul uses the emphatic *ego* that points to his personal stand: *I for my part* (as opposed to Peter).[11] The word *for* in v. 19 is causal. It relates back to v. 18 and also introduces an idea that explains the statement of v. 17: *we cannot think of Christ as an agent of sin for we are dead to the law and we are alive to God*. "Living for God is hardly sinful."[12] The meaning of v. 19 therefore lies in its place in Paul's response to the accusation that Christ is an agent of sin. Paul's answer is that he cannot re-establish or again build up the law, believers in Christ cannot be considered as sinners, and Christ is not an agent of sin because *I died to the law*.

The concept of dying to one power and living to another is at the heart of Gal 2:19. The contrast that Paul introduced in 2:16, between works of the law and faith in Christ, is a contrast that is carried forward in 2:19, as living to the law is placed in contrast to living to God.[13] This polarity is signified both by the nouns in the dative case and the verbs, *die* and *live*.[14]

1. There are a number of passages in Galatians and Romans where Paul uses a verb connoting dying, followed by *sin*, *law*, or *world* in the dative case: (1) dying to sin, Rom 6:2, 10-11; (2) dying to law, Gal 2:19; Rom 7:4, 6;

---

9. Guthrie, 89; against Lambrecht, 495. Martyn, 256.

10. Fitzmyer, *JBC*, 241, calls v.18 Paul's 1st reason and v.19 his 2nd reason for rejecting the argument of v.17.

11. Lambrecht, 493 n. 35.

12. Fitzmyer, *JBC*, 241. Martyn, 256: "For whoever re-erects the Law's distinction between Jew and Gentile, as though God were making things right via observance of the Law, rather than in Christ, has thereby shown himself to be a transgressor."

13. Paul oscillates from *works of the law* in particular to *the law* in general in 2:19. See 3.1 below.

14. BDAG, 111, *dying* with the dative is peculiar to Paul in the NT, and indicates the thing from which one is separated by one's own death; Martyn, 256.

(3) crucified to the world, Gal 6:14.[15] These texts speak of *dying to* or being *crucified to* in contrast to *living to* or *belonging to*.

Datives of (dis)advantage "designate the person whose interest is affected."[16] They show for whose sake the action of the verb is intended. In 2 Cor 5:13, for example, Paul says, "If we are beside ourselves, it is for God (i.e., it happened for God's sake); if we are in our right mind, it is for you (i.e., in your interest)." But there are some datives that introduce the idea of ownership. In 2 Cor 5:15, for example, Paul says of Christ that "He died for all that those who live might live no longer for themselves but for him." These are datives that express *more the possessor* and *living for God* in Gal 2:19 is best understood in this way. But when the verb is not only *living* but also *dying* and when the noun is *sin, law,* or *world,* then the datives are of an even more specific type. Datives of *relation* designate respect, *in the sight of,* or, *in relation to*.[17] This relationship is to be understood in terms of *possession* or *rule*. Since the implication of ownership is clear, God and sin, or God and law, to whom one lives or dies, "are not beings of the same level as the one who dies or lives, but are slave masters who rule" over people.[18] In Gal 2:19 Paul says that he has *died to the law*, meaning that the law is the possessor out of whose ownership he has passed by death. This dying is *with respect to one specific entity*, the law. Dying is made relevant in one particular relationship. It is not dying *as such* about which Paul is concerned, nor is it living as such. "Living and dying are defined with reference to an outside object totally external to the subject."[19] It may be understood, *In relation to the law, I died*. Although Paul does not refer to a physical or natural death,[20] this is not merely a figurative death either. Paul does not use *figurative, inauthentic language*.[21] The connection, *crucified with*, keeps the language from being figurative, just as for Paul Christ's death was never docetic, and *it is Christ's death in which this death of the self is grounded*. This dying does not refer

---

15. Moule, "Certain Datives," 367.
16. BDF, §188.
17. Moule, "Certain Datives," 370, is nearer the dative of respect (BDF §197). Wedderburn, *Baptism*, 43 n. 1, says that the verbs for *being* and *becoming* are characteristic of datives of possession (BDF §197) but are missing from datives of advantage or disadvantage that have *more the possessor* (BDF §188) quality to them, such as Gal 2:19. So it is apt to compare them to datives of relation or respect (BDF §197). He also notes the fluidity of usage that likely was there for the native Greek speaker, thus indicating that the categories are not *watertight compartments*.
18. Tannehill, *Dying*, 18.
19. Ebeling, 138.
20. Luther, *Galatians* (1519), 233.
21. Ebeling, 144.

to the satisfaction of the demands of the law, by way of a costly death, but rather it means that "we have been placed where the law no longer operates: 'we are dead'... or 'we have been put to death'... *so far as law is concerned, with reference to law*; our relationship with the law has been annulled."[22] In Rom 7:4 this annulment by death happens *through the body of Christ!*.[23] In Gal 2:19 it happens *through law*. But the same condition is described by both texts: the believer has become non-existent or annihilated so far as the law is concerned.[24] Paul thus speaks of freedom by death. Just as any debtor who has died is freed from the creditor, so to die to the law is to be made free from the law.[25]

2. Annulment by death, annihilation in relation to the law, or dying to the law in Gal 2:19, can be understood as *a decisive past event*.[26] The aorist of the verb distinguishes the event from dying with Christ as a present experience, especially as that experience is encompassed in the believer's suffering. The event is past in the sense that it *took place in Christ's death* on the cross. It is decisive because *that death includes the believer* in its effect.

3. The concept of dying to the law and the concept of dying with Christ (or in Gal 2:19, being crucified with Christ) are distinct but related ideas. If Gal 2:19 were understood in connection with 3:10–13 and 4:4, the identification of the two concepts in Paul's argument would become explicit: to be crucified with Christ would mean to die to the law and under the law as Christ did. Paul grounds his statements in Gal 2:19–21 in sentences that are first-person statements, but their real subject is not only Paul as an individual, as for example, distinct from Peter. The logic of Paul's statements is based on both his individual experience and his Christology. The statements about dying and living have the same structure as the christological statements that tell of Jesus' death and resurrection: Christ was dead and now lives, I was dead but now I live to God. This is further grounded in *I have been crucified with Christ*.[27]

22. Moule, "Certain Datives," 372. Martyn, 256–57, it is not a life of violation of the law, but a life of separation from the law, of which Paul speaks.

23. See 2.4 below.

24. Moule, "Certain Datives," 373; Bruce, *Galatians*, 144, "A change of lordship, from law to Christ, has taken place..." The converse is suggested by Gal 6:14: relation to the cosmos is non-existent so far as the believer is concerned. Tannehill, *Dying*, 6, 84, 130, notes that besides (1) dying with Christ as a decisive past event (Gal 2:19-20; Rom 7:1–6), and (2) dying and rising with Christ as a present experience, as in suffering (2 Cor 4:7–14; 12:9; 13.4), there is also (3) being with Christ in the future resurrection (1 Thes 4:14; 5:10).

25. Luther, *Galatians* (1519), 234–35.

26. Tannehill, *Dying*, 7.

27. Lührmann, *Galater*, 45. Mußner, 179, Paul has taken a path that Peter and the

Bultmann spoke of participation in the saving significance of the cross as what happens when (1) one is confronted by the kerygma; (2) one acknowledges the question by which one is addressed in the kerygma; (3) one gives up one's old self-understanding.[28] Such an interpretation, however, limits the meaning of *dying with* or being *crucified with* to personal human experience. The concept is then limited to what happens in a person when that person hears the gospel and comes to faith. It is a view that more describes *believing* than it does *dying* or *dying with*. Such anthropological interpretation understands divine action in terms of what it means for human life.[29] Similarly, both *dying* and *dying with* have often been interpreted to signify what has happened in baptism.[30]

Although *crucified with* is used in the Gospels regarding the criminals who were crucified along with Christ, Paul likely does not have in mind in Gal 2:19 the actual scene on Calvary nor an early account of it as relating to the other two victims.[31] All that the Gospel texts state about Jesus and the criminals is that they were crucified together, and even though *crucified with* is used in those texts, it seemingly knows nothing of a special relationship between them and Jesus.[32]

Paul seems to mean that he was included in that death on the cross when on that cross his representative died.[33] Thus, Paul understands himself

---

others must also tread.

28. Bultmann's view of the cross: *Faith*, 208–9, 214, 306–10; *Myth*, 36–8; *Theology* 1:292–314.

29. Bultmann, *Theology*, 1:191: "Thus, every assertion about Christ is also an assertion about man and vice versa; and Paul's Christology is simultaneously soteriology." Käsemann, *Freedom*, 61–5, rightly criticizes this view.

30. Schneider, *TDNT* 7:582–83; Schlier, *Galater*, 99–100; Oepke, *Galater*, 94–5; Mußner, 181. Borse, *Galater*, 117; Tannehill, *Dying*, 59; 2.2, for the view that this is not a reference to baptism.

31. See Mt 27:44; Mk 15:32; Jn 19:32.

32. Dietzfelbinger, 32.

33. On Paul's eschatological orientation in Gal 2:19, Oepke, *Galater*, 95, suggests that one understands it best in light of the Adam-Christ parallel. (Röm 5:12–21; 1 Kor 15:22, 45–57). Tannehill, (1963), 134–35: "The believers were put to death with Christ because they were included in the collective man or body of the old aeon which was crucified with Christ." More than that, Martyn notes: "Paul's perception of Christ's crucifixion is thoroughly apocalyptic, in that it is both this-worldly and other-worldly. (1) On the one hand, it is the real death that was carried out with literal nails on a literal piece of wood, a gruesome spectacle that Paul can portray literally in sermonic form (3:1) . . . (2) On the other hand . . . the crucifixion of Christ is entirely real as the cosmic event that cannot be truly seen by those who look only at human actors who employ literal nails and pieces of wood. Paul identifies those who crucified Christ as 'the rulers of this age', referring to supra-human powers."

to have been struck with Christ on the cross, just as in the death of Christ Paul has also been crucified to the world, and all believers for whom Christ are dead as well (Gal 6:14; 2 Cor 5:14).[34] *I have been crucified with Christ* could be paraphrased, *When Christ was crucified on his cross, I was crucified, too.* The concept of participation of this kind is not really a formula, because a formula expresses a clear tendency in a set phrase. Rather, the idea appears in various ways, expressed by the word *with* as an independent preposition, or compounded with a verb, or in phrases in which the preposition is absent. Therefore, Tannehill says,

> The motif of dying and rising with Christ may be said to be present when Paul refers to the believer's participation in Christ's death or resurrection by means of a construction which relates two elements which stand in the same contrast to each other as "death" and "life" and are related in thought to these terms.[35]

All texts referring to dying with Christ as a decisive past event use the type of dative construction that has here been described as the dative of *relation* or *reference*. This dying is simultaneous with and included in Christ's dying. The references are to dying in relation to an old power or master and living to a new master. Two dominions are involved, and two aeons, and release from one and transfer to the other is indicated. In Gal 2:19 Paul refers to the law as part of the old dominion. He has undergone a radical break from life under the law in the old dominion, to allow for the newness of Christian existence, that for him means to *live to God*. The believer's present life cannot be characterized as either a life of works of the law (Gal 2:16) or a life of sin as a law-breaker (2:18), because the relationship to the old dominion has been annulled.[36]

So far as the law of the old aeon is concerned the believer is dead, and therefore free from the master who formerly ruled. Death to the law occurs solely because the believer participates with Christ, having died with Christ in Christ's death, on the cross, under law. The first half of the if-then clause in Gal 2:18, *But if I build up again the very things that I tore down/*, is negated by the first half of 2:19, *For through the law I died to the law*. Paul died in relation to the law, and therefore he does not build up again what he has torn down.[37]

34. Borse, *Galater*, 117.
35. Tannehill, *Dying*, 6.
36. Tannehill, *Dying*, 6–18, 57; Weiß, *History* 2:603–5; Keck, *Paul*, 77.
37. Martyn, 278, notes that Paul views the crucifixion of Christ as an active event of the law but *not* as a Jewish event: ". . . The Law is a cosmic power affecting Gentile no less than Jew. Thus, Paul does not say that the Sanhedrin worked through the Law

2.2. Crucified-with

The term, *I died*, in Gal 2:19 relates to dying to one power or dominion and living to another. In Galatians this meant death to the rule of law and transfer to faith in Christ, which for Paul meant living to God. What then is the relation between *I died* and *I have been crucified*?

1. The old aeon, in which law ruled, is the realm in which and to which *I have been crucified with Christ*: *I died* and *I have been crucified* explain one another. The aorist points to the event of dying for Paul. *Dying* is further specified by the perfect passive compound verb that refers to the cross of Christ. The aorist tense "contains no action on Paul's part ... he has been drawn into an event in which the *nomos* itself was dethroned and robbed of its sovereignty."[38] Paul's participation with Christ includes the experience of Christ under law and on the cross. The aorist has no significance regarding a thing's endurance and is ambiguous about its time of occurrence. It attests the action of the verb as attained, the fact of the action or event, but without regard to its duration nor to the actual point in time of its accomplishment.[39] The perfect tense is specific regarding both these matters: the event took place when Christ was crucified, and it is still presently in effect.[40] When Christ was crucified so was, and still is, Paul crucified with him.[41]

2. Compound verbs using *with-*, (συν, *sun*) are one way in which dying with Christ is expressed.[42] Schweizer maintains that the original meaning of *with Christ* was eschatological, that is, it first referred to the future life with Christ after his advent (*parousia*).[43] In some texts, however, Schweizer

---

to bring Christ to his death. He attributes the active role to the Law itself as one of the enslaving elements of the old cosmos (3:13)."

38. Schnackenburg, 62–3. Betz, 122.

39. BDF §333. Dana and Mantey, 193. The aorist tense is like the past tense in English. But there are gnomic or futuristic aorists where the author had a specific case in mind in which the act had been realized.

40. Bruce, *Galatians*, 144: "The perfect tense ... (sic, *sunestauromai*) emphasizes that participation in the crucified Christ has become the believer's settled way of life. 'Union with Christ is nothing if it is not union with Christ in his death' (Dunn, *Unity*, 195)." Oepke, *Galater*, 94–5; Borse, *Galater*, 116–17; Lührmann, *Galater*, 56; Schlatter, *Galater*, 63; Benoit, 33; Fitzmyer, *JBC*, 241; Blank, *Paulus*, 299.

41. Martyn, 279–80, says, Paul's "perception of himself is as thoroughly apocalyptic as is his view of Christ's death itself ... the crucifixion is *the* apocalyptic, cosmic event in which God confronts the powers that hold all of humanity in subjection ... In this event Paul was torn away from the cosmos in which he had lived, and it was torn away from him. For in dying with Christ on Christ's cross, this zealous Pharisee suffered the loss of the Law, surely his earlier guide to the whole of the cosmos."

42. Tannehill, *Dying*, 6; Bouttier, 45; Schweizer, "Dying," 1–14.

43. Schweizer, "Dying," 1–2, refers to 1 Thes 4:17; 2 Cor 13:4; Rom 6:8b; Col 3:4;

maintains that this post-*parousia* being *with Christ* is extended back into the period between death and the *parousia*, and back even into the earthly life of the believer, and so the phrase occurs only in either apocalyptic or baptismal contexts.[44] Thus, ". . . in the work of the Spirit given by baptism the coming aeon has broken into this present."[45] Schweizer sees Gal 2:19 as one such text, in which the post-*parousia with Christ* is interpreted back into crucifixion with Christ, and therefore, ". . . Paul uses the perfect tense in order to emphasize the continuing validity of what happened once in baptism."[46] But Schweizer's conclusion about baptism in this text is not mandated by the eschatological understanding of *with Christ*. Certain interpretations of *I have been crucified* in 2:19 are precluded by syntactical constructions within the verse. A baptismal reading is precluded by *through law*, for Paul does not mention baptism in this context, and to understand 2:19 as representing baptism means that the law would have to be the power operative in baptism.[47] Death, Paul says, was through law: "The phrase 'through law' also makes clear that Paul is not speaking of baptism in Gal

---

Phil 1:23; 3:20; 2 Cor 4:11, 14; 1 Thes 5:10. Generally, he says, *in Christ* refers to the believer's earthly life as a member of the church, while *with Christ* is eschatological.

44. Schweizer, "Dying," 3, refers to 1 Thes 5:1f; Rom 14:8-9; 8:32. Tannehill, *Dying*, 7, 59, shows that not all texts relating to dying with Christ as a past event belong to a baptismal interpretation: see Rom 6:3-5 and Gal 2:19.

45. Schweizer, "Dying," 6; Tannehill, 4 n.2, notes that most Paul passages quoted by Schweizer do not emphasize baptism; an eschatological text or motif (in the sense that it represents the future life as having broken into the present) is distinct from making those same texts representative of baptism, although baptism may indeed signify that eschatological break-in. The terms *eschatology/eschatological* are used in this discussion in a limited way, as defined by the concept of two ages. The old world or aeon has reached its end or destruction for the believer. The event of Christ is eschatological because what normally was thought to apply to the end of the world has now occurred in Christ's death and resurrection, by which the natural world's time and rule are over for the believer. Dahl, "Messiahship," 43; "Eschatology," 130; Bultmann, *Word*, 35; *Eschatology*, 23; *Theology* 1:306; Keck, *Paul*, 81.

46. Schweizer, "Dying," 3: "Rom vi.4-8 and Col ii.12f; iii.1 clearly describe baptism. For Gal ii:20 the same may be true." Similarly: Schnackenburg, 63; Mußner, 181. Schlier, *Galater*, 98-100, understands Gal 2:19 explained by Rom 6:3-14; Duncan, 71. Kertelge, "Rechtfertigung," 242, rightly sees that the relation of faith and baptism here is not explicit, but a hint of baptism as the sacramental grounds of the new life may be present.

47. Betz, 123, notes that Galatians expresses the same restraint about baptism as 1 Cor 1:13-17. Paul mentions baptism only once, at 3:27, where he does not mention dying with Christ. Paul speaks of dying with Christ in 5:24 and 6:14 but there does not mention baptism. None of the Galatians passages show reference to the concepts of Romans 6, such as resurrection; Gal 2:19 may be "the theological principle by which Paul interprets the ritual of baptism in Romans 6," and not vice versa. Kertelge, *Rechtfertigung*, 242.

2:19. This reference to the law can be understood only in connection with Christ's death under the law's curse on the cross. The law does not bring about a sacramental death in baptism."[48]

The aorist, *I died* (*apethanon*), is best understood as part of Paul's response to the statement of v. 18. The thought of returning to something to which he has died is absurd. This is not to deny that faith, justification, and baptism are always related or referred to one another, for, ". . . Paul knows no faith without baptism . . ."[49] But this is a different conclusion from saying that Gal 2:19 *means* baptism, or is explained by Romans 6. Furthermore, if Gal 2:19 refers to baptism, one wonders why Paul did not explicitly mention baptism in the verse. There is in fact no hint in the epistle that the Galatians should know that in baptism they died to the law. Paul, on the other hand, pinpoints the termination of the rule of law in Christ's coming (3:24; 4:4) and in his salvific death (2:21; 3:13).[50]

Interpretations that see a reference to baptism in 2:19 tend to approach the text by way of Romans 6. The same question may be asked of Rom 6:1–14 as of Gal 2:19, namely, whether it is a baptismal text in the strict sense of the word. It is not.[51] The real point of connection between the two texts is freedom by death: death to sin in Rom 6:6, 11, and death to law in Gal 2:19. In Gal 2:19 Paul makes no reference to baptism, but sees himself nailed to the cross with Christ, and so included in the death of Christ, he died to and through law.[52] The prefix *with-* (*sun*,) echoes a *being with Christ* that points to the inclusive and representative nature of Christ's death on the cross. When he died, Paul died with him. Baptism may signify this dying,

---

48. Tannehill, *Dying*, 47, 59. Baptism is a manifestation of the eschatological power of the cross and an event by which one enters the people of the new age. But baptism does not repeat the event of the cross nor make it present. Martyn, 279, may be close to this understanding. The link between participation in Christ's death and being *with Christ* or *in Christ* is key.

49. Kim, 305; Kertelge, *Rechtfertigung*, 247.

50. Carlson, 295.

51. Käsemann, *Romans*, 163, the motif that is emphasized in Romans 6 is, "the fellowship of our destiny with that of Christ." This is not an explicit statement of Paul's doctrine of baptism. The text says nothing about the usual things the church tends to ask in relation to baptism in the early church: conferring of the Spirit, incorporation into the body of Christ, the necessary preparation, the rite as such, the gathering of the community, the administration of baptism by office bearers, invocation of the name of Jesus, the use of vows, hymns, laying on of hands, immersion or aspersion, whether many people or families were baptized together, and the baptism of infants.

52. Borse, *Galater*, 117; Tannehill, *Dying*, 59.

serving as the Word of God under a sign (water), but dying itself is linked to Christ's death on the cross.[53]

3. An apocalyptic interpretation of Gal 2:19 and of the perfect tense, *I have been crucified with*, in particular, is appropriate. The revelatory language with which Paul counters the Sinai tradition of his opponents (1:12, 16, 21), and the two-aeon theology by which he asserts a discontinuity between Sinai and the cross, between the old aeon of law and the new aeon of Spirit, indicate a breaking into the present of what had been future expectation (1:4).

Despite the first-person statements Paul does not speak in a purely individualistic way. A psychological interpretation is precluded by the *dying to* and *living to* construction. The release from one lordship and entry into another, with the dative indicating the lord in question, points to law as the power of the old aeon. The old dominion does not die because one becomes conscious of bondage and the law's inability to justify or make alive.[54] The old dominion ended with the coming and death of Christ. Law ruled and was operative in the old aeon, but with the birth of Christ under law (4:4) and his giving himself for us (1:4), deliverance from the law and the old aeon was given. Christ's death is the ground and cause of this deliverance. The phrase, *through law*, directs us away from a subjectivity that would limit 2:19 to the personal experience of Paul.

But Paul's own experience is involved. Paul speaks of his call, his being set apart, his reception of revelation, his being sent to preach (1:15–16), and his death to the law (2:19). Paul could have been speaking for Jewish Christians in general, but the emphatic *ego* (*I*) of v. 19, which may anticipate that of v. 20, "suggests that he knew in a special way what it meant to die to law 'through law.'"[55] In relation to Christ and grounded in his own experience of call and revelation on the Damascus Road Paul's new view of law came forth.[56] In his new view Paul sees the law and the cross beside one another, and speaks of their respective work as being related, so that what God did through law and what God did through Christ are effectively in harmony.[57] Thus, we see the likeness of Paul's death through the law and Jesus' death under the law, as Jesus has pulled Paul with him into his death. *Through law* can be understood on the basis of *I have been crucified with* (*Christ*). Paul's death to and through law can be understood in Christ's death to and

---

53. Bruce, *Galatians*, 144; Betz, 123; Kertelge, 242; Oepke, *Galater*, 96.
54. Tannehill, 58.
55. Bruce, *Galatians*, 143.
56. Ibid., 144. Schlatter, *Galater*, 61.
57. Ibid., 62–3.

through law. This points to the role of the law in Jesus' death. Paul dying to and through the law was Paul's transfer to the lordship of Christ.[58] In Christ, Paul was in Christ's death crucified with Christ.[59]

2.3. Through Law

We have seen that Paul's statement about *dying to the law* means death in the particular relationship of Paul and the law, and transfer to a new dominion. We have seen that this death is qualified by his phrase *crucified with Christ*, meaning that Paul was included in Christ's death on the cross. We turn now to Paul's enigmatic phrase *through the law*. What does Paul mean by saying that he died *through the law*? Two aspects of our investigation are the involvement of the law itself in Paul's death to the law, and the involvement of the law in the death of Jesus.

1. Paul asserts that the very death (in relation) *to* law that he has died is a death in which the law itself is somehow involved.[60] This involvement is represented by *through law*. There is nothing in the verse or its context to warrant distinguishing two laws or referring only *law* to the Law of Moses and *through law* to the law of faith or Law of Christ.[61] Both terms refer to the law of Moses or the law as such. It is this one law *to which* and *through which* death occurred. Räisänen summarizes three diverse interpretations for the abbreviation *through law* in Gal 2:19 that can be categorized as psychological, preparatory, and causative.[62]

---

58. Tannehill, *Dying*, 59, and 3.2 below.

59. Oepke, *Galater*, 95; Lührmann, *Galater*, 45; Blank, 299; Bruce, *Galatians*, 143.

60. Räisänen, *Paul* (1983), 53–6, concludes that *telos, end,* in Rom 10:4 means termination. The polemical language about the law shows that righteousness from law is contrasted to righteousness from faith, the *law* of v. 4 is associated with the law righteousness of v. 5 because of the explanatory *for* connecting the two verses and so ". . . with regard to such a law Christ can only be its end!" In response to, "Why was the law abolished?" Räisänen, 56–62, asserts three summations of Paul's position: (1) the law was given for a limited period of time, stated in Gal 3:19, assumed by Gal 3:23–5, and supported by 2 Cor 3:3–13; (2) according to Gal 2:19 the abolition of the law was due to the law itself; (3) the death of Christ freed us from under the law, Gal 3:13 (cf. 4:4; Rom 7:1–6), and so has made the law a thing of the past for the Christian. It is the second of these answers that concerns us here.

61. Luther, *Galatians* (1519), 161–3, sees *through law* as law of Christ or law of faith. Lagrange, 51, agrees. Aquinas, 60, "*I by the law* spiritual *am dead to the law* carnal."

62. Räisänen, *Paul* (1983), 57; Betz, 122, says that this *abbreviation* must be *decoded*. Martyn, 257, summarizes three interpretations of *through the law*: (a) as pedagogue, Gal 3:24; (b) as related to *through the commandment* in Rom 7:4; (c) as actively involved in Christ's crucifixion, evidenced in Gal 3:13, and because of which Paul was separated from the law. Martyn refers to the *shocking motif* of the law's *collision with the Messiah*.

1.1. A psychological understanding of Paul's statements about dying through the law would emphasize Paul's own bitter experiences under the law.[63] Räisänen says that this explanation *can be safely dismissed*, but he later speculates that Paul's conversion was perhaps not so sudden a thing as it seemed to Paul himself, and *some psychological commonplaces are probably applicable* to Paul, even though we cannot penetrate his psychic life twenty centuries after Paul lived.[64] Plausible as such speculations seem (rendering credible a former fear of punishment in Paul, pointing to Paul's chafing under certain unmotivated precepts of the law, or indicating that Paul embraced the views of the very people he once persecuted, thus accepting the Hellenists' relaxed attitude toward the law in their inclusion of Gentiles and circumcision-free mission)[65] they are matters about which Paul himself offers no clear explanation. Accordingly, the texts with which we have to deal relate to situations in the churches to which Paul is applying the gospel. They are not primarily intended as windows into the personal life of the apostle. To make them such is to shift attention from the author's intention to that of the interpreter. Some distinction must be maintained between understanding Paul (the person) and understanding Paul's letters.

1.2. A preparatory understanding of dying to the law through the law would emphasize that for Paul the law pointed beyond itself to Christ. This pointing to Christ happens in the law's pronouncement of the death sentence over the sinner, or in its confining all people under sin.[66] If Gal

---

63. Räisänen, *Paul* (1983), 57, discusses a psychological interpretation; cf. 229-36, especially n. 1-17. Such interpretation tends to be based on an autobiographical understanding of Romans 7, and is represented by Deißmann, Klausner, Dodd, Davies, and Buber. In fact, (1) whether Romans 7 (or Galatians 2) is to be taken as autobiography or an intended inclusion of all believers, and (2) whether Romans 7 is a pre-conversion or post-conversion Paul, are in both instances alternatives too narrowly conceived. There is a case to be made for the paradigmatic nature of Paul's experience. Cf. Eichholz, 224, regarding Phil 3:4-11. It is true also of Gal 2:19.

64. Räisänen, *Paul* (1983), 232: "It is one such commonplace that the unconscious can break through in opposition to the conscious belief to which one clings. There is a 'polarity, a kind of opposition, between unconscious experience and consciousness' so that 'the more we are unconsciously smitten with doubts about an idea, the more dogmatically we fight for it in our conscious arguments ... A dynamic struggle goes on within a person between what he or she consciously thinks on the one hand and, on the other, some insight, some perspective that is struggling to be born.'" Räisänen is citing May, *Courage*, 59, and Beker, *Paul*, 237, who says, "How could the Christophany have been so traumatic and so radical in its consequences unless it lit up and answered a hidden quest in his (Paul's) soul?"

65. Räisänen, *Paul* (1983), 234, 236, 251-56.

66. Ibid., 57: "Perhaps the general and somewhat vague idea that, by pointing to Christ as the redeemer, the law pointed beyond itself and thus paved the way for the Christian's liberation from it, is a sufficient explanation." Lietzmann says that here is

3:19 were understood to mean that the law produces transgressions, then a preparatory sense could be inferred. So also, 3:22 may implicitly have within the purpose clause the sense of law (here Scripture) preparing for the promise of faith. On the other hand, 3:24 uses the term for *custodian* or *disciplinarian*, but this does not indicate a preparatory role for the law. Primarily these texts are part of Paul's argument about the temporary and inferior nature of the law. An implicit preparatory function could be seen in 4:4, relative to Christ's birth under law: he was born under law *so that* those under law could be redeemed. The preparatory function of the law can be inferred from 3:13–14. But Paul does not make explicit statements in Galatians about the preparatory function of the law.

1.3. A causative understanding of Paul's statement about dying to the law through the law would emphasize that the law in fact caused the death of Christ, and because believers were crucified with Christ it has caused their death, too. Räisänen's response to this is, "It is difficult, however, to find in Paul the idea that the law *caused* the death of Christ . . ."[67] But how difficult is it? What follows is our investigation into the causative role of the law. There are three interpretations of *through law* in Gal 2:19 worth considering. Finally, Paul's view of the character of law is a consequence of how the law was involved in the death of Jesus.

1.3.1. Oepke has categorized five different uses of the preposition *through* (*dia*) with the genitive.[68] He classifies it, in Gal 2:19 as instrumental, with genitive of cause, showing the means by which a thing occurs (Gal 1:15; 2:16, 21; Rom 3:22, 25, 27; 5:10; 1 Cor 4:15; Col 1:20, 22; Mk 16:20; Acts 15:11). This is distinguished from a causal sense that points to origin or author as primary cause.[69] The distinction is between cause of death and means or agency of death.

Benoit systematizes this distinction. He takes Gal 2:19 to be a commentary on Rom 7:1–4, where the plural *you have died* is in fact with reference to the death of Christ himself. This is a death in which believers participate, a death in which they are included. Christ died to the law by undergoing its sentence. In union with him, believers undergo the same sentence of law and the same death: through crucifixion with Christ the believer dies to the law through the law. Romans 6:11 and 8:10 are analogous to Gal 2:19,

---

pronouncement of the death sentence. Betz interprets it as all people confined under sin. Räisänen, 58 n.76, cites Gyllenberg, who assumes intentional ambiguity behind the abbreviation.

67. Räisänen, *Paul* (1983), 58.

68. Oepke, *TDNT* 2:65–70. The five are spatial, temporal, modal, instrumental, and causal.

69. Ibid., 2:67–68; cf. BDF, 119, for the distinction between agent and originator.

as they speak of the death of the Christian to sin and through sin. Benoit points to the difference between *through* (or *because of*) *sin* in Rom 8:10 (that he takes to be causal, pointing to origin) and *through law* in Gal 2:19 (instrumental with genitive of cause). That is, sin caused the death but law was the agent or instrument of death. Benoit then moves to the death of Christ (the event in which the believer's death is included and the paradigm by which it is understood) and says, ". . . Sin was the cause of the death of Christ but not the instrument of it as was the Law."[70] Benoit maintains the distinction between primary cause on the one hand, and agent (instrument or means) on the other. He sees Gal 2:19 in the second sense. His interpretation is dependent on Romans texts.

Schlier also sees dying to law (Gal 2:19) as analogous to dying to sin (Rom 6:2, 10). It is repeated in the passive formulation of *you have died*, Rom 7:4. Such becoming free from the law is mediated through the law. It is the agent of death, through which I die to it. This is explained by the parallel passage in Rom 7:4, where the body of Christ (on the cross) is the actual point through which Christians become dead through the law. The *law* brought death to Christ, and by our inclusion in his death the law brings death to us. So the mediation of death is through the law, and the meaning of Gal 2:19 relates to Rom 7:7-20, in that in the sphere of sin the law represents sin's hold. Sin is thus the primary cause behind the mediating instrument or (in Gal 2:19, death-bringing) agent, the law. When sin is made powerless, the law has no more power.[71]

Sanders also speaks of the law as an agent of death. He sees Paul, in Gal 2:19, placing law in the old world order, along with sin and the flesh, and hence representing something which Christians must escape. Christians die to sin (Rom 6:5-11), are no longer in the flesh (Rom 7:5, 9), and are dead to or freed from the law (Rom 6:14-23; 7:4, 6). Sanders adds,

> The law is different from sin and the flesh, however, because it is an agent of death, probably because of its power to condemn: it kills (2 Cor 3:6; cf. Rom 7:9-13). It is probably for this reason that Paul can say both that he died to the law and that he did it through the law (Gal 2:19), although the formulation is difficult. It seems to agree more with his general view of escape from the powers hostile to God to say that Christians die through Christ (Rom 7:4).[72]

70. Benoit, 33.
71. Schlier, 100.
72. Sanders, *Paul* (1983), 83. To this view it should be added that Paul remembers the God-given nature of the law, and therefore he will not treat it as the personified active malign power that he does regarding sin and flesh.

Sanders is reluctant to ascribe a causative role to the law regarding the death of Jesus: "... While it is reasonable to surmise that Paul saw a fault in the law for its supposed role in Christ's death, neither he nor other first-century Jewish Christians—or non-Christian Jews—seem to have reasoned in this way."[73] Sanders doubts that when Paul wrote Gal 3:13 he was actually thinking about the causes that historically led to Jesus' death.[74]

But in fact the use of Deut 21:23 (Gal 3:13), initially perhaps by Jews who disputed that Jesus was the Messiah, is based on their presumption of Jesus' guilt under law. Paul's acknowledgement of their textual argument, and his application with the addition of *for us* indicates his acceptance of Jesus' guilt under law. But Jesus' acceptance *for us* of the guilt and the curse becomes the point of Paul's kerygma.[75] Paul's saying *through law* may indicate that he is thinking about the causes that led historically to Jesus' death.[76]

1.3.2. Fitzmyer distinguishes between a primary and secondary cause, that is, between cause as origin, and cause as instrument or agent, by speaking of a proximate and a remote cause of dying to the law.[77] He translates this verse, "... Because of the Law I died to the Law." His rendering of the preposition with cause and effect terminology is in accord with the two reasons for which Fitzmyer thinks Paul uses the prepositional phrase *through law*. What Fitzmyer calls the proximate cause for death to the law, "... is the crucifixion of Christ himself, but its remote cause is the Law, the curse of which was leveled against Christ (3.13). It was the Mosaic Law and the mentality it produced among men that was responsible for the crucifixion, and indirectly for the emancipation of Christians from it."[78] By *remote cause* Fitzmyer points to the primary cause or power behind the scenes that brought about both the *proximate cause* (the crucifixion of Christ) and its consequence, freedom from the law for believers. He does not speak of the law as means or agent of sin, but as primary cause (Oepke's fifth category), referring to author or origin.

Ebeling also speaks of the law as cause of death in a similarly direct or primary way. It is in Gal 3:13 that Paul describes what actually happened

---

73. Sanders, *Paul* (1983), 25.

74. Sanders argues against Harvey, *Constraints*, 22–25, who presents Paul as believing that Jesus was guilty under the law and was handed over by a Jewish court as the result of a decision based on law.

75. Schnackenburg, 63.

76. Oepke, *Galater*, 95, says that because Paul thinks concretely and objectively, the second half of 2:19 shows a historical connection, with the law as the warden of the law's curse (3:13).

77. Fitzmyer, *JBC*, 241.

78. Ibid., 241.

in the death of Christ. The law played a part in that death, "... because it was the crucial factor that sent Christ to his cursed death on the cross (Gal 3:13)."[79] So Paul says in Gal 2:19 that *through the law he died to the law* to express that the law is not only affected by his death, but also functions as its cause.

1.3.3. There is yet another interpretation of *through law* that must be considered. Borse, in line with Rom 3:27; 4:11; 2 Cor 5:7, understands the phrase in Gal 2:19 as the accompanying conditions or situation *in law* from which one is released. Paul may be speaking, in line with his own Jewish background, of the condition in which he lived. Law as an active realm or condition accompanied his life. Thus, in spite of the instrumental understanding of the preposition *through* that makes proper sense in 2:16 and 2:21, the same sense ought not be presupposed for 2:19.[80] This same modal understanding of *through law* would then also have to be considered when speaking of the historical events and forces under which Jesus lived and which led to Jesus' death. Respect for law had been translated into practices, actions, and a particular religious way of life for Paul. Respect for law was, for him as for Pharisees generally, not a generic principle but specific and prescribed courses of action in compliance with Torah conditions. Paul's concern in Galatians is not only with theological convictions regarding the law in the church, but with particular practices being observed or proposed. This would correspond to the rather precise meaning of *works of the law* as we meet it in 2:16 and the situation to which it speaks. *Works* were the conditions that the Judaizers wanted to impose on the Galatians. Thus when Paul says that he died *through law* it would mean that only in relation to Christ, in revelation on the Damascus Road, was the *moral bankruptcy* of the law disclosed. So ended the old life under the conditions and constraints of law and so began the new life under Christ.[81]

However, the weakness of this modal understanding of the law is that it identifies the law with *life* and the accompanying conditions under which one *lives*. The phrase *through law*, if it meant the accompanying conditions or manner of life, would relate to Paul's previous existence, prior to the death to which he refers in Gal 2:19. The phrase would then become

---

79. Ebeling, 147.

80. Borse, *Galater*, 117; Galatians 4:4 could be read this same way. Lightfoot, *Galatians*, 118, speaks of three stages (prior to law, under law, free from the law) through which believers pass. This indicates a modal interpretation. Harvey, ch. 3; O'Neill, "Blasphemy." On Rome's responsibility in the death sentence, Winter, *Trial*, 62; Rivkin, ch. 7.

81. Bruce, *Galatians*, 143.

disconnected from the action of the main verb, *I died*.[82] But Paul separates life from the law, and speaks of the law in terms of death: *I died through the law*. Therefore, it is best to confine the understanding of what Paul means by *through law* to a causative role in the sense of either origin or agent of death. Then *through law* is understood in its appropriate connection with *I died*, with the emphasis, as Paul seems to intend it, on the death-bringing character of the law.

2. Is the law therefore the cause as origin, or the means as agent, in the death Paul, of the believer and behind that, the death of Christ? Paul is flexible on this point. In Rom 7:7–12 he clearly has the law in the power and service of sin, with law as the agent and sin the cause. But in Galatians he does not speak so explicitly of this relationship between cause and agent. He may be close to such a concept in 3:19, where he likely means that the law produces transgressions, and in 3:22, where the law (Scripture) locked up all things under sin. In such texts it is logical to think of the law as being under the power of sin, or in service to sin, even though in Galatians Paul's focus is not on death to sin or through sin, but on death to and through law. The inclusiveness with which he can speak of sin, death, law, or flesh as aspects of the old aeon, or the present evil age, may allow him to focus on any single one of those aspects as the need arises, and allow the item to take on proportions generally appropriate only to the age or dominion itself. Technically each of those aspects could be thought of as a means or agent of the forces and power of the old aeon, with the old aeon itself being the cause or origin of the characteristics operative in the various means. But it is a separate question whether in Galatians Paul has allowed the law to rise to the position of cause or origin for death, even though he seems clearly not to do so in Romans. Paul in fact makes no explicit statement in Galatians about the law as the origin or source of death. The law as an agent of death, in the service of sin, is an understanding not prohibited by Galatians. That is, contrary to its purpose and against its God-given nature the law is exploited by sin to bring death. This is clearly the view in Rom 7:8–13, and this view does not seem to be incompatible with Galatians. It may be best to say that in Galatians the law is the cause of death at least in the agency or instrumental sense. If Gal 3:19 were taken to mean that the law produces sin (that is, causes sin) then it could be inferred that the law is also the cause or origin that produces death as well. Paul places sin and death together (along with law and flesh) in the old aeon. If the law is the cause or origin of one (sin) then it could be assumed that he would say that

---

82. The prepositional phrase functions as an adverb. What verb does it modify? BDF §184, 203, 214–16.

the law is also the cause or origin of the other, namely death. But this is not explicitly stated in Galatians.

2.1. And yet whether the law is the origin or the agent, it has a death-bringing character. Lührmann points out that as for Christ, so also for the Christian, the law not only does curse, but also kills.[83] Thus, 3:13 becomes instrumental in understanding 2:19, as the law in both instances is presented as death-bringer.[84] This death-bringing character of law is not grounded in human failure to keep the law perfectly, but is an attribute of law itself.[85] This death-bringing character of the law is over against the belief that the law brings life. The antithesis of *I died through law* would be found in the *righteousness through law* of 2:21 (cf. 3:21), in which case Christ's death would have been in vain. But in fact the law brings death, not the life it promised.[86]

Linton has pointed out that the end of the law occurs because of the law's death-bringing character. If one is dead one can no longer be reached by the law.[87] A dead person cannot be brought into a juridical process. Death is the only way to be free from the law. This concept of freedom from the law by death is so important that Paul applies it universally. The expression is not meant as philosophical symbolism, illusion, nor as though one only seems to be dead. The expression is meant in a juridical sense: one no longer exists under law because one has died to the law. Linton maintains that Paul is consistent regarding this fundamental juridical principle: the law can be removed from power only in a *lawful* way. Law can come to an end only if it is over-ridden by something greater. God as law-giver (and therefore only God) can bring the law to an end. That Paul speaks of the law as he does means that he has had to suppose that God never intended the law to be everlasting. From its beginning the law had a limited time to be in effect. Linton thus maintains that the law had its own demise built into the very work (bringing death) that the law does. Hence, the law could not have been given for more than a limited period of time.

In light of Linton's helpful comments it is important to remember the connection between Paul's view of the law and the turn-around that happened in his view and in his whole life following the revelation to him of

---

83. Lührmann, *Galater*, 45.

84. Weder, *Kreuz*, 177. Calvin, *Galatians*, 41-2, speaks of the law slaying its own disciples.

85. Mußner,180, says that the promise of life, given in the law, was only for those who fulfill it; the one who does not fulfill it falls under a curse; no one fulfills its strict requirements. Perfect law observance, however, is not Paul's argument in Galatians 2-3. Sanders, *Paul* (1983), 25.

86. Lührmann, *Galater*, 45.

87. Linton, "Paulus och Juridiken," 184-85.

God's Son (Gal 1:16). That is, Linton's analysis pertains to *Paul's view* (as opposed to Paul's pre-conversion view, the traditional Jewish view, and even the Jewish Christian view) of the law, a view to which Paul came in or after the call to faith in Christ. Bruce rightly sees this fact pointing to the "the logic of Paul's Damascus-road experience—the experience which brought home to him in a flash the 'powerlessness' of the law to accomplish what it was designed to do."[88] A strength of Bruce's position is that it connects Paul's own experience, signaled by the *ego*, of 2:19, to his central conviction about the Crucified Christ, in whose crucifixion Paul has participated or been included. That is, the turn-around (conversion, call) that happened to Paul corresponds to the turn-around in his view of law, that he then saw to have brought death, not life, to him.

Related to this turn-around is interchange in Christ, wherein Christ's death under law brought life and blessing to believers. Paul shares in that blessing, or *lives to God*, by being crucified with Christ. The believer's death to law comes because of inclusion or participation in Christ's death to law. It was therefore in the cross of Christ that the law met its end and in that sense repealed itself. Paul shows this in 3:13.[89] The law removed Christ from the sphere of its influence. This is also true of the believer, who meets freedom from the law by death to the law. By involvement in the death of the believer who dies to the law, the law is involved in its own demise and end. In Paul's view the law is, in this way, turned against itself.[90]

And yet, it was not the law itself that brought Paul to see that it brings death.[91] After his conversion Paul came to see his previous life as a persecutor of the church as unspeakably sinful (1 Cor 15:9). It had not been the law that had shown him this or prevented him from previously persecuting the church. In fact it had been his respect for the law that had led him to such sin even as the law brought death to him.

2.2. How then does the death-bringing character of the law relate to the death of Jesus? What was the involvement of the law in the death of Jesus? The statements about dying and living have the same structure as the christological statements that tell of Jesus' death and resurrection: Christ

---

88. Bruce, "Research," 124.

89. Lührmann, *Galater*, 56.

90. Oepke, *Galater*, 95. Weder, *Kreuz*, 177; Schlatter, *Galater*, 61. Bruce, *Galatians*, 143; Schoeps, 193: "With death obligations towards the law have ceased."

91. Burton, *Galatians*, 133, says that it was Paul's experience under the law that had taught him his own inability to meet its spiritual requirements and its own inability to make him righteous. In fact, Paul's view of the law in Galatians is grounded in God's revelation of the Son to Paul (1:16).

was dead and now lives, I was dead but now I live to God.[92] Christ's experience is the paradigm for the believer's experience. The death of Christ under the law and the death of the self of which Paul speaks in Gal 2:19 correspond to one another. As for Christ, so also for the Christian: the law not only brings curse, it also brings death. Galatians 3:13 is instrumental in understanding 2:19, because what is true of the believer in relation to law is true *because* it was true for Christ.[93]

The passage, 3:10-14, serves as a basis for understanding 2:19, as what first happened to Christ is that which Paul declares also of himself.[94] Paul's life is no longer directed by law. He is free from the lordship of the law, because the law brought death to Paul as it did to Jesus. In faith Paul understands himself thoroughly in terms of what happened to Jesus, and this is the way that he perceives his relationship to the law. But Paul's relation to the law is primarily the result of the law's relation to Christ, not primarily because of the relation of the law to the individual. It was, therefore, Jesus' birth under law (Gal 4:4) and his death under law (Gal 3:13), and this *for us*, in which Paul's death through law happened. Christ was born under the law to redeem those who were under the law (Gal 4:4) and this redemption becomes the christological–soteriological core of Paul's theology.[95]

2.4. Comparison to Romans 7:1-6

Romans 7:1-6, and especially v. 4, may be compared to Gal 2:19. The two texts have both a similarity and dissimilarity between them, although finally comparison rather than contrast is the appropriate word. The similarity is death to the law: *you* (plural) *died to the law* (Rom 7:4) and, *I died to* law (Gal 2:19). Freedom by death is common to both phrases. An important dissimilarity lies in the words that follow *through* in both texts: *through law* in Gal 2:19, and *through the body of Christ* (Rom 7:4). It is important that we do not use an interpretation of Rom 7:4 as a key to understanding Gal 2:19. But we can see that the comparison draws attention to a basic pattern

---

92. Lührmann, *Galater*, 45.

93. Ebeling, 147; Oepke, *Galater*, 95; Schnackenburg, 63; Weder, 177; Fitzmyer, 241; Schlier, *Galater*, 101.

94. Blank, 299, sees this connection to 2:19; thus, 300, from the understanding of what happened to Christ follows Paul's new self-understanding, realized in faith.

95. Blank, *Paulus*, 301. Tannehill, *Dying*, 58-9. Sanders, *Paul* (1983), 83, Christians escape the powers hostile to God in dying through Christ (Rom 7:4=Jesus' death on the cross). Death to law is by inclusion in Christ's death.

with which Paul worked in dealing with the law.[96] This thought pattern of *dying to the law through the law* or *through the body of Christ* points to the transition from one lord to another, one age to another, and one central conviction to another.

1. Romans 7:1-6 shows continuity with the preceding argument. Its basic pattern of thought continues that of Romans 6, as bondage, release from bondage, and entry into a new bondage is the decisive transition through dying with Christ. Tannehill notes four concepts common to Romans 6 and 7:1-6.[97]

1.1. The verb for *be destroyed* in 6:6; 7:2; 7:6 describes the end of the old bondage.[98]

1.2. The old and new bondages are described with *be enslsaved* in Rom 6:9, 14; 7:1, and with *enslaved* or *slave* in 6:6, 16-23.[99]

1.3. The same datives indicate the lord to whom one lives or dies, 7:4; 6:2, 10-11.[100]

1.4. The idea of *bearing fruit* connects 6:21-2 to 7:4-5.[101]

In Rom 7:4 it is the law to which one dies, while in Rom 6:2-11 it is death to sin. Paul connects subjection to sin with subjection to law.[102] Ro-

---

96. Gaventa, "Methods."

97. Tannehill, *Dying*, 43.

98. Rom 3:3, 31; 4:14; Gal 3:17; 5:4. Sanday and Headlam, 158, 71; Cranfield, *Romans* 1:181; Delling, *TDNT* 1: 453-55; Tannehill, 43. Hultgren, *Romans*, 249, refers to Rom 6:6, *the body of sin*: "In this context Paul does not refer specifically to the anatomical body as such . . . By 'the body of sin' in this context Paul refers to the life of the Christian prior to baptism, a life that has now been put to death through baptism into the death of Christ. Crucified, it has been destroyed. Once destroyed, it is no longer enslaved to sin." Fitzmyer, *Romans*, 436.

99. Foerster, *TDNT* 3:1097, *enslsave (kurieuo)* refers to powers that rule human life. Rengstorf *TDNT* 2:279, sees *(doulos/douleuo)* servant/serve referring to human obligation, either to God or to God's opponents. Hultgren, 250: "The believer's union with Christ in his death opens up union with him in life." Hultgren notes likenesses of expression in 6:5-7 and 6:8-10.

100. BDF, §188, §197; 2.1 above. Fitzmyer, 432-33, cites four senses in which *dying to sin* and *rising to life* may be understood (Cranfield, *Romans*, 299-300): juridical, baptismal, moral, and eschatological.

101. Cranfield, *Romans* 1:337, argues that *bear fruit for God* is not governed by the image of v. 2-3 (Sanday and Headlam, 174) but by *you died*, with much the same meaning as *enslave* in v. 6 (Cranfield, 336-37). But these contrasting alternatives are too sharply drawn, in view of the dominance of Paul's illustration in v. 2-3 and the use of the verb with *to death* in v. 5. The being put to death in v. 4a is purposive, as shown by the purpose clauses. These clauses govern grammatically the form of the verb. But the image of bearing fruit may well come from the marriage analogy in v. 2-3. The question is by whom one shall be ruled. Hauck, *TDNT* 3:616.

102. Dodd, *Romans*, 102, says that here Paul equates subjection to law with

mans 7:1-6 reaches back to 6:14-15, and beyond there to 5:20.[103] In 5:20 Paul refers to *law, trespass,* and *sin,* placing them all on the same side against *grace, justification/righteousness, eternal life,* and *Jesus Christ* (5:21). In 6:14 law and grace are opposing dominions. Paul uses a word crochet in 6:14 (not under law but under grace), as he shifts the focus from sin to law and so prepares the way for his argument in ch.7.[104]

Romans 7:1-6 is a clear instance of the interchange of ideas, as liberation from sin changes to talk of liberation from law.[105] By such interchange and word crochet Paul's argument is continuous from Romans 6 to Romans 7: "With respect to the ideas of the two bondages and dying with Christ, Rom 7:1-6 continues the thought of chapter 6. With respect to the question which is treated in these terms, that of law, it begins the discussion which follows."[106]

2. Paul's illustration from marriage in 7:2-3 uses a mixture of motifs. Paul's main point is in v. 4: you have died to the law. This would have easily followed from v. 1: the law is binding on a person only during a person's life.[107] But in 7:2-3 Paul introduces a picture that might confuse more than clarify his point. In v. 2 the married woman becomes free from the law because of her husband's death. To correspond to the main point in v. 4 it should have been the woman who is freed by dying. In Paul's illustration it is not the dead husband but the living wife who is freed from the obligations of the law.[108] But in Paul's main argument, 7:1, 4, it is the one who has died who is

---

subjection to sin. However, the wording of 7:5 is telling: *sinful passions aroused by the law*. The passions are those of sins (gen.) but they are through the law (with gen.). The implied relationship is that the passions originate in sin, and the law is the agent that arouses them.

103. Tannehill, *Dying*, 43. The role of law in 5:20 informs the sense of 6:1—7:6 as a whole.

104. Harrisville, 99.

105. Reicke, "Law," sees such interchange also in Galatians, where liberation from flesh changes to liberation from law (5:18), being under the law is synonymous with being under the elements (4:3), flesh and Spirit are opposed (5:17), as are law and Spirit (5:18).

106. Tannehill, *Dying*, 44. Nygren, 268, compares parallel themes in Romans 6 and 7. Dahl, *Studies in Paul*, 79-82, Rom 7:5-6 concludes what precedes and introduces what follows.

107. Räisänen, *Paul* (1983), 61 n. 91 notes that these two points could plausibly have conformed to Rabbinic premises and the Rabbinic rule that "as soon as a man has died he is free from the Torah and from the commandments." Hultgren, *Romans*, 269: "Although the issue was debated (at least within rabbinic Judaism) as to whether the law has an abiding significance in the world to come, the meaning is clear here. Once a person has died in this age, he or she is not subject to the law." Fitzmyer, *Romans*, 454-62.

108. Dodd, *Romans*, 101.

freed from the law and, "Ye are under law *as long as* ye live, but only *as long as* ye live."[109] If the illustration and main point were followed in a straightforward way the married woman (v. 2) would be the person who is bound under law during life (v. 1) and she would also represent the believers who have died in order to be free from the law (v. 4a). The woman's husband (v. 2a) would represent the law. She would be bound to him during life (v. 1b) but could be free only by *her* death (v. 4b). If one pursues the logic between the main argument (v. 1, 4) and the illustration (v. 2–3) it seems to have *gone hopelessly astray*,[110] so that *the analogy is simply confusing*.[111]

And yet Paul needs both the argument and illustration to make his point, as "*both* the maxim of v. 1 and the illustration of v. 2–3 correspond in detail to what happens to the Christian."[112] For on the one hand, the introduction in v. 1 (freedom from law comes only by death) matches the main point in v. 4 (Christians have died and been released from law). On the other hand, the woman in v. 2–3 who is free from the law, free to marry another, matches the believers' experience in v. 4b-c: they are free from the law so as to belong to another, to him who has been raised from the dead.

> No example will quite fit what Paul wishes to say, for Christians are both the ones who die and the ones who live on under a new master. Dying with Christ is something more than a figure of speech which can be changed to fit Paul's illustrations. Instead, Paul uses two different ideas to illustrate what he wishes to say about dying with Christ to the law.[113]

The same pattern of *dying to–living to* is in Rom 7:1–6 as in Gal 2:19. With it is bound up the idea of freedom by death.[114]

3. Freedom by death to the law happens through the body of Christ.[115] The terminology of Rom 7:4 differs from that of Gal 2:19, in that Gal 2:19 says that death to the law happens *through law*. Romans 7:4 says that death to the law happens *through the body of Christ*. The sense of the preposition *through* in Gal 2:19 is causal, referring to the death–bringing character of the law. For Paul, death to the law happened because of Jesus' death through

---

109. K. Barth, *Romans*, 233. Romans 6:7.

110. Dodd, *Romans*, 101.

111. Räisänen, (1983), 61. Reicke, 267, Paul missed the transition from one motif to another.

112. Tannehill, *Dying*, 44.

113. Tannehill, *Dying*, 45; Althaus, 64; Hultgren, *Romans*, 269–71.

114. Cranfield, *Romans*, 336; Best, 77; Tannehill, 43; Räisänen, *Paul* (1983), 58; D. Davies, 157.

115. Hultgren, *Romans*, 272.

and to law and Paul's participation or inclusion in that death. Paul could therefore have said, *I died to the law because I am united with Christ who died under or because of law*. Paul's thought is christological. Christ's death on the cross included Paul (and believers) and so Paul attests to having been crucified with Christ. Christ's death under or through (διά, *dia*) law on the cross is the paradigm for Paul's relation to the law.

But the same cannot be said for the use of *through* in Rom 7:4. There Paul does not mean that he died to the law through the death-bringing character of the body of Christ, anymore than in Gal 2:19 could it be understood that the law was his representative, whose death included Paul. But this representative sense is present in Rom 7:4. What does *body* refer to in Rom 7:4? Schweizer describes three ways in which Paul uses the term *the body of Christ* in the generally accepted epistles: (1) the body of Jesus offered up for people on the cross; (2) in such eucharistic texts as 1 Cor 11:24, where Paul or the community before him added *which is for you* to *body*, thereby stressing the act and not the substance of the offering; (3) the community (Rom 12:5; 1 Cor 10:17; 12:13) is not merely like a body, it *is* a body. The plural *you are* in 1 Cor 12:27 is also to be noted, referring to the community.[116] Nothing in Rom 7:1-6 seems to warrant taking *body* in the eucharistic sense, and so it has been interpreted as either (1) the body of Jesus on the cross,[117] or (2) the community, the church, as forming his mystical body.[118] Robinson combines the two meanings, and takes *through the body of Christ* to mean "*both* 'through the fact that Christ in this flesh-body died to the law' *and* 'through the fact that you now are joined to and are part of that body.'"[119] With this combination of ideas many interpreters assume that Rom 6:3, and baptism, is the key to Rom 7:4, and that one dies to the law by being joined to the body of Christ in baptism.[120] Baptism then becomes the means by which participation in the death of Christ is affected.[121] However, to understand what Paul is getting at in Rom 7:1-6, and what he means by *through the body of Christ* in v. 4, we note several key features of the text.

3.1. In 7:4a Paul uses the passive, *put to death*, instead of the active, *you died* (as in 6:2). He likely does so because he has in mind the act of Christ

---

116. Schweizer, *TDNT* 7:1067-71. Hultgren, 269-71.

117. Cranfield, 1:336; K. Barth, *Romans*, 232-3; Michel, *Römer*, 167; Sanday and Headlam, 174.

118. Dodd, *Romans*, 101-2; Schweitzer, 188 n. 1; Best, 77.

119. Robinson, 47.

120. *Romans*: Harrisville, 101; Käsemann, 189, Nygren, 274; Black, 100.

121. Nygren, *Romans*, 274.

being violently put to death in execution on the cross.[122] The passive corresponds to the passive *we are discharged* in 7:6. This death, like the release from the law, is ultimately God's doing, and so is freedom from sin (Rom 6:7). It is Christians who have been killed, but the backdrop of this death is the death of Christ on the cross.

3.2. The words *the body of Christ* are best understood as referring to the body of Jesus on the cross.[123] Although it is natural to assume an interpretation of Rom 7:4 on the basis of Rom 12:5 or 1 Cor 12:12-13, where *body* has a corporate sense, the word in those texts functions only to emphasize the relation of members to the whole, nothing is said about the dying of the body, and in Rom 7:4 no other function of the body except dying is mentioned.[124] *Body* does not function in v. 4 as a metaphor for the whole, the community, but speaks of what has been done to us *in* or *through* the flesh of the incarnate and crucified Christ.[125]

3.3. The interpretation of *body of Christ* requires a corporate sense for *you* who were put to death through that body. It therefore seems best to take *body* to refer to Jesus Christ in his humanity: "His cross performed and completed a perfect work . . . a unique, powerful, perfect event in history: Christ crucified . . . Paul asserts that in the crucified body, then and there, the curse, guilt, sin, division of mankind was summed up, gathered in, and put to death . . ."[126]

The full sense of the term *body* in v. 4 asserts that both (1) the physical body of Christ that died on the cross, and (2) the corporate body in which believers are present were included in that death on the cross. Karl Barth translates v. 4, *through the slain body of Christ*, and interprets it to

---

122. Cranfield, *Romans* 1:335. Bultmann, *TDNT* 3:7-25.

123. Schlier, *Römerbrief*, 217, sees in 7:4 a reference to the body of Christ on Golgotha and by baptism one enters the death of Christ as such, not only a present likeness of his death. Thus, it is more clear to speak of baptism as signifying the inclusiveness of what happened on the cross, so as to keep from any concept of repeating in baptism the cross event. Wilckens, *Römer* 2:64-5, sees the aor. pass. in v. 4 as a reference to the baptismal event in 6:3-11: *through the body of Christ* is a precise statement of what Paul means by *through the death of Christ*. Baptism does not give a corporate-inclusive quality to Christ's dying on the cross: the cross has that in and of itself.

124. Tannehill, *Dying*, 45. Wedderburn, "Body," 78-80; Robinson, 55, lists 5 studies of derivation for *body*.

125. M. Barth, "Church," 142.

126. Ibid., 143.

mean, *Comprehending Him, ye are comprehended in His death.*[127] Paul says of Christians' former selves, "They died in his death."[128]

3.4. Christ acted as humanity's representative.[129] When he died, believers died. When he was crucified *our old self was crucified with him* (Rom 6:6). In like manner Paul has said in Gal 2:19, *I have been crucified with Christ.* That is, the believer is included in the death of the representative. It is a death *to* law (Rom 7:4; Gal 2:19). It is a death *under* law (Gal 4:4). It is a death *through* law (Gal 2:19). One has died, therefore all have died (2 Cor 5:14). The inclusive nature of Christ's representative death, indicated in Rom 7:4, corresponds to the *I have been crucified with* of Gal 2:19. The prepositional phrases of Rom 7:4 and Gal 2:19 both refer to death under law, but do so differently. Romans 7:4 refers to Jesus' body, dying under law on the cross, in a death that includes Paul. Galatians 2:19 refers to the law's bringing death to Paul, and behind Paul's death through law is the death of Christ through law on the cross.

The cross is *itself* an inclusive event. Baptism does not make it so, nor does baptism give the cross its character and power as an inclusive event by repeating this event or making it present in the believer. Baptism signifies and makes that power and event manifest in the life of the church. But the cross itself is an inclusive and representative event of its own accord. Paul is speaking of the significance of the cross. This was God's eschatological act that took place only once, and it involved the old and new worlds as wholes. By that event the Christian is no longer enslaved to the powers of the old world (Rom 6:2-11; 7:1-6; Gal 2:19; 5:24). The believer is no longer bound by the values and judgments of the old world (Gal 6:14; 2 Cor 5:14-19). The believer walks in newness of life (Rom 6:4), or in the Spirit (Rom 7:6), or lives by the Spirit (Gal 5:25), and is a new creature (Gal 6:15; 2 Cor 5:17). Christ now lives in the believer (Gal 2:20).

Such statements bear witness to the time of God's decisive act in Christ's cross. Second Corinthians 5:14 emphasizes in a particular way the time of transition from old to new as it happened in the cross of Christ: *because he died, all have died.* Here is the inclusive nature of the decisive past event, the

---

127. K. Barth, *Romans*, 232-3. Tannehill, *Dying*, 146. Schlatter, *Gerechtigkeit*, 226, put it beautifully: "In das, was Jesus tat, hat er aber alle eingeschlossen, die ihm gehören. Seine gottheitlich starke Liebe macht seine Gemeinschaft mit allen total und für alle wirksam." (*In that which Jesus did he has included all who believe in him. His divine, sturdy love empowers his community with all fullness, and for all included.*)

128. Cranfield, *Romans*, 1:336. Tannehill, *Dying*, 47.

129. Wedderburn, "Body," 78; *Baptism*, 37-69, 342-55. Thrall, *Corinthians*, 149: "The belief that Christ acted representatively on behalf of the whole human race is the key principle of Paul's theology."

purpose clause, and the indirect object that could be rendered, *no longer live to themselves*. The transfer to living *to him*, resulting from participation in Christ's death on the cross, more than referring to the time of conversion, is the sense of the words *from now on* in 2 Cor 5:16.[130] The death of Jesus is the turning point.[131] Second Corinthians 5:16 therefore corresponds to Gal 2:20: *the life I now live in the flesh I live by faith in the Son of God.*

Summary

The dying of which Paul speaks in Gal 2:19 is death within a particular relationship, namely that to law. The dative of relation expresses dispossession: Paul has died to the dominion of law. The aorist points to death as a past experience that together with the perfect passive is identified with Christ's death on the cross. Christ's death is the frame of reference for Paul. He understands his own experience in terms of Christ's experience. He also sees Christ as his representative whose death included Paul in death. Christ's death under law is the source of Paul's conviction about the law. Paul does not mention baptism when he speaks of being crucified with Christ and dying to the law. The law was the power operative in this death. But law is not the operative power in baptism. This *dying to* is not brought about by one's own consciousness of the law's weakness. It is Christ's dying and living that engenders the new age.

The same *dying–to, living–to* pattern of thought in Gal 2:19 occurs also in Rom 7:4. The pattern points to the transition from one lord to another, and uses the dative to indicate the lord to whom one lives or dies. In Romans Paul interchanges ideas, from death to sin in 6:2–11 to death to law in 7:4, and so equates the two subjections as one and the same thing. Paul's point in Rom 7:4, death to the law, is served with a seemingly contradictory double illustration from marriage that describes what happens to the Christian: one is free *from* the law by death, one is free *for* living to and belonging to him who has been raised from the dead.

This same pattern exists in Gal 2:19. The two passages do not contradict one another, even though dying through the law in Gal 2:19 is replaced by dying through the body of Christ in Rom 7:4. The *body* of Rom 7:4 seems best understood as the actual body of Jesus on the cross. When he was crucified Christ died as humanity's representative. Through his slain body

---

130. Tannehill, *Dying*, 47, 70–4.

131. Georgi, *Opponents*, 278, Paul's opponents did not recognize this about Jesus' death: the turning point was in Christ's cross. Plummer, 176: *from now on* refers not to the present moment, but to the death of Christ.

believers were included in his death to the law. That is, through union with and representation by the body of Christ, which was put to death to the law for us, we are dead to the law. For Christ and for the believer the death on the cross was to, through, and under law. The cross of Christ was a decisive event for the believer by which the believer is no longer enslaved to the powers of the old aeon.

But the phrase *through law* in Gal 2:19 does not refer to union with or representation by the law, but rather shows how Paul disassociates the law from life, and associates it with death. The law does not make alive but brings death. In this way Paul counters the position of his opponents in Galatia who were promoting law observance as the necessary condition for membership in the church, for righteousness, and for living to God. *Living to God* in Gal 2:19 corresponds to *belonging to another . . . who has been raised from the dead* in Rom 7:4. In both texts dying to the law happened so that life in this new lordship could come about. In Gal 2:19 the dying was through the agency of the law. In Rom 7:4 the dying was through the means of Christ's body on the cross, as he died through law. Galatians 2:19 and Romans 7:4 may be understood as referring to the same event, namely the death of Christ under law on the cross. But whether *through law* in Gal 2:19 can be understood to mean more than that the law is the agent or means of death cannot be concluded from 2:19 alone, nor from its immediate context in 2:11–21. Another step is required, and for this step we must turn to Gal 3:13 to consider Christ's death under law.

And yet there is a significant difference between Christ's death under law and our death through law. Christ's death under the curse of law was *for us* (Gal 3:13), just as Christ's birth *under the law* was *so that* he might redeem those under the law (4:4). Paul can say of us in relation to law that *the sinful passions aroused by the law were at work in our members to bear fruit for death* (Rom 7:5). But the sense of Christ's death under law is quite different. It is a death under law not as though he deserved death, not because sinful passions were aroused by the law in him, but because of the death-bringing character of the law itself, and because Christ who did not deserve to die, died for us in whom sinful passions were aroused *through the law* and who do deserve to die. But Christ's death under law was because the law kills, and he was born under law so that he could redeem those who are under law. There is therefore an interchange in Christ, as the one in whom there was no sin that was aroused by law nevertheless died under the law, so that we who are under the law and in whom sinful passions are aroused so as to produce death, nevertheless are blessed. The law cannot and does not make alive or bring righteousness. This thought informs Paul's emphasis on the specific works of the law in Galatians 2 and 3. Galatians 3:13 speaks of the relation of the law to the death of Jesus, and exemplifies the interchange in which he became a curse so that we might be blessed. It is to these explications of Paul's doctrine of Christ and his work that we turn in Part 3 of this study.

3
Galatians 2–3

3.1 Works of the Law in Galatians 2

PAUL CONTENDS WITH THE theological terms, *work*, *works*, and *works of the law*, as the polarizing antagonism toward his received revelation of Jesus Christ. The terms represent a significant part of the faith and history of his own people, Israel.[1] The issues that had become problems in Galatia are attached to these terms. That *works of the law* had been promoted by Paul's opponents as necessary conditions of faith for new believers in Christ indicates the common currency the concepts had in the history of the opponents.[2] In a persistent way the *works* represented equivalence to doing God's will. Cultic service is indicated as an expression of *works* required by God or the Mosaic Law and necessary to Jewish piety. The *works* are in contrast to works that originate in human self-will. For Paul's people, Israel, and for those with whom he argued in Galatia, the fulfilling of such requirements was a holy work, related to righteousness.[3]

---

1. The single term is ἔργον (*ergon, work*); the plural is ἔργα (*erga, works*); the phrase is ἔργα ἐξ νόμου (*erga ex nomou, works of law*). See Hatch and Redpath, 1:541–44.

2. Martyn, *Galatians*, 250–53, 268–71, translates *by works of the law* as *by observance of the law*.

3. Bertram, *TDNT* 2:646, says that the eschatological expectation was that God Himself will write the works of the law (*erga nomou*) on the fleshly tables of the heart (Jer 31:33). It is in Paul's use of Jer 31:33 (Rom 2:15) and not in Jer 31:33 itself, that *works of law* occurs. What God will write upon the heart, Jeremiah says, is *my laws* (NRS 31:33 = LXX 38:33). The connection for Judaism was works of the law, righteousness, and fulfillment of requirements as fulfillment of the will of God. The concept of *works of the law* is found in the literature of Qumran; Fitzmyer, *JBC*, 240; Hultgren, *Romans*, 171–4.

Such works of the prescriptions of law correspond to what Paul calls the *works of law* in the Letter to the Galatians.[4] The succinctness and force with which Paul uses the phrase suggests that it was a commonly used formula, indicating acts that had been prescribed by the Mosaic law and its Pharisaic interpretations, and that by the time of Galatians *works of law* was a conflicted issue.[5] When Paul first uses the expression in Gal 2:16, he does so three times in succession within the verse, each time to emphasize that justification is *not by works of law*. The expression occurs again in 3:2, where Paul appeals to the experience of the Galatians themselves who received the spirit by *hearing with faith* and *not by works of law*. Again in 3:5 the same rhetorical question asks whether reception of the Spirit and working of miracles happened *by hearing with faith* or *by works of law*. Finally, in 3:10, Paul uses the phrase in a straightforward declarative statement: all who rely on works of the law are under a curse. Works are thus contrasted to faith and miracles and associated with curse (that Paul in turn connects to death by crucifixion, in 3:13). Paul does not return to the expression in Galatians, but moves from it to the single term, *law* (*nomos*), throughout his argument about the law.[6] The introduction of the phrase *works of law* in 2:16, is the first mention of either works or law in the letter. It follows the reports of two separate debates, that in turn each focused on a distinct issue and specific aspect of law. These were at Jerusalem, 2:1-10, the question of circumcision of Gentile converts to Christianity, and at Antioch, 2:11-14, the question of table fellowship of Jewish Christians with Gentile Christians.

1. Galatians 2:1-10 reports Paul's second visit to Jerusalem. The first visit to Jerusalem following his conversion is mentioned in 1:18, and was made three years after the conversion, for the expressed purpose of *visiting Cephas*.[7]

1.1. The timing of the second visit is unclear. *After fourteen years* could mean after the visit to Syria and Cilicia (1:21), after the first visit to Jerusalem

---

4. Betz, 116 n. 35, refers to *ex ergon vomou* (*by works of law*, "on the basis of [the] works of [the] Torah") as an abbreviation that occurs only in Pauline theology, representing "fulfilling the ordinances of the Torah."

5. Paul's references to *works of law* occur only in Galatians and Romans, in six verses: Rom 3:20, 28, Gal 2:16 (3x); 3:2, 5, 10. The singular, *the work of the law*, occurs at Rom 2:15, referring not necessarily to a single work but to the Gentiles who have an inner inclination to law practice, to doing the law's work. Cf. Rom 3:27; 4:2, 6; 9:11, 32; 11:6.

6. Paul is flexible in generalizing from particular works to the whole law. See 1.4 above.

7. Betz, 76 n. 190-1, the time period of the first visit is imprecise. Three years could mean starting from the revelation *or* the return to Damascus. Stendahl, *Paul*, 7, reminds us that it was *call* and not *conversion* for Paul.

(1:18), or after the revelation of Christ (1:16).[8] Paul went *with Barnabas*, and *took Titus along with him*.[9] The purpose of the visit was that Paul could lay before those of repute the gospel that he had been preaching among the Gentiles.[10] Paul went in accord with revelation, from a higher authority by whom he had been commissioned, *sent neither by human commission nor by human authorities* (1:1).[11] Paul was sent *through Jesus Christ and God the Father*. Such was the basis of his apostleship, and he went to Jerusalem in response to it, not to carry out the requirements of those *from* whom he came in Antioch, but to enable recognition of the truth of the one and only gospel (1:6-9, 11; 2:2, 5) by those *to* whom he went in Jerusalem (2:2).[12]

Apostleship for Paul means acting in accord with what had been revealed to him, and is understood via the content of that revelation. When he speaks of having been set apart (1:15) so that he could proclaim the Gospel (1:16), Paul alludes to Jer 1:5 and Isa 52:7. These texts emphasize the

---

8. Betz, 83; on chronology, 9-12, 63-4. Jewett, *Chronology*; Georgi, *Kollekte*, 91-6. Lüdemann, 71-7, dates the incident in Antioch (2:11) before the Jerusalem conference (2:1-10). But differently, Barrett, *Freedom*, 10-14; Suhl, 43-77; Wedderburn, "Chronologies," 103-8.

9. We note, *with Barnabas*: Barnabas was senior to Paul at this point. Betz, Excursus: Barnabas, 84; Meeks, *Christians*, 10-11; Weiß, *History* 1:207; Räisänen, *Paul* (1983), 253. Note also: *taking Titus along with me*: Titus was taken along as a test case. They who came to Antioch from Judea had probably insisted on Titus' circumcision. Duncan, 41-5, reads 2:3-5 to mean that Titus *was* circumcised after coming to Jerusalem, but not because he was compelled. Paul then would mean in 2:5 that he *did* momentarily yield so that in the long run his law-free gospel would be allowed to continue unimpeded. Thus, Weiß, *History* 1:271. But Linton, "Aspect," 87-9, and Barrett, *Freedom*, 11-12, 112, rightly disagree because of Paul's main argument.

10. Acts 15:2 has Paul as a delegate from the Antioch church. This could mean that: (1) Paul was in Jerusalem at the behest of Antioch; (2) Antioch was unable to make a decision by itself about circumcision-less faith; (3) supremacy of the Jerusalem church or its pillars is assumed. Paul's report in Galatians corrects all three. That he went *by revelation* implies its negative aspect: it was not at someone's behest, nor because he was summoned. Barrett, *Freedom*, 10.

11. *Revelation*, 2:2, contrasts to *human origin*, 1:11; cf. apocalyptic terminology (ἀποκάλυψιν, *apokalupsin*) 1:12, 16; 2:2; 3:23. Betz, 71; Oepke, *TDNT* 3:582-87. Lührmann, *Offenbarungsverständnis*, 41, says that in 1:12 and 2:2 the meaning *ecstatic vision* is ruled out in accord with Rom 16:25. Paul is not clear about the kind of experience he had.

12. In Gal 1:1(*resurrection*) Paul signals the cleavage between *through man* and *through Christ*, between the old aeon and the new. God's defeat of death is accomplished in raising Christ, and is the foundation of Paul's being an apostle. His reception of the gospel (1:12), recognition of Jesus as Son of God (1:16), and going to Jerusalem (2:2) are all events of the new age. Lührmann, *Offenbarungsverständnis*, 145-46: Paul announces God's righteousness in the gospel, and with the language of *apocalypse* declares the turning of the ages, from old to new.

prophet's appointment (even before birth) to preach to *the nations*, and the good tidings that he was to bring. For Paul, the revelation of God's Son was a means to an end. The end was that Paul would proclaim the Son of God (the *content* of the revelation) to *the nations*. Paul thus speaks of preaching to *the nations* as the purpose of his call to faith in Christ.[13] With this allusion to Jer 1:5 and Isa 52:7, the work of a prophet passes to the apostle.[14]

Paul does not appeal to the consensus of church leaders to legitimize his gospel.[15] He represents what he has already said in 1:12: what had happened to him as a break between two worlds has become a break with tradition in his own life and person.[16] Galatians 1:12 contrasts what might have come from *a human source* to what Paul had in fact received through *a revelation of Jesus Christ*, and sets the tone for what follows in three ways.

1.1.1. The meaning of *apocalypse* in 1:12 ought not be limited to a vision.[17] Paul could have a visible and audible event (Damascus Road experience) in mind, but his real point is to set the origin of his Gospel against his opponents' theological tradition.[18] Theirs was a law-abiding tradition, grounded in Torah, Moses, and Sinai. It led back to Jerusalem as the measure of legitimate teaching.[19] Paul had broken with this. The criticism against him was that he lacked legitimacy because of that break.[20] Paul's concern

---

13. Elliott, *Nations*, 46, renders τὰ ἔθνη (*ta ethnaē*) as *the nations*: "The unfortunate proliferation of Gentiles in recent translations is a lexically and exegetically dubious practice and one to be resisted." He agrees (n. 130, 131) with Esler, that no ethnic group ever identified themselves as *ethnē*.

14. Lührmann, *Galater*, 32.

15. The background of 1:15 is decidedly Jewish, the content of 1:16 peculiarly Christian. Betz, 69–70: "Paul had not ceased to formulate his task in terms of a Jewish eschatological universal mission . . . in line with the tradition of the prophetic vocation." For Paul this vocation meant conformity to the Crucified and Risen Christ in both his preaching content and way of life. We note *to me*, as the revelation was obtained by a particular recipient, namely Paul. Lührmann, *Offenbarungsverständnis*, 78. The revelation is not the Christ-event as such, but the interpretation received by one who has a new beginning because of the new activity of God. Burton, 41, "He is speaking neither of an epiphany of Jesus as a world event, nor of a disclosure of him which, being made to men at large, as, e.g., through his life and death, might be perceived by some and fall ineffectual upon others, but of a personal experience, divine in its origin . . . personal to himself and effectual."

16. Lührmann, *Galater*, 32.

17. Lührmann, *Offenbarungsverständnis*, 40–44, refers to 1 Cor 14:6; Rom 16:25; Eph 1:17; 3:3. Gaventa, *Light*, 23, notes that Paul does not just write about a personal event, but about God's revelation, usually linked to God's action in the end time, and about the attack of that revelation on Paul's prior life.

18. Lührmann, *Offenbarungsverständnis*, 74.

19. Ibid., 72–3.

20. Lührmann, *Offenbarungsverständnis*, 71–4; Georgi, *Kollekte*, 36 n. 113;

was for the unity of the church, with Jews and Gentiles, founded on faith in Christ without conditions of law. Paul received this as "divine direction . . . the standard by which he himself and all others are to be judged."[21] Paul's conflict was with a tradition of revelation fulfilled only in Moses, with the Torah as valid for all ages.[22] Revelation thus has to do with disclosure of the world to come, the unveiling of what is hidden, and requires a divine act.[23] Paul asserts that his gospel has been that of justification without law from the beginning of his ministry. This emphasis does two things: it identifies his Christ-position as over against his opponents law-tradition; it affirms that his gospel is no different from what it has always been since God revealed it to him.[24]

1.1.2. The new tradition given to Paul (1:16) in accord with which he acts, is Jesus Christ, the Son of God. That Paul speaks here of Jesus as the Son of God is not coincidental.[25] It is not only that Jesus was revealed to Paul (1:12) but that he was revealed as God's Son:

> . . . Jesus Christ himself was revealed to him in such a way that as a result he now had a gospel to preach . . . All that Paul subsequently preached was determined by his experience on the Damascus road, when Jesus Christ was revealed to him in His true significance. Jesus was to be thought of no longer merely as one who had been crucified and was therefore accursed; He was the Christ, the Son of God, who had died to win men's salvation, and who was now exalted as Lord.[26]

The revelation that opposes the tradition of Paul's opponents is the revelation of Jesus Christ in his role as bringer of salvation. Christ is the eschatological bringer of salvation because he has superseded the epoch of the law and brought about justification without works of the law. The eschatological nature of Paul's speech is manifest. The new tradition signals

---

Stuhlmacher, *Evangelium*, 67. It was this legitimacy question, and not merely whether Paul had suited his gospel to human wishes (Kim, *Origin*, 67-8) that is at the heart of this struggle.

21. Bornkamm, *Paul*, 38, 166.
22. Oepke, *TDNT* 3:575, 577. Stuhlmacher, *Evangelium*, 107-8, 67.
23. Oepke, *TDNT* 3:582-83.
24. Wilckens, "Development."
25. Betz, 70; Hahn, *Titles*, 279-80; Kramer, 108-9; 183-84; Schweizer, *TDNT* 8:383; Lührmann, *Offenbarungsverständnis*, 76-7; Cullmann, *Christology*, 293: "Here lies the key to all New Testament Christology. *It is only meaningful to speak of the Son in view of God's revelatory action* . . . as God reveals him in redemptive action."
26. Duncan, 23.

the end of the old, and that new tradition is described as Jesus Christ the Son of God.[27]

1.1.3. Paul's argument in Galatians moves to the soteriological level from the start. Even before specifically mentioning particular works of the law (2:3; 2:12), and thereafter generalizing to the whole law (2:19), Paul's christological tradition is implicitly opposed to the law tradition. His use of the key word, *revelation*, in Gal 1:12, 16, and again in 3:23, connects his gospel with Jesus Christ, and connects revelation with faith.[28] This points to justification through faith, as over against law. There is for Paul a material connection between the christological title, *Son of God*, and justification. This title is used again at 2:20, in connection with the saying about Jesus *given up* in death, and at 4:4 and 4:6, in the sayings about the sending of the Son whose Sonship makes possible the sonship of all believers. At the same time Paul declares that this sending of the Son who gave up Himself is the conclusion of the time of the law, and the facilitation of justification apart from the law (4:5). Paul's choice of the title, *Son of God*, indicates his attitude to the law. For him, the revelation of the Son of God is the boundary between law and faith.[29] This central conviction was signaled in Paul's break with tradition that he reports having happened when he became an apostle to the Gentiles.[30] So Paul could not seek legitimization of his Gospel from those in Jerusalem. The gospel itself legitimizes him, and it is not dependent on human discussion or validation.[31] His experience of the end of the old aeon could not be measured by the standards that he perceived as *according to the flesh* (1:16). With this phrase the discussion moves from Paul's stand against his Galatia opponents and their law-tradition, to what he reports as the stand taken against Jerusalem.

27. Lührmann, *Offenbarungsverständnis*, 75-8.

28. Betz, 71, notes that in Rom 1:3-6 Paul similarly connects *Son of God* and his Gospel, as he quotes a christological formula as that Gospel's content. Lührmann, *Galater*, 32-3, says that Paul uses *the Gospel of his Son* still again in Rom 1:9, and in 1:7 names the revelation of God's justification by faith as the content of the Gospel.

29. Lührmann, *Galater*, 32-3. We could infer from 1:16-17 that Paul, having been called to preach, carried on this purpose in Arabia. In accord with his call it was to the Gentiles, while in accord with his theology it was a gospel of the Son of God and freedom from the law. But Paul does not explicitly say this in 1:17.

30. Watson, 21, sees Galatians as Paul's legitimization of a reform-movement that has decided to become a separate sect. The mission to *ethnē* arises from a failed mission to Jews in which Paul had participated and preached. This argument is based mostly on other epistles and Acts, fails to take into account Paul's two-aeon view, dismisses Paul's teaching about new creation as sectarian sentiment (68), and ignores that the theological concern for the truth of the gospel and sufficiency of the Christ event for faith and salvation have any other than sociological grounds.

31. Lührmann, *Galater*, 33. Schlier, *Galater*, 58.

Against the opponents, Paul's two-aeon scheme stands behind his statements about the revelation of the Son. The scheme has in it the nature of apocalyptic: this age has been superseded through God's manifestation in Christ. This manifestation has initiated the new age. The scheme represents God's eschatological work: the discontinuity to history is in the salvation brought by the new age that has been established without the law of the old age. We can see three differences between Paul and these opponents. First, there is a christological difference. For Paul the Christ-event signifies the cancellation of continuity. For the opponents it was the confirmation of the law. Second, there is a difference in understanding of the law. For Paul revelation has annulled the tradition of law. For the opponents it was through the mediation of Moses that law was given for all time. Third, there is a difference regarding the meaning of revelation. For Paul it was the working of God with people, and it meant the end of the old cosmos. For the opponents the revelation implemented by Moses mediated between divine power and people, but effected no such discontinuity. Paul herein denies the authority of the opponents' tradition.[32]

1.2. But Paul does not deny the authority of the apostles of the Jerusalem church. He does deny that his Gospel originated with them or needs to be validated by them. He therefore seeks to establish a distance and independence from them, not totally, but on this point: the validity of his Gospel. He has a dialectical relationship with the "highest but human authorities in the church."[33] It is a "dialectic between being independent of and being acknowledged by Jerusalem."[34] Four verbs point to this dialectical relationship.[35]

1.2.1. The (aorist) verb in 1:16 is negative: *I did not confer*. Paul begins his denial of dependence first by stating what he did *not* do following his new call, and secondly by indicating the immediacy of his response, *immediately* (*I did not straightaway confer*).[36] The (aorist middle) verb also implies denial, as "there is no object, about which such consultation could take place."[37] Paul defends the independence of his commission as he indi-

---

32. Lührmann, *Offenbarungsverständnis*, 78.

33. Betz, 73, ". . . Paul does not identify these apostles with the Twelve or any other group. There was no definition of apostleship which all could agree upon." Betz' Excursus, 74; Rengstorf, *TDNT* 1:420; Kirk, "Apostleship"; Kertelge, "Apostelamt," 161-81; Barrett, *Signs*, 1.

34. Holmberg, *Power*, 16.

35. Dunn, "Relationship."

36. Betz, 72; BDF, §102:2; Mußner, 89: *from the beginning on* . . .

37. Betz, 72, 95; Behm, *TDNT* 1:353. Acts 9:10-19 substantiates that Paul had a human teacher.

cates a meaning somewhat more technical than simply taking counsel with a person. The verb here means a consultation with one who is a recognized or qualified interpreter of the significance of a sign.[38] This fits the sense of 1:1, 11-12, as Paul did not deem it necessary to seek out anyone even from among Jesus' followers to give an authoritative verdict on the revelation and apostolicity that had come to him without human agency. In contrast then to the *flesh and blood* (1:6) and *Jerusalem* (1:17) with whom Paul did not consult for a verdict, he went away into Arabia. The sense of the alibi is likely that he was in Arabia and consequently *not* in Jerusalem.[39]

1.2.2. In 1:18 the (aorist) infinitive of *visit* has an ambiguity to it, as it can mean either, (1) get to know someone, or (2) get information from someone.[40] Indeed, *visit Cephas* is prudently, carefully spoken; the search had a purpose in seeking out information. It brought him to Peter.[41] It does not undermine Paul's argument of independence that he got information from Peter. He was not altogether aloof from Jerusalem, but wanted to clarify his distance on a specific issue: the revelation of his gospel. The point having been made that Paul's apostolicity was not attributable to human authority, he can freely acknowledge his indebtedness to Peter for information to which Paul would not have had access, namely, information regarding the ministry of Jesus while on earth. This is the kind of information that had not come to Paul with the revelation. That Paul should go to the chief Apostle to get to know him and learn something from him, and at the same time preserve his own experience, revelation, and gospel from a verdict by

---

38. Dunn, "Relationship," 462.

39. Linton, "Aspect," 84. This also points to the problem of the relationship to Acts 9:26-30, that has Paul going to Jerusalem and attaching to disciples. Linton, 85, points out that this does not necessarily make the Acts material later, for the Galatian adversaries of Paul had already reported a similar thing: "For when Paul denies that he has gone to Jerusalem it is because they have said that so he had done. And when Paul maintains that he came to Jerusalem only after three years, it is because the 'Galatian' version runs thus, that he went to Jerusalem immediately (or very soon). And when Paul asserts that he was in Jerusalem a very short time, it is while it was said that he stayed there for a long time. And, finally, as Paul denies that he communicated with the Apostles—save only Peter and James, the Lord's brother—he is refuting the opinion that he was a docile disciple of the Apostles." Suhl, 46-51.

40. BDAG, 483, adopts (1). Betz, 76, sees "a non-committal phrase," renders it, "pay Peter a visit," and thinks it out of keeping with Paul's defense if he were to admit getting information from Peter. But Paul wanted a particular kind of independence. Kilpatrick, 148, sees it in contrast to *I saw . . . James*, "St. Peter had been an eyewitness and disciple of Jesus. St. James could not claim to be a comparable informant about the teaching and ministry." Dunn, "Relationship," 465-66, agrees. Walter, 506-7.

41. Schlier, *Galater*, 60.

that chief Apostle, would have been as careful a maneuver as Paul's choice of language indicates, not seeking legitimization but needing to know Peter.[42]

1.2.3. Paul says in 2:2, regarding his Jerusalem visit, that he *laid before them the gospel I preach*. He uses a neutral verb that relays nothing of the relative status of the parties involved.[43] He does not seek approval for validity but recognition for effectiveness and holds a delicate balance in describing his relationship with Jerusalem. He laid his gospel out before them, but he was already convinced of the truth of it (1:8). He could now help its cause.[44]

1.2.4. In 2:6 the active sense of *they added nothing to me* relates to *the ones of repute*,[45] who neither corrected nor completed Paul's gospel, imposing on him no new burden of doctrine or practice.[46] The sense of the verb cannot mean *in addition* to what they had already imparted as either revelation or correction, for this would counter Paul's previous argument for independence on just that point. Hence all they could give was recognition of what had happened.[47] Paul here connects the demand made in Antioch

---

42. Lührmann, *Galater*, 34, puts both issues together: Paul is already an apostle before coming to Jerusalem, he is already more than two years into his Gentile mission in Arabia, he already has had exposure to what he is now about, and he has no need of legitimization, but only acquaintance. Dunn, "Relationship," 463–64, has too narrow a choice between Chrysostom's *to see and honor Peter*, and, *to inquire into or about*. Peter could have been the object of Paul's visit for the sake of information, and that "not just about the weather." Dunn, "Gal 1:18...once more," in response to Hofius, "Gal 1:18," who denies the *get information* sense in classical usage. The contrast here is not between various renderings of a word but between the fact that a visit was made, and all that is entailed in Paul's revelation that was not received from human authority (1:12). Josephus, *Bell* 6:81.

43. Dunn, "Relationship," 467.

44. That Paul gave a second reading before those who were of repute is seen by Betz, 87, as analogous to Plato's use of *men of eminence* to grant recognition of authority without compromise of one's personal conviction. Klausner, 581; Barrett, "'Pillar' Apostles," 4; Plato, 21B–22B; 29A; 36D; 41E; Bruce, *Galatians*, 109: "It is most unlikely that Paul would have modified his gospel had the Jerusalem leaders *not* approved it—he had higher authority than theirs for maintaining it unchanged, and 'no one is likely to want the *independence* of his gospel to be confirmed' (Schmithals, 43)." Barrett, *Freedom*, 11, notes that Jerusalem authorities could prove him neither right nor wrong but could ruin his work by failure to affirm it (2:2).

45. Paul alludes to Deut 10:17, for his attitude toward the leaders. Lührmann, *Galater*, 38: Paul will not have legitimization from humankind; it can come only from God, and so Jerusalem *cannot* be against him.

46. Burton, *Galatians*, 89–91.

47. Weiß, *History*, 1:270. Betz, 95: the addition could only be "to subject the Gentile Christians to Torah and circumcision (cf. 4:9; 5:16)...he is able to report and substantiate that at the Jerusalem conference his gospel was approved as is and that no additional requests, such as the opponents are now making, were made. Thereby the present demands of the opponents are declared illegitimate." Schlier, *Galater*, 74–5; Mußner,

for circumcision with the same demand in Galatia by his opponents. That demand was not laid on him by the leaders in Jerusalem and he cannot capitulate to it now. The pillar apostles had already acknowledged the validity of his circumcision–free gospel.[48] That the demand for circumcision was the central issue in Jerusalem that Paul relates to the Galatian situation is seen from two other items of context.

First, the mention of Titus in 2:3 is in light of *added nothing to me* in 2:6.[49] Titus was taken along as a test case.[50] He was not compelled to be circumcised, meaning either that he was not circumcised, or that he was circumcised but not compelled.[51] In any case, the verse stands in sharp contrast to Peter's inconsistency, as demonstrated in Antioch and described by *compel* in 2:14. Titus was not *compelled*, 2:3, and the force of the contrast to the two situations is carried by this verb.[52]

Second, in 2:7-8, the reference is neither to two gospels nor two missions or apostolates. *Circumcision* is an abbreviation for the Jews, and Peter is to go to them, while Paul goes *to the nations*.[53] It is a division of labor or

---

114–15; Georgi, *Kollekte*, 19–20.

48. Dunn, "Relationship," 469.

49. Meeks, *Christians*, 230 n.2.

50. Betz, 84 n. 252, sees *taken along* as an indication of inferior rank, "take along as an adjunct or assistant." Georgi, *Kollekte*, suggests that Titus was taken along as a test case to be decided at the meeting. Compare Luther, *LW* 27:200, whose *all things to all men* view of Paul's attitude to the law may be right generally, but not in this context. Betz' *Excursus*, 84; Barrett, *Freedom*, 10–11.

51. Was Titus circumcised? Linton, "Aspect," 87, ". . . how could such a deviation from the straight way be said to preserve for the church the truth of the gospel?" And 89, "that the truth of the gospel might continue with you" fits with the view that Paul gave way not at all, made no concession, but was strictly steadfast. Weiß, *History* 1:271, adopts the *not compelled* rendering, accepting the alternate reading (D, p46, et al) that omits οἷς οὐδε (*to them*), meaning that Paul conceded as a practical accommodation and to disparage fault–finding. Duncan, *Galatians*, 41–5. Betz, 91, accepts the text as it stands, n. 313 for bibliography. Barrett, *Freedom*, 112 n. 12, finds the majority reading to be defective Greek because it lacks a main verb, while the alternate reading shows Paul making a tactical submission, and concludes: "The whole of Galatians 2, indeed the whole of the epistle, expresses an adamant refusal to compromise on the issue of circumcision. It seems very much more probable that Paul wrote (or his amanuensis took down) a piece of bad Greek than that he gave way in the test case of the Gentile Titus."

52. Howard, 24–7, sees the verb pointing not merely to the implications of Peter's actions but that "Peter was teaching outright that Gentiles had to be circumcised to be saved." Peter thus is breaking faith with the agreement at Jerusalem, an agreement already in effect. But see Dunn, "Incident," 4–11, on the fact of limited (table) fellowship between Jews and Gentiles.

53. Betz, 96 n. 370. Schlier, *Galater*, 76: It is a Gentile mission but not a different gospel. Two different gospels would render nonsensical Paul's argument in Galatians for equal status of all people. It is possible that Paul and the others understood both the

responsibility, but not a distinction in what shall be proclaimed. As *gospel* applies to and binds the two categories of people together, so also *mission* (*apostolate*) pertains to both ministries, including that of Paul.[54]

Having described his gospel and its recognized authenticity, Paul speaks of the *fellowship* (2:9) that was extended from James, Cephas, and John, to Barnabas and himself.[55] That is, having heard his gospel's content and seen the independence with which Paul preserved it from any attempts to legitimize it, they accepted him and his gospel not only without further requirements, but offered the *right hand of fellowship*. Paul's two-fold point is that, (1) the pillars have recognized the grace given him,[56] and (2) the equality of partnership is clear in the agreement. Having understood his law-free proclamation they accepted it without qualification.[57]

1.3. Paul's report of the meeting in Jerusalem (Gal 2:1-10), as well as the events leading up to and following it, brings us inevitably to comparison and contrast with the reports of Acts. But aside from the contrast between Paul and Acts, Linton has detected yet another view of his theology and ministry that Paul is battling against as that view circulated in Galatia. As over against the conflict-synthesis theory that Baur proposes, Linton maintains, "In fact the unity existed from the very beginning, and the conflicts did never disappear."[58] That is, already in Paul's time there were current reports of his life and teaching that he was anxious to correct. Some of the traditions that Paul energetically repudiates occur in Acts, and there are

---

agreement and his apostolic status differently.

54. Betz, 96-8, understands the passage as a quotation of the Jerusalem agreement. The agreement may indeed have referred only to Peter's mission in terms of an apostolate, and yet here Paul asserts an equality of authority and legitimacy. Schlier, *Galater*, 78 n. 2, and Mußner, 116 n. 91, say that the term *apostolate* here includes Paul and his mission. It is not likely that Paul would make such a point of his own apostolicity, grounded in revelation and identified with justification, and also emphasize his dialectical relationship to Jerusalem as evidence of his gospel's recognized authenticity, and then *not* apply *apostolate* to himself as well. What Paul argues about apostolicity and gospel in Galatians governs the inclusiveness of *apostolate*. BDF §479.

55. Betz, 99, James appears as the leading figure in this triumvirate of *the pillars*. Wilckens, *TDNT* 7:732-36; Barrett, "Apostles," 5-6.

56. 2 Cor 8:9; Phil 3:10: Acts 15:11; 2 Cor 13:6. Betz, 99, because of the theological insight of God's redemptive work as grace, "the apostles at Jerusalem understood and approved Paul's message and his theology."

57. Grundmann, *TDNT*, 2:38, calls this a sign of agreement and alliance. But the consequences of this decision had not been perceived, as seen from the difficulty in Galatia (Antioch, too). The single condition, remembering the poor, is something to which Paul eagerly subscribes, and it highlights the difference between his view of the proceedings and that of his opponents.

58. Linton, "Aspect," 79.

certain affinities between the later literary image drawn by Acts and the earlier representation of Paul's person and activity that are contested by Paul himself. There are three accounts of the relations between Paul and the Jerusalem apostles: (1) the version circulating in Galatia is that against which Paul struggles in Galatians 1 and 2; (2) the version given by Paul himself in Galatians; (3) the version of Acts. Scholars have tended to discuss the relationship of (1) and (2), or (2) and (3), but seldom (1) and (3).[59] Because of the importance of how each view relates to the others, and the relation of each to the law, it will be helpful to sketch how the three views compare and contrast to one another. All three versions agree that Paul had been a zealous champion of the law, and that he had been a fanatic persecutor of the church.[60]

1.3.1. There are also points in common between the Galatian version that Paul repudiates, and the Acts version. These can be inferred by omitting the negatives in Gal 1:15–20: Paul *has* received his gospel from men; Paul *has* been taught by them; therefore Paul is *not* an immediate apostle of the Lord; Paul went to Jerusalem and remained a longer time.[61] But there is not full agreement between the Galatian version and Acts: the Galatian version has circumcision necessary for salvation; the Acts version refutes the claim for the necessity of circumcision. And yet, ". . . all accounts emphasize that the Church cannot have but one standpoint as to the question of circumcision and Law."[62] The Galatian description of Paul is not that he is a false apostle because he has forsaken circumcision, but rather that he acknowledged circumcision at Jerusalem (with all the Apostles) and now preaches it.[63]

1.3.2. Paul and Acts agree that concord was reached in Jerusalem, but of that concord: (1) Paul says there were no conditions; (2) Acts (15:28; 16:4) says there were certain conditions and these in fact were inculcated by Paul himself. Thus we can understand Paul's sharp rebuke in Gal 5:11. The opponents now expect him to remain within the bounds drawn up by the Apostles, and to which (his opponents say) Paul once subscribed.[64]

---

59. Ibid., 80.

60. Gal 1:13–17; 1 Cor 15:9; Phil 3:5–6; Acts 7:58; 8:1; 26:12; Linton, "Aspect," 82; Kim, 46; Hultgren, "Persecutions," 100–102.

61. Linton, "Aspect," 83. Acts 9:19–25 agrees with the inferred version that circulated in Galatia: "To the author of Acts there is, however, evidently nothing disparaging in Paul being instructed by Apostles or other good Christians." Acts seems to correct and improve Paul as a means of defending him.

62. Ibid., 92.

63. In Acts 16 Paul circumcises Timothy, "son of a Jewish woman," after the decision of Acts 15.

64. Linton, "Aspect," 92, says that the Judaizers have not rejected Paul because he

1.3.3. The view of the Judaizers is that: (1) they would not compel Gentile Christians to keep the whole law, but only those regulations that are necessary to distinguish the people of God from the Gentiles; primarily this means circumcision and dietary regulations; (2) they see Paul as an evangelist but not an Apostle; he is subordinate to the Apostles, and the Judaizers portray Paul as a Judaizer, too; (3) they have a version that differs from both Acts and Paul (both of whom said *no* to circumcision) and this difference existed already at the time Paul wrote the epistle.[65]

1.3.4. The view of Acts is that: (1) in agreement with Paul, circumcision is not a requirement; (2) in disagreement with Paul, Acts reports Paul going to Jerusalem because Antioch sent him (15:2); (3) the Apostles and elders in Jerusalem have a kind of supremacy over the whole church, with Peter and James as pillars; (4) the resolution of the question has some conditions. Thus the account of Acts is not identical with but is akin to the Galatian version and sources.[66]

1.3.5. The Acts account was preceded by the Galatian version that was already current when Paul wrote to the Galatians. It is the version against which he struggles to make a correction. He appeals to the Galatians for three main changes. They ought: (1) recognize his authentic and reliable apostleship; (2) abandon their form of the gospel; (3) be free from the law.[67] This fits the thesis of an existing and established law-observant Gentile mission.[68]

1.4. What was the *gospel* that Paul called on them to abandon?[69] The Judaizers found the absolute point of departure for their theology in the law (5:3–4), and may have coined the phrase *law of Christ* (6:2) to indicate that

---

is a heretic, but "... have modeled him according to their own intentions and depicted a good Paul—in their eyes—subordinate to the Apostles at Jerusalem and preaching circumcision."

65. Ibid., 93.

66. Ibid., 95: "The Author of Acts belonged ... to those Christians who wanted to correct Paul slightly in order to make him better ... The Paul of the Church is to a great extent a corrected Paul, the Paul of Acts and not the Paul of history ... he is not only defamed by his enemies but also corrected by his friends."

67. Galatians 1:6, the Galatians had either gone over to the opponents' view or were considering doing so. Meeks, *Christians*, 116.

68. Martyn, "Mission," 323, notes that prior to this problem Paul made no use of Abraham or Genesis texts, had not dealt with the descendants question, and in response to the problem of the law offered the cross as the solution.

69. Ibid., 314–16; *Galatians*, 18, 117–26; Martyn prefers the term *Teachers* for Paul's opponents, rather than Judaizers, because of their thorough-going program of evangelism, with a particular theological content: connected to the Jerusalem church, centered in the Sinaitic Law.

their teaching was God's law as interpreted by God's Messiah. This *good news* is for Gentiles and the whole of humankind, and involves a genuine mission outreach through the law of the Messiah. In Gal 3:1–5 Paul contrasts his teaching with that of the opponents and emphasizes the cross, which elicits faith and the Spirit coming upon the hearers. The opponents, using texts to which Paul must respond, quote and interpret the Scriptures with a firm conviction that their theological position is supported by Scripture itself. In their position there is a strict condition laid down for the granting of the Spirit. It indicates the thoroughly conditional nature of the *good news* that they teach. The congregations, they charge, have been misled by Paul, and need to be woken up with threats to shut the gate to salvation.[70] Gentiles must pass through the *gate* by circumcision, signifying full participation in the people of God.[71] Christ is viewed in the light of God's law, rather than the law in the light of Christ, and this means that Christ is secondary to the law. "Paul thus seems to have no fear of being contradicted when he repeatedly says they avoid taking their theological bearings from the cross."[72]

The question that arose in Antioch and was sent to Jerusalem for adjudication was that of the terms of admission into the church for Gentiles, with circumcision as the focal issue.[73] Acts and Paul agree that the decision meant that circumcision was not necessary. The Galatian version differs on that key point, and it is against this version that Paul writes Galatians. Acts reports the addition of certain kosher-type conditions. Paul's report in Galatians contains no such conditions.[74]

---

70. See references to frighten, disturb, trouble, intimidate, 1:7; 5:10; 4:17 for *shut out*.

71. Martyn, "Mission," 316, calls circumcision the *commandment par excellence*.

72. Ibid., 315. The thing they do not have is a crucified Messiah: "Presumably they understand Christ's death to have been a sacrifice for sins . . . in harmony with God's law . . . they consistently avoid every suggestion that God's Law and his Messiah could even partially conflict with one another . . . In a word, when they speak of the Messiah they do so in a way which takes for granted that the Messiah is the Messiah of the Law."

73. Meeks and Wilken, *Antioch*, 16.

74. On the background of the conditions in Acts, Wilson, 68–102; 92–3; he draws two conclusions about the conditions. First, it is likely that by the time Luke wrote Acts abstention from such things as banned by the decree was an established part of Christian mores, and so Luke can present the decree as in no sense a burden but as likely to be welcomed by Gentile churches. The terms of the decree were obligations of a customary but not of a legal sort. Second, if there had been a connection between the decree and the Mosaic law (and a background in Leviticus 17–18 would still not necessarily be implied) the connection is obscured both by Luke's insistence that the decree was apostolic in origin and inspired by the Spirit and by the way in which the terms of the decree were probably understood at the time Luke wrote. But two important issues remain separate. First, whether at the time Paul wrote Galatians the banns of the decree

Acts and the Galatian version agree that Paul's apostleship is subsidiary to the Jerusalem apostles, as he has received and been taught his Gospel by them. Paul's defense is that his Gospel came by revelation. This apocalyptic Good News replaced the tradition of law and set him in opposition to law right from the start.[75] He argues that his Gospel was known and affirmed by the Jerusalem pillars. Later action by them to the contrary would be inconsistent with the Jerusalem accord. This is part of the significance of his report of the Antioch incident in 2:11-14.

2. Galatians 2:11 begins Paul's report of what happened when Peter came to Antioch.[76] The report runs at least through v. 14.[77] It focuses on the question of table-fellowship, as represented by Peter first eating with and then withdrawing from Gentile Christians (2:12).[78]

2.1. There were substantial numbers of both Jews and Greeks within the population of Antioch.[79] Jews and Gentiles combined within the Antioch Christian congregation.[80] Within this first mixed church the conversion of Gentiles seems to have come about without accommodation to the law.[81]

---

were established part of Christian mores is a separate question from that regarding the time in which Luke wrote. Second, it would not have served Paul's argument to include anything in his report of the decree which even remotely sounded like extra conditions to his gospel.

75. Did Paul know from the start that such theological consequences were inherent in the new faith, or did he come to see it only later? What we have is his report in Galatians. Räisänen, *Paul* (1983), 254-56. In Galatians Paul has the advantage of past experience clarified by present questions. Watson, *Paul* (1986), 30, 54.

76. Acts reports no visit of Peter to Antioch. Paul reports no reason for Peter's visit. Betz, 105.

77. Opinion is divided whether Paul's report of the Antioch episode ends at 2:14 or includes 2:15-21, which would then be a summary of the speech Paul made in Antioch. Bligh sees Paul's speech, delivered to Peter at Antioch, extending to Gal 5:13a. But see Barrett, "Allegory," 157-58. Betz, 113-14, refers to 2:15-21 as the *propositio*, whose function is to summarize an easy transition to the (following) *probatio*. Whether the function of the text can be that systematically categorized Paul's purpose in relating the Antioch confrontation is to apply its point to the Galatian situation. Schlier, *Galater*, 88, notes that the statements in 2:14-21 have the character of an applicable summation, as both the concrete situation in Antioch and the developments Paul is aiming at in Galatia are in his mind.

78. Gentiles (2:12) and Jews (2:14-15) means Gentile Christians and Jewish Christians, an inner Church conflict.

79. Moe, 1:156, "Next to Alexandria, Antioch had the largest Jewish population of any city outside Palestine." Meeks and Wilken, 3; Josephus, *Jewish War* 7.3.3:44-5; Harnack, *Expansion*, 1:2-3, 10; Meeks, *Christians*, 10; Acts 11:19-26. Moe estimates a population of 500,000.

80. Moe, 1:156-57.

81. Weiß, *History* 1:172, sees the analogy to the God-fearing Gentiles in relation

When this practice was questioned, the Jerusalem Conference affirmed that circumcision was not necessary for membership and Gentile Christians' entrance into the church.

2.2. At Antioch the question was primarily one of fellowship within the church, as certain dietary regulations, re-imposed on Jewish Christians, would have precluded fellowship between Jewish and Gentile Christians.[82] The two occasions, Jerusalem and Antioch, were enough like what was happening in Galatia, with an attempt to impose certain features of the law, for Paul to apply the histories of the two cases to the present situation.[83] The relationship of the Jerusalem report in 2:1-10 and the Antioch report in 2:11-14 is one of both similarity and dissimilarity. The two occasions are contrasted in that the meeting in Jerusalem reached accord and gave affirmation, resulting in fellowship, while the events in Antioch represented confrontation and conflict, because of broken fellowship.[84] The two occasions have in common that both focused on specific questions of the law, in Jerusalem as it related to Gentiles and circumcision, in Antioch as it related to Jewish Christians and eating with Gentiles.[85] That Gentile Christians were not required to observe Jewish food laws in Antioch indicates

---

to Jewish communities of the Dispersion. Such were admitted to worship without circumcision, and observed only some of the ceremonial commands. Harnack, *Expansion* 1:60, thinks the title *Christians* was given to the uncircumcised converts in the Antioch church, itself evidence that the new Christian community in Antioch stood out in bold relief from Judaism: "The name of Christian was the title of Gentile Christians." It was later that Jewish Christians were also designated by this name. Meeks and Wilkens, *Antioch*, 1, see that implicit in this Antioch situation is the fact that here Christianity is first perceived as a distinct movement, and that it thus here first crossed the boundaries of Judaism in seeking Gentile converts on a law-free basis. A related question concerns the extent of the influence of Hellenistic Christians on Paul. Räisänen, *Paul* (1983), 251-56; "The Hellenists."

82. Weiß, *History* 1:274.

83. Ibid., 1:299; Harnack, *Expansion* 1:60-1.

84. Antioch is evidence that the implications of Jerusalem were not thought out and that the consequences of the conference were not self-evident in Antioch or Galatia. Lüdemann, 71-7, dates the Antioch incident before the Jerusalem conference. But see Meeks, *Christians*, 81. Meeks and Wilkens, 16, note that Antioch, "... was also the place where controversy between Jews and Gentiles first erupted within the church." This is not surprising, for Antioch was the first deliberate mission to Gentiles that made Gentile Christianity "visible to outsiders as a distinct movement very early in its history. Antioch was the birthplace of 'gentile Christianity.'" Harnack, *Expansion* 1:59, traces the faith of the Greeks in Antioch to the "scattered adherents of Stephen (Acts xi 19f)" who were "the first missionaries to the heathen; they founded the Gentile church, that of Antioch. In this work they were joined by Barnabas and Paul." Paul was then not the first apostle to Gentiles, but joined a movement already in force.

85. But interestingly, Paul does not mention *law* until 2:16.

that their liberty had not been restricted, and yet no social intercourse was possible with Jewish Christians under such conditions.[86] When the men from James came to Antioch (2:12) they found it unacceptable that Jewish Christians were eating with Gentiles, and the Mosaic food laws were being disregarded. The food laws regulated clean and unclean foods, proper slaughter of animals for table meat, tithing, ritual purity, and avoidance of food that had been offered to idols. Under this pressure Peter and other Jewish Christians withdrew. Loyalty to their ancestral faith made them want to show that belief in Christ made them no less Jewish than before.[87] That is, the biblical commands of such explicit stipulations as Gen 17:9-14, Lev 11:1-23, and Deut 14:3-21 could not be ignored by anyone who wished to be identified as a faithful member of God's covenant people.[88]

2.3. Table-fellowship, of which the *eating* in Gal 2:12 is an example, may be understood according to both its religious and social functions.

2.3.1. The laws governing table-fellowship included food regulations.[89] The food laws for Judaism had a religious meaning, signifying "fellowship before God . . . all have a share in the blessing which the master of the house has spoken over the unbroken bread."[90] The limits of table-fellowship were determined partly by the commands laid down in the explicit laws of the Torah concerning unclean foods (Lev 11:1-23; Deut 14:3-21). This had been one of the *make or break* issues of the Maccabe rebellion, for which principle many had chosen to die rather than be defiled by eating.[91] Food should not be tainted by the abomination of having been offered to idols.[92] Food must be avoided from which the blood has not been drained in strict accord with the Mosaic commands.[93] Pharisees in Palestine were particu-

---

86. Weiß, *History*, 1:274: "It was equivalent to a division of the church into two separate groups." Lührmann, "Abendmahlsgemeinschaft?" 277, speaks of the relation of the Antioch problem to church unity, which had been concretely realized when Peter adopted the form of life of the Antioch congregation. Jewish and Gentile Christians sat at the same table no longer hindered by the law. Unity is neither the goal nor means of communion, but its foundation. Barrett, *Freedom*, 12-14, for these conditions relative to the Eucharist.

87. Dunn, "Perspective ," 103.

88. Ibid., 108: especially since the Maccabees (1 Macc 1:62-3; Dan 1:8-10; Tob 1:10-13; Judith 10:5; 12:1-20) the observance of laws regarding clean and unclean food was a basic expression of covenant faithfulness.

89. Dunn, "Antioch," 4; Burton, 104; Oepke, *Galater*, 51; Bruce, *Spirit*, 176; Betz, 107 n. 448.

90. Dunn, "Incident," 12.

91. 1 Macc 1:62-3; Josephus, *Antiquities*, 11.8.7:346; Dunn, "Incident," 12.

92. 4 Macc 5:2; 1 Cor 8-10; Acts 15:20, 29.

93. Lev 3:17; 7:26-27; 17:10-14; Deut 12:16, 23-24; 15:23; Acts 15:20, 29.

larly pre-occupied with defining these limits for the practice of table-fellowship, and 229 of the 341 rulings (67%) pertain to table-fellowship.[94] Two particular aspects of ritual purity emerge: (1) cleansing of hands was intended to safeguard from uncleanness due to an unintentional touching;[95] (2) tithing, not just of money but of food for the table, was necessary to render food ritually acceptable.[96] The idea was to apply to everyday life the purity laws that governed temple ritual. This has to do with Israel's faith and covenant-keeping.

With respect to observance of such laws there was a variety of different attachments to Judaism on the part of Gentiles, and different levels of acceptance of Gentiles on the part of Jews. Adherence to the law governed behavior, as strict Jews would have avoided table-fellowship with Gentiles, and those less scrupulous about tithing and purity would have been willing to share meals with Gentiles.[97] There were three different possible forms of the relationship between *goyim* and Judaism.[98] The *proselyte*, or full convert, was a Gentile who had been won over to Judaism.[99] The proselyte observed the law, including circumcision, and was within the same limits of table-fellowship as a native-born Jew. The *resident alien*, a Gentile who lived within the borders of Israel, accepted only some of the commands of the Torah, including at least the seven Noachic laws.[100] The *God-fearers* attached themselves to Judaism in differing degrees.[101] Of the three categories they were generally the most acceptable to Jews, frequently found to observe the law

---

94. Neusner, *Pharisees* 3:297; Dunn, "Incident," 14.

95. Mk 7:2-5; Matt 15:2; Lk 11:38; Dunn, "Incident," 14.

96. Mt 23:23; Lk 18:12; Dunn, "Incident," 15. Neusner, *Piety*, 83, distinguishes (1) Pharisees, who practiced ritual purity outside as well as inside the temple, and (2) lay-people who practiced it only in the temple but not in the non-cultic activities of everyday life. Paul (80) was trained as a Pharisee, was knowledgeable about that tradition, and it seems to be that against which he argues in Antioch and Galatia. Dunn, "Incident," 17, notes that Mk 7:19 and Matt 15:17, 20 attest to discrepancy of views among Jesus' followers regarding his teaching on cleanliness. The incident at Antioch attests to the same debates. It is clear that the men from James wanted greater definition and observance.

97. Dunn, "Incident," 23.

98. Ibid., 18-22.

99. Lake, I, 5:82-4; Kuhn, *TDNT* 6:736-37.

100. Noachic laws legislated: (1) subjection to established courts of justice; (2) against blasphemy; (3) against idolatry; (4) against adultery; (5) against bloodshed; (6) against robbery: (7) against eating flesh from a living animal. Moore, 1.339; Str-B.2:729-39; 3:37-8; Kuhn, *TDNT* 6:740-1.

101. Lake, 5:85.

as native-born Jews.¹⁰² Judaism likely reflected varying attitudes toward the qualifications for belonging to each of these categories, as well as toward persons in each category. But the fact remains: each level or category of belonging involved the essential element of affiliation or unity, to whatever degree, with the actual *faith* of Israel. In some sense the heart, mind, soul, and strength were involved. This was the religious question. The question follows as to what extent God-fearing Gentiles were expected to observe laws of ritual purity and tithing in the Antioch situation.¹⁰³

2.3.2. The nature of table-fellowship also included the identity-defining function of the law. In a sociological way a group may be marked off as distinct from other groups by its peculiar beliefs and practices. The boundaries established by such beliefs and practices serve the group's definition of identity, and these boundaries will be emphasized the more a group senses that it is under threat.¹⁰⁴ Along with circumcision, the food laws, which set the limits to table-fellowship, were widely regarded as characteristically and distinctly Jewish. They were the *identity markers* or,

> ... peculiar rites which marked out the Jews as that peculiar people... These identity markers identified Jewishness... They functioned as badges of covenant membership. A member of the covenant people was, by definition, one who observed these practices in particular.¹⁰⁵

Again, performance of these laws was seen by the Jews themselves as fundamental observances of the covenant (the religious question). And said performance could also be seen by others who would thereby distinguish Jews from other people (hence, the social or public identity question).

2.3.3. There are three alternatives for understanding the quality of table-fellowship at Antioch before the arrival of men from James.¹⁰⁶

---

102. Josephus, *Apion*, 2.38:282.
103. Dunn, "Incident," 21-3.
104. Dunn, "Works," 524; Mol, 57-8, 233. Dunn, "Incident," 7-11, describes the threats to Judaism's distinctive religious and national identity under Rome, and how the followers of Jesus would have been affected by this same pressure, so that as Judaism struggled to emphasize its boundaries by way of ritual law, some Christians also sought to be defined as loyal nationalistic Jews by means of the same laws. Pressures against the new sect's beliefs or practices were perceived as threats to Jewish institutions and traditions. Dunn asks whether the men from James sensed this threat and reacted to table-fellowship as they did in Antioch. Reicke, "Hintergrund," 172-87; Jewett, "Agitators," 204-6.
105. Dunn, "Perspective," 108; Sahlin, 89, adds that proselyte baptism was required.
106. Dunn, "Incident," 29-36.

2.3.3.1. Table-fellowship at Antioch as practiced by Jewish Christians, including Peter, meant a total abandonment of laws governing table-fellowship. What the men from James could then have insisted was that the decree described by Acts 15:29 be enforced.[107] The Jewish Christians at Antioch were *living like Gentiles*, that is like Gentile *sinners* who were outside the law. This would fit with: (1) the use of *like a Gentile, like a Jew* in 2:14, *sinners* in 2:15; (2) Acts 10–11, Luke's account of Peter's vision at Joppa, and the subsequent lesson that the law of clean–unclean no longer applies; (3) the Antioch incident preceded the Jerusalem council, with the council called to resolve the problem of the incident.[108]

Having laid out this alternative Dunn shows three problems with it. First, he says that it is unlikely that Jewish believers at Antioch abandoned the law so completely, and cites Rom 14:1–2 and 1 Corinthians 8 as indicators of such reluctance among some Jewish Christians. Dunn thinks that total abandonment would have caused problems among the Antioch Jewish believers even before the arrival of men from James. It is clear that for some Antioch Christians as well as for Paul relation to the law was a problem in the church. But that it was a problem does not preclude abandonment of the law, but more likely indicates that abandonment was taking place. In seeking to understand what happened in Antioch, as reported in Paul's letter to Galatia, the attitudes and events described in Romans or 1 Corinthians are not adequate standards of explanation. Paul's apocalyptic gospel, described in Galatians 1–2 as having been laid out for the pillars of Jerusalem, and from the start replacing the tradition of law-keeping in Paul's life with the central conviction of faith in Christ's redemptive death, indicates law abandonment during Paul's Antioch years. We may infer a congregation where such a position was acceptable, if not expected.

Second, Dunn suggests that the first Gentile converts came almost exclusively from among the God-fearers, who were already accustomed to observing dietary laws in some measure. He cites Acts 6:5. We note, however, that Acts 6:5 mentions a proselyte, not a God-fearer. Furthermore, the distinct self-identity that the *Christians* gained in Antioch (Acts 11:26) indicates more of a break with Judaism and its laws and traditions, rather than continuity.[109] This fits with what Paul says in Gal 1:15–24 about himself,

---

107. Catchpole, "Decree." Lührmann, "Abendmahlsgemeinschaft?" 277, Peter came to Antioch and assumed the life that was observed by the church. See Wilson, 68–70, for what may have been Luke's view of the Cornelius episode.

108. Dunn, "Incident," 29 n. 95. But how was Peter's behavior inconsistent? Galatians 2:10=Acts 11:30 *only if* 11:30 and Acts 15 do not refer to the same event. Barrett, *Freedom*, 111; Wilson, 71–84.

109. Räisänen, "Paul's Break," 548–50. Gager, 54–66, argues: Paul wrote only to

his independence, and his proclamation. The impression (2:3) is that Paul's proclamation had been law-free from the outset of his apostolic activity.

Third, Dunn says that it must be doubted that Paul would have reacted so strongly if only a requirement for observance of the Noachic laws had been laid on by the men from James. But Paul argues against the whole law, following the instigation of any aspect of law whatever, and the whole tone and content of the letter to Galatia leaves very little room for minor observances of the law. Paul never distinguishes Noachic or any other particular aspects of law once he moves to arguing against the whole law, as in the move from 2:16 to 2:19.

The Christians of Antioch, including Peter, likely had adopted a manner of life aside from law. The boundary distinguishing Jew from Gentile, inside the law from outside the law, and the threat to Jewish covenant-keeping and identity were too great for Peter and the others to ignore.[110]

2.3.3.2. An alternative interpretation is that table fellowship at Antioch involved a fair degree of observance of food laws, and the men from James wanted a greater observance, with the God-fearers being fully proselytized by circumcision.[111] This interpretation would match Gal 2:12 and Acts 15:1. It would explain the Jerusalem council as having been called to resolve the Antioch incident, and it would allow for the number of Gentiles at Antioch who were willing to Judaize.

But the weaknesses of this interpretation, Dunn suggests, are two-fold. First, it does not fit with the language used by Paul. The term, to *judaize/live*

Gentiles, applying only to fellow Christians; Jews of Judaism were not part of his argument in Galatians; the law remained valid for them but it brought a curse (as it always had) to Gentiles. The argument in Galatians, Gager, 77–80, is not a fight with Judaism, but with anti-Pauline apostles who wanted greater (but selective) law observance. Paul knew that the law remained valid for Judaism. However clear the dynamics and contestants in the Galatian context may have become in recent years, it remains a separate question how clearly the distinction between the Jesus movement and Judaism was and was seen to be, even by Paul, at the time. Gager, 59–64, comments about *Two Ways?* Aageson, 21, notes, "In Paul's theology, apostolicity and being Jewish are not to be construed as fundamentally opposed or mutually antagonistic to one another. To be sure, the attempt to hold these together causes Paul some religious and theological difficulty. But this difficulty itself . . . testifies to the breadth of Paul's religious commitment. He will not—indeed cannot—abandon Israel and its God. He cannot forsake his conviction that the God of Israel has acted to bring salvation to the nations in Jesus Christ. Thus, he is compelled to reshape his religious worldview and the moral order that undergirds it. He is forced to reinterpret the character of God's covenant with Israel. Or, as Paul might say, he has been given to understand the essential meaning of the covenant, which has been hidden from all eternity."

110. Dunn, "Works," 528–29.

111. Mußner, 145 n. 53; 146–67; Gutbrod, *TDNT*, 3:371–91; Reicke, "Hintergrund," 184.

like a Jew refers to the adoption of Jewish customs and is to be distinguished from circumcision, which was the final step in the process of becoming a proselyte. It is not likely that Paul would use the term *to judaize* with reference to that final step for Gentiles who were already *judaizing* to a considerable extent. Second, it would be difficult in this interpretation to understand the Antioch episode as the sequel to the Jerusalem agreement of Gal 2:1-10 (as it in fact was).

2.3.3.3. The third alternative has in common with the second the suggestion that the Gentile believers were already observing basic food laws, but the men from James wanted a *more scrupulous observance* of what these laws involved, especially with regard to ritual purity and tithing.[112] Dunn would see a match of Gal 2:14-15 with interpretation (3), as Peter demanded a greater ritual purity, or *judaizing*, regarding laws that were in some measure already observed.

In both interpretations (2) and (3), however, Dunn argues backwards, beginning with the notions that *like a Gentile* means a limited observance of the law, including at least the Noachic rules and life-style; *judaize* meant enough affiliation with Judaism to make table fellowship possible for Gentiles;[113] consequently, there had been some measure of law observance by the Antioch Gentile Christians for the sake of fellowship with Jewish Christians, and there was no real break with the law or with Judaism prior to the incident of 2:11-14. The term, *like a Gentile*, usually refers to one who no longer observes Jewish customs and law, or who lives in contrast to them.[114] Paul thus seems to use the term in Galatians in accord with the general argument of law versus faith. With the term *like a Jew* Paul indicates observance of Jewish customs and law and uses the term as a synonym for *judaize*.[115] The connection to the occasion of his taking Titus with him to Jerusalem, where Titus was not compelled to be circumcised (2:3), is made by the repeated use of the verb *compel* here in 2:14. Two ways of life are being contrasted. For church unity on Peter's terms full adoption of Jewish ways, including circumcision, would have been necessary. Dunn's categories tend to blur this contrast.

2.3.3.4. If we are to approach the problem as Paul did it means moving outward from the same center from which he proceeded. Paul's gospel had

---

112. Dunn is imprecise here, but probably means that the men from James called upon the Antioch church to move from a partial to a complete observance of the law. Weiß, *History* 1:244.

113. Dunn, "Incident," 25-6.

114. Betz, 112; Bruce, *Galatians*, 133; BDAG, 276; Schmidt, *TDNT* 2:372.

115. Gutbrod, *TDNT* 3:383, conversion to Judaism is indicated, particularly including circumcision; Bruce, *Galatians*, 133.

at its center *the Son of God who loved me and gave himself for me,* (2:20) who was revealed to Paul so that Paul might preach him among the Gentiles (1:16). This news Paul declares by way of contrast to the law-keeping tradition that had been his own past (1:13), and that had from the beginning of his new faith been replaced by the revelation of Jesus Christ (1:12). As Paul argued from the Galatians' own experience, so would he also argue of himself, that he received the Spirit by hearing with faith, and not by works of law (3:2-5). Although there is a distinction to be made between *judaize* and circumcision, the latter being the final step of the former, an over-lapping of *judaize* with *like a Gentile* is thereby neither ensured nor implied. Paul uses *judaize* in contrast to *like a Gentile*, not as a synonym for receiving circumcision.[116]

The terminology of 2:14-15 can be understood in light of Paul's law-free gospel. It cannot be the starting-point for an argument that leads to defining the degree of either law-observance or freedom from the law within that gospel. In the light of that gospel, *I tore down* (2:18), perhaps a technical term for abandoning the law,[117] reflects Paul's previous break with Judaism. This sense of discontinuity is heightened if 2:18 is taken as part of Paul's report of what he said to Peter at Antioch, a statement he made *then* about a break that was already real at that time. Any action regarding aspects of the law, not in keeping with the break necessitated by the new tradition that replaced it, would not be in accord with the truth of that gospel.[118] Hence, Paul intervened and publicly confronted Peter at Antioch.[119] Peter no longer proceeded *on the right road*, nor was he going *straight toward the goal*, and so his orthodoxy had *gone lame*.[120]

2.3.4. The horns of Peter's dilemma are stated according to Paul's evaluation. Peter's religious status is *that of a Jew* who, having given up his Jewish way of life, lives *like a Gentile*, no longer observing the Jewish law.[121] *Way of*

116. Against Dunn, "Incident," 31.

117. Büchsel, *TDNT* 4:338; Räisänen, *Paul* (1983), 47.

118. On *the truth of the Gospel*, Betz, 92; Schlier, *Galater*, 73; Mußner, 111 n. 58; Lightfoot, *Galatians*, 107; Burton, 86. It can mean, (1) *true Gospel* versus *false gospel* (1:6-9); (2) integrity of the Gospel; (3) consequences of the Gospel. The doctrine of grace is denoted. Ebeling, 117, notes that the expression, ". . . does more than raise the question whether the gospel is true in itself, in contrast to other messages and doctrines; it emphasizes the obligation that the gospel be proclaimed and preserved in all its purity and inward consistency. Cephas' conduct had the opposite effect . . ."

119. Galatians 2:14; Mußner, 143 n. 43, *but*, as signifying the turning point.

120. Betz, 111 n. 483; Preisker, *TDNT* 5:451; Mußner, 144.

121. BDAG, 1029; BDF §414:1. The form, *like a Gentile*, is a *hapax legomenon* in the NT, and signifies contrast to the Jewish way of life of obedience to the law. BDAG, 276; Schmidt, *TDNT* 2:372. The advantage of being *Jewish* is in having the law. The

life is emphasized here. "The present tense . . . (*you are living*) implies much more than an act of table fellowship with Christian Gentiles. It suggests that the table fellowship was only the external symbol of Cephas' total emancipation from Judaism."[122]

And yet, having broken with a former way of life, Peter is demanding (compelling) that Gentile Christians now *judaize*.[123] In 2:3 the demand was for circumcision of Titus. In Galatia the agitators' demand is also for circumcision (6:13). Therefore, *judaize*, for Paul, means more than submission to Jewish dietary laws, for such submission carries the obligation to keep the whole law (5:3), that is, fully to *judaize*, and through circumcision become a proselyte. Paul assumes the obligatory nature of a single aspect of law, and he would argue that selection of special laws is illegitimate. For Paul only God can exempt from any part of the law, and this God has done by dethroning the law in Christ.[124]

Summary

Paul's use of the expression, *works of the law*, in Gal 2:16, is best understood in relation to two occurrences.[125] First, Gal 2:1–10 relates to the Jerusalem conference that decided in favor of Paul's law-free, circumcision-less gospel, regarding the entry of Gentile converts. Second, Gal 2:11–15 relates to the Antioch incident that focused on table fellowship between Jewish and Gentile Christians. The theme of justification, as Paul begins to speak of it in 2:16, is set in the context of that confrontation at Antioch.[126] By the expression, *works of law*, Paul seems to have very specific aspects of the law in mind, namely circumcision and dietary laws, and these particular obser-

---

distinction from *Gentile* is not of race or nationality, but is grounded in revelation and the will of God. One is Jewish, according to Paul, by attachment to the law, and one may convert to Judaism by adopting the law. Gutbrod, *TDNT* 3:381–83.

122. Betz, 112; Burton, 112; Schlier, *Galater*, 86; Bousset, 44.

123. Betz, 112; 1 Macc 2:25; 2 Macc 6:1, 7, 18; 4 Macc 5:2 27; 8:1.

124. Linton, "Aspect," 90–94: "Paul admits no distinction between indispensable and dispensable commandments. The law is to Paul, as to his rabbinic compatriots, one and indivisible. Therefore, if a man is circumcised, he is a debtor to the whole law. And why does Paul so severely emphasize this? Evidently because there was a tendency in Galatia to oblige Gentile Christians to some commandments of the Mosaic law and not to others. The Judaists were thus not so rigid Judaists as generally supposed."

125. Dunn, "Perspective," 107. Would *special days* (4:10) have included the Sabbath? If so then Schlatter, *Galater*, 64, is poignantly correct (we paraphrase): I am dead to the law and it will have no more hold on me; it has no access to me and it will have nothing more to say to me; I am entirely free from the law.

126. Wilckens, "Werken," 86.

vances of the law were characteristically definitive of Jewish identity. The very issues that were problematic for the life of the church were the badges by which Israel had signified its covenant membership.[127] These specific works typified the observance of law that represented the standard response to God's covenant. Law-observance as standard response to God's covenant has been called *nomism*, as over against *legalism*, the term customarily ascribed to an attitude that would gain divine favor by law keeping.[128]

Paul rejects works of law as a standard of faith and so undercuts law as constituent for self-identity. The self-understanding of the believer, he teaches, is found in Christ, who is our righteousness.[129] Paul's response to the problem of law is set in the context of his gospel (1:7), received by revelation (1:12, 16), in accord with which Paul now lives (1:16b, 23; 2:2). This gospel of God's Son (1:16a) is the standard of Paul's apostolicity and that to which he calls the Galatians (1:6-9). It places him in a dialectical tension with Jerusalem (1:16c, 18-19; 2:2b, 6c) and open opposition to the teachers in Galatia who sought to re-impose the law (2:3-5). The revelation of the gospel was the transition from a law tradition to "life . . . by faith in the Son of God, who loved me and gave himself for me" (2:20b). The replacement of the old tradition with the new is seen in the contrast between works and faith (2:16). The contrast is the chief reason for which Paul introduces justification (2:16-17, 21).[130]

Paul's break with his past relation to the law is brought to light in this argument. It is not abused or misunderstood law against which he argues, nor does he seek to clarify and establish the true law. As one who has not remained a law-observant Jew and who has undergone conversion, Paul saw the need for both Jew and Gentile to "enter the new community."[131] The

---

127. Dunn, "Perspective," 107-8. And yet we ought not confine the law to identity issues only. Many OT texts clearly indicate law as instruction, about which the writer can express love. Paul could argue for the necessity of law as a death bringer (*through law*) so that new life in relation to God, through Christ, could come about.

128. Longenecker, *Paul*, 78, refers to an *acting legalism* and a *reacting nomism*. Paul's relation to the law (86-155) is a rejection of nomism as well as legalism. Sanders, *Paul* (1977), 75, 420, 544, describes *covenantal nomism* as the obedience to law which maintains but does not earn one's inclusion in the covenant. Related to this is the question of whether Paul distorts the Judaism of his day. See Räisänen, "Legalism," 63-83, and "Difficulties," 301-20. A distortion could be argued if Paul were setting up the straw-man of legalism, but he does not do so. Childs, *Canon*, 301-10.

129. Blank, "Werken," 91; Wilckens, "Werken," 88; Kertelge, "Rechtfertigungsbegriffs," 215.

130. Galatians 2:16-17 contrasts how justification does not happen (works of law) to how it does happen (faith in Christ). A fuller exposition of justification is in 3:6-14, as Paul refers to Abraham-blessing-curse material.

131. Räisänen, "Break," 548-50, says of the Jew, "In a word, *conversion* was as

break with the law was not only an example of Paul's flexible generalizing from particular works to the whole law. It is also a break that is implicitly expressed by the theological motifs present from the opening sentence of the letter. Of particular significance, however, is the fact that it was the specific works of circumcision and table laws from which Paul generalized in his speaking about the law as a whole. Such works represent the active realm of law, respect for and practice of whose conditions describe Paul's former life.

It was these same conditions that Paul's opponents in Galatia sought to impose on Gentile converts to faith in Christ. This imposition was reminiscent of Peter's vacillating behavior, which would have brought disintegration to the Church. Such conditions of law bring death. This is reflected in Paul's view of the law, expressed in a phrase that is both a full and final statement: he has died to it (2:19). This death was Paul's break with the law. He has died to the old tradition so that he could live to God. The old tradition was not an option but a barrier. Because the old tradition was divinely ordained, freedom from it could come only by death.

But along with his reference to his own death to law Paul alludes to the death of Christ, as he says that he has been crucified with Christ. What then is the connection between the death of Christ and the law, and between the death of Christ and Paul's death to the law? To examine these problems we turn to Paul's statement about the death of Christ in Gal 3:13.

3.2 Curse of the Law

Paul continues to expound his gospel by laying out two arguments that defend the replacement of the rule of law by the reign of faith in Christ. The argument from experience, in Gal 3:1–5, challenges the Galatians to look at their own experience of Christian faith with a series of questions. The argument from Scripture in 3:6–29 develops texts and exposition into a response to the opponents' view, to their use of Scripture, and to the practices of law that they prescribed.

1. Paul's argument from experience is in Gal 3:1–5. The position of the perfect passive participle, *crucified*, at the end of 3:1, is emphatic. Its perfect tense alludes to what took place on Calvary and is also the present status of Christ.[132] Together with the aorist (past) passive, *publicly displayed*

---

necessary for him as for a Gentile . . . Even he had to become a (*new creation*). It was a new beginning."

132. Fitzmyer, *JBC*, 241; Betz, 128, 256–57, *crucified* is an abbreviation for "Christ's redemptive act of liberation, his crucifixion and resurrection (cf. 1:1, 4; 2:20; 3:13; 4:5) . . . In the Pauline sense, 'to be free' means to participate in Christ's crucifixion and

(or, *placarded*) it points to, (1) the message of The Crucified One that was publicly proclaimed to them;[133] (2) the message that they had heard and believed from the very beginning. In view of that firm beginning Paul asks, *who has bewitched you?* The verb's meaning in this question signifies the current "spiritual infancy of the Galatians" as well as the "envious spirit of the agent."[134] Paul turns to a contrast, like that in 2:15, as he continues in 3:2. In 2:15-16 the contrast was about the means of justification. In 3:2 the contrast questions how they received the Spirit. Spirit (3:2) and faith (2:16) are thus placed on the same side.

Paul continues his reference to *spirit* in 3:3, associating it with the their beginning of faith, and emphasizing the initiative of the verb, *placarded*, in v. 1. The word *flesh* is introduced to the contrast, against Spirit, and thus on the side of law. *Flesh* alludes to the flesh that was cut in circumcision.[135] In 3:4 the translation, *experience* (RSV), is too weak, as the Galatians have in fact suffered trauma in their faith, which Paul interprets theologically for them in ch. 5. There we notice: (1) the pressure to receive circumcision (5:3), that Paul sees as a hindrance to their faith (5:7); (2) a view other than Paul's (5:8, 10) has troubled and unsettled them (5:10, 12); (3) the message of the cross is a necessary scandal (5:11b) and issues in freedom (5:13) but is in danger of being lost; (4) behavior in the congregation that lacks love (5:13-14) is linked to the fleshly life (5:16-21), precludes the Spirit (5:16-17), and so needs to be crucified (5:24). The NT does not use the verb, *endure* or *suffer* (3:4), relative to spiritual blessings.[136] Should they yield to present pressure the past trauma will be *in vain, for nothing*. Paul has associated justification with faith and faith with Spirit. In 3:5 he adds miracles to that same side of the contrast, against *works of law*. The phrase, *hearing with faith* is in 3:2 with *you received the Spirit* and in 3:5 with *supply you with the*

---

resurrection." 1 Cor 1:13, 17, 18, 23; 2:2, 8; 2 Cor 13:4; Gal 5:11, 24; 6:12, 14, 17; Phil 2:8; 3:18; Col 1:20; 2:14; Eph 2:16; Bultmann, *TNT* 1:292-306; Käsemann; "Death," H-W Kuhn, 31-7.

133. Lightfoot, *Galatians*, 134; Fitzmyer, *JBC*, 241; Schrenk, 770-72; Schlier, *Galater*, 120; Burton, 144; Oepke, *Galater*, 100; Mußner, 207; Betz, 131; Borse, 123; Bruce, *Galatians*, 148; Bornkamm, 159.

134. Lightfoot, *Galatians*, 133. Neyrey, 73: "... Paul is arguing that the false teachers spreading 'another gospel' in Galatia are either Satan himself or persons possessed and controlled by Satan."

135. Fitzmyer, *JBC*, 241; Jewett, *Terms*, 19, 98-100, notes that here Paul is arguing against trusting in circumcision. "Paul's aim is not to argue that (*flesh*) cannot be justified by any means at all. It can be justified when it depends solely on Christ ..." (98); "Trust in the circumcised flesh became, on account of the agitators' efforts, synonymous with trust in the law as such!" (100).

136. Lightfoot, *Galatians*, 135.

Spirit and work miracles. It serves as Paul's point of departure for the Abraham midrash that begins in 3:6. He draws no line between experience and Scripture, nor between theology and proclamation. The arguments stand side by side, without conflict. He upbraids the Galatians for being *foolish*, (*ignorant*, 3:1, 2) and without understanding. They have not judged their situation correctly: "Spirituality is defective when, as is so often the case, it lacks the capacity for clear and sober theological judgment."[137]

Behind Paul's series of questions in 3:1-5 are really two things that the Galatians must answer: (1) how the gift of the Spirit has come, and (2) where will they end up in the dispute between antithetical proclamations.[138] In view of the justification–Spirit–faith association that Paul has constructed, the two mutually exclusive possibilities that they may provide are cast in the single rhetorical question of v. 5. It is the question that Paul answers in 3:14b: ". . . that we might receive the promise of the Spirit through faith."[139] It is also seen by this association that the Spirit is identified as something experienced: (1) the gift of the Spirit had a clear beginning, and was a unique event (hence the past tense of v. 2) and yet is presently effectual (hence the present tense of v. 5); (2) the Spirit is recognized by the working of miracles, and yet the signs are themselves distinguishable from the Spirit. Paul traces the Spirit back to its origin: *hearing with faith*. In contrast to *works of law* this phrase emphasizes the centrality of faith and the proclaimed word as source of faith. The Galatians' experience of the Spirit, traceable back to *hearing with faith* is linked to the fact of proclamation with which Paul began this argument from experience (3:1). The message of Christ crucified is linked to proclamation (3:1), and Spirit is linked to hearing with faith (3:2). Faith was linked to justification already in 2:16.[140] The Spirit belongs not to a second or higher stage of faith than justification, but to the foundation of the gospel. The gift of the Spirit and justification belong on the same side, with faith, gospel, the cross, and miracles, against law (3:2), the flesh (3:3), and curse (3:10).[141]

---

137. Ebeling, 156.

138. Ibid., 158.

139. Weder, 186, notes that the entire section (3:6-14) answers the question in 3:5. Lührmann, *Galater*, 54.

140. Ebeling, 160. *Hearing*, from Isa 53:1 (LXX); Bruce, *Galatians*, 149: Paul quotes in Rom 10:16, "as referring to the gospel and treats [it] as a premise leading to a conclusion: 'so faith comes from what is heard' . . ."

141. Bruce, *Galatians*, 149-50; 151-52, notes "the unmistakable sign that the new age has dawned" (Joel 2:28) is "the presence of the Spirit in power" which rules out "righteousness by works which the law prescribes."

2. Paul's argument from scripture is in Gal 3:6-29. Paul uses a series of midrash developments in Galatians 3 to make a scriptural and doctrinal defense of his gospel. The form of the scriptural (OT) argument in Galatians 3 is similar to that in 1 Corinthians 1-3.[142] There are three common characteristics in such presentations of Scripture.[143] First, an OT quotation introduces the theme that is to be addressed. This is the opening statement. In the case of Galatians 3, it refers to Abraham (3:6). Second, subordinate quotations support and develop the argument that was introduced in the opening statement. Catchwords or key words link the initial quotation to the exposition that follows and to the subordinate OT quotations. There is a concentration on key words that are linked in paraphrase, but not every word or phrase of the texts plays a part in the argument. Third, a final OT quotation alludes to the initial quotation and/or summarizes the argument. The initial quotation is often introduced with an introductory formula using verbs such as *it is written* or *it says*, with subjects such as *God, law, Scripture, David,* or *Isaiah*.[144] Galatians 3:8 refers to *the Scripture . . . saying*, and *it is written* appears in 3:10. *It is written* also occurs in 1 Cor 1:19; 2:9; 3:19. Such formulae indicate the accepted authority of Scripture as the declaration of divine will.[145] Paul generally quotes from the LXX, but with a freedom that allows him to modify texts to suit his argument.[146] This indicates the subordination of the exact wording of a text to the subject matter and need at hand, as Paul's christological convictions are given precedence over the OT text's literal precision.[147] Original contexts of OT quotations may also be ignored, along with exact renderings, for the sake of what Paul calls

---

142. Fitzmyer, *JBC*, 241-44, with Ebeling, 163, divides the scriptural argument into segments that extend through Gal 4:31. However, Gal 3:29 clearly marks the end of the Abraham material begun in 3:6, although 4:1-6 plays on words and themes introduced in 3:6-29 that are related to the Abraham story.

143. Ellis, *Prophecy*, 156; Borgen, *Bread*, 47-50.

144. Ellis, *Old Testament*, 22-5, *it is written* occurs 29 times in Paul. Metzger, "Formulas"; Goppelt, *Theology*, 2:51-5. Fitzmyer, "Quotations," 8, lists *to write, to say* references in Paul's intro formulae.

145. Ellis, *Old Testament*, 23, 25; Wilcox, "Old Testament," 241, ". . . the primitive church's acceptance of the authority of Jesus . . . enabled it to *pesher* the OT in terms of him."

146. Ellis, *Old Testament*, 83-4, for Paul the true meaning of OT is in Christ. After conversion the OT became a new book for Paul. On Paul's typology, Ellis, 127-46: Paul's meaning is primary, the exact wording is secondary; Ellis, *Prophecy*, 147-54. However, Paul's omission of *by God* in Gal 3:13 shows the influence of MT as over against LXX, which includes the phrase; Fitzmyer, "Crucifixion," 510.

147. Ellis, *Old Testament*, 28-9, cites Michel, *Bibel*, who says that the Spirit must speak from the Scriptures.

his gospel.[148] Texts, therefore, must carry the gospel, and no other standard seems to take priority over that in his use of texts. Galatians 3:6-29, 1 Cor 1-3, and Rom 4:1-22 are examples of this exegetical method.[149]

2.1. The main argument from Scripture in Galatians 3 is opened and closed with references to Abraham, faith, righteousness, and promise.[150] "That in Christ Jesus the blessing of Abraham might come upon the Gentiles" through faith, is the christological conviction served by the OT texts from which Paul argues (Gal 3:14). After alluding to Ps 143:2 in Gal 2:16,[151] Paul's OT references in Galatians 3 are predominantly texts from the Pentateuch.[152] In Galatians 3 the OT references include: Gen 15:6=Gal 3:6; Gen 12:3=Gal 3:8; Deut 27:26=Gal 3:10; Hab 2:4=Gal 3:11; Lev 18:5=Gal 3:12; Deut 21:23=Gal 3:13; Gen 22:18=Gal 3:16.[153]

These developments have in common that they all concentrate on Abraham, and show Paul's concern with what it means to have the right of appeal to Abraham.[154] The question of Gentile righteousness without the law corresponds to the extension also to the Gentiles of the promise made to Abraham. If the righteousness question were answered exclusively in terms of the gospel then there would inevitably come a conflict with traditional

---

148. Goppelt, *Typos*, 127, Paul's "basic view of the OT text is that its content corresponds to the gospel . . . its task is to present the gospel . . ." Paul's writings show consistency of occurrence for *gospel* and *preach the gospel*, with gospel as event, content, and power. Friedrich, *TDNT* 2:729-35.

149. Ellis, *Prophecy*, 156-57, 213-14; *Old Testament*, 119-25; Weber, *Cross*, 77-91; Wuellner, "Homily," 199-204, sees in 1 Cor 1-3 a homiletical pattern as noticed in Gal 3:6-29, Rom 4:1-22 by Borgen, *Bread*, 43-6. The pattern of the scriptural arguments in Galatians and 1 Corinthians are much the same. But in Galatians Paul seems to argue from the OT because his opponents have done so, and he responds to their use of particular texts. In 1 Corinthians his argument is not based on the biblical texts in so fundamental a way. If 1 Corinthians were written soon after Galatians, then it is reasonable to think that these two aspects of Paul's approach carried over from one letter to the other. That is, he used Scripture in Galatians because he had to, and used it in 1 Corinthians because it was an argument thus fresh in his mind. In Galatians the crucified Messiah who died as one who became a curse epitomized the reversal of values that also informed Paul's approach to the wisdom problem in Corinth.

150. Borgen, *Bread*, 48.

151. In Gal 2:16 Paul is flexible in using Scripture to support his argument: *works of law* is not in Ps 143:2, but Paul adds it against the inconsistency of Peter. Barrett, *Freedom*, 19; Lindars, 224-25.

152. In 1 Corinthians the argument is predominantly based on prophetic texts, as Paul acts in the tradition in Israel that was critical of wisdom. McKane, 102-12; Wuellner, "Homily," 203-4.

153. On whether Paul is using Gen 12:3 or 18:18 at Gal 3:8, see Sanders, *Paul* (1983), 21 n. 24.

154. Ebeling, 164.

interpretations of the Abraham story. These traditional interpretations were in line with the Jewish view of Abraham that "... allowed for faith as trust in the divine promise (and especially the monotheistic confession as the sum of faith) to be itself a work; and the divine acceptance was hence considered as a juridical ratification of an existing piety."[155] The faithfulness of Abraham was emphasized in a view that shows up in the Apocrypha, the New Testament, and Philo.[156] Paul's interpretation of Abraham is according to his own theological understanding of faith. Paul uses the Abraham material in accord with his law–faith contrast, and may have used the story because his opponents had introduced it.[157]

According to the Jewish or traditional interpretation, Abraham's faith is not at all opposed to his deeds. His works included steadfastness in the midst of temptations and his abiding trust in the promise of God.[158] A similar view of Abraham occurs in James 2:21–3. It is contradicted by Paul.[159] Paul understands faith, in his interpretation of Abraham, not as a *work* of human faithfulness, but rather as faith in Jesus Christ, in whose crucifixion God's saving act has taken place, "that in Christ Jesus the blessing of Abraham might come upon the Gentiles" (Gal 3:14). But Paul's thought here also seems to be, *if blessed, then not cursed*. This, together with the possibility that his opponents introduced the notion of curse relative to failure to keep the law (3:10), leads Paul to deal with curse in 3:10–14. To get to the point of freedom from curse in 3:13 Paul's argument utilizes three stages.[160]

First, in 3:6–9 the catchwords are *faith* and *blessing*. Two quotations are used: Gen 15:6 in v. 6, followed by a conclusion in v. 7 that is introduced by *you know therefore that*; Gen 12:3 (or 18:18?) in v. 8, followed by a conclusion in v. 9 that is introduced by *so that*. The subject of both conclusions is *those of faith*, of whom two things are declared: *they are sons of Abraham*, and *they are blessed with Abraham who had faith*. Those who are of faith belong to Abraham and share his blessing.[161] Paul does not discuss

---

155. Käsemann, "Abraham," 81; Heidland *TDNT* 4:286–92. Betz, 140, notes that Paul uses a text (Gen 15:6) that was famous to (1) Jews: Str-B 3:199–201 and (2) Christians: Hahn, "Gen 15:6," 97–100.

156. Sir 44:19–21; 1 Macc 2:50–2; James 2:21; Heb 11:17; *De Abrahamo*, 262–76. Ebeling, 166.

157. Betz, 141 n. 19; Burton, 153, 156; Barrett, "Allegory," 158; Bruce, *Galatians*, 154–55; Oepke, *Galater*, 102; Michel, *Bibel*, 91.

158. Betz, 139; Bultmann, *TDNT* 6:197–228.

159. Hahn, "Gen 15:6," 97: While the Letter of James speaks of works, Paul avoids their possibility.

160. Ebeling, 167–68.

161. Mußner, 222–23, when later generations believe, they are in community with

the figure of Abraham first (as he does in Romans). He focuses on *those of faith*.[162] Abraham has become the prototype of people of faith. This does not mean faith generally or generically, but faith *in Christ* (2:16), as attested by the kind of faith that Paul establishes in opposition to works of the law, in Gal 2:16 and 2:20. Paul also attributes to Abraham the unique role of being the only person before Christ who knew and believed the gospel. Paul explains that this happened because (1) Scripture foresaw, thus acting in a personified manner,[163] and (2) Scripture proclaimed the gospel beforehand to Abraham (v. 8).[164]

Second, in 3:10-12 the catchwords are *works of law* and *curse*. The structure of the previous stage is reversed, with a thesis followed by a supporting quotation. Each quotation is preceded by an introductory formula: (1) *for it is written that*, in v. 10, introducing Deut 27:26, and (2) *it is evident that*, in v. 11, introducing Hab 2:4.[165] Three propositions take the law as their starting point, and use similar catchwords: v. 10, *by works of law*; v. 11, *by law*; v. 12, *law*. Each of these is followed by an assertion that is negative in content or meaning if not in form: v. 10, *cursed is everyone*; v. 11, *no one is justified before God*; v. 12, *is not of faith*. The unifying theme of righteousness before God is answered positively in 6-9 and negatively in 10-12.

Third, in 3:13-14 Paul uses a chiasmus to cover in reverse order the same ideas that occurred in 3:6-12. The first two sections are opposite one another: in 3:6-9 Abraham and blessing are central; in 3:10-12 law and curse are central. In this third section Christ is central, and unites the opposite topics of sections one and two by becoming a curse himself, so as to bestow the blessing of Abraham. In this way Paul shows how the curse is removed (v. 13) and how the blessing is fulfilled (v. 14). The section's quotation in the middle (v. 13b: Deut 21:23) substantiates the preceding assertion (v. 13a) and leads to the following statement (v. 14).

Hellenistic Jews and Jewish Christians may have used this same material in such a way as to show the continuity from Abraham to Christ, thus

---

Abraham.

162. Betz, 141: the phrase is used only here, and stands in contrast to *those of works of law* in 3:10, and *those of circumcision* in 2:28. On sons of Abraham see Schweizer, *TDNT* 8:365; Str-B 3:263.

163. Betz, 143; Str-B 3:538; Michaelis, *TDNT* 5:381-82. The rabbis personified Scripture.

164. Betz, 143; BDAG, 712; Friedrich, *TDNT* 2:737; Luz, *Geschichtsverständnis*, 111. The verb is a *hapax legomenon*.

165. Paul quotes Deut 27:26 in a form found only in Gal 3:10; Rom 12:19; 14:11; 1 Cor 1:19; 3:19; Michel, *Bibel*, 72; Ellis, *Old Testament*, 22; Fitzmyer, "Quotations," 9; Betz, 144.

skipping from Abraham in 3:6–9 to Christ in 3:13–14. The continuity would be from latent blessing to fulfillment. Paul, however, inserted his complex assertions about the law in 3:10–12 in order to point "to the crucified Christ who bears the curse. There is no other way he can account for the fact that only now does the blessing of Abraham come to the Gentiles."[166] Previously the promise had been barred by law and the blessing barred by curse. Faith that justifies comes only through deliverance from the curse of the law.

2.2. In Gal 3:7–14 Paul uses subordinate texts together with theological tradition and word plays to link together his argument. The subordinate texts and tradition that we will examine here include, (1) Hab 2:4, in contrast to Lev 18:5; (2) Deut 27:26 and 21:23; (3) the *for us* tradition of Isa 53:9b–11. But besides these supporting texts and tradition in Paul's argument there is another structural element that gives continuity and direction to his case. Brinsmead describes Paul's use of a *word crochet* as the literary device that holds together the argument that runs from 3:1 to 4:11.[167] By this means the entire passage is divisible into smaller pericopes, each using a particular word in the last phrase of the pericope. The word will have been used infrequently or not at all in the preceding lines of the pericope. After use in the final phrase, the word crochet will repeat the word in the first phrase of the next pericope, where it then becomes a key word used several times. In the last phrase of that pericope a new word appears, and this becomes the key word in the next pericope. Paul uses word linkage to move through the various stages and texts of his argument. In 3:1–5 *faith* occurs only in 3:2, and again in the final phrase of 3:5. But then the word is picked up in 3:6, Abraham *believed/had faith in God*, and thereafter it appears eight times in 3:6–14.

In 3:14 *promise* appears in the final phrase of the pericope. It is repeated in the beginning of a new pericope (3:16), and thereafter occurs seven times in 3:15–22. In the same pericope *faith* is not used until 3:22. In 3:23 the word is picked up once more, and used five times in 3:23–9. In the same pericope *promise* is not used until the very end, in 3:29. Then 3:29 introduces *heir* (also used previously in 3:18) which recurs in 4:1 and 4:7, where it functions as a bracket. In 4:7 *heir* is associated with *God*, and 4:8 begins with the question of the believer's relation to *God*. This word, *God*, is part of the word crochet that ties 4:8–11 into the entire argument.[168]

---

166. Ebeling, 170.

167. Brinsmead, 82–4. Mußner, 244, sees a unity of 3:19–29, 4:1–7 on the basis of themes and presence of *heir*. The argument about Abraham extends beyond the formal argument from Scripture.

168. Brinsmead, 83, sees the entire sequence bound together by *in vain/for nothing* in 3:4; 4:11; the meaning in 4:11 mirrors 3:4, since both are "based on the same pathetic

Galatians 3:1-5 and 4:8-11 are reaffirmations of the *causa* (1:6-10). The two pericopes are "... carefully placed at the beginning and end of a sequence of argument. Both immediately after the first statement of the *causa* and immediately before the second, the issue is sonship ..." (*those of faith are sons of Abraham* [3:7]; *because you are sons,* [4:6]; *so you are no longer a slave but a son* [4:7]).[169]

Abraham has an essential function throughout the argument. He does not appear before chapter 3 nor after chapter 4, but holds the whole section together, from 3:6 (the issue of the sons of Abraham) to 4:21-31 (the two *children*, 4:25, 28, as paradigms of the two spheres of *flesh* and *spirit*). Abraham's role is also heightened by the way Paul negates almost all other aspects of Jewish salvation-history.[170] *Faith alone*, rather than *faith and obedience*, is pre-eminent.[171] Moses and Israel have been dropped out completely (as positive factors), as Moses becomes a symbol for slavery (3:19; 4:24), and stands alongside a whole series of enslaving powers.[172] These powers include *law* (3:24); *guardians and trustees* (4:2); *elements of the world* (4:3); *beings that by nature are not gods* (4:8); and the *angels* (3:19), through whom the law was given.

In Paul's eschatological scheme *cosmos* is identified with the present evil age and brings bondage. Eschatology is central to Paul's argument, as chapter 3 is built around a particular time sequence, climaxing in 4:4. "This last text grounds eschatology in Christology ... The law is elevated

---

contrast." See nn. 195, 196: in both pericopes, the Galatians who had known God (4:9) and entered the sphere of *spirit* (3:3) are turning to the powers of the old *cosmos* (4:9) and the sphere of *flesh* (3:3).

169. Ibid., 83.

170. Brinsmead, 84 n. 200: Paul uses a different salvation history in Galatians than elsewhere. See Conzelmann, *Outline*, 255. In Galatians 3 the period from Abraham to Moses is missing. This heightens the pre-eminence of promise. In Romans 5 there is a sweep from Adam to Moses, and no Abraham. In Romans 4 Abraham is placed alongside David to illustrate the witness of the law to the gospel. Galatians 3 contrasts law and promise. Romans 5 contrasts law and sin. Beker, *Paul* (1980), 99-104.

171. In Romans 4 Abraham first believes and then is circumcised. In Gal 3:15-22 the covenant with Abraham is confirmed with the promise, not with circumcision. In late Judaism Abraham's faith, in obedience to God's will, was a meritorious work; Jub 23:10; Pr Man 8; 2 Bar 57:2; 58:1. In 1 Macc 2:52, Gen 15:6 is attached to Gen 22:15-18, as in James, showing that Abraham's righteousness was his obedience to the will of God; Str-B 3:188-94. This emphasizes faith as obedience. Romans emphasizes faith and obedience. Galatians emphasizes faith alone. Brinsmead, 84 n. 201.

172. Brinsmead, 118, sees comparisons and contrasts between Galatians and Romans regarding law and Israel. In Romans 9-11 Israel is part of salvation-history and the oracles of God are part of Israel's treasure. In Gal 4:21-31 Israel is in a Hagar-bondage, brought about by the enslaving Sinai covenant. Rom 4:16 speaks of the *seed* of both the law and faith; Gal 3:16, 19 speak of only one seed.

particularly in terms of its role in the death of Christ (3:10–14)."[173] The time sequence involves the fulfilling of the time that coincides with the sending of the Son (4:4). These in turn coincide with the coming of the time of faith (3:23, 25) and thus the end of the rule of law (3:23, 24, 25). Paul's use of Hab 2:4 supports the argument about faith that he began in 3:6. It also supports both the development of that argument in such texts as 3:23, and the conclusion of the scriptural argument, about being Abraham's offspring (by faith), in 3:29.

2.2.1. Paul uses Hab 2:4 in opposition to Lev 18:5 to support his argument that Gentiles are justified by faith and not by (works of) law. Because the argument is terminological it is necessary for Paul to use texts in which the root for the words *righteousness* or *justification* is connected with *faith*. The LXX has only two passages in which this linkage occurs, and Paul uses both of them in Galatians 3. Genesis 15:6, containing *believe* and *righteousness*, is Paul's lead text in Gal 3:6. Habakkuk 2:4, containing *righteous* and *belief*, quoted in Gal 3:11, supports Paul's argument that no one is justified by law. It may have suited Paul's purpose better if Hab 2:4 had a passive form of the verb instead of the adjective, but the verse nevertheless connects righteousness with faith.[174] What 3:11 has in common with v. 10 and v. 12 is a negative assertion about the law, answering negatively the question of righteousness before God.[175] Each assertion in 3:10–12 is then followed by a supporting quotation. By terminological association faith is first linked to righteousness in 3:6, and then *belief/faith* or *believe/have faith* forms are used eight times in 3:6–14.[176] Having associated righteousness and faith in 3:6 the linkage is repeated in 3:8 and 3:11. In 3:8 *Gentiles* and *blessing* are also included with the mention of faith and Abraham from v. 7. Only in 3:11 do *faith* and *righteousness* occur alone together, without Abraham, blessing, or Gentiles. The significance of this limitation is seen in the relation of 3:11 to 3:12, or, in the relation of Hab 2:4 to Lev 18:5. For Paul Hab 2:4 opposes Lev 18:5 because faith and works of law exclude one another.[177]

---

173. Brinsmead, 84 n. 203; Schlier, *Galater*, 134, Duncan, 124. Bornkamm, "Colossians," 124, notes that there is an identification between *the elements of the world* and the angels who give the law; existence under the *elements* is existence under the law (4:5; 3:13, 23).

174. Sanders, *Paul* (1983), 21 n. 23, whether *by faith* modifies (1) *will live*, or (2) *righteous*; (1) if *by faith* modifies *will live* it refers to the manner of life by which one lives who is righteous; Hanson, *Studies*, 41; Cavallin; (2) if *by faith* modifies *righteous* it refers to one who is righteous because of faith, and *will live* becomes a promise of life to the one who is righteous by faith. Burton, *Galatians*, 166–7. See Rom 1:17.

175. Ebeling, 167–69.

176. Brinsmead, 82–4.

177. Dahl, "Justification," 106; "Contradictions," 170.

They exclude one another, Paul argues, because righteousness (justification) is based on faith (Hab 2:4=Gal 3:11), while the law is based on doing (Lev 18:5=Gal 3:12). Leviticus 18:5 was the biblical evidence for a particular Jewish view of the law: "It was a basic presupposition for every Jew that God's power to give life was closely connected with the law."[178] In this view it was through the law that God gave and preserved life. The law served as a barrier against the destructive powers of sin and evil. Paul's rejection of this claim informs his polemics against the Judaizers. He refers to it in connection with its biblical evidence, Lev 18:5, "You shall therefore keep my statutes and ordinances, by doing which a man shall live: I am the Lord."[179] In each case Paul counters this verse with another text from Scripture. In Rom 10:5–8 he quotes Deut 30:12–14. In Gal 3:10–14 he quotes Hab 2:4. In Galatians Paul's exposition of Gen 15:6 contrasts Lev 18:5 and Hab 2:4.[180] The contrast rules Paul's interpretation of Hab 2:4.[181] "In the LXX there is only one occurrence of the words *by faith* and that is precisely in Hab 2:4."[182] There are two fundamental features of Paul's use of Hab 2:4 in the NT. First, his use is limited to Gal 3:11 and Rom 1:17, corresponding to his concern with the topic of *faith* in the two epistles. The word *faith* occurs twenty-two times in Galatians and forty times in Romans, but very few times in 1 Thessalonians (8), 1 Corinthians (7), 2 Corinthians (7), Philippians (5).[183] Second, in keeping with Paul's frequent use of *faith* in Galatians and Romans, and the use of Hab 2:4 in only those two epistles, the Habakkuk phrase *by faith* likewise occurs only in Galatians (9 times) and Romans (12 times). In both uses of Hab 2:4 the *by faith* formula modifies the adjective *righteous*: "he who through faith is righteous shall live."[184] Paul links faith and righteousness in order to describe the true nature of righteousness. Within

---

178. Moxnes, 263. Sir 17:11; Bar 4:1; Pss Sol 14:2; Str-B 3:129–31.

179. Lindars, 228–32; Sanders, *Paul* (1977), 483.

180. Beker, *Paul* (1980), 120–1; 246, Paul differs from Jewish hermeneutics, citing no third text to mediate conflicting texts: "Paul simply allows the contradiction to stand for the sake of his Christocentric argument . . . Hab 2:4 agrees with the gospel . . . Paul audaciously quotes Scripture against itself in order to create the antithesis between 'the work of the law' and 'faith-righteousness' . . . (and) deletes 'doing the law' from his canon of Scripture."

181. Moxnes, 264: ". . . the virtual identity between *righteousness* and *life* is presupposed (cf. Gal 3:21)." Sanders, *Paul* (1977), 503–8, modifies his view from "Method," 470–4, that the *real* meaning of righteousness is *life*, to speak instead of the virtual identity of righteousness and life. If identified with one another then one could replace the other in a text that could empty such statements of their force.

182. Corsani, 87.

183. Morgenthaler, 132.

184. Corsani, 89 n. 6. Longenecker, 123.

Paul's theological argument the formula relates to the saving acts of God in Jesus Christ and to justification. It "has more to do with the objective fact of Christ's coming, dying and rising from the dead than with the subjective attitude of man."[185] It is therefore faith, not law, that achieves righteousness, and this again stands over against the tradition in rabbinic literature about Abraham's faith.[186] Paul's interpretation of Abraham's faith differs from the traditional Jewish interpretation of his opponents, *and* his use of Hab 2:4 differs from both the LXX and the quotation by the author of Hebrews.[187]

There are four different views of Hab 2:4.[188] First, the Hebrew points to the faithful person, *the righteous will live by his faithfulness.*[189] Second, the LXX points to the faithfulness of God: *the righteous one will live by my faithfulness.*[190] Third, Hebrews 10:38 moves *my* from *faithfulness* to *righteous one*: *my righteous one will live by faith.* Fourth, Paul omits the possessive pronoun, leaving the verse open to his own interpretation and theological understanding of faith: *the one who is righteous by faith will live.*[191] The origi-

185. Corsani, 91; Kramer, 19-44, 45-48.

186. Ellis, *Old Testament,* 93, 56. Rabbinic literature sees Abraham's faith: (1) as a work of merit; (2) inherited by Israel; (3) not contrary to justification by works. Str-B 3:186.

187. Dodd, *Scriptures,* 50-51. Ellis, *OT,* 152, Paul varies from LXX and MT where they vary from one another.

188. BDB, 53: אֱמוּנָה can refer either to the *fidelity* of human conduct or the *faithfulness* of God.

189. Jepsen, *TDOT* 1:318-19, reads Hab 2:4 as "that inner attitude which is prerequisite to a genuine life . . . Such v*emunah* is peculiar to the *tsaddiq* and brings him to life." Szeles, 30-33. Gaster, 253, translates 1 QpHab 8:1-3: *"But the righteous through his faithfulness shall live.* This refers to all in Jewry who carry out the Law (*Torah*). On account of their labor and of their faith in him who expounded the Law aright, God will deliver them from the house of judgment." Brownlee, *Habakkuk,* 55.

190. Jepsen, *TDOT* 1:319, says that LXX could assume a different Hebrew text or a well-known interpretation that makes the life of the righteous dependent on God and not on its own quality.

191. Bonsirven, 327, notes that Paul is materially unfaithful to the original sense of Hab 2:4, as he invests *faith* with the full sense given by the doctrine of justification. Ellis, *OT,* 121, notes that the original context of Hab 2:4 was a prophetic complaint: Chaldeans triumphed and God has allowed it. The hope that followed predicted that the vision would be fulfilled in the future when the righteous will triumph, and in that triumph the earth will be filled with the knowledge of God. For Paul the messianic age is inaugurated by Christ and ushers in fulfillment of the vision, while faith in Hab 2:4 is defined by the Abraham story (Gen 15:6), and means faith in Christ. But J. Sanders, 233, observes that Hab 2:4 emphasizes faith in the sovereignty of God through adversity. Paul, like Qumran, used Hab 2:4 to speak of obedience and responsibility; the distinction is that Paul's point was responsibility *after* justification, and he applies the passage to Christ's atoning death (240). Stendahl, *Scrolls,* 17: "It is Jesus that makes the difference." Fitzmyer, "Hab 2:3-4", 240-2; "Theology," *JBC* 79:125-7. On differing

nal context and sense of Hab 2:4 are laid aside, as Paul rephrases and reinterprets the verse to serve his theological argument about faith in Christ. This same method of dealing with Scripture prevails in Paul's use of support texts from Deuteronomy.

2.2.2. Deuteronomy 27:26 and 21:23 are central to Paul's argument about curse in Gal 3:10 and 3:13, as he connects law with curse and then curse and law with crucifixion.

2.2.2.1. Deuteronomy 27:26 reads, "Cursed be he who does not confirm the words of this law by doing them." The verse is the final declaration in a series of twelve curses pronounced by the Levites on Mt. Ebal, in Shechem.[192] This Shechemite Dodecalogue may have been periodically repeated as part of a covenant renewal ceremony.[193] Corresponding blessings occur in Deut 28:1-6. The entire Dodecalogue deals with crimes that convey the curse regardless of whether the perpetrator ever submitted to due process before a human court.[194] The curses were automatic and there is no specific penalty prescribed for each offence. Yahweh is called upon to execute divine curse on the wrongdoer. The curse effectuates itself through the threat of each command.[195] The curse involves exclusion from the covenant community.

The LXX makes the text more emphatic than the MT with the addition of *every* after *cursed* and *all* after *not obey*. Paul takes over this twofold *all*, and replaces *all the words of this law* (in LXX) with *all the things written in the book of the law* (in Gal 3:10). In both LXX and the MT the curse is pronounced on the one who *does not confirm the words of this law by doing them*. The Dodecalogue points to itself as the standard to be upheld and the measure of offense.[196] Paul generalizes to the whole written Torah.

The context of the Dodecalogue mentions both blessing on the law-keeper and curse on the law-breaker. But this duality is not Paul's interest in the text and its context.[197] He overturns the original sense of the text

---

uses between Galatians and Romans of Hab 2:4, Ellis, *OT*, 117–24; Beker, *Paul* (1980), 95–96. Dodd, *Scriptures*, 51, says that the various uses of Hab 2:3-4 suggest that it belongs among traditional testimonia from the church's earliest period. Barth, *Romans*, 41.

192. Lewy, 207–11.

193. Bruce, *Galatians*, 158, refers to an elaborated form that was used by the covenant community at Qumran (1QS 2:1-8). On the relationship of curse and covenant see Fensham, 1–9.

194. Driver, 299–300.

195. Bruce, *Galatians*, 158; Alt, 115; Lührmann, *Galater*, 55.

196. Scharbert, 410, v. 26 is "against anyone who transgresses the entire Torah corpus of Dt. 6–26."

197. Lührmann, *Galater*, 55.

and connects curse not to failure to keep the law but to attempting to live under the law. That *curse* and *law* occur in the same text is one of Paul's chief interests in using this quotation. Paul, however, does not diminish the force of the *all* added by LXX, even though he could legitimately have removed it in keeping with the sense of the Hebrew text. The presence of *all* in Paul's use of texts does not make it the main point of his argument.[198] It is not Paul's argument that God has offered the way of faith because the way of law-keeping is impossible.[199] It is central to his theology that faith is the way God has decided people shall be related to God. If the *all*- character of law-keeping were his point then Lev 18:5 and Deut 27:26 in the original sense would suit him. Paul quotes the verses only to lay them aside.[200]

Why should he bother thus with these verses, and Deut 27:26 in particular? Likely the law-keeping texts were first part of the argument of Paul's opponents. Such texts would have fit well with the tradition against which Paul lays out his apocalyptic gospel from the outset of the epistle. There are three places in Galatians 3 where Paul responds to the exegesis of his opponents and re-interprets their proof texts to serve his side rather than theirs.[201] First, in Gal 3:6 Paul quotes Gen 15:6. He follows it with Gen 12:3 (or 18:18) to show the interest of the Gentiles in the promise to Abraham. Their participation in the promise must be due to faith, since they are uncircumcised and not keepers of the law.[202] Second, in 3:10 Paul quotes Deut

198. Sanders, *Paul* (1983), 21.

199. Wilckens, "Development," 21, argues in a nearly cause and effect manner: because no one can keep the law perfectly, and Torah grants life only to those who do, therefore life can come only by faith, for which reason Paul quotes Hab 2:4. But this ignores the fact that Hab 2:4 is subsidiary to Paul's main argument, based on Gen 15:6, with faith in Christ contrasted to works of law. Faith is not a stop-gap for failure, but the essential factor in divine-human relationship. Law is impotent (Gal 3:21). It is faith that participates in Christ's atoning death.

200. Bruce, *Galatians*, 160. Regarding Gal 3:6-14, Räisänen, *Paul* (1983), 94-96, agrees with interpreters who assume that Paul is thinking here of the impossibility of fulfilling the Torah. He rejects the interpretation of v. 10 that understands Paul's main point to be the problem of doing (as over against believing) and not the problem of impossibility: "Had Paul wished merely to emphasize the falsity of the principle of 'doing', the best method would have been to omit v. 10 altogether; the idea would then have been clear enough from verses 11-12." But what if Paul dealt with Deut 27:26 because (1) his opponents quoted it against his view, and (2) the verse is unique for bringing together curse and law? The way of law-keeping may be impossible, and Paul may have had that in mind, but it is not his argument that plan A (law) has failed, so God has had to fall back on plan B (Christ-faith).

201. Barrett, "Allegory," 158-60. Stuhlmacher, "Ende," 29-30 (ET, 139-40).

202. Barrett, "Allegory," 159: Paul uses Gen 15:6 also in Rom 4:3, and supports it with Ps 32 to show the non-imputation of sin, equivalent to *the gratuitous imputation of righteousness*, rather than careful account-keeping of Abraham's good works. Black,

27:26. His opponents would have supported this text with Lev 18:5, which Paul counters with Hab 2:4. The opponents would have applied Deut 27:26 to Paul himself, who in their estimation failed to keep the law and did not require his Gentile converts to do so either, to whom their quotation would also apply. They are not denying that faith is necessary, but they are asserting that law-keeping is also necessary for membership in the church.[203] Third, Gal 3:16 is based on Gen 12:7; 13:15; 17:7; 22:18; and 24:7. Here Paul first gives a singular sense to the normally collective *seed* before coming around to a new collectivity (3:28). The singular refers in Paul's argument to Christ, in and through whom the promises are fulfilled. The collective sense refers to the new covenant community, based not on racial, social, or physical divisions but on unity in Christ.[204]

Paul could use OT texts that had already been quoted by his opponents. These opponents were Christian missionaries who could agree with Paul about the basic principle of *faith in Christ*, and this may explain why Paul does not explicitly deal with the ideas of sin-offering or day of atonement, even though such provision was granted by the law itself. "One reason may be that the sacrificial ritual had not been mentioned by the agitators. Even they knew that this part of the law at least had been rendered obsolete by the death of Christ."[205]

Romans, 75–6: "The verb *logizomai* (count, reckon) occurs 29 times in Paul (apart from OT quotations)—11 times in Romans alone and only 6 times elsewhere in the New Testament. For the metaphorical use of the word in Paul, see W. H. Griffith Thomas, *ET*, XVII (1905-6), 211–14. The view that Abraham's *faith* was *reckoned to him* as *equivalent* to *righteousness* is less convincing than to take *for righteousness* as meaning that Abraham's faith was counted to his credit *with a view to the receiving of righteousness*. (Cf. for this use of *eis* ('*for*'), Rom 1:16; 3:22; 10:10."

203. Sanders, *Paul* (1983), 19: ". . .the rival missionaries did not argue against 'faith in Christ . . . The argument of Galatians 3 is against Christian missionaries, not against Judaism, and it is against the view that Gentiles must accept the law *as a condition* of or as a basic requirement for membership." Sanders sees *faith in Christ* as "a common Christian formulation." Bultmann, *TDNT* 6:203–19; Sanders, *Paul* (1977), 441 n. 54; 445. Hooker, ΠΙΣΤΙΣ ΧΡΙΣΤΟΥ, argues for the subj. gen. understanding of Gal 2:16, 20; 3:22 (Rom 3:22, 26; Phil 3:9), referring to Christ's faith as the basis for ratification of the promise. Then the faith of believers is really a sharing in Christ's faith; 331, "Thus even the faith they have is *reckoned* to them." For the present point it is not necessary to settle this question, although it seems reasonable that if being crucified with Christ (Gal 2:19) means inclusion in the cross of Christ then the faith of Christ (Christ's own faith) might also be the basis of the promise and justification in which one shares by believing. Hooker, 342: "to believe is to share in the faith of Christ himself." Paul's point is that faith, not law, is the basis of justification.

204. Barrett, "Allegory," 160.

205. Bruce, 160–1. Harnack, *Christianity?*, 159: "Those who looked upon this death as a sacrifice soon ceased to offer God any blood-sacrifice at all." Sacrifice, not as

2.2.2.2. Paul quotes Deut 21:23 in Gal 3:13. It is not likely that Paul took over *this* OT text from his opponents in Galatia. Christian opponents would not have attached Deut 21:23 to the crucifixion of Jesus, for Deut 21:23 is not *by itself* useful in Christian preaching.[206] Paul introduces the text into the argument for the purpose of showing how the curse of the law has been borne by the innocent Jesus. It is, "... a scriptural citation of Paul's own choosing, the only scriptural text, in fact, by which Paul ever interprets Christ's death."[207] The curse is nullified for people of faith in Christ. "It was the cross that put the promise of Gen 18:18 into effect."[208]

Deuteronomy 21:23 may have been used by Jewish opponents to Christianity and by Paul himself previous to his conversion.[209] Paul twice mentions his previous law-abiding zeal in Judaism together with his persecution of the church (Gal 1:13; Phil 3:5-6).[210] This could indicate that one of the main reasons for Paul's persecution of the church was the criticism by Christians of, or relaxed attitude towards, the law.[211] It is also likely that Paul would have understood, on the basis of current Jewish interpretations of Deut 21:23, that a crucified man could not be the Messiah.[212] By the time of Jesus some Jews had already interpreted Deut 21:23 as applying to crucifixion, even though the original sense of the text means hanging

---

continuing practice but as explanation for the death of Christ, was within the inherited tradition with which Paul had to deal, beyond which his own interpretation would go. See 1.5 below.

206. Dietzfelbinger, 36.

207. Martyn, *Galatians*, 319; see Martyn's n. 111, summarizing three possible Early Christian understandings of the relation of scripture/Law and Christ's death. These include: (a) Christ's death as a Jewish martyr who was crucified by the Roman military establishment; (b) Christ's death as a fulfillment of the Law as scripture, a fulfillment of prophecy; (c) Christ's death as conflict with the Jewish Law. In line with interpretation (c), "... Paul explores the view that Jesus died in *conflict* with the Law insofar as it had the power to pronounce a curse." Thus, Galatians 3:13 signals Paul's understanding of Christ's death, as does Gal 1:4, as well.

208. Barrett, "Allegory," 160.

209. Dietzfelbinger, 37-8; Lindars, 233.

210. Kim, 46.

211. Hultgren, "Persecutions," maintains that Paul did *not* persecute the church because it taught a way of salvation apart from law, but because the church's faith, centering on Jesus crucified and raised, was offensive to Paul. That is, Paul, as a Jew, did not see Christianity as a competitor to, but a movement within, Judaism. Later, his Christian view (102) saw the church as "a new community no longer subject to the parent body." But crucifixion and law criticism related as causes of Paul's persecuting the church. Belief in a crucified messiah was contrary to interpretations of the law (Deut 21:23); the factors of law criticism and crucifixion so closely connect as to be hardly separable.

212. Dietzfelbinger, 33-6, 38.

after death.[213] When the Christian church proclaimed the crucified Jesus of Nazareth to be the Messiah it provoked offence among Jews, who would have interpreted Deut 21:23 to mean that Jesus was cursed and so could not be the Messiah. To them the Christian message of the crucified Jesus as the Messiah was a contradiction in terms. Jewish sentiment about the crucified Jesus is represented by Trypho when, pointing to Deut 21:23, he rejected the messiahship of Jesus.[214] Christians from the beginning of the movement met opposition from Jews based on Deut 21:23. Law criticism could have been inferred from the induction of Gentiles into the church without law observance. This, together with the proclamation of a crucified Messiah, had likely once made Paul part of that opposition.[215] Paul and his opponents would have been cognizant of the history of interpretation of Deut 21:23. We note three aspects of that history.

First, the meaning of the Hebrew text in its original context has been interpreted according to either a subjective or an objective genitive. The subjective genitive would indicate a curse coming from God: *for a hanged man is accursed by God* (RSV).[216] The objective genitive would indicate an offense against God: *for a hanged man is offensive in the sight of God* (NEB). The meaning of curse or ridicule *against God* seems more probable.[217] Deuteronomy 21:23, Josh 8:29 (the battle at Ai), and Josh 10:26-27 (the five fugitive kings) all indicate a great concern that the land not be defiled by the hanging overnight of the criminal's dead body. It would have been this defilement that was an insult against God, and this corresponds to the sense of curse which is represented by the hanged man, a curse, offense, or sign of disrespect directed against God. This is the objective genitive interpretation, and is that generally adopted by rabbinic readings.[218]

Second, the LXX adopts a subjective genitive interpretation. The curse is *from God*, a curse generated by God against the accused. In Judaism the association of Deut 21:23 with crucifixion, and the connection of

---

213. Lührmann, *Galater*, 55–56. Kim, 46; Yadin, "Nahum"; *Scroll*, 204–16; Hengel, *Crucifixion*, 84–85; Wilcox, "Tree"; Fitzmyer, "Crucifixion," 125–46.

214. But did they choose to interpret Jesus' crucifixion as proof that he was accursed because the fact of being crucified proved it, or because their perception of his attitude toward the law motivated them to chose such an interpretation? Kim, 46, citing Justin Martyr, *Dial.*, 39:7; 89:1—90:1. Dietzfelbinger, 35.

215. Blank, "Werken," 91; Dietzfelbinger, 37–38.

216. Driver, 248–49; Phillips, 143–44; Mayes, 305.

217. Dietzfelbinger, 35. Brichto, 194, understands the noun via the verb that is best understood against its antonym, *to fear, to reverence*, hence "behavior in regard to a fellow human being which constitutes an offense in the eyes of (hence, against) the Deity."

218. Barrett, *Freedom*, 30.

crucifixion to the curse of the law, was first made during the time of the Jewish ruler, Alexander Jannaeus (103–76 BCE). He used crucifixion against Jews.[219] He could have justified this by perceiving the victims as traitors who had brought shame upon their own people. The punishment intentionally conveyed the greatest shame and dishonor to the one crucified and was thought fitting for the crime of treason: the victim had brought curse upon himself by deserving the punishment in which God's curse was incorporated. It signified a curse going out from God, with the emphasis on the one being crucified as deserving this sentence and penalty.[220] The crucified is at fault. By contrast, the Romans used mass crucifixion against Jewish freedom fighters, for whom *traitors* would not have been an appropriate designation from the Jewish perspective. In this case, the interpretation of Deut 21:23 would be an objective genitive (curse against God), with the emphasis on the crucifixion itself. The ones doing the crucifying had discharged a curse against God. Here, the crucifier is at fault. Any of these interpretations was available, depending on the situation to which and perspective from which one must speak. Finally, however, the horror of a curse from God being pronounced against a crucified man first led to questioning and then rejection of such an interpretation. It was thought to be incompatible with the belief in God's divine image that the hanged man (crucified man) should be a curse from God. Herein also is grounded the fact that the cross never became a symbol for Jewish suffering, and that a crucified messiah was considered an absurdity in Judaism. In later conflicts between church and synagogue this rejection of a crucified messiah, grounded in Deut 21:23, was strengthened, and no doubt lay behind the Synagogue's reaction to the post-Easter preaching of the early church.[221]

Third, Paul omitted the words *from God* in his use of Deut 21:23 in Gal 3:13. This serves to distance God from the law. It also serves Paul's view, which is to *negate* the idea that God cursed Jesus and Jesus could therefore not be the Messiah. Paul implicitly puts the work of cursing Jesus on the law itself, thus emphasizing the fate of those who would live under law. It does not serve Paul's purpose to connect the curse to God. Because he wants to put distance between God and the law (3:19) he here omits *from God*. It is likely that Paul has incorporated the verse from a previously worked out answer to Jewish polemic, and used it here to strengthen his case. The Christian opponents of Paul in Galatia would not have used Deut 21:23 for

---

219. Josephus, 379–83. Feldman, 810, doubts that the Lion of wrath of 4QpNah is Jannaeus.

220. Dietzfelbinger, 34.

221. Ibid., 35–6.

exactly the same reason Paul himself once had. They would not have wanted to associate Jesus' death with curse.

> The allusions to Dt 21:23 in Acts 5:30; 10:39; 13:29; 1 Pet 2:24 suggest that from the beginning the Christians encountered Jewish opposition based upon Dt 21:23 to their proclamation of Jesus as the Messiah. The Christians would hardly have applied Dt 21:23 to Jesus on their own initiative. Rather, they must have taken it from their Jewish opponents, and turned it into a weapon of counter-attack.[222]

Paul likely had used Deut 21:23 in his own Christian counter-attacks against Jewish opposition before re-using the text and argument in Galatians.[223] If Deut 21:23 had been a catch-phrase for Paul the persecutor, it became a guerilla tactic for Paul the apostle. He took that weapon from his adversaries and turned it against their anti-Christian Jewish polemic prior to Galatians. He uses Deut 21:23 in Gal 3:13 in order to get to the *pro me* nature of the gospel. He does not use it primarily to associate law and curse, as he has done that already in 3:10, using Deut 27:26. Now he must associate curse with cross, having first said that Christ has become a curse *for us*. Paul must therefore make a connection between Deut 21:23 and Deut 27:26. This he does by free association and play on the word *curse*. In quoting Deut 27:26 and 21:23 Paul modifies the LXX to make the texts correspond to the facts of Jesus' case, and serve the connection Paul establishes between law and curse, and curse and cross. The play on *curse* involves two different words in the two texts of MT, two different forms of the same word in both texts of LXX, and the same form of the same word in Paul's two quotations.[224]

The two different words in the Hebrew (MT: Masorete Text) represent two different senses of *curse*. Deuteronomy 27:26 is the concluding curse pronounced against those who do not live according to the teachings of the Shechemite Dodecalogue. The sense here is *cursed*, that is, it denotes a curse coming from God.[225] It ought really to be followed by a participial construc-

---

222. Kim, 46. Dietzfelbinger, 36–7. Deuteronomy 21:23 *by itself* is not useful as a Christian argument. It would not have been useful for early Christian preaching to introduce the text in discussion with the synagogue.

223. Dietzfelbinger, 38–39. Haenchen, Acts, 251; Acts 5:30 and 10:39 may be understood as the answer of early Christian apologetic to the early synagogue polemic that used Deut 21:22–3 against the Jesus-message. The answer in Acts is that God has overturned and invalidated the curse by raising the Crucified One.

224 Bruce, "Curse," 30; *Galatians*, 163–67. Thus:

Text	MT	LXX	Paul
Deut 27:26	ארר	ἐπικατάρατος	ἐπικατάρατος
Deut 21:23	קללת	κεκαταραμένος	ἐπικατάρατος

225. Scharbert, 408; *BDB* §779. Brichto, 77–96.

tion. In Deut 27:26 certain sins are punished by automatic curses, latent within the threat of the laws themselves. But in Deut 21:23 the reference is either to the individual who has been executed for blasphemy or avoidance of due process, and whose dead body is thereafter hung on a tree as a public sign of ignominy,[226] or it refers to the act of hanging. The sense of the noun here is either (1) *accursed*, that is, it refers to the object of curse, the person smitten by curse, or the destructive power of curse,[227] or perhaps (2) an *offense* against God in whose image the hanged man was *created*.[228] Although it may have been a Jewish objection that Jesus' death on the cross rendered him accursed of God, the context of Deut 21:23 did not have to do with the manner of execution but with what happened *after* execution. "The man is not accursed because he has been hung, but hung because he is already accursed on account of his crime."[229]

The LXX (Septuagint) enhances the association of these two different senses of curse by rendering both of them from the same root, and giving to both texts the sense of a cursing action which comes from God. This is strengthened by the LXX use of *from God*, subjective genitive, in Deut 21:23. Paul goes one step further than LXX by using the same form of the adjective, based on the same root, in both quotations, thus differing from LXX where it has already differed from the MT.[230] But Paul's purpose is to connect the curse of the law in Deut 27:26 with the curse of the cross in Deut 21:23. This serves to attribute Jesus' death on the cross to the cursing power of law. The association is not an exact example of the exegetical device, *equal category*, but Paul depends on the presence of a nearly common term in the two LXX texts that he brings together.[231] Although Paul's word association is dependent on the Greek text, ". . . Paul probably reveals his awareness that the Hebrew text of Deut 21:23 shows a substantive meaning *curse* rather than a participial meaning *cursed* when he speaks of Christ as (*became a curse*)."[232] This thought goes beyond the concept of substitutionary atonement: "To be sure, Christ became the Law's curse *in our behalf*. But he did that not simply by taking onto himself a punishment due us but by

---

226. Von Rad, 167-68. Fitzmyer, "Crucifixion," 139. Dietzfelbinger, 33-5 (Deut 21:23), Driver, 248-49.

227. Scharbert, 415; *BDB* §7045.

228. Brichto, 191-95.

229. Lindars, 233.

230. Ellis, *Old Testament*, 155.

231. Fitzmyer, "Crucifixion," 138; Bruce, *Galatians*, 35, 165.

232. Bruce, "Curse," 30; contra Lindars, 235: "The meaning is similar to the idea of the sin-offering, and there is probably an intentional reference to the theory of sacrifice."

embodying the curse, in such a way as to be, in his crucifixion, *victorious over its enslaving power.*"[233]

Paul's version of Deut 21:23 in Gal 3:13 has the same verbal adjective that LXX has in Deut 27:26, which replaces MT noun; he omits *from/by God*, to avoid saying that Christ was cursed by God: "It was impossible now for Paul the Christian to say that Christ was cursed by God; he was not. Paul (whether he remembered the Hebrew or not) chose to use the word expressing a relation. Christ came to stand in that position in relation to God that was rightly ours."[234] But Paul's use of the quotation has another effect, too. He limits his citation to Deut 21:23b: *cursed is everyone who hangs on a tree*. This associates the hanging body with the law and its curse and dissociates the curse away from God.[235]

It can therefore be said that just as Christ embodied real and true faith, so also he embodied the law's curse: "When one looked at him, as he was being crucified (3:1), one saw the only juncture at which that embodied faith met that embodied curse in all of its power."[236] That Christ took the position in relation to God defined by curse, which was rightfully ours, was so that we may stand in the relation to God that is defined by the word

---

233. Martyn, *Galatians*, 318, n. 110, continues: "Paul places the thought of apocalyptic warfare in the foreground. There are not three actors—the guilty human being, Christ as the substitutionary sacrifice for that person's guilt, and God, who, accepting that sacrifice, forgives the guilty human being. There are four actors: the powerful, enslaving curse of the Law, human beings enslaved under the power of that curse, Christ, who comes to embody the enslaving curse, and God, who in this Christ powerfully defeats the Law's curse, thus liberating human beings from their state of enslavement. Central to the action in this apocalyptic struggle is, therefore, not forgiveness, but rather victory, God's victory in Christ and the resultant emancipation of human beings."

234. Barrett, *Freedom*, 30, sees 2 Cor 5:21 using a word of relation: "Christ stood in that position in relation to God that is defined by the word sin." Bruce, "Curse," 32. Weder, 191, Paul may be thinking of the resurrection here in Galatians but he does not speak of it.

235. Martyn, *Galatians*, 321. "The voice of God and the voice of the Law are by no means the same. It was the Law, not God, that pronounced a curse on the crucified one."

236. Ibid., 318, notes the analogy of 2 Cor 5:21, Christ *made into sin* in our behalf; Israel's sacrificial language as likely used by early Jewish–Christian confessions which included two key convictions: (1) sin can be transferred from one person to another; (2) our sin was transferred to Christ, thus freeing us from enslavement to the power of sin. For sin transferred by laying on of hands see the scapegoat account in Lev 16:20–22; for such transfer affecting persons see Lev 24:13–16. The *sin* is transferred and sent away to the wilderness, or the community is purified by putting to death of the sinner (in this case for blasphemy which pollutes the community). Ibid., 318, "By laying his hands on the animal that was to be sacrificed a man transmitted his sin to it, the result being that the animal, having become sin, was itself called 'sin' (often translated as 'sin-offering')."

righteousness. Christ did this on our behalf. By this strange interchange Christ redeemed us.[237]

If one were working only with the alternative interpretations that were then currently available regarding Deut 21:23, Paul's statement in Gal 3:13 would be very perplexing indeed. It would seem that his omission of *from God* would indicate that he had elected the objective genitive interpretation, wanting to absolve God of having cursed Jesus. But then it would not make sense to say that Jesus had become an offense against God, although it would be understandable to say that the act of crucifying Jesus was an offense or sign of disrespect before God. But in fact Paul's point rests on neither of these alternatives. He removes *from God* so that in Jesus' case he locates the cursing power within the law, and not within God's activity. Thus for Paul whether the act of crucifying Jesus is an offense to God or Jesus himself has taken the position before God of one who is the object of curse, it is the law that has done this. The law thus retains a place in the plan of salvation, but it is a negative place. In view of Deuteronomy texts in Gal 3:10 and 3:13b one might have expected the same word in v. 13a.[238] The original sense of Deut 27:26 is that they are cursed who do not do the whole law. The quotation in 3:10 is therefore a statement of the law's real power and true work. Galatians 3:13b states that the cursing power of law came upon the Crucified One. But in 3:13a Paul switches to the noun: from the standpoint of the gospel Christ is seen as a *curse*. Christ has taken the cursing power of the law into himself, and become a curse.[239] The idea of interchange is instrumental here, and so is the idea of the law's participation in its own demise.[240] This does not elevate the law, but makes the law clearly show that it has turned against itself, runs its course, and has its effect in the death of Jesus as the work to which the law is put.[241] That he speaks of Jesus as a curse is the foundation of Paul's use of *for us* (or *in behalf of us*). His use of the *for*

---

237. Barrett, *Freedom*, 30-31, calls ἐξηγόρασεν (*exēgorasen, redeemed*, Gal 3:13) the verb of freedom.

238. Weder, 188, sees the change to the noun as more than mere *Metonymie*. The change from *accursed* to *curse* conceals within itself the change from the opponents' law-perspective to Paul's gospel-perspective. This change is the christological point of the passage: from the standpoint of law Christ is deservedly accursed by God, but from the standpoint of the gospel he is a curse on our behalf.

239. Second Corinthians 5:21 is analogous. Weder, 188 n. 251, the entire power of sin became so concentrated on Christ that Christ himself became sin. Schlier, *Galater*, 138; Riesenfeld, *TDNT* 8:512-13; Betz, *Galatians*, 150. Dietzfelbinger, 37, is also to the point, Christ not only bore the curse but became the curse for humankind.

240. Hoad, "Isaiah 53." Hooker, "Interchange"; *Servant*, 121-23.

241. Weder, 189, 191, notes how the law is against itself, in that it has come to its own death and its own end.

us formula indicates the unique interpretation Paul gives to the texts about curse, as he speaks of redemption from the curse of the law through Christ's coming to be a curse under the law.[242]

2.2.3. The tradition of Isa 53:9b-11 lies behind Paul's reference to Christ becoming a curse *for us*. Hoad recognizes in 2 Cor 5:21a point by point description of the situation portrayed in Isa 53:9b-11.[243] There is a three-fold presentation of Christ: (1) *the one who knew no sin*, corresponds to Isa 53:9b; (2) *in our behalf (God) made him to be sin*, corresponds to 53:10; (3) *so that in him we might become the righteousness of God*, corresponds to 53:11. The three-fold pattern underlies the plan of redemption in Rom 8:3-4: (1) *in the likeness of sinful flesh*; (2) *to deal with sin* (or, *concerning sin*); (3) *so that the just requirement of the law might be fulfilled in us*.[244] Two characteristics are in both texts. There is a final *so that* of redemptive purpose that describes the effects of the death of the sinless Christ for sinners. There is a re-application to present readers of the *many* of the Servant song: *for us—so that—we* (2 Cor 5:21), *in us* (Rom 8:4). The primary pattern may be recognized according to its three parts: (1) Christ who had done no wrong, (2) entered into our experience, (3) in order that we might enter into Christ's experience and through him be in a right relationship with God.

The same pattern is similarly detected in Gal 3:13-14, where Paul uses proof texts from Scripture and is dependent on Isaiah 53 *only* for the phrase, *for us*.[245] The Servant who had done no wrong (Isa 53:9b) suffered in the

---

242. Martyn, *Galatians*, 317, "... *hyper hêmôn*, 'in our behalf,' [is] a phrase that refers in Paul's mouth to the redemptive act Christ has performed for *all* human beings ..."

243. Hoad, 254-55. Betz, 126 n. 109. Furnish, *II Corinthians*, 339-40. Bultmann, *Second Corinthians*, 164-66.

244. Hooker, *Interchange*, 349, says that *for sin* can be understood as the comparable texts of Gal 3:13 and 2 Cor 5:21, namely becoming or being made sin or curse. This is different from *sin offering*, a common translation. Hooker thus sees similarity in language, form, and theme, in Gal 3:13; 4:4; 2 Cor 5:21; 8:9.

245. Deut 21:23 also influenced 1 Peter's description of Christ based on Isaiah 53: *on the cross* in 1 Pet 2:24 (see Acts 5:30; 10:39). Cullmann, *Christology*, 76-7, sees *ebed Yahweh* (*servant of the Lord*) Christology extending back to the earliest period of Christian faith, its first exponent was Peter, and the christological use of *for us* goes back to Jesus himself. Riesenfeld, *TDNT* 8:510 notes that the prepositional phrase is also in the Last Supper logia that Paul has in common with 2 Synoptics; *TDNT* 2:133.12; 5:716 n. 484; Jeremias, *Words*, 101, 165, 171. The texts involved are 1 Cor 11:24; Lk 22:19; Mk 14:24. Hoad, 254, needs qualification: the preposition *for*, *in behalf of*, does not occur in Isaiah 53 (v. 5) where a different word (*peri*) of like meaning is used. Paul's substitution came from early Christian formulae which spoke of the vicarious death of Jesus, of benefit for the many, based on Christian interpretations of Isa 53:11-12. Statements with *for us* show salvation *for* humankind. There was flexibility in the use of prepositions to signify Christ's death. The *thought* of Isa 53:11-12 is represented by

same way as one who had committed a crime that was punishable by death (Deut 21:23). Therefore, the death was not for his own sin, but was for the sin of others. Vicarious atonement is indicated.[246] Although the concept of substitution is near to Paul's view of atonement in Galatians 3, his understanding of Christ is that he suffered as humanity's representative, rather than as substitute.[247]

In keeping with the characteristic re-application of the Servant Song's concept of *many*, Paul asserts that the curse rests on all who are under the law. Christ comes under the curse in order to set people free. As in Deut 21:23 the hanging on the tree of a criminal's dead body was the public display of one on whom the curse *already* rested, so also Paul may mean that Christ was already under curse by entering the human situation: ". . . we ought not drive a wedge between the incarnation and the crucifixion in Paul's thought."[248] For Christ to enter the experience of the human condition meant for him to be born under law (Gal 4:4) and its power of curse.

The atoning significance of the cross is also explained in statements about the justice of God. This concept is present in Gal 3:10 and Paul's use of Deut 27:15-26. Paul saw that all people who lived under the law's order of retribution (everybody: Rom 2:6) were under curse. To this thought Paul added Gal 3:13, Christ became a curse (came into that relation to God of one who is accursed), although not as one who was deservedly accursed. This is in accord with 2 Cor 5:21, Christ became marked by sin, but did not become a sinner. Sin separates a person from God, and delivers one over to dying. Christ suffered this separation, and was delivered over to dying as representative and as atonement.

> Because this representative bearing of the curse was at the same time atonement it "redeemed us," as it says in Gal 3:13. It brought freedom from the curse of the Law and—according to Gal 4:5—at the same time from its claim by having placed us in the relationship of sonship to God.[249]

In keeping with the characteristic *so that* of redemptive purpose, there is a purposive, means-to-an-end pattern in this aspect of Paul's thought in Galatians. The pattern is similar in 4:4 and 3:13. Christ redeemed us from

---

Paul's different wording.

246. Goppelt, *Theology* 1:94-7.

247. Hooker, "Interchange," 358; contra Morris, *Preaching*, 55-9; *Cross*, 220-4.

248. Hooker, "Interchange," 351. Käsemann, "Significance," 47-8, cautions not to turn the story of salvation into a chain of events, in which the cross is secondary either to incarnation or resurrection.

249. Goppelt, *Theology* 1:96-97.

the curse of the law (3:13a), having become a curse for us (3:13b), *so that the blessing of Abraham might come upon the Gentiles* (3:14a), and *so that we might receive the promise of the Spirit* (3:14b). Thus, "... Christ became what we are, in order that we might become what he is... not a straightforward exchange. Christ does not cease to be Son of God, and we receive the Spirit of the Son."[250] Paul's view of the Torah is uniquely Christian:

> Paul's doctrine of the Law deviates radically from the common Jewish view ... He does not give a historical, objective description of the Jewish view of the Law; that was clearly not his intention. On the contrary, in Galatians 3 and elsewhere he constructs a specifically Christian view of the Law and of its function as part of Scripture ... (his argument persuades only when approached with specific Christian assumptions.[251]

Paul the Apostle and Paul the persecutor *did* have something in common regarding the law. This was the conviction that the Law of Moses and faith in Christ mutually exclude one another as grounds for righteousness.[252] This conviction lies behind the contrast of Hab 2:4 with Lev 18:5, as well as the material regarding curse in Gal 3:10, 13. Paul's use of early Christian traditions that stem from Isaiah 53 serve this same contrast. It makes gospel proclamation out of texts that had been used to promote law observance and that pronounced a curse on the crucified.

2.3. Galatians 3:15-29 continues Paul's exposition and arrives at his concluding statement.

2.3.1. In 3:15-18 Paul moves to a new stage in his series of proofs, as he uses legal terminology to support his theological point.[253] The argument is

---

250. Hooker, "Interchange," 352. Dahl, "Preaching," 35: there is a teleological pattern common to preaching and hymnic texts that is characterized by christological statements with a purpose clause, as Gal 3:13-14. Stauffer, *Theology*, 343, observes a paradox: "... the protasis speaks of 'the burden of the unencumbered', and the apodosis of the 'unburdening of the encumbered.'" The purpose clauses show that the pattern confirms to the goals of Christ's saving act, thus: "Christ ... for us—so that we ..." This is one of several patterns that characterized *community* preaching, as over against *missionary* preaching. Bultmann, *Theology* 1:105; Reicke, "Synopsis." Dahl, "Atonement," 153-54, suggests that the Akedah tradition of Genesis 22 lies behind this representation or substitution; Gal 3:13-14, along with Rom 3:24; 4:25; 8:32; 1 Cor 5:7; Eph 1:3, 6; cf. John 1:29; 1 Pet 1:19; Rev 5:6. Such texts, however, are not explicit references to the Akedah. Dahl, "Promise," 131. Betz, 151 n. 126, rightly disagrees with Dahl's thesis. Ziesler, *Righteousness*, 183 n.1.

251. Dahl, "Promise," 134-35.

252. Dahl, "Contradictions," 170. And yet righteousness and law are related, Rom 3:21.

253. Gal 3:1-5 appeals to experience; appeal to Scripture begins in 3:6, recapitulated

cast in the negative, as Paul says that the law does not annul God's covenant of promise (v. 17b, corresponding to v. 15), does not add a codicil to it (v. 15b), nor does it secure the inheritance (v. 18). In 3:15 Paul speaks *according to human standards* (NRS: *an example from daily life*). The phrase is usually in contrast to God's will, as in 1:11 Paul was emphatic that the gospel that he preached was *not according to human standard*. But in 3:15 it refers to Paul's analogy from human life (see Rom 6:19) and judicial practice, as Paul speaks of the will or covenant.[254] Whether the word in 3:15 should be rendered in the secular sense (*will* or *testament*) and in 3:17 in the biblical sense of *covenant*,[255] Paul clearly uses the legal example in a specific way: (1) he applies it to the argument about the *promises* to Abraham; (2) both senses, *will/testament* and *covenant*, are concerned with *inheritance* (v. 18);[256] (3) the *will* or *covenant* is not changeable;[257] (4) the covenant is related to the *seed/offspring*, in Gen 17:1-11, and in v. 16 by way of the middle term, *promises*.

Paul first used *promise* in 3:14, connecting it there with the blessings given to Abraham, which, through Christ, are intended for the Gentiles. In

---

in 3:29. Betz, 20-21; Fitzmyer, *JBC*, 241. Martyn, *Galatians*, 337, Paul argues in 3:15-18 against the idea that promissory blessing and covenantal law are an indivisible whole, for they are distinct from one another, and law lacks power to specify or alter the promises; thus, 325, "God blesses; the Law curses . . . Paul sees that the blessing and the curse do not come from the same source."

254. Bruce, *Galatians*, 169; Betz, 154-55 (see n. 20), distinguishes terms between what cannot be changed and is immediately effective, independent of the donor's death, and on the other hand what, in Greek and Roman law, can be changed at any time. Paul may have the former in mind here. See Räisänen, *Paul* (1983), 129.

255. Bruce, *Galatians*, 169; Betz, 157; Schlier, *Galater*, 146 n. 4. Burton, 182; Behm and Quell, *TDNT* 2:129, say *testament*: Paul speaks in the sense of Hellenistic law, but his theological sense is shaped by the LXX.

256. The term is introduced in v. 18 and plays a major role through 4:8. Foerster and Herrmann, *TDNT* 3:784: in 3:18 the *inheritance* "is the portion assigned to Abraham and his seed." But the promise to Abraham and his seed, given as a testament before the law was given, is in force because God uttered it and does not add to it. Paul is not thinking of a prohibition against adding to a testament in Hellenistic law, which defines no age of majority. His illustration is legal, his thinking about covenant is theological.

257. Betz, 156. It is not clear whether the *hapax legomenon*, *add to*, refers to the action of the donor or another. The simpler form of the compound verb occurs in 3:19. Schlier, *Galater*, 143-44; Delling, *TDNT* 8:34-36: the law was not just mediated by angels: they decreed it. But it remains God's law. Bruce, *Galatians*, 170, notes that not even the original owner can change it, and that Paul's concern relates to the unilateral covenant that graciously bestows blessing. Mendenhall, *Law and Covenant*, "Covenant"; Anderson, *Old Testament*, 95-106. Hübner, 26-30, argues that the angels are demonic beings who authored the law with the evil intention of causing sin in humans, and *ordained by angels* indicates God's lack of involvement in the giving of the law. But see Räisänen, *Paul* (1983), 131.

3:16 Paul again picks up the term, but ignores the content of the promises (multiplication of offspring, gift of land) in order to move immediately to the phrase, *and his seed*.[258] He insists that the biblical texts use the singular, and in fact they may be interpreted as using a collective singular. Traditional Jewish exegesis usually refers its word, *seed*, to a plurality of descendants. Paul takes the word as a singular, excludes the traditional Jewish interpretation, and reserves the role of heir for Christ. Paul's point is that the promised blessing has been fulfilled in a single descendant, Christ, and through him it comes to all who belong to him and so also are Abraham's offspring.[259] In 3:17 Paul emphasizes the absolute priority of the promise over the law: the promises were made (implied: by God) to Abraham (v. 16), but the law *came* 430 years later. The way in which Paul speaks here of the law (using a participle), "gives the impression that the law had come on the scene independently, on its own initiative, unlike the *covenant/will* based on promise which was 'confirmed by God' (v. 17) . . . Gal 3:17 serves to create a distance between God and the law."[260] Paul distances the law from God, even as he separates the law from promise. It was the normative Jewish position that both law and promise belong together. The promise to Abraham and the Sinai Torah were held together because Abraham knew the law, (1) out of himself; (2) from secret writings; (3) or by special revelation from God.[261] However, in Paul's argument the promise was complete in itself, validated long before the law was given, and the law cannot *annul* the covenant or *nullify* the promise.[262]

---

258. Betz, 157. References to *seed/offspring* (σπέρμα, *sperma*) include Gen 12:7; 13:15; 17:7; 24:7. Martyn, 339, notes that in 3:16 Paul skips mention of the promise of a land and the command for circumcision, and focuses only on God's blessing for the Gentiles; 340, God's promise is spoken only to Abraham and his singular seed, Christ. Plural offspring exist by being incorporated into the singular *offspring/seed*, Christ.

259. Bruce, *Galatians*, 172–73; Quell and Schulz, *TDNT* 7:545; Daube, 438–44; Wilcox, "Seed," 2–20. Betz, 157, rightly contests that Gal 3:16 points to Isaac or an Isaac–Christ typology, as Dahl, "Akedah," 153–54, asserts; Moule, *Christology*, 61; Wedderburn, "Body," 84 n. 3, 88.

260. Räisänen, *Paul* (1983), 128–29, notes a "correspondingly active expression" in Rom 5:20: the law came *between*; cf. Gal 2:4. Hübner, 17, 87–8, in 3:17 wants it (*will* or *testament* but not *covenant*) interpreted as promises and set against the Mosaic law, which cannot annul God's will made 430 years earlier: "Thus the promises to Abraham acquire temporal and therefore substantive priority over against the *nomos* (*law*). It is therefore not Moses but Abraham who has relevance for salvation!"

261. Betz, 159 n. 57; Mußner, 271; Schlier, *Galater*, 147 n. 1. Romans 4:13. Martyn, *Galatians*, 341, n. 165: "Divorcing the covenant from the Law is a move with profound implications for the view of Israel as God's corporate people." Ibid., 341, n. 166; 341–43, 431–57, for Martyn's comments about the two-covenant view of Gal 4:21—5:1.

262. Behm, "κυρόω"; Delling, "καταργέω"; Schlier, *Galater*, 148 n. 2; Bruce,

There may be an OT antecedent to Paul's contrast. The Deuteronomic emphasis on the covenant of Horeb-Sinai, in contrast to the Priestly interpretation that gave primacy to the Abrahamic covenant and its permanent validity, represent a juxtaposition of the conditional and unconditional views of covenant within the OT.[263] The difference is represented by "if you obey ... (then) your God will set you high above all the nations of the earth" (Deut 28:1-2), and the unconditioned *I will bless* (Gen 12:2-3), *I will make, I will establish, I will give* (Gen 17:1-8).[264]

In 3:18 a juxtaposition of *from law* and *from promise* leaves no room for compromise: "Paul polemically separates what Judaism tries to hold together."[265] Paul speaks of the present situation: if the inheritance is by law, it is no longer by promise. With the use of *grant/bestow* he correlates the promise made to Abraham with God's present work of salvation also for the Galatians. The continuity is implied by the perfect tense. The law and the promise are conflicting principles. If the inheritance is not *from law* then it excludes those who are *of works of law*.[266]

2.3.2. Galatians 3:19-20 is part of the concise digression that Paul lays out in 3:19-25. The whole section of seven verses is not a new argument, but is intended to prevent the wrong conclusion that Paul is an enemy of the law.[267] Paul defends himself against the accusation that may be inferred from Gal 2:17; 5:23; Rom 3:5-8; 6:1; 1 Cor 9:19-23. Luke also defends Paul against such accusations: Acts 18:13; 21:21, 24; 24:5, 13; 25:7.[268] Having made the negative statements about what the law does not and cannot do (3:15-18; cf. 2:16; 3:10) Paul poses the question. In response to, "*Why then*

Galatians, 173; Betz, 158; Duncan, 109-10. Martyn, *Galatians*, 342, notes that the issue here for Paul is power: the law is not sufficiently powerful to invalidate or nullify the promise and its true reference: "Christ as the singular seed of Abraham."

263. Clements, *Abraham*, 57; Anderson, *Old Testament*, 357-58.

264. Anderson, *Old Testament*, 460: "The covenant with Abraham, like that with Noah, is also an 'everlasting covenant', unconditional in character ... circumcision is not a condition of this covenant but is a physical *sign* of membership in the covenant community." He notes, 462, that P has no independent account of the Sinai covenant.

265. Betz, 159. There is an even sharper rejection in Rom 4:13-15. Martyn, *Galatians*, 342, n. 171.

266. Conzelmann, *TDNT* 9:396 n. 193. Betz, 160-2; Bruce, *Galatians*, 174; Duncan, 110.

267. Betz, 162, nn. 9, 10; 163; Mußner, 245-48, 277-90.

268. Linton, "Aspect," 83, sees that Paul is not merely defended but is corrected in Acts, and this corrected view of Paul has prevailed in the church. Betz, 163, n. 13; 119-20 regarding Gal 2:17.

the law?"²⁶⁹ (that is, why was it given?)²⁷⁰ he gives two answers about the law's purpose: (1) it was added to multiply and stimulate transgressions (v. 19a); (2) it confines and restrains (v. 23). The presence of *promise* is one of the connecting links in the progression of Paul's thought, appearing in 3:14, 16, 17, 18, 19, 21, and 22. And yet, within that progression there is a distinct reference to the law in 3:19-20, expressed with specific arguments: (1) it was a late addition, it was for the *purpose of* transgressions, and it was temporary and intended to last only *until* the offspring would come; (2) it was inferior because of having been ordained by angels, and because of being given through an intermediary.

2.3.2.1. Paul's reference to the law as having been *added* (3:19b) does not indicate the addition of law to the promise for the sake of making the promise effective.²⁷¹ The whole argument about the validity and sufficiency of promise-covenant precludes that meaning. He means the law was added to the human situation for a purpose different from that of the promise. The abiding validity of promise is emphasized by the perfect passive verb, *had been promised*, in 3:19c.²⁷² That the law was added (later) corresponds to v. 17. The context preceding v. 19, especially v. 15, suggests that the law is "an invalid addition not willed by the testator; (*no one*) in v. 15 makes one think of someone other than the testator himself—of an outsider."²⁷³ The question of who gave the law is not explicitly answered, as Paul affirms that it was given as an addition even though such is against the will of the testator behind the *testament/will*. Paul's point does not hinge on the logic of his application of the legal argument. He wants to assert the inferiority of

---

269. BDF §480:5.

270. Betz, 162, reads, *What, then is the law?* Oepke, *Galater*, 114-15. Rom 3:1. Sanders, *Paul* (1983), 65.

271. Hübner, 32-3, points out that the idea of the law being *added* (*to*, i.e. *later*) would have been particularly offensive to the Jewish notion of the pre-existence of the law.

272. Bruce, *Galatians*, 176.

273. Räisänen, *Paul* (1983), 129. Hübner, 26-31, says: "...the *nomos* is a Law negotiated between the angels and Israel and not between God and Israel ... That God did not institute the *nomos* is a constitutive element in Paul's proof." Hübner distinguishes between the life-giving intention of the law itself, the evil intention of the angels to provoke human transgression of the law, and the intention of God to save, which is accomplished by God's taking up all intentions into justification by faith. Hübner is committed to showing that there are no contradictions in Paul's argument in Galatians 3, and his notion of a three-fold intention makes this possible. But as we have seen, consistency is not Paul's best suit, and his message springs more freely to life when this is recognized.

the law: "... the logic which impelled him to the conviction that Christ had displaced the Torah was the logic of the Damascus-road experience."²⁷⁴

It is an untraditional position for Paul to say that the law was added for the purpose of stimulating transgressions.²⁷⁵ The Jewish view was that the Torah provides an impenetrable fence of protection around Israel, to prevent transgressions, and the un-Jewishness of Paul's position is to be noted.²⁷⁶ Paul does not speak of *sins* here, but *transgressions*, referring to "the conscious disobeying of definite commandments."²⁷⁷ There are three alternatives for what Paul means with, *because of transgressions*: (1) the revelatory or cognitive interpretation would mean that in the light of the law one learns what is sin and that one is a sinner; (2) the definitional interpretation would mean that the law defines sin as transgression, specifying it as conscious and willful action; (3) the causative interpretation would mean that the law brings about sinning. This third view is most in line with what Paul says in Rom 7:5, 8, 9; 1 Cor 15:56; 2 Cor 3:6. There is a causative sense in 3:19, *because of*. Paul's concept of the law as not being able to *give life* (v. 21) but rather bringing death (Rom 7:10) parallels Paul's concept of the law as bringing curse (Gal 3:10) rather than blessing. The death of Christ may be echoed in Paul's own death *through law* (2:19).²⁷⁸

Even so this transgression-producing law ruled only until Christ, "*the eschatological seed of Abraham*" came.²⁷⁹ The reign of law is temporary by design, and was not the fulfillment of the promise anymore than were the material blessings of land and nationhood.²⁸⁰ This counters the orthodox Jewish view of the law as eternal.²⁸¹ Paul's view that the death and resurrection of Christ mark the end of the old aeon and the rule of law is extended back into the time before Christ's coming, wherein Paul devalues the law in

---

274. Bruce, *Galatians*, 176. Paul emphasizes the temporary nature of law. Maurer, *TDNT* 8:167-68: law "is only a temporally restricted interlude which began after the promise"; Burton, *Galatians*, 188; Schlier, *Galater*, 151.

275. Hübner, 32-3: "there was already in the first century A.D. a belief in the pre-existence of the Torah." Paul counters this belief. Mußner, 245, says that *added to*, in Paul's question at the beginning of 3:19, is adverbial, *Why was the law added?*, not as a predicative that inquires about the nature of the law.

276. Betz, 165; Schoeps, 182. Martyn, *Galatians*, 355-57, 364-70.

277. Cranfield, "Law," 46; Bruce, *Galatians*, 175; Schneider, *TDNT* 5:739-40; BDAG, 758.

278. Räisänen, *Paul* (1983), 140-1, 144.

279. Mußner, 246.

280. Duncan, 113.

281. Betz, 168, discusses the possible pre-Pauline tradition at work here.

terms of purpose and function.[282] His reference in 3:19b, a statement relating to the time of the giving of the law, is consistent with his view that to be under law until (i.e., before) Christ came (v. 24) was a negative, confining, and restraining state of existence.[283]

2.3.2.2. But if the law is subsidiary and temporary it is also inferior: it has not been given by direct revelation, but only indirectly through angels, by way of a mediator. Thus, 3:19d–e is in sharp contrast to 3:18c: *God* gave the promise to Abraham.

The tradition that angels attended the giving of the law is preserved in the LXX (but not in MT) version of Deut 33:2.[284] God would normally be the subject of *ordained/founded*,[285] but here Paul avoids speaking of God as law-giver or the law as revelation, and instead indicates the law as a mere ordinance,[286] in contrast to the gospel which was a revelation of Jesus Christ (1:12), and in contrast to the promise with which Abraham was *graced* (v. 18). It is also difficult not to see in the passive, *had been given*, of 3:21b, a reference to God as law-giver, and it is *God's* overarching plan in which an answer must be found for the place of the law (v. 21).[287] Paul does not say that the angels authored the law, that it was they who added it, nor that the angels were of either good or bad character.[288] Paul's point seems not so much to be that of disparaging the origin of law by denying divine authorship, but rather to contrast its inferior nature to the direct gift and revelation of gospel-promise.[289]

282. Betz, 166; Schoeps, 168.

283. Callan, "Midrash," this text is one of only two (2 Cor 3:7–18) wherein Paul cites the circumstances of the giving of the law in his argument against imposing the law on Gentiles; he cites the reference to angels in particular; the implicit references to the giving of law in the words, *added*, (3:19) and *came* (3:17) are also devaluing comments.

284. Duncan, 114: cf. Acts 7:38, 53; Heb 2:2; Jub 1; Josephus, *Ant* XV.136. Betz, 169 n. 63.

285. Dahl, "Contradictions," 173, especially n. 22.

286. Duncan, 113–14, also points out that in accord with Deut 8:3, only by the word of the Lord could one live, and so of the law, "Had it been a direct communication from God, it would have brought *life*, as experience showed that it did not." Mußner, 247.

287. Räisänen, *Paul* (1983), 132.

288. Hübner, 26–31, asserts that the demonic angels act with evil intention, contrary to God's will; it is in the *giving* of the law, not in law as such, that evil intention was expressed. See criticism by Räisänen, *Paul*, (1983), 131–3; Bruce, *Galatians*, 175. Lührmann, *Galater*, 63, recalls Paul's assertion, that not even an angel from heaven could change Paul's gospel as proclaimed to the Galatians (1:8). Sanders, *Paul* (1983), 67, notes that for Paul to deny divine authorship of the law would mean he must deny what he had been taught and believed all his life, "that God gave the law."

289. Sanders, *Paul* (1977), 550, suggests that Paul has here made an extreme statement in the heat of argument, but gives *soberer reflection* in Romans and Philippians 3;

The second way in which Paul here speaks of the inferior nature of the law is with the reference, *by the hand of a mediator*. The phrase may be an allusion to Ex 34:29. Moses came down from Mt. Sinai, for the second time, after the incident of the golden calf, *with the two tables of the testimony in his hand*. Moses is never spoken of as a mediator in the OT, but midrash developments did speak of him as such.[290] Paul here assumes knowledge of that tradition.[291]

The mediator to whom Paul refers is Moses.[292] Paul's phrase, *by the hand of a mediator*, corresponds to the saying, *through*, or *through the hand of*,[293] as in Ex 34:29.[294] But interpretation also depends on grammatical structure, because "meaning and structure are conditioned by one another."[295] What may be working in v. 20a is an example of "the stylistic figure of ellipse . . . a dominating word, which appears only once in a clause, will sometimes have to be supplied once more especially when the predicate has to be supplied from the subject or the subject from the predicate."[296] This text would then have to be analyzed as though it read: *Moses is the mediator, but the mediator is not just relative to one party*. Thus, v. 20a is an assertion about Moses. It is not a general statement about mediators. Then the definite article of v. 20a corresponds to Moses, who is the mediator of v. 19. The adversative particle, *now* (beginning of v. 20) marks a limitation in the mediating role of Moses: *(But)* the role of Moses as mediator is depreciated because he is a mediator *not of one*, that is, he does not represent a single individual but a plurality of angels. A missing link in the argument must therefore be supplied from the preceding, *ordained through angels*. We can understand the sentence to say: *the intermediary (i.e. Moses) is an intermediary not of one single person*

---

see also *Paul* (1983), 67. Räisänen, *Paul* (1983), 133, speaks of this as an ad hoc adaptation of Jewish tradition about angels at Sinai (see references in his n. 29), but it was an idea to which he did not return.

290. Callan, "Midrash," 550, 555-64.

291. Dahl, "Atonement," 153-54; "Contradictions," 169-74; Str-B 3:554-56; Schlier, *Galater*, 159-60; Callan, "Midrash," 555-64.

292. Mußner, 248. Lührmann, *Galater*, 63, also refers to Moses, who here is meant as the mediator; Betz, 170; Jeremias, *TDNT* 4:870; Oepke, *TDNT* 4:618-19.

293. Lohse, *TDNT* 9:430-1; Burton, *Galatians*, 189; Schlier, *Galater*, 155, 158-61; BDAG, 1082; Betz, 170.

294. Callan, "Midrash," 561, on Ex 34:29 the midrashic literature speaks of Moses as mediator. If Paul is alluding to Ex 34:29 he is speaking instrumentally, not locally; (Dahl, "Contradictions," 172); he equates Moses' (2nd) coming down the mountain with giving of the law, as 2 Cor 3:7-18.

295. Riesenfeld, "Mediator," 405; he cites Lightfoot, Zahn, Burton, Oepke, Schlier, Mußner.

296. Ibid., 407; for examples of ellipse in Paul, 410-12.

but of a plurality of angels. Paul's purpose is to focus on the contrast between law and promise: the promise was given to Abraham directly from God; the law was given indirectly by way of angels and an intermediary. This, not that Moses acted as a mediator, is the focus of thought here, and while Paul uses common Jewish tradition about angels attending the giving of the law, he *dissimulates the fact* that God gave the law to angels to give to Moses.[297] The argument uses the concept of oneness as expressing perfection and plurality as expressing imperfection: "anything that stands in contrast to the oneness of God is inferior."[298] Paul has taken material that his opponents knew and accepted, by which their positive attitude towards the law could be supported, and turned it against them to speak of the inferior nature of the law as contrasted to the promise given to Abraham and fulfilled in Christ, the Offspring.[299]

2.3.3. In 3:21-2 Paul denies that the law and the promises are truly opposed, because they serve different functions in different spheres. An affirmative answer might have been expected from 3:10 and on.[300] But the affirmative answer could only come if it were accepted that the law is able to do what Paul maintains is only the gospel's power and purview. Paul has said of the law that it: does not grant the Spirit (v. 5); brings curse (v. 10); does not justify (v. 11; cf. 2:16); does not rest on faith (v. 12); is that from which Christ redeemed us (v. 13); came 430 years after the promise (v. 17); does not annul the covenant of promise (v. 17); does not convey the inheritance (v. 18); was added to the human situation to produce transgressions (v. 19); lasted in rule only until Christ came (v. 19, 24); is inferior by virtue of not being direct revelation from God (v. 19d) and because of being mediated by Moses (v. 19e, 20).

The covenant of promise, on the other hand, reckoned righteousness to Abraham (v. 6), was the preaching of the gospel (v. 8), brought faith and blessing (v. 9), was fulfilled in Christ (v. 14, 16), includes the Gentiles (v. 14),

---

297. Ibid., 407-8.

298. Betz, 171-72; see his n. 85, regarding the *no intercessor* tradition of 1QH 6:13f; Riesenfeld, "Mediator," 407; Stauffer, *TDNT* 2:434-42; Deut 6:4; Eph 4:3-6; 1 Cor 8:6; BDAG, 292.

299. Moses was regarded as a divine man, especially in Hellenistic Judaism, because of his role as mediator. Betz, 170; Tiede, *Charismatic Figure*, 101-37; Riesenfeld, "Mediator," 409.

300. Burton, 192. Martyn, *Galatians*, 358, it is not an antithesis but an *antinomy* to distinguish God's promise and angel-generated law; 570, n. 79: "Throughout the present volume I use the term 'antinomy' in an idiosyncratic way, namely to render the numerous expressions by which the ancients referred (in many languages) to a pair of opposites that inheres in the *cosmos*—in Greek an *enantion*—an oppositional pair so fundamental to the cosmos, being one of its elements, as to make the cosmos what it is."

and was the vehicle of inheritance (v. 18). The law and promise, therefore, do entirely different things. Paul summarizes this thought in v. 21b: the law cannot make alive. If it could, *then* it would compete with the promise. It was *never* the purpose of the Torah to give life, according to Paul, and it is unable to do so.[301] Paul shifts in 3:22 to speak of *the Scripture*. The logic for this shift lies in the contrast just mentioned: blessing, Spirit, life, righteousness all belong to the side of faith, while curse, flesh, and death are all related to the law.[302] Therefore, the law cannot be a positive subject in the process of salvation. The role of law, here spoken of as Scripture, is to shut up all things under sin.[303] That this imprisonment *under sin* is a means to an end, subject to the rule of promise, is shown by the purpose clause in v. 22b, the end of which is in sharp contrast to *the unreal hypothesis of v. 21*.[304] The recipients of the promise, the members of the new age, are represented by *those who believe*.[305]

2.3.4. Galatians 3:23-9 is characterized by: *before* (v. 23); *but now* (v. 25); *you are* (v. 26, 29). There is a clear before and after, as the duration of the law's curse is ended by the revelation of faith (v. 23). Two periods of time are distinguished.[306] The former time was *under sin* (v. 22); *under law* (v. 23; cf. 4:4); *under guardians and trustees* (4:2); *under elements of the world* (4:3).[307] Although this guardianship may in itself be understood as a protective guard, its proximity to v. 19 and to imprisonment in v. 23,[308] as well as its belonging to the former time which was characterized by negative statements

---

301. Bultmann, *TDNT* 2:855, 874, Paul's view contradicts that of Judaism, that one lives by law, and the Torah is the tree of life; Lührmann, *Galater*, 64, notes that for Paul the connection to curse is not caused by his disobedience against the law; the law itself is not able to deliver righteousness. But Räisänen, *Paul* (1983), 128-54, notes that Paul oscillates on why God gave the law: was it meant to save or was it not?

302. Lührmann, *Galater*, 64.

303. Michel, *TDNT* 7:746; Schlier, *Galater*, 164 n. 2. Paul often speaks of law and Scripture as interchangeable or at least overlapping terms (Räisänen, *Paul*, 16; Bruce, *Galatians*, 180) and that the two are identified here is indicated by his assertion that Scripture (law) did not make alive; Rom 3:19.

304. Burton, 195. Compare the parallel purpose clause in v. 24.

305. There is similarity to Rom 10:4, if that verse means *termination*. Badenas, *End*, 118-20, asserts that Paul's view in Rom 10:4 and its context is that "the law led to Christ and Christ was the true *end* of the law." This would indicate Christ as the *goal* of the law. Paul could assert this in Romans, if law were not the contest for Gentile church membership, but it is not an appropriate scheme for interpreting Galatians.

306. Lührmann, *Galater*, 65. Betz, 175 n. 119.

307. Bruce, *Galatians*, 181.

308. Burton, 199.

about the law, give it here a restrictive sense.[309] There is a temporal meaning, *until*, regarding this imprisonment, similar to the temporal way Paul refers to the coming of Christ, *until* he came (v. 24).[310] The law's restrictive, rather than educational, nature is emphasized by *pedagogue*. The term relays the negative experience of being under the custodian.[311] The custodianship was a means, the end of which is parallel to that in the purpose clause of v. 22, even as the means is similar in both clauses. The purpose clause of v. 24, and the implicitly limited role of the *pedagogue* who functions only until the child reaches the age of majority, beyond the time of *minors* (4:1), relays the limited duration of the law's role. It ends with the coming of faith (v. 25, i.e. faith in Christ, as identified in v. 26). But is this an end for believers or for the cosmos?[312] The answer is in *the ones who believe* (v. 22) and the *we* (v. 25), for whom faith has come.[313]

Galatians 3:27 has the only reference to baptism in the epistle.[314] Galatians 3:27-8, could have come from an early Christian baptismal liturgy.[315] Both at their baptism and now in hearing the liturgy again, the Galatians will have noted that in form the text presents what numerous thinkers of their day understood: there is a table of certain pairs of opposites that were named and identified as the *elements*. These give to the cosmos its dependable structure. To pronounce the nonexistence of these opposites is to announce nothing less than the end of the cosmos.[316] Paul reminds the Galatians of their standing before God as members of the new age in which old contraries no longer prevail. The reference corresponds to 3:1-5, where he reminds them of their experience of beginning in the faith, and 3:27-8, the "decisive ceremony which made them members of the Christian

---

309. BDAG, 1067.

310. Burton, 200; BDF §474:5.

311. Burton, 200-201; Betz, 177; Bertram, *TDNT* 5:620-1; Oepke, *Galater*, 120-2; Schlier, *Galater*, 168-70; Lührmann, *Galater*, 65, says that the pedagogue was not such in our sense but was a slave who was responsible for discipline of a child for the sake of instruction, but who was not himself a teacher.

312. Betz, 179.

313. Stuhlmacher, "End," 143; Luz, *Geschichtsverständnis*, 157; Betz, 179.

314. Betz, 181.

315. Meeks, "Androgyne," 180, calls it a *baptismal reunification formula*; *Urban Christians*, 88: "The natural kinship structure into which the person has been born and which previously defined his place and connections with the society are here supplanted by a new set of relationships."

316. Martyn, *Galatians*, 376.

Church."[317] Unity in Christ is particularly pertinent in view of divisions that the law would sustain if imposed on Gentile converts.[318]

The argument about Abraham began in 3:6.[319] Paul cited the *inheritance* in 3:18 and closes the argument about Abraham in 3:29. He thus prepares us for the inheritance and sonship themes of Galatians 4 that come about with the end of the rule of law.

Summary

Sanders makes three comments about Galatians 3 that are helpful to this discussion.

1. Regarding the way in which *Paul chooses the quotations in Galatians 3*, Sanders points out that the argument is terminological, and therefore it depends on finding proof texts for Paul's view that Gentiles are justified by faith. Sanders sees Paul choosing the Abraham story for the purpose of linking *Gentiles* and *faith*. In that link Abraham is the middle term, connected to Gentiles in one proof-text (Gal 3:6/Gen 15:6) and righteousness by faith in another (Gal 3:8/Gen 18:18).[320] Deuteronomy 27:26 is the only LXX passage in which law and curse are connected, in the sense that law brings a curse.[321] It is questionable, however, whether Paul *chose* all of these texts. They likely were chosen for him, in the sense that his opponents used them and he had to respond. In fact, as Räisänen has pointed out, Deut 27:26 taken at face value is against Paul's point of view: *cursed is every one who does not abide*, would imply *not cursed is everyone who does abide*.[322] Paul does make use of the law–curse association, but he gives it his own theological interpretation: law and faith are exclusive of one another (3–12); Christ redeemed us by becoming a curse for us (3:13).[323]

---

317. Betz, 185.

318. Martyn, *Galatians*, 377: "Religious, social, and sexual pairs of opposites are not replaced by equality, but rather by a newly created unity."

319. Borgen, *Bread*, 48.

320. Sanders, *Paul* (1983), 21, says that Paul's major intention is to include Gentiles, and since the term *ethnē* does not appear in Gen 12:3, Paul uses 18:18, even though by so doing he must settle for the presence of *blessed* in 18:18 when the presence of *dikaioun* (*justify*) would have been better. Sanders, *Paul* (1983), 53 n. 24, 25.

321. Sanders, *Paul* (1983), 21, says that because of this connection and the priority for which Paul chose the text, the thrust of Gal 3:10 is borne by *law* and *cursed*, not by *all*.

322. Räisänen, *Paul* (1983), 95 n. 13.

323. Paul's Christian opponents could have argued that it is necessary to do the law in order to avoid curse. In response, Paul interprets Deut 27:26. But Christian opponents

2. Regarding the relationship of the argument of 3:10-12 and the proof-texts, Sanders rightly holds that Paul's theological position governs the use and interpretation of the texts.[324]

3. Sanders regards 3:10-13 as subsidiary to 3:8. The choice of Gen 18:18 to prove the justification by faith of the Gentiles includes the presence of *blessed*. This ". . . naturally leads to its opposite: cursed. Galatians 3:10, then announces the negative proof of the positive statement of 3:8."[325] Then to prove that no one can be made righteous by the law Paul quotes Hab 2:4. Faith excludes the law. Galatians 3:13 explains how God has provided for the removal of the curse. Galatians 3:14 summarizes the argument in chiastic fashion: the first purpose clause reiterates the positive part of 3:8, and the second purpose clause the positive assertion of 3:1-5. Paul makes Christ central as the one who became the curse in order to bestow the blessing on the Gentiles (3:13-14). Paul does not speak of God as having generated the curse. He omits *from God* and thus attributes curse to the inherent power of the law itself. He also uses common terminology to connect curse of the law and curse of the cross, thus attributing the death of Jesus on the cross to the cursing power of the law. To be under law is to be under curse. Paul links Gentiles and faith (Gen 15:6; 18:18) and law and curse (Deut 27:26). Paul does not explicitly say that the law caused the death of Christ. But he does lay the power to curse exclusively on the law. Even as he makes the law responsible for producing transgressions he also indicates law as the origin or cause of curse, and hence also in the death of Jesus. Law in Galatians is not the agent of sin, as it is in Romans; it is its source, even as law in Galatians is also the origin or source of curse. Since law, sin, and curse are aligned by Paul on the same side, we may understand him to indicate law as a cause of death, even as it is of curse and sin. In order to deal with the power sphere in which sin, curse, and death are members, Christ entered into that sphere, in order to die under the law, and dying, to redeem those under the law.

What then is the relation of this material to 2:19? We saw that Paul's statement about being crucified with Christ points to his being with Christ and dying with Christ when Christ died on his cross. Christ's death was through the curse-bringing, death-bringing power of the law, even as Paul

---

would not have used Deut 21:23. Paul's interpretation in Gal 3:13 may be a carry-over from established arguments against Jewish polemic. Kim, *Origin*, 46.

324. Sanders, *Paul* (1983), 54 n. 28; Betz, 144, notes that Paul "states his conclusions first." The meaning "is simply that exclusion from 'blessing' (cf. 6:16) equals 'curse.'" Schlier, *Galater*, 133. Sanders (22) sees that Paul's emphasis is not on the word *all*. The law for Paul does seem to be indivisible. The *all things* of Gal 3:10 can be present and true without being the decisive factor, as Sanders points out, 27-9.

325. Sanders, *Paul* (1983), 22.

also says of himself that he died *through law*. We could paraphrase Paul's thought, "I died to the law, through the law, inasmuch as I am united with Christ who also died under or because of the law." But Christ died under the law, having been under the law's curse, not because he deserved to be cursed for failure to keep the law, nor because he was in need of being redeemed from the law. Rather, Christ became like us although he was unlike us, so that we might become like him. The final part of this thought pattern therefore relates to Christ's own coming to be under the law, as Paul speaks of that in Gal 4:4. This verse is in the context of Paul's argument about inheritance and the sonship that become ours in Christ. Paul places this two-fold status in contrast to infancy and slavery, which come to an end with the end of the rule of law. The end of that rule of law allows for the new community.

4

End of the Law

4.1 Sons, not Slaves, Galatians 4:1-7

PAUL'S TWO-AEON THEOLOGY IS the proper context for interpreting his view of the law in Galatians. Galatians 6:14-15 represents Paul's two-aeon perspective, as the new creation is in contrast to the circumcision-uncircumcision distinction. The cruciform life is in contrast to Torah-based existence. Galatians 6:14-15 explicates Paul's previous statements in 4:1-11 about his understanding of all people together in the old aeon under law, and the sending of God's Son to be under law for the purpose of redemption and adoption into the status of sons. It is Christ's coming to be under law for this very purpose that is the turning point of the ages. In this final part we will first examine Paul's statements in 4:1-7 and then examine his summary statement in 6:14-15.

In Gal 4:1-7 Paul discusses implications of 3:26-8. He first uses an illustration from the practice of law (4:1-2), and then applies that comparison to the present situation of the Galatians (4:3-7). His conclusion in 4:7 connects this section to 3:29, which connects 4:1-6 with 3:1-28.[1]

1. Paul changes analogies in 4:1, from the prison-warden and custodian of 3:22-6, to the guardian and trustee of 4:2. The theme about *heirs* was used in 3:29, and is carried forward in 4:1.[2] The contrast in 4:1 is be-

---

1. Betz, 202; Martyn, *Galatians*, 392; Mußner, 276, notes that 4:7 does not say *minor*, but *slave*.

2. Bruce, *Galatians*, 192. Duncan, 125, says, "His new point is the positive one that even tutelage suggests a future period of emancipation . . ." Lührmann, *Galater*, 68, notes that in 4:1 Paul reaches back one more time to the example of inheritance in 3:15-17, a legal order of more Hellenistic than Jewish form, and yet he assumed it had convincing power for the Galatians. Paul's point is that in this time the heir has no right of disposal over himself and over his future position; he is stuck in the position of a slave.

tween two times or states of being, that of *infancy* (or *minority*, the *before*) and that of *heir* (the *after*).³ The key words in 4:1 are *heir, child, slave,* and *owner*, with *heir* corresponding to *lord* (NRS 4:1, *owners*), and *child* (NRS, *minors*) corresponding to *servant* (NRS, *slaves*), in an A-B-B-A pattern. The passing role of law is represented by the three terms *guardians, trustees* and (corresponding to them), *disciplinarian* (3:24), a role that held sway until the date/time fixed by the Father.⁴

The pre-Christian situation of minority applies to all believers. The application in 4:3 of the comparison made in 4:1-2 fits both Jewish and Gentile Christians, as indicated by Paul's shift to the emphatic *us*. Paul switches to the first person plural. The juxtaposition of *us* to the imperfects, *we were minors* and *we were enslaved*, and to the perfect passive, *(we were) enslaved* contrasts the time in which *we were* to the time now indicated in v. 4. The former time was characterized by the words, *minors... enslaved to the elemental spirits of the world*. The fullness of time (v. 4) is characterized by, *receive adoption as children*. To be under the custodianship (3:24) of the law, during the period of infancy (4:1, 3) meant enslavement to the *elements*. Thus, law and *elements* are lumped together as part of the old aeon, and the words, *under the law*, in 3:23 correspond to *enslaved to the elemental spirits* in 4:3.⁵ This is in contrast to the freedom through Christ, a theme implicitly introduced in 4:3, 5, 7.⁶ The common denominator of slavery under the *elements* was the pre-Christian condition of all believers, a time ended by the time of faith in the Christ-event, which corresponds to the revelation of 1:12, 16 and 3:23.⁷

---

3. Martyn, "Antinomies," 417; *Galatians*, (1997) 387, 570-4, 587.

4. Bertram, "νήπιος," the concept of childhood as a status to be left behind, and according to 4:1, 3 has already been left behind, is in tension with sonship as the supreme gift of the Spirit. We may note that Paul's point is perhaps as likely to be obscured as secured by inclusive language for *sonship*, which is granted to all, male and female (3:28) in the new age, while childhood is that which has been left in the past order. Martyn, 386, "Paul has no intention of implying that human beings have been God's sons all along, only waiting for the day of their majority. On the contrary, they have been actual slaves and have therefore to be made into sons ... Paul uses adoption into sonship to define liberation." For the *hapax legomenon*, (*set time*), Betz, 204 n. 20; Schlier, *Galater*, 189 n. 6. BDAG, 671.

5. Bruce, *Galatians*, 193; Davies, *Studies*, 237; Lührmann, *Galater*, 69, also notes the surprising replacement of the expected confinement under law (3:23), with confinement under the elements (4:3), with no middle step in the argument, since, although it is an idea that Paul has not clarified for his readers, "they know what is meant."

6. Betz, 202, 204.

7. Oepke, *Galater*, 129; Lührmann, *Galater*, 69. Martyn, *Galatians*, 370-2.

2. The word, *elements* (*stoicheia*), occurs in the NT at Gal 4:3, 9; Col 2:8, 20; Heb 5:12; 2 Pet 3:10.[8] Only the three references in Galatians and Colossians use the word together with *of the world*.[9] Of the various meanings that *elements of the world* could have, Burton offers four as worthy of consideration for this letter to the Galatians: (1) physical elements of the universe; (2) heavenly bodies; (3) spirits or angels; (4) elements of religious knowledge. Because the phrase is used in connection with the law, Burton concludes that it is to be understood as, "the rudimentary religious teachings possessed by the race."[10] But this interpretation does not adequately understand the elements as belonging to pairs of opposites that make up all things, that include opposition to the new being in Christ, and that no longer define life in the world for the believer, who now lives life in the flesh by faith in the Son of God (Gal 2:20). Only so can the elements be inclusive enough to be the elements of the world, against which Paul sets the new age, new creation, and life of faith.

The interpretation of *elements* in this passage should conform to the context, in which *world* is spoken of negatively, as that to which Paul has been crucified, and in which both Jew and Gentile were in bondage in their pre-Christian existence. The slavery of v. 3 refers to Jews under law, and the slavery of v. 9 refers to idol worshippers who had been enslaved (v. 8) to beings who were no gods. The *elements* in both v. 3 and v. 9 refer to that to which both groups were enslaved.[11] That Paul does not refer only to Gentiles and the former paganism of the Galatians is indicated by his connection of life *under the elements* and life *under the law*.[12] The elements to which the Gentile Galatians are in danger of returning are not the same as those to which they were formerly in bondage. The phrase is descriptive, and "denotes a category inclusive of those things to which the Galatians were enslaved and those to which they are now in danger of returning."[13]

---

8. Carr, 72. The Greek term translated as *elements* is στοιχεῖα (*stoicheia*). BDAG, 946.

9. Burton, 514; Delling, *TDNT* 7:683-87.

10. Burton, 510-15. Martyn, *Galatians*, 393-406; 394, cites four possibilities: fundamental principles, elemental substances, elementary spirits, heavenly bodies.

11. Burton, 516; Betz, 213-15: of the Galatians' past paganism Paul says they *did not know God*, a phrase likely from missionary language and rooted in the OT and in Hellenistic Judaism. See Betz, n. 7, 8.

12. Bruce, *Galatians*, 194. Martyn, *Galatians*, 393, the elements enslave, affect all human beings, and had some connection to the law, but God has terminated the slavery by sending the Son.

13. Burton, 517; Köster, *TDNT* 9:272: ". . .Paul uses the typical vocabulary of mission here . . ." As ignorance of God was equal to bondage to beings that were no gods so now acceptance of law would become as a return to slavery under the elements.

The actual situation in the pre-Christian existence of both groups was that Jews were under the law and Gentiles were under the beings that were not real gods:

> Paul cannot be thinking here in terms of explicit identification. Although paralleled with both, the *stoicheia* cannot simultaneously be the law and the beings ... The point of the parallel between the *stoicheia* and the law is perceived when one focuses on Paul's conviction that the plight of Jew and Gentile must be the same, since Christ saves all on the same basis. The common denominator is bondage and the equation of law and *stoicheia* is material. Thus Paul can go back and forth from "we" to "you" and also from pagan deities to the law. Everyone needs to be liberated from bondage by Christ. The argument that being under the law is the same as being under the *stoicheia* is driven home by the statement that both require the observation of special times: accepting the law is materially the same as resuming worship of beings which are not gods (4:10).[14]

And so the situations of Jew and Gentile, although different, melt together. Although Paul's reference to *law* means the Mosaic Law of Sinai, and parts of his argument are based on dating that law from the time of Moses (3:17, 19), he is thinking of something that concerns all people. Thus, the law assumes much wider dimensions.[15] Galatians 4:5–6 shows that Paul's thought locates the Gentiles under the law. Here Paul says that God sent the Son to redeem those who were under the law, seeming to refer to Jewish Christians. But he continues by saying that this happened *so that we* might receive adoption as sons. "Because *you* are children, *we* have received the Spirit."[16] *We* here clearly includes Gentile Christians. The whole force of Paul's argument is that the blessing of Abraham has come upon the Gentiles (3:14), this status is by faith in Christ (3:7), the blessing of Abraham was bestowed so that *we* might receive the promise of the Spirit (3:14), and both 4:5b and 4:6b correspond to that argument of inclusiveness. Paul works with a double sense of law, as "a historical and particularist Torah and ... a universal force."[17]

Bultmann, *Theology* 1:67.

14. Sanders, *Paul* (1983), 69; Fitzmyer, "Paul and the Law," 27. Jews and Gentiles were both subject to the law and to the *elements*. Reicke, "This World," 273; Howard, 78. By *no gods* Paul does not mean that they have no existence, but that they are demons rather than gods. See Deut 32:17. The demonological interpretation is supported by the identification of these beings with the elements. Betz, 215; Duncan, 133.

15. Räisänen, *Paul* (1983), 22.

16. Ibid., 21.

17. Ibid., 21.

As the Gentiles are under *law*, so Jews are under *the elements*. Paul includes himself in the plight of his readers when he says that *we* were enslaved under the elements (4:3), and *we* became sons when redeemed from under the law (4:5b). The Galatian Gentile Christians who as pagans had been under the *stoicheia* would turn again to bondage under *stoicheia* by submission to the Jewish law (4:9). Once having been slaves to the beings which were no gods, they would now become slaves to the elements by becoming slaves of the law. Subjection to Jewish law, represented also by calendar piety (4:10), is the same as a return to former bondage.[18] Paul thus associates their pre-Christian pagan existence and subjection to the elements with turning to the Torah. Paul's identification of being under the law with being subject to the elements corresponds to his aligning the law and the flesh. Paul has played on the word *flesh*, meaning at one time the physical flesh that was cut in circumcision, and at another time the power of evil and sin. He has played on the word law, as when he speaks of law as such, after generalizing from the specific practices of circumcision, table regulations, and calendar piety as conditions of life in the world under law. So when he speaks of the elements, which he aligns with law, the physical world is included, but the inclusion also of his reference to the beings to which the Gentiles were once subject indicates a realm greater than but including the physical. It is a demonized physical world.[19] The elements were in contention, and their *mighty strife* threatened the existence of the world and the soul after death. People lived in fear of the elements.[20]

The Jewish submission to Torah is associated with bondage to the elements.[21] A clue to this merging of Jewish and Gentile bondage may be seen in Gal 3:28. Just as in Christ the distinction from one another of the two groups has been eliminated, so also there was a previous common need: all were under bondage. Galatians 3:28 corresponds to what Paul says about the crucifixion of the world in 6:14. And yet Paul does not identify Torah with the elements: "Paul's point in Gal 4 is probably only the polemical one of suggesting that man's plight under the law is identical with his plight under the elements ... Paul's 'description of the human plight

---

18. Ibid., 21.

19. Schweizer, "Slaves," 455, argues that philological evidence from the literature of Paul's time indicates that the word, *stoicheia*, when used with *the world* refers to the basic four elements: earth, water, air, and fire.

20. Ibid., 466.

21. Hübner, 33, "A demonic and pagan character or power may be attributed to the elements of the world ... for the Jews something monstrous is being said: the function of the Torah is identical with that of the pagan deities."

varies, remaining constant only in the assertion of its universality."[22] The pre-Christian situation of Jew and Gentile, actually different with respect to the powers that controlled each group respectively, is viewed the same way from Paul's Christian law-free perspective: deliverance is for all, therefore all were under bondage, and to return to the law is to return to bondage.[23]

3. What makes the *time* of 4:4 complete, in contrast to the inadequate and rudimentary *elements*, is the coming of Christ. Deliverance from the rule of law and assumption of the role of sons marks the end of the age of infancy or minority, a purpose indicated by the two purpose (means-to-an-end) clauses in 4: 5. The double ends of the clause, *in order to redeem those who were under the law*, and *so that we might receive adoption as sons* are ends achieved by the one means to which the clause refers, *God sent his Son*. Paul has used the same term for redemption in 3:13 to describe Christ's work. In 4:5a the first purpose clause could, by itself, be taken to refer to Jewish Christians. And yet in 4:5b the second purpose clause includes all Christians. In the context of the letter's argument, the two clauses summarize the sequence of Gal 2:15—3:25, and 3:26–29.[24] "There is here the same sense of a pivotal event in history as there was in the statement about Christ's ransoming work in iii:13."[25] We note four things about the relation of 4:4 and 3:13.

---

22. Räisänen, *Paul* (1983), 23, quoting Sanders, *Paul* (1977), 474; Sanders, *Paul* (1983), 69.

23. Does the close connection in v. 3 of *when we were children* with subjection *to the elements* suggest *elementary teachings*? The adjectives, *weak* and *beggarly* are appropriate when used of a religious system, but not of heavenly bodies. Burton, 517, says that the contrast in v. 9 is to "the full truth of the revelation in Christ." What is common to the *elements* in both Colossians and Galatians is application to an imperfect type of teaching, to a relapse into a dogmatic system, as contrasted to the completeness found in Christ. According to Carr, 75–6, Paul may be thinking of a contrast between *elements* and *fullness*. The *fullness of time* in 4:4 corresponds *to the date set* by the Father, 4:2. Burton, 515, 518, suggests that in view of the way Paul refers to *elements* to apply to both Jews and Gentiles before faith in Christ, and speaks in ways indicating a two-aeon thought pattern, the word is best understood as *elements of religious knowledge . . . the rudimentary religious teachings possessed by the race*. Similarly, Carr, 75. But this definition of *elements* as religious teaching is too restrictive, as it does not adequately take into account that these are elements of *the world*, by which the citizen of the Graeco-Roman world likely understood something like, *those powers, dominions, and orders that make life in the world what it is*.

24. Betz, 208. Compare the double ἵνα (*hina, in order that*) clauses in Gal 3:14. Lührmann, *Galater*, 69: the first clause (in 4:5) repeats the expression of a slave's redemption from slavery to law (3:13), and the second clause corresponds to the comparison of the heir and status as a son (3:26).

25. Duncan, 128.

3.1. The emphasis in 4:4 is on the sending of the Son and the help from God that this sending brings.[26] Here Paul points to the true humanity of the Son, with terminology about birth by a woman that is terminology applicable to any and all humans.[27] The birth coincides with the sending for a mission, and this is reminiscent of Isa 49:1,5; Jer 1:5,7; Gal 1:15.[28]

3.2. That Jesus was sent to be *under the law* indicates that he was not only born a man amidst humanity, but was also born as a Jew who was obligated to observe the law.[29] The purpose of this sending, it could be thought, was that he might then win law-true Jews.[30] But being under the law meant that he was also under the elements of the world, and consequently was in solidarity with all human life.[31] Paul indicates that birth by a human mother and being put under law form "a definition of human life."[32] "The *nomos* has the function of serving as the sphere of enslavement for man. Man's existence before Christ is a state of *'being under the Law.'*"[33] Into this existence under the law the Son has been sent, born, therefore, into slavery.[34]

---

26. Betz, 207; Schlier, *Galater*, 196; Mußner, 270; Bruce, *Galatians*, 194–95, regarding both pre-existence and virginal conception of Christ. Paul indicates neither knowledge nor denial of a tradition of virginal conception of Jesus. Regarding sending for redemption, Oepke, *Galater*, 132–33, Mußner, 271–73; Bruce, *Galatians*, 194–96.

27. Schlier, *Galater*, 196; Bruce, *Galatians*, 195.

28. Bruce, *Galatians*, 196. *Sending* likely refers to the pre-existent state. Burton, 217; Phil 2:6.

29. Mußner, 270; Schlier, *Galater*, 196: It is not only Christ's nature but also his history that belongs to his humanity. The phrase *under law* may be Paul's addition to the pre-Pauline formula about the sending of the Son. Bruce, *Galatians*, 196. Schlatter, *Galater*, 106, notes that a woman gave Jesus life, and the law was his master.

30. Borse, *Galater*, 143.

31. Schlatter, *Galater*, 106; Mußner, 270. Martyn, *Galatians*, 390, "... God sent his Son ... into the malignant orb in which all human beings have fallen prey to powers inimical to God and to themselves."

32. Schweizer, *TDNT* 8:383: *born of woman* was used traditionally for all men. Mußner, 269. Betz, 207: the sense of the phrase is birth from a human mother, the conditions of human existence. Duncan, 129, notes that the assumption of human nature meant coming under law. In connection with 3:13 does 4:4 support viewing the law as a cause of the curse? Schweizer sees 4:4 as a development of 3:13. Betz reads Schweizer to say that 3:13 is a development of 4:4, and does not think this plausible. But Schweizer speaks of 3:13 as the outgrowth of an earlier tradition of the sending of Jesus in terms of the incarnation, here developed by Paul as a statement of the sending in terms of substitutionary death on the cross (3:13b), further developed in 4:4. Harvey, 11:35, 21–5. Paul presses the traditions of the *sending* and *redemption* into his argument against the law.

33. Mußner, 255, points out that the phrase *under law*, with the accusative rather than the genitive, means the sphere or dominion of law. Lightfoot, *Galatians*, 168.

34. Borse, *Galater*, 143. See Phil 2:7.

3.3. This being born under the law is here the same as becoming a curse, for with the mention of Christ's placement under law, Paul makes a connection with the context of his entire argument, in which promise is contrasted to law, blessing is contrasted to curse, and law and curse are placed together on the same side of things.[35] What it meant for Jesus to be under the law Paul has already spelled out in Gal 3:13.[36] The similarity of thought between 3:13-14 and 4:4-5 is paralleled by the similarities in structure.[37] The participle, (*being* or *having been*) *born*, is in both 3:13 and 4:4, relating to Christ's becoming a curse, becoming human, and becoming (or getting) under law.[38] The verb for redemption by Christ refers to his redeeming from the curse (3:13) those under law (4:5).[39] Parallel dependent purpose clauses show the results of Christ's becoming curse, human, and under law.[40] The promise of the Spirit is received by faith (3:14), as righteousness is by faith (3:11; 2:16). The Spirit is sent by God (4:6), as God sent the Son (4:4).[41]

3.4. Redemption from under the law is redemption from the curse of the law and bondage to the elements.[42] Christ frees all people for whom adoption as a son is effective by faith in him.[43] Here Paul develops a traditional line of thought about the sending of the Son for the purpose of redemption.[44] The sending of the Son is the arrival of the new age, "the nodal point of salvation history . . . the divinely ordained epoch for the people of God to enter into their inheritance."[45] The contrast between the old and the new is emphasized in 4:7: those who have received the status of adoption and the Spirit are no longer slaves but sons, and if sons then heirs.[46] This sta-

---

35. Betz, 151; Kramer, 25; Bruce, *Galatians*, 196. Mußner, 270.

36. Lührmann, *Galater*, 69; Schlier, *Galater*, 196; Schlatter, *Galater*, 106; Oepke, *Galater*, 133.

37. Hooker, "Interchange," 352.

38. Betz, 150 n. 121, cites analogous formulations.

39. Büchsel, *TDNT* 1:126-28.

40. Lightfoot, *Galatians*, 140, 168.

41. Barrett, *Freedom*, 113 n. 29, 114 n. 38.

42. Bruce, *Galatians*, 196.

43. Borse, *Galater*, 144. Martyn, *Galatians*, 390, notes that *adoption* in 4:5 is "a term consistently used in Paul's time to refer to the event of adoption as a son (not the abstraction 'sonship')."

44. Schweizer, *TDNT* 8:374; Rom 8:3; John 3:16, 17; 1 John 4:9.

45. Bruce, *Galatians*, 194. Hooker, "Interchange," 351-52, notes that this interchange involves Christ entering into our experience in order that we might enter into his. The structure of 4:4 is parallel to 3:13.

46. Martyn, *Galatians*, 391, for *you are sons* in 4:6: "Does Paul here rescind the formula of 3:28 with its affirmation of the erasure of sexual distinctions in Christ? No. He uses the words 'sons' inclusively in order to draw the link between God's Son and

tus of sons, or inheritance, is not by law but by promise (3:18). The contrast is sharpened by Paul's use of a verb similar to the noun (*stoicheia*), *elements*, to indicate the new life: *let us also walk* (*stoichomen*) by the Spirit (5:25); peace and mercy be upon *all who walk* (*stoichēsousin*) by this rule (6:15). Being subject and in bondage to the elements (*stoicheia*) is in opposition to living, walking, or corresponding (*stoicheo*) to the characteristics of the new age.[47]

4.2 Paul's Summation, Galatians 6:14-15

Galatians 6:14-15 is within the postscript of the letter and, "... serves as the *peroratio* or *conclusio* ... It contains the interpretive clues to the understanding of Paul's major concerns in the letter as a whole and should be employed as the hermeneutical key to the intentions of the Apostle."[48] Galatians 6:14 may thus be seen as a summary of Paul's position, and v. 15 states the consequences of v. 14. Paul speaks of 2 different worlds in Gal 6:14-15. The old world is that from which Paul has been separated by a three-fold crucifixion (6:14). The new world is that of which Paul speaks when he refers to the new creation (6:15b).[49]

1. The three crucifixions to which Paul refers pertain to Christ, the world, and Paul himself.[50] The latter two proceed from the first, and the first rules out *glorying* in either the world or the self. Paul glories (or, *boasts*) only in the cross of Christ (6:14a). By crucifixion of the world Paul does *not* mean: (1) the heavens, earth, or physical universe; (2) the earth as the stage of human history or the home of humankind; (3) outsiders to a religious

---

God's family, the members of which are sons by being incorporated into the Son."

47. The present Jerusalem corresponds to Hagar and Mt. Sinai in Arabia (4:25). The Hagar–Sarah contrast in 4:21-31 serves the same pattern of pairs of opposites and of two aeons, discontinuous with one another. Martyn, "Antinomies," 418; Minear, "World," 399; Barrett, "Allegory," 164: Paul places Hagar, the slave woman, in the same category as Mt. Sinai, the place of the giving of the law. Both are in contrast to law-free Christian Isaacs.

48. Betz, 313.

49. Martyn, "Antinomies," 412; *Galatians*, 381-82, the new creation is, "the eschatological family ... the new-creational community that God is calling into being in Christ ... The church, in short, is a family made up of former Jews and former Gentiles ... For the old pairs of opposites are not discrete sins to be washed away or simply renounced. They are the basic building blocks of a cosmos from which one is now painfully separated by death."

50. Minear, 396.

community; (4) the realm of sin, death, or unredeemed creation.[51] What he *does* mean is something similar to *sarx (flesh)*.[52]

By crucifixion of his own self Paul seems to assert that the same is true for every believer. Paul's experience is a paradigm for all believers, and here he speaks to those who have not yet realized that crucifixion of their world and of self are realities derived from the crucifixion of Christ, even though they had expressed faith in Christ.[53] The derivation of the crucifixions of the world and the self from the crucifixion of Christ is implicit in the verb, *crucified*, in 6:14b:

> The tense of the verb is perfect: though occurring in the past, presumably at the time of Christ's death, that past action still determines the present situation. The voice of the verb is passive: the two entities (the kosmos, I) have been acted upon. Neither the world nor the self has initiated its own crucifixion.[54]

Galatians 6:12–13 shows that for people to whom the world has not yet been crucified, circumcision (and so, the law) retains its earlier significance. Galatians 6:11–16 provides a composite profile of the *kosmos* that has been crucified to Paul: (1) this *kosmos* is characterized positively by a reliance on circumcision, the flesh, the law, and the covenant community which

---

51. Ibid., 403–4.

52. Oepke, *Galater*, 203. Luther, *Galatians*, 249, took crucifixion to the world to mean *hatred of the world*. This does not explain what *world* means. Minear, 395, 397: "... the crucifixion of the world is an event that marks the total devaluation of both circumcision and uncircumcision. Kosmos is a realm where people set a high value on those distinctions. It is in the destruction of those distinctions that the new creation emerges. Where *kosmos* ends, καινὴ κτίσις (*kainē ktisis, new creation*) begins. The two are mutually exclusive realities." See Jewett, *Terms*, 101, for σάρξ (*sarx, flesh*). Sasse, 885–93, notes that κόσμος (*kosmos, world*) refers not just to the universe as the sum of all created things, but to the world now estranged from its creator, and therefore the early Church did not use the word for the eternal world of eschatological hope. In Paul it is identified with this age. In Gal 6:14 it is the epitome of unredeemed creation. Burton, 514, refers to *kosmos* as, "The mode of life which is characterized by earthly advantages, viewed as obstacles to righteousness: Gal 6:14." For Paul, the advantages to which he was crucified included Israelite descent, circumcision, rank and dignity as a Pharisee, and righteousness in the law. In 6:14 the first person singular pronoun (*I, me*) is emphatic by position: Paul's ground for *boasting* or *glorying* was in *the central fact of his gospel*, the cross, in contrast to his Judaizer opponents, whose basis was in the flesh. *Flesh* and *world* inform one another in 6:12–14, and this *world* informs the use of *stoicheia*.

53. On Paul as a paradigm, Eichholz, 224; Betz, 122. Minear, 396.

54. Minear, 396. We note the similarity to the verb in 2:19; relating *crucified* to *the time of Christ's death*, gives the death of Christ a representative quality, similar to that expressed in 2 Cor 5:14: *one has died for all, therefore all have died*. This interpretation sheds light on *I have been crucified with*, in 2:19. Cousar, 61.

was bound by those standards; (2) this *kosmos* is constituted negatively by its opposition to new creation, avoidance of persecution for the sake of Christ, and rejection of *the Israel of God* that walks by this rule.[55] The Israel that Paul means in 6:16 is to be identified with the new creation. It is not continuous, but is discontinuous, with the Israel of Judaism.[56] Accordingly, "... in the new creation the boundary between Jew and Gentile has been obliterated. We can safely infer that wherever that boundary becomes obsolete, the sovereignty of that *kosmos* has been terminated."[57]

2. Between his references to the old cosmos (6:14b) and the new creation (6:15b) Paul places a statement about circumcision, "the sign par excellence of observance of the Law."[58] The neither–nor statement in v. 15a is of the same form as Gal 5:6 and 1 Cor 7:19, both of which texts negate any significance to either *circumcision* or *uncircumcision*. Since there is no necessary validity to either of these categories, "... that to which Paul denies real existence is, in the technical sense of the expression, *a pair of opposites*, what Aristotle might have called an instance of (*the contraries*)."[59] It was a widely held belief in the ancient world that such pairs of opposites were the fundamental building blocks of the cosmos. This is the pattern of thought that Paul seems to presuppose in these verses. This pattern was likely known in some form by the Galatians. The use that Paul makes of this theory is to deny real existence to a pair of opposites in order to emphasize that the old cosmos has suffered its death. Paul has frequently spoken of pairs of opposites throughout the letter. These include the God–human pair in 1:1 and 1:10, flesh–cross in 6:13–14, flesh–Spirit in 3:3 and 5:16–24, law–faith in 3:2–4 (see 2:16), opposing adverbs, *Gentile-like, Jew-like* in 2:14, and opposing datives in 2:19.[60] In 6:13–16, however, Paul asserts that the world defined by the pair, circumcision–uncircumcision, has been crucified to Paul and Paul to it. Three other examples of literature show reference to pairs of opposites as fundamental to ancient world cosmology.

---

55. Minear, 398.

56. Davies, *Paul* (1948), 119, shows that the concept of new creation is rooted in Judaism and rabbinic thought, where it refers to making a proselyte for Judaism. Although this may be the source of Paul's terminology, he uses it in Gal 6:16 as the antithesis of circumcision, and hence *not* for the sake of continuity with old Israel.

57. Minear, 399. The Greek term is τὰναντία (*ta[a]nantia*).

58. Martyn, "Antinomies," 413. The issue in 6:13–16 is the Galatians' willingness to accept circumcision.

59. Ibid., 413.

60. Ibid., 414, 423 n. 15.

2.1. Aristotle spoke of the *the contraries* in describing the polarities that constitute existence.[61] This Pythagorean theory holds that these contraries are both, (1) the first or fundamental principle, by which life is governed, and (2) the matter of which things are made.[62] Aristotle lists ten principles, recognized by the Pythagorean philosophers as a series of *corresponding pairs*.[63] Heraclitus also spoke of opposites, which in their combinations formed the world's unity. Because of cosmic justice dominating all things, the strife between the opposites never issues in the complete victory of one over the other. The world's unity results from this diversity, as opposites continue in tension.[64] These *contraries* are first principles, that upon which the nature of all other things is modeled. First among such principles are numbers. The *elements* of the numbers are assumed to be the elements of everything. The *stoicheia* are the particular sides of the contraries and a series of corresponding pairs was called *sustoichian*.[65]

2.2. Philo of Alexandria also speaks of both human nature and the nature of the universe as being mixed and constituted of opposing powers. In the case of the human soul the opposites vie with one another for control, and the soul that attains to the characteristics of the positive side gains immortality:

> Into every soul at its birth there enter two powers, the salutary and the destructive... These powers are not to be identified with the two chief powers or attributes of God... They correspond more closely to the good and evil cosmic powers, identified with good and bad angels (or demons) respectively... But the nation is a mixture of both (these powers), from which the heavens and the entire world as a whole have received this mixture...[66]

Furthermore, Philo comments on Gen 15:10, and maintains that Scripture teaches this theory of the composition of the world: "... the Scripture leads us on to the knowledge of opposites, by telling us that `He placed the

61. Aristotle, *Metaphysics* I:986a.

62. Ross, I:142. This double nuance may apply to *elements* (στοιχεῖα, stoicheia) in Gal 4:3, 9. The key is elements *of the world*.

63. The list of ten paired opposites includes: limit–unlimited; odd–even; one–plurality; right–left; male–female; at rest–in motion; straight–crooked; light–darkness; good–evil; square–oblong.

64. Russell, 60–3; Kirk and Raven, 190–1, 240–1. The patriarchal order of the gods also reaffirms itself through its opposite. Burkert, 219. On the fear–producing tension of the opposites see Schweizer, "Slaves," 466–68, and "Versöhnung," 493–97.

65. Aristotle, 1–3; 24, στοιχεῖα (the sides of the contraries); συστοιχίαν (series of pairs of contraries)

66. Philo, *Exodus*, 23.

sections facing opposite each other' (Gen xv.10). For in truth we may take it that everything in the world is by nature opposite to something else."[67] He lists some of the opposites, including corporeal–incorporeal; living–lifeless; mortal–immortal; beginning–end; life–death; justice–injustice; law–lawlessness. Philo explains: "... the two opposites together form a single whole, by the division of which the opposites are known."[68] Philo also asserts the priority of Moses to Heraclitus on this teaching: "... it was Moses who long ago discovered the truth that opposites are formed from the same whole, to which they stand in the relation of sections or divisions."[69] Philo relates the positive side of moral opposites to life, the negative side to death:

> "Behold, I have given before thy face life and death, good and evil (Deut XXX.15)." Accordingly, thou wisest of Teachers, goodness and virtue is life, evil and wickedness is death. Again, elsewhere: "This is thy life and length of days, to love the Lord thy God (Deut XXX.20)." This is a most noble definition of deathless life, to be possessed by a love of God and a friendship for God with which flesh and body have no concern.[70]

Philo here makes use of the Pythagorean tradition of opposites, ascribes it to Moses, and uses it in the exposition of Scripture.[71]

2.3. The same cognizance of opposites is found in the Old Testament. The light and darkness of Gen 1:3–5 are both the results of God's creative work (Amos 5:18–20). Amos 3:6 ascribes evil to God's doing and a similar thought occurs in Job's response to his wife's advice to curse God and die: "Shall we receive good at the hand of God, and shall we not receive evil?" (2:10b; see 42:11). These two pairs occur together in Isa 45:7: "I form light and create darkness, I make weal and create woe, I am the Lord, who do all these things." The passage (44:24—45:13) tells of the commission of Cyrus, the Lord's *anointed*.[72] Although not a member of the covenant people, Cyrus is an instrument in God's hands, whom God will surely give success: "I gird you, though you do not know me" (45:56). Cyrus, a non-believer, as well as both good and evil, are seen here by the prophet as subject to God's supremacy: "In Israelite thought nothing, not even evil and darkness, could be

---

67. Philo, *Heir?*, 207.
68. Ibid., 213.
69. Ibid., 214.
70. Philo, *Flight*, 58.
71. Wolfson, *Philo*, 1:334.
72. Hebrew (MT), משיח (*mashiach*, messiah); Greek (LXX), χριστός (*christos*, christ, anointed one*); Isa 45:1.

removed from the dominion of Yahweh."[73] The work of Cyrus is a manifestation of God's power, and history itself is a mingling of light and darkness, good and evil, all reflecting God's creative power and God's will. Israel's view of life and life's mixture of opposites are lodged in Israel's thoroughgoing monotheism.[74] For Israel the pairs of opposites are real and under God's reign.

3. This theory of pairs of opposites was widespread in the ancient world. Paul uses it in a very specific way: the old cosmos has been crucified; life can no longer be defined in terms of the old pairs of opposites. New pairs now prevail. Paul's teaching at this point is *not* about the failure of Judaism, but about the death of the world, whose old structures are gone for believers in Christ. Among the Galatian churches the old definitional structure whose demise Paul asserts is the particular pair of opposites, circumcision–uncircumcision. Galatians 3:27-8 and the pairs contained there can also be seen in this same way: the old world had pairs of opposites, but the New Creation, marked by anthropological unity in Christ, is not defined in the same old way.[75] That is, the new world does not have the *same* pairs of opposites. And yet there are certain pairs of opposites that not only have not departed, but which were established by God's new creative act in Christ. In Gal 5:16-17 Paul speaks of Spirit and flesh as corresponding to the new aeon and old aeon, respectively. In 5:17 he speaks specifically of flesh and spirit, and says that *these* (emphatic) are *against* one another. He twice uses a preposition (*kata* with genitive means *against*) to declare that each of the two powers is against the other, and then he strengthens his statement the third time with a verb that implicates an enemy: the two are *opposed*. That is, Spirit and flesh are opposed, not law and flesh.[76] It may be conjectured that Paul's opponents

---

73. McKenzie, 77.

74. Bright, 24: "Whether the Israelite ... denied that other gods existed is a point that has occasioned much debate." For our purposes the question need not be settled. No pantheon surrounded Yahweh. Yahweh created without assistance or intermediary and alone rules over *all*. McKenzie, 78; Westermann, 161-62.

75. Martyn, "Antinomies," 415. See Gal 3:28.

76. Schweizer, *TDNT* 6:424-31, notes that *spirit* signifies the new existence, the new existence is related to the Redeemer, and it is not merely the preliminary sign of what is to come but is new existence as such. He also notes that: (1) *spirit* is in contrast to *flesh*, 3:3; (2) *flesh* is parallel to *by works of law*, 3:2,5, while *spirit* parallels *by hearing with faith*; (3) *the one born according to the flesh* is contrasted/opposed to the one who is *through promise*, 4:23, 29; (4) the person is the battlefield of the two powers, 5:17; (5) *love* is life in the Spirit, which is life freed from the *flesh*; it is *faith* at work, 5:6; (6) to live *according to the Spirit* is to live in freedom from *law*, and wholly by *Christ*, *grace*, *cross*, 5:19-23; (7) *flesh* (5:13,16), *law* (5:2-4, 18), *circumcision* (5:6, 11), *slavery* (5:1), interpret one another on one side, while *spirit* (5:5, 16-18), *Christ* (5:2-4), *grace* (5:4), *cross* (5:11) *love* (5:6, 13) *freedom* (5:1, 13) interpret one another on the other side.

had been teaching that the evil impulse must be opposed and checked by the law. For them the fleshly impulse and the law would have constituted a pair of opposites, with the law as the antidote to the evil impulse.[77]

Not every branch of early Christianity came under influence by Paul, and subsequent to him there were churches that had not done away with works, did not trust their salvation to faith alone with the same energy as he had, and had not undergone a radical break with Judaism. The letter of James may have originated on such soil, in which such thought and literature the law is seen as the means for overcoming the evil impulse or the flesh.[78] Then James belongs in the broad category of wisdom teaching for which the person who attains wisdom is the person who observes the law. Such a person is the one who overcomes the fleshly impulse, or evil inclination. The person who overcomes the (*yeser, impulse*) is "above all a doer of the law, which is the law of freedom from the *yeser* (1:22–5)."[79]

For Paul it is the Holy Spirit that is opposed to the flesh. There is nothing distinctively Christian about the usage here (nor throughout the NT) of *spirit*, *except* that it is related to Jesus Christ, and the pattern of death and resurrection. As such the Spirit becomes the instrumentality of right conduct and of life, and to walk by the Spirit (Gal 5:16) or to be led by the Spirit (5:18) stands in opposition to walking, living, or being according to the flesh. Orientation to the flesh is signified by circumcision (5:3). It is to be *under the law* (5:18). Flesh and spirit are contrasting powers, demonic and divine, respectively.[80] The fleshly impulse is opposed not by the law, but by the Spirit. The flesh and the law are a pair of opposites of the old order, not a pair that has totally disappeared but that has been realigned so as to stand together opposed by the Spirit.[81]

For Paul the new age is characterized by the three connected realities of the Son, the Spirit, and faith. When the time of the rule of law had come to its completion, according to God's discretion, then God sent the Son (4:4). Corresponding to this decision, *God sent the Spirit of his Son* (4:6),

---

Therefore, Schweizer, 424, says: "... the event which had been the decisive stumbling-block for Paul could now be regarded as the decisive event of salvation. This was the cross." Schlier, *Galater*, 250.

77. Martyn, "Antimonies," 416.

78. Dibelius, *James*, 118–19.

79. Marcus, 620, regarding יצר (*impulse*). Martyn, "Mission." The roots of this concept are in Rabbinic theology, which speaks of God creating the evil impulse and then giving the law as an antidote, so that the words of the law are likened to a medicine of life. *Baba Batra* 16a, *Kiddushin* 30b; Montefiore and Loewe, 295–96.

80. Meyer, 4, 5, 11.

81. Martyn, "Antimonies," 416.

with the double action of God and the relation of Spirit to the Son signified by the repeated use of the same verb.[82] The role of the law was only *until faith should be revealed* (3:23), and the revealing of faith corresponds to the coming of Christ. This again indicates that when he says, *faith*, Paul means faith in Christ.[83]

The presence of the Spirit and of faith are connected to the coming of Christ, that is, to God's new creative act in the Son.[84] The opposition of Spirit to flesh is grounded in this *new* creative act, *not* in God's creative act at the beginning.[85] Paul shows a discontinuity with what has gone before, as Christ is "the God-given alternative to everything that has gone wrong since Adam."[86] Paul's thinking at this point is of a piece with apocalyptic theology, wherein God's future could only be discontinuous with the present (old) order.[87] The theme of two aeons therefore becomes fundamental, as the present order is not hospitable to divine presence, God is radically transcendent, and knowledge of God and the true situation depends on apocalypse, on revelation as alternative and disjuncture.[88] Paul can therefore say that for Gentiles to accept circumcision, and so be obligated to obey the whole law (5:3), amounts to a relapse to the former situation of bondage that was characteristic of the human situation *before faith came* (3:23). Beker sees Paul's gospel as apocalyptic "because it looks forward to the final triumph of God in Christ over all those powers . . . that resist his redemptive purpose."[89] Keck responds,

> Suffice it to say that Paul's theology . . . is apocalyptic not because it includes "vindication, universalism, dualism and

---

82. Burton, 216-17, 221; Rengstorf, *TDNT* 1:406.

83. Galatians 3:24 reads, *to/unto Christ*, the sense of which is governed by the preposition *before* (πρό, *pro*) in v. 23, and *no longer* in v. 25. Note the word order of the Greek text in 3:26; NRS reads, *for in Christ Jesus you are all children of God through faith*; the Greek order is, *for you are all children of God through faith in Christ Jesus*. Räisänen, *Paul* (1983), 57; Betz, 178.

84. Theißen, *Aspects*, 260-4, 353 n. 1, 385.

85. Martyn, "Antinomies," 416.

86. Keck, "Apocalyptic," 234.

87. Martyn, *Galatians*, 563. "Paul redefines the word 'boast,' so that, in his case, it does not mean what it means in the case of the Teachers . . . the ground of Paul's boast is not some accomplishment of his own. That ground is rather an event that happened apart from him—Christ crucified (3:1)." See Paul's use of καυχᾶσθαι (*kauchasthai*, boast) in Gal 6:14.

88. Keck, 234-37.

89. Beker, *Apocalyptic*, 19. Käsemann, "Apocalyptic," 109 n. 1, primitive Christian apocalyptic is "the expectation of an imminent Parousia," unchanged even by extension to the future because of disappointed hopes.

imminence"—some of these categories apply also to other theologies—but because it shares with apocalyptic theology the perspective of discontinuity. Over against all theologies which see continuity between God and world (whether focused on nature or on the history of a people) Paul sees disjuncture. God and the redemptive future stand over against the world and its history, including the history of Israel (Rom 9–11) and the future of the church (1 Cor 10:1–22).[90]

Paul's unique and creative grasp of the meaning of the Christ event transformed Christian tradition and experience, as well as former apocalyptic theologies. He saw the dawn of the new creation in God's sending of the Son. In Gal 3:23 Paul connects the coming of faith with the revealing of faith, even as he previously spoke of the revealing of the Son (1:16) in contrast to his own former life (1:13–14). Even so the cosmos in which Paul previously lived met its end in the apocalypse of Jesus Christ (1:12, 16; 6:14). This apocalypse was also the birth of Paul's gospel mission (1:16), in which he asserted that flesh, law, and bondage are aligned together, in opposition to Spirit, the Son, and faith.[91] The law is not arraigned against the flesh, but is aligned with it, and therefore also with death. This is the context and summary for what Paul means when he says in Gal 4:4 that Christ was born under law. It was bound to bring death to him, even as the law brought death to Paul (2:19).

Summary

In Gal 4:1–11 Paul uses guardian and trustee terminology, parallel to the custodian and prison warden of 3:22–6, to speak of that from which the believer is free. The believer, or heir, has come of age and with the sending of Christ and giving of the Spirit has received the full inheritance. The common situation of Gentiles under the elemental teachings and Jews under the law has ended with the passing of the old aeon. Believers now know God in Christ and have gained the status of sons through him. Paul argues that we were slaves to the elements as long as we were children and slavery was dependent on being children. We were children until the time set by the

---

90. Keck, "Apocalyptic," 241. Beker, *Apocalyptic*, 30–53, speaks of vindication, universalism, dualism, and imminence as, "The Basic Structure of Paul's Apocalyptic Gospel." But none of these categories distinguish the new era from the present age, as Keck's view more appropriately does.

91. Martyn, "Antinomies," 417; Keck, "Apocalyptic," 241; Minear, "World," 406.

father. That time has been fulfilled with God's sending the Son to be fully human, under the condition of law.

Galatians 4:4 and 3:13 can be understood together. The law brings curse to those who would live by it (3:10) even as it brought curse to Jesus, who became a curse (3:13). For Jesus to be born as a human being meant he was under the condition of law (4:4). To be under the law meant for him to become (to embody) a curse. This three-fold description, *born* (or *became*) *of woman, born/became under law, became a curse* indicates both the nature of human life in the world and the character of the law's work. When Christ redeemed us from the curse it was redemption from the law and freedom from the elements to which we were formerly subject. The elements have to do with the old world.[92] To that world Paul has been crucified: he is dead to it and free from it. The era of the rule of the law is over for those who have died to the law and are crucified with Christ (2:19; 6:14–15).

In Gal 6:14–15 Paul speaks of the crucifixion of the world to him, and of himself to the world, as realities proceeding from the crucifixion of Christ. By crucifixion of the world Paul means the old world as characterized by circumcision and the flesh. Behind Paul's neither–nor statement in 6:15a lies his short list of pairs of opposites in 5:6. This common ancient view of defining the world by pairs of opposites is a device Paul uses to explicate his view that the old aeon has ended in the Christ-event, and with it has also ended all necessity of imposing the law on those who are in Christ. Paul points to a radical discontinuity between the old world and the new creation, and between law, flesh, circumcision on the one side, and Christ, faith, and freedom on the other. In the sense of this discontinuity between old and new, Paul's gospel is apocalyptic.

Paul's crucifixion to the world (6:14) corresponds to his dying to the law (2:19). Paul's dying to the world was included in the event of Christ's cross. It was Christ's cross through which (6:14) Paul's crucifixion to the world also occurred, and in which Paul's death to law was also included. Christ's cross, by which the rule of the old world, law, and flesh came to an end, was an inclusive event: in it, or by it, Paul also died to the law and to the world. Galatians 6:14 thus informs our understanding of *crucified with* and dying *to the law* in 2:19.

---

92. Reicke, "Law," 259–65. Reicke, 262, would identify the elements of 4:3, 9 with the angels of 3:19. But it is likely that Paul simply established distance between God giving the promise directly and the law given indirectly.

5

Sacrifice and Deliverance in Galatians 1:4

5.1. He Gave Himself, Galatians 1:4a

GALATIANS 1:4 IS THE middle part of Paul's salutation and doxology in 1:3–5. The verse has a significant message in and of itself, with three clauses that each relay a particular aspect of 1:4 as a whole. But the verse does not stand on its own. It occurs amidst an extended theological statement that commences with the *grace and peace* formula in 1:3 and ends with a doxology and *amen* in 1:5. In this way the prescript in Galatians differs from that of other letters. Romans, 1–2 Corinthians, Philippians, 1 Thessalonians, and Philemon all *end* the salutation with the *grace and peace* formula. But Galatians uses the *grace and peace* greeting to *commence* the clauses of 1:4 that are clearly doctrinal, have theological emphases that vary from one clause to another, and enable foresight of the letter's message as a whole. The extended statement then ends with the *doxology* and *amen* in 1:5, and concludes the prescript that opens the letter (1–5).[1] The *grace and peace* pronouncement of 1:3, as in other letters, mentions and thereby clearly distinguishes the personages of *the Lord Jesus Christ* along with *God our Father*.[2]

Galatians, however, is alone among Paul's epistles in that it proceeds after the salutation with no thanksgiving![3] The short doxology replaces the

---

1. Betz, 43, language of doxology, "must have originated in liturgical contexts of a Jewish background." Kittel, *TDNT* 2, 247, 250, speaks of δόξα (*doxa*, glory) as "the divine mode of being—Participation in δόξα, whether here in hope or one day in consummation, is participation in Christ." BDAG, 257.

2. Rom 1:7; 1 Cor 1:3; 2 Cor 1:2. Betz, 40, calls *grace and peace* "a form of prayer." Furthermore, 41 n. 48, "The acclamation 'Lord [is] Jesus Christ' (Κύριος Ἰησοῦς Χριστός) is reflected here." Cf. 1 Cor 12:3; Phil 2:11; Rom 10:9; Cullmann, 195; Hahn, *Titles*, 68; Kramer, *Christ*, 65.

3. Bruce, *Galatians*, 77. Bring, *Galatians*, 18–21, notes that Paul writes not as a private person with his own ideas, but as an authorized representative of God and Christ.

longer thanksgiving usually found in the letters, as Paul apparently wants to get quickly to the issues that already impact the Galatian church.⁴ Because the clauses in 1:4 follow the *grace and peace* pronouncement, and in turn are followed by the attribution of *glory* to the Father in 1:5 and the *amen* that finally concludes the entire salutation (both of which terms invite worship and praise), we are given to wonder what this difference of greeting might signify.⁵ Paul clearly has a particular objective! *Deliverance* in Christ is his emphatic message, especially given "the immanent danger that this gospel of Christ will be perverted and turned into its opposite."⁶

Paul connects three clauses in 1:4 that together relate to God's redemptive mission in Christ. He cites Christ's *self-giving* (1:4a), believers' *deliverance* (1:4b), and *God's will* to act in Christ for deliverance (1:4c). Paul affirms that the Lord Jesus Christ *[gave himself for our sins] [to set us free from the present evil age] [according to the will of our God and Father]*.⁷ We will study each of these three clauses in turn.

Behind Paul's words is the power of his apostolic call, attended by questions about the same. Roetzel, 57, 66.

4. Mußner, 52. Martyn, *Galatians*, 91. "Paul ends the prescript with a doxology, something he does in none of his other letters. The doxology, brought into Christian worship from long usage in the synagogue, serves as the climactic exclamation at the end of a hymn or prayer in which the magnitude of God's deliverance has been celebrated, *doxa* ('glory') being God's power in action."

5. Martyn, *Galatians*, 81–6, 87, notes three criteria in the prescript: (1) Paul as author, 1:1; (2) the Galatians as addressees, 1:2; (3) the formula *grace and peace*, 1:3. But, "Paul does not place a stop after this formula. He pauses only after he has developed a fairly long and complex sentence which reaches through vv 4 and 5. The weighty elements that make up the latter part of this sentence are nowhere else found as parts of an epistolary greeting. We have to ask, therefore, whether in hearing them, the Galatians will have sensed that Paul has changed the expected salutation into something else."

6. Ebeling, 37.

7. Galatians 1:4, NRS (brackets added); NRS 1:3–5 reads, *(3) Grace to you and peace from God our Father and the Lord Jesus Christ, (4) who gave himself for our sins to set us free from the present evil age, according to the will of our God and Father, (5) to whom be the glory forever and ever. Amen.*

The Greek text says, (3) χάρις ὑμῖν καὶ εἰρήνη ἀπὸ θεοῦ πατρὸς καὶ κυρίου ἡμῶν Ἰησοῦ Χριστοῦ, (4) τοῦ δόντος ἑαυτὸν ὑπὲρ τῶν ἁμαρτιῶν ἡμῶν ὅπως ἐξέληται ἡμᾶς ἐκ τοῦ αἰῶνος τοῦ ἐνεστῶτος πονηροῦ κατὰ τὸ θέλημα τοῦ θεοῦ καὶ πατρὸς ἡμῶν, (5) ᾧ ἡ δόξα εἰς τοὺς αἰῶνας· ἀμήν.

Martyn, *Galatians*, 81, translates *(3) May grace and peace come to you from God our Father and from the Lord Jesus Christ, (4) "who gave up his very life for our sins," so that he might snatch us out of the grasp of the present evil age, thus acting in accordance with the intention of God our Father. (5) To God be glory throughout the whole of eternity. Amen!*

Martyn, 88, supplies quotation marks around the clause, "*who gave up his very life for our sins,*" in order to indicate that "Paul draws these words from an early Christian

5.1.1. Galatians 1:4a affirms the self-giving of Christ as faithful voluntary mission.

The affirmation in 4a that Christ *gave himself for our sins* is present in the similar formulaic statements of Gal 2:20; Rom 4:25; 8:32 (see Eph 5:2, 25; 1 Tim 2:6; Titus 2:14). That such statements may be considered *formulaic* relates to a history of reception and use in the early church's theology, faith, and worship. The formula helped to explain the death of Christ and by Paul's time the formula was well established within Jewish-Christian tradition.[8] The formula may have roots in a Jewish blessing that was adapted for Christian usage.[9] The formula may also have roots in the piety of pre-Christian Jewish lament.[10] Several things can be said favoring the probability of such a development.

First, the laments that were part of Jewish piety carried the voice of pain that kept prayer anchored in real life experiences.[11] These laments would then have been the familiar experience of the first Jewish Christians who had revered and attached themselves to Jesus. In struggling with the distress of his death and their own grief, the laments came readily to use as calls for God's help in the midst of trouble, suffering, and loss.

Second, the early history of such laments, in Judaism and in the nascent church, likely had no sense of a redeeming value or meaning ascribed to the suffering itself or, for that matter, to Jesus' death. Such understanding of the redemptive character of Jesus' suffering and death came later. But first, the cry was for justice in the face of injustice, and for God's presence and help in the face of God's hiddenness. The ancient words are pertinent

---

hymn or (eucharistic?) confession . . ." The words are not originally Paul's own; the thought is not characteristic of his theology.

8. Martyn, *Galatians*, 89. "From its inception the church made various efforts to interpret Jesus' death, and the present formula arose in the course of these efforts." Betz, 41; Dahl, "Akedah"; Bruce, *Galatians*, 77.

9. Bring, 22–23, "These words had a greater sense of reality to the readers of the letter than it may have to modern man. This greeting was not merely a pious phrase, it was an actual bestowal of grace and peace . . . The word 'peace' represents the Hebrew *shalom* . . . 'Grace' is closely related to mercy and compassion . . . Grace and peace had their foundation in the fact that Christ had come and had accomplished his work."

10. Westhelle, 16, "The early Christian development of a 'theology' of the cross took place largely within the context of Jewish piety as it unfolded during the intertestamental period and well into the second century of the Common Era. These 'Jewish insights acquired down the centuries (independent of Jesus of Nazareth)', writes Edward Schillebeeckx, 'are something [that] is impossible to dismiss. On the contrary, these already existing ideas helped the Jew, now become a Christian, to place in context and understand the life and destiny of the Master he already venerated and worshipped; they were not the cause of that veneration.'"

11. Billman and Migliore, 33.

for Jesus and his followers: "How long, O LORD? Will you forget me forever? How long will you hide your face from me?" (Ps 13:1); "My God, my God, why have you forsaken me?" (Ps 22:1).[12]

Third, martyrdom was the mark of a true prophet. The death of a prophet, in this case Jesus, attests the righteousness of the prophet's life. And yet the death cannot be justified: "it remains a tragic event, the outrageous price charged to the One who was righteous."[13] But the vindication of the prophet's life, signaled by his faithful death, is the real truth of the tragedy.

5.1.2. The formulaic phrase, *who gave himself*, indicates that Christ freely gave his life—it was not taken from him against his will.[14] His was an active compliance with the will of God.[15]

> Behind the drama of the self-giving Christ is the self-giving love of God ... Even in a text such as Gal 1:4, which affirms Jesus' own initiative ("who gave himself ... "), the initiative comes in compliance with God's intention ("according to the will of our God and Father"). There is no notion of Jesus as a lonely and courageous hero, taking up the cause of humanity in its brokenness and forcing God's hand to change the course of history.[16]

Christ gave himself to a mission and purpose to which he had been called and for which he had been sent. He complied fully with the will and intention of the Father who assigned the mission and sent him into it. But that he took up the mission indicates no death-wish on Christ's part nor divine will for appeasement of the Father. At some point did death seem to him truly possible, then probable, then finally certain? But Jesus set his face towards

---

12. Westhelle, 17; Schillebeeckx, 291, holds that the suffering servant of Isaiah 53 is not a frame for the early passion narratives and so, "the salvific implication of Jesus' suffering and death" was not part of the early Christian picture. Rochford, 251, argues that Schillebeeckx fails to see the methodological limitations imposed for today by his reliance on frameworks of interpretation that too narrowly freeze experiences of salvation within the biblical and traditional horizons of experience." We note the word *paradidomi* (*give, turn over, betray*) in Isaiah 53, that repeatedly functions in the gospels as the verb that carries Jesus through his passion experience. This linguistic linkage elucidates the connection between the ancient prophetic text and the self-giving, crucified Servant, Jesus. Gunton, 173–75.

13. Westhelle, 19.

14. Martyn, *Galatians*, 89. BDAG, 242.10: dedication of oneself for a purpose or cause.

15. Green, 34, notes that Jesus himself could have pioneered the combination of non-masochistic intention with absolutist commitment, "for the construction of a soteriology in which affliction might be understood not only as a condition from which to be delivered but also the means by which deliverance might come."

16. Cousar, *Cross*, 26–27.

Jerusalem in faithfulness to his mission. That is, *he gave himself* to the mission, no matter what might be forthcoming.

Jesus' own teaching points in this direction of self-giving to a mission. All three of the Synoptic Gospels (Mk 12:1-12; Lk 20:9-19; Mt 21:33-46) recount the expectation of the Father in sending the Son. The parable they record portrays this mission in terms of the landowner who sent his servants to collect the produce from the tenants who had farmed his land. The unfaithful tenants beat and killed the servants. The landowner thereafter sent his own son on the same mission, saying, "They will respect my son." Luke's account (20:13) is even more poignantly expressive: "I will send my son, the beloved." This is close to the identifying terminology used of Jesus at his baptism.[17] In the parable of the vineyard the outcome of violent death was the work of wicked servants. The will of the owner/Father was respect for the son/Jesus, that is, that the Son be recognized and honored as the rightful heir who was sent by the Father. The sacrifice was decided and executed by the unfaithful tenants. The heir, the beloved son, carried out his mission even in the face of such danger and threat.

The verb for *giving* (δίδωμι, *didomi*) in Gal 1:4a, together with the pronoun (*himself*), represents this self-giving of Christ. The clause in 1:4a has this verb as an active participle with the definite article. It could be translated, *the one who gave*. It is a frequent verb in the NT, used of God's giving of grace, or the pillar apostles giving the hand of fellowship to Paul (Gal 2:9).[18] Paul sometimes uses the compound form, with the prefix *para-* (παρα-), signifying *give over, hand over, give up, deliver up*. This form can indicate God's action to *give up* or *deliver up* certain persons (i.e., to their own devices, Rom 1:24, 26, 28). It is also used to show self-giving, as Gal 2:20 speaks of the Son of God, *the one who loved me and who gave himself for me*.[19]

---

17. Gen 12:2 (re: Isaac), λαβὲ τὸν υἱόν σου τὸν ἀγαπητόν ὃν ἠγάπησας, *take your beloved/only son whom you love*, may show that the covenant people do not sacrifice their children, and God does not do so, either. See "beloved son" re: Jesus (Οὗτός ἐστιν ὁ υἱός μου ὁ ἀγαπητός, *who is my beloved son*), Mt 3:17; Mk 1:11; Lk 3:22.

18. The NT uses of the verb include Matt. 4:12; 5:25; 10:4, 17, 19, 21; 11:27; 17:22; 18:34; 20:18f; 24:9f; 25:14, 20, 22; 26:2, 15f, 21, 23ff, 45f, 48; 27:2ff, 18, 26; Mk. 1:14; 3:19; 4:29; 7:13; 9:31; 10:33; 13:9, 11f; 14:10f, 18, 21, 41f, 44; 15:1, 10, 15; Lk. 1:2; 4:6; 9:44; 10:22; 12:58; 18:32; 20:20; 21:12, 16; 22:4, 6, 21f, 48; 23:25; 24:7, 20; Jn. 6:64, 71; 12:4; 13:2, 11, 21; 18:2, 5, 30, 35f; 19:11, 16, 30; 21:20; Acts 3:13; 6:14; 7:42; 8:3; 12:4; 14:26; 15:26, 40; 16:4; 21:11; 22:4; 27:1; 28:17; Rom. 1:24, 26, 28; 4:25; 6:17; 8:32; 1 Co. 5:5; 11:2, 23; 13:3; 15:3, 24; 2 Co. 4:11; Gal. 2:20; Eph. 4:19; 5:2, 25; 1 Tim. 1:20; 1 Pet. 2:23; 2 Pet. 2:4, 21; Jude 1:3.

19. Betz, 125-26. Bruce, *Galatians*, 145, ". . . here, Christ is the subject and the action is reflexive"; 146, quoting Hooker ("Interchange"), "Jesus own role is understood as less passive and more active . . ." Mußner, 183.

The reference to self-giving raises the question of how sacrifice fits the message of the cross, and what place sacrifice has in the church's interpretation of the death of Christ. "Who is this Son of God, and what is his faith? He is the one who 'loved me and gave up his life for me,' and his faith *is* that sacrificial act . . ."[20] And yet, Paul never called Jesus' death a sacrifice.

> The cross's consequences for men (*sic*) dominate all Paul's statements to such an extent that the consequences for God simply do not enter his field of vision, and other concepts occupy the foreground so exclusively that for this reason alone no essential significance can be attributed to the theme of sacrifice . . . the decisive point, at all events, is the ending of our separation from God. It is only the idea of vicariousness that has Christological importance.[21]

Christ's *faithfulness* informs the self-giving that eventuated in his death. The *consequences* of Christ's death inform the proclamation of Paul. Paul retains the message of self-giving (Gal 1:4a) and adds the purpose statement (1:4b) that proclaims the end result: *deliverance*.

5.1.3. The same verb as 1:4a is found also in Gal 2:20, and likely has roots in Isaiah 53:12 (LXX). Isaiah says of the Servant that, *he (poured out) himself to death, and (made intercession) for the transgressors*. Paul speaks of Christ, the Son of God, *who loved me and (gave himself) for me*.

Such early references to the *servant* (as found in Isa 53:12) were sometimes designations for Israel.[22] The early church applied the *Servant* passages to Jesus as a way of understanding his mission, suffering, and death.[23] A similar and likely connection of the phrase in Gal 1:4a to Isa 53:12 is the common use of the same verb, to *give*, by Paul and Isaiah.[24] The connection is also signaled by the concept of self-giving *for the sake of others* who will benefit from, live, or be saved by the self-giving of the martyr-servant. It was well-rooted in Judaism that the death of a righteous martyr, "would

---

20. Martyn, *Galatians*, 259; 89.

21. Käsemann, "Significance," 43: "Thus, according to 1 Cor. 5.7, Jesus is the Paschal lamb slain for us. But in the context the point is not the sacred rite but its result: for Christians, Easter has begun."

22. Isaiah 53:12 is among four *Servant Songs* in Isaiah: 42:1–4; 49:1–6; 50:4–11; 52:13—53:12.

23. Hoad; Heim, *Sacrifice*, 96–101; Anderson, *Understanding*, 500–2; Brueggemann, 650–4, 666–67.

24. The verb, δίδωμι, *didomi*, is used by Paul as an aorist active participle: τοῦ δόντος, *tou dontos*, and by Isaiah as an aorist passive indicative: παρεδόθη, *paredothē*. Hearers would have recognized the common root.

expiate the sins of others."[25] The christological statement of Gal 1:1 affirms the divine origin of Paul's apostolic call, tells what God has done *to Jesus* in raising him from the dead, and anticipates the formula in 1:4 and its message of what has been done *for us*:

> "Christ gave himself up for our sins" implies an old christology which understood Jesus' death as an expiatory self-sacrifice. This christology is likely to have originated in Judaism . . . according to Jewish belief the righteous man, when he suffered martyrdom, would expiate the sins of others. We may suppose that in the pre-Pauline period Jewish Christianity interpreted Jesus' death in this manner, so that we have here one of the oldest christologies of the New Testament, perhaps the oldest one of all.[26]

We note, however, that the Isaiah text does *not* make the connection between the Suffering Servant and the anticipated Messiah.[27] Although the expiation of others by way of the martyr's death was a theme in Judaism, and the church's understanding of Jesus' death may have been considerably explicated by this theme, the connection of the servant-martyr theme to the concept of Messiah was a step that the church itself would take, and did so in what was finally to become a traditional view of his sacrificial and atoning death:

> In the final hour of awareness the nations come to realize that the Servant is bearing their griefs and carrying their sorrows, but, beyond that, that God is working out his purpose through him, that it is his purpose that the Servant should suffer and die for them, and that it is through the suffering and death of the Servant that they are to be healed and made whole. The hour of deepest humiliation and degradation and rejection is the hour when the Servant rises to his highest elevation as the

---

25. Betz, 42. Hooker, *Servant,* discusses whether Jesus saw himself in terms of the Servant. The church has come to understand him in such a connection. Jeremias, "παῖς θεου," 706, sees *according to the Scriptures* in 1 Cor 15:3-5 as undoubtedly referring to Isaiah 53 because of the phrase, *for our sins.* Hengel, *Atonement,* 59, " it should no longer be doubted that *Isa. 53 had an influence on the origin and shaping of the earliest kerygma.*"

26. Betz, 41-2, cites Bultmann, *TNT* §7,3; Riesenfeld, "ὑπέρ," 507; Dahl, "Atonement." Mußner, 50, n. 38; Moore, *Judaism,* 546-49; Williams, *Jesus' Death.* For, "Christ gave himself up," Gal 1:4; 2:20; for, "God gave him up," Rom 8:32; for, "Christ was given up," Rom 4:25.

27. Mowinckel, 196-206, 325-33; 329: "In the time of Jesus . . . a suffering and dying Messiah was quite alien to the normal Jewish view. For many it was not merely incomprehensible, but offensive."

commissioned instrument of God. The words were meant for the future, but for the future made present by faith. In the passion and death of Jesus, the Christian community confesses that in him the words are fulfilled, and in so doing it confesses that the whole meaning of Israel from its earliest beginnings finds in him its ultimate revelation.[28]

5.1.4. The tradition of Jesus' death as atoning sacrifice is not where Paul concludes the subject of Jesus' self-giving. The second phrase in Gal 1:4a, *for our sins,* could be read, *in order to remove the deadly effects of our sins.*[29] Paul seldom speaks of *sins* in the plural, as he does in Gal 1:4. He usually utilizes the singular: *sin.* The plural form occurs only four times in the undisputed letters: (1) 1 Corinthians 15:3 is an early Christian confession, wherein Paul refers to the message that he *received* and *handed on*; (2) 1 Corinthians 15:17 is within the broader context of said message and thus corresponds to 15:3; (3) Romans 7:5 is an adjectival plural modifying a plural noun and therefore its form is ruled by the noun it serves; (4) Galatians 1:4 reflects the tradition or confession that Paul inherited.[30] Thus, it seems that Paul speaks of Jesus having died for our *sins* only when he is quoting a traditional formula which, in other words,

> ... is to a significant degree foreign to Paul's own theology ... Paul, when he is formulating his own view, consistently speaks not of *sins,* but rather of *Sin,* identifying it as a power that holds human beings in a state of slavery. And he sees liberation rather than forgiveness as the fundamental remedy enacted by God.[31]

The *dying for our sins* clause in Gal 1:4a is unlike Paul as to origin and content.[32] Paul uses the phrase and so acknowledges the tradition. But he builds on it, as he renders the tradition to a respectful displacement as a *means* to the *end* that he wants to proclaim. That *end* is *deliverance.* The inherited formula regards *sins* as the fundamental human problem and *forgiveness* as

---

28. Muilenburg, 149. *The final hour of awareness* refers to final reckoning and accounting.

29. Martyn, *Galatians,* 89; *for our sins:* (ὑπὲρ τῶν ἁμαρτιῶν ἡμῶν, *hyper tōn hamartiōn hēmōn*).

30. In the undisputed letters, Rom 3:9, 20; 4:7; 5:12, 20; 6:1, 6, 10, 16, 20, 22f; 7:5, 7, 11, 13, 17, 20, 23, 25; 8:2, 10; 11:27; 14:23; 1 Cor 15:3, 17, 56; 2 Cor 5:21; 11:7; Gal 1:4; 2:17; 3:22; 1 Thess 2:16. In the disputed letters, Eph 2:1; Col 1:14; 1 Tim 5:22, 24; 2 Tim 3:6. Wall, 4, speaks instead of *historical* Paul and *canonical* Paul.

31. Martyn, *Galatians,* 89, 90. Green, 25, there was no singular line of understanding about Jesus' death.

32. Mußner, 50, n. 38, "die Sprache in Gal 1:4, ‚ganz unpaulinisch' ist."

the necessary divine remedy.³³ For Paul, the fundamental human problem is enslavement to the *power of sin*, and consequently *deliverance* is the necessary divine remedy. We could say that Paul's paradigm is not the altar, but the Exodus.

Word combinations suggest this perspective of the development in Paul. The preposition, *for (hyper)*, when used following terms of dedication or sacrifice, is understood in the sense of *for someone else*. For example, in Rom 16:4 we are told that Aquila and Priscilla have been ready to give their lives *for* Paul. Paul would have been willing to risk his own connection with Christ *for the sake of* his own people, kindred according to the flesh (Rom 9:3). In a similar way we note of Christ, in relation to his giving or dying *for* others: *Christ died for us* (Rom 5:8); *Christ died for our sins* (1 Cor 15:3); *This is my body that is for you* (1 Cor 11:23-4). The verb of giving, (*didomi*), used with the preposition *for/in behalf of*, forms a special group of texts that speak of Christ's *self-giving*. These include Rom 8:32; Gal 1:4; 2:20.³⁴ Galatians 1:4, besides its connection to the Servant of Isa 53:12, is also explicated with the interpretation of *for (hyper)*:

> When used with such a word as "sin," the normal meaning of *hyper* (on behalf of) becomes modified into the ideas of deliverance and relationship (Burton). Hence Christ's work is inseparably connected with sin. The nature of the connection is not precisely defined, but the following phrase (*sic*, Gal 1:4b) throws valuable light upon it.³⁵

But can *more* than "not precisely defined" be said regarding the connection between Christ's work and sin? The four Gospels can answer *yes* to that question.

---

33. Betz, 41, "'Christ gave himself up for our sins' implies an old christology which understood Jesus' death as an expiatory self-sacrifice. This christology is likely to have originated in Judaism." Bultmann, *TNT* §7, 46-7: "Then Jesus' death would already have been conceived as an expiatory sacrifice in the earliest church . . .The interpretation of Jesus' death as an expiatory sacrifice for sins was, in itself, not unnatural to Jewish thinking. For in it the idea of the expiating power of the suffering of the righteous, especially of the martyr, had been developed." Mußner, 50-2; Dahl, "Atonement."

34. The self-giving of Christ is for us, for many, for all; Riesenfeld, "ὑπέρ," 508-10. BDAG, 1030.

35. Guthrie, 59. Riesenfeld, 511: "No matter how one may assess the direct influence of Is. 53:11f. on the self-awareness of Jesus and primitive Christian christology, the beneficial quality (ὑπέρ) of the death of someone, even in the categories of Jewish martyr theology, can be understood only against the background of the sacrificial concepts of the OT. Exclusively an act of self-sacrifice, the negative fact of death can become a positive event which may produce fruitful results for others."

> One detail on which all four Gospels agree is that Jesus was literally exchanged for another condemned prisoner, Barabbas. Barabbas, like the two thieves on Calvary, underlines the point that sacrifice is already going on. Victims are going to be offered this Passover week; only their identities are at issue. There is a real person whose place Jesus takes and for whose sake he dies. That person is redeemed and the price is Jesus' blood. All the traditional language is here simply, descriptively true. It has a concrete, historical application. Barabbas can say, with no theological overlay at all, that Jesus died for him. Jesus bore the punishment for Barabbas's sins.[36]

The Barabbas detail in the four passion narratives enhances our understanding of the meaning of Christ's death. Matthew (27:15-26), Mark (15:6-15), Luke (23:13-25), and John (18:40) report that one person could irrefutably have argued that Jesus died *for* him, that Jesus died *for* that man's sins. Barabbas was caught in the consequences of his own sins of rebellion and murder, resulting in a death sentence. Matthew identifies the key elements of the scene: Pilate had the authority of office and custom to release a prisoner, 27:15; Pilate's wife acknowledged the innocence of Jesus, v. 19; the crowd chose the release of Barabbas, v. 21, thus ensuring Jesus' death, v. 21-2; Pilate released (*loosed, set free, forgave*) Barabbas, v. 26; freedom, deliverance, came to one for whom Jesus died. Innocent blood—the guilt and responsibility—was on the crowd who had decided the sacrifice, v. 25.[37]

5.2. To Deliver Us, Galatians 1:4b

5.2.1. Galatians 1:4b affirms the meaning of Christ's death on behalf of others. The clause in 4b, *to set us free from the present evil age*, completes a *means to an end* statement. It is a purpose clause. The means in 4a, *Christ gave himself for our sins*, leads to the purposeful end in 4b, *to set us free from the present evil age*. The first phrase in 1:4b, *to set us free*, initiates and elucidates the purpose statement in terms of rescue, liberation, or deliverance. The conjunction, *so that*, with the subjunctive, signals the purpose, showing design and intention.[38] The purpose of liberation or deliverance is signaled

---

36. Heim, 304.

37. Luz, *Matthew* 3:499-511, indicates that Matthew "wants the guilt of the Jews to be understood as a strictly christological rather than a moral issue. It is not that they affirmed solidarity with a bandit but that they had their own Messiah crucified." See his comments regarding the role of the Jews.

38. BDF, §369, ὅπως (*hopos, in order that*), rather than the usual ἵνα (*hina*) is parallel to it in meaning as a means to an end, or purpose clause; see Gal 1:16; 2:16, 19; 3:14,

by the verb (*exelētai, set free*) in this means to an end construction.[39] The word is common in the LXX, although Paul uses this term only here in his writings. The verb occurs in Ex 3:7-8, within God's promise of rescue for the Israelites.[40] Paul and his readers would recognize *exelētai* as an echo of the story about God's deliverance of the covenant people from oppression and misery in Egypt. It is at Horeb (Sinai), the *mountain of God*, that Moses is drawn to the burning bush, and the Lord announces the divine intention of deliverance: *Then the LORD said, "I have observed the misery of my people who are in Egypt . . . I have come down to deliver them from the Egyptians . . ."*[41]

The Exodus story demonstrates that God's deliverance is not only *from*, it is also deliverance *to: from* oppression, *to* the land that had been promised: "The act of salvation is not simply about being removed from the oppressive situation. It is also the gift of a land, a new place for life and blessing. *God's redemptive acts lead to a new creation . . .* enabling the people to move from redemption to creation."[42] The tradition of deliverance elucidates the atoning work of Christ in a way that the concept of sacrifice alone could not. God's solution for the problem of human sin is not simply forgiveness *for* transgressions, but rescue *from* bondage.[43]

22, 24; 4:5. Abbott-Smith, 321.

39. Betz, 42, n. 59, recognizes the Pauline *hapax legomenon*, as does Bruce, *Galatians*, 75, who adds, "Paul's use of ἐξαιρέομαι here adds weight to the opinion that he is quoting a form of words well known to his readers, which summed up the gospel which they had received and from which, he feared, they were now departing." The word, ἐξέληται (*exelētai*), in 1:4b is the aorist middle subjunctive form of the verb to which Bruce refers, expressing *deliverance, rescue:* "Christ's self-oblation not only procures for his people the forgiveness of their past sins; it delivers them from the realm in which sin is irresistible into the realm where he himself is Lord." BDAG, 344.

40. LXX examples: Gen. 37:21; Deut. 32:39; Ps. 30:2-3; Job 5:4, 19; Isa. 31:5; 43:13.

41. Exodus 3:7-8 (NRS); Ex 3:8a (LXX) reads καὶ κστέβην ἐξελέθαι αὐ τοὺς ἐκ χειρὸς Αἰγυπτίων (the verb is middle aorist infinitive); cf. 18:4,8,9,10. JPS Tanakh has *rescue* for the Hebrew לחציל Ex 3:8; NRS, RSV, KJV say *deliver*. The same verb occurs in Acts 26:17, in Paul's defense before Agrippa, as he recounts God's promise in the Damascus Road experience.

42. Fretheim, *Exodus*, 58-9. See his, "Whole Earth," 230, regarding the Book of Exodus: "The book moves from Israel's servitude to Pharaoh to its service to Yahweh, from the enforced construction of buildings for Pharaoh to the willing assemblage of a dwelling place for God. Walter Brueggemann speaks of a flight 'from Pharaoh to Yahweh, from one master to a new one' (NIB 834). Yet, the new master differs from the old one. A difference exists in the kind of sovereignty exercised."

43. Käsemann, "Significance," 44, "It is striking that Paul hardly ever uses the expression 'forgiveness', although he must have been familiar with it from the context of the message of the Lord's Supper and probably also from baptism, and although he of course adhered to what was meant. But for Paul, salvation does not primarily mean the end of past disaster and the forgiving cancellation of former guilt. It is, according to

Martyn questions why Paul quotes this formula of *sins* (requiring forgiveness) when Paul's own view is consistently that of *sin* as a power that holds human beings in bondage and God's liberation from that bondage is the content of Paul's proclamation. Martyn's answer to this question is, "Paul quotes the Jewish–Christian formula in order affirmatively to correct it by means of an additional clause."[44] The additional clause is 1:4b. The clause has roots in Israel's covenant history: *so that he might snatch us out of the grasp of* the present evil age.

The verb (*exelētai*) that Martyn renders as *snatch* is translated in KJV and RSV as *deliver,* and reads *set us free* in the NRS. The use of this verb, and the concept of freedom issuing from rescue's action, is in keeping with Paul's sense of sin as a power that holds humanity in captivity, a power that only God can break. It is a power that God *has* broken and in breaking it God has surpassed the human performance of sacrifice:

> Jesus giving up of his own life for our deliverance was not simply a deed of his own, but rather an act carried out in faithful obedience to God . . . It was, in fact, an act intended by God . . . .The death of the Son is therefore a sacrifice enacted both by him and by God; and as such it breaks the mold of the old sacrificial pattern. The cross, that is to say, is not a sacrifice human beings make to God; it is fundamentally God's act, and as such the inversion of the sacrificial system.[45]

If *deliverance from the present evil age* represents Paul's corrective addition to a piece of the early tradition, (namely, he *gave himself for our sins*) what can be said of the tradition he corrected? Is Christ's self-giving synonymous with blood sacrifice? What is the place of sacrifice in our understanding of the biblical story, and with respect to the death of Jesus in particular?

Bernhard Anderson reflects on the Servant concept of Isaiah as it relates to Israel. He concludes that the Servant—when in exile, then in movement along God's royal highway of justice, thence into freedom and a new life—was not victim, but victor! Deliverance from exile and alienation was not to be only a deliverance from bondage (that might have been too easily understood as nationalism)—it was also to be a walk of justice and service

---

Rom. 5.9f.; 8.2, freedom from the power of sin, death and the divine wrath; that is to say, it is the possibility of new life. He therefore gave a more radical turn to the tradition which he took over."

44. Martyn, *Galatians*, 90.

45. Martyn, 91. Two diverse thoughts need not be confused: (a) the self-giving of Christ/God's giving of the Son and, (b) that self-giving as determining violence of torture and death.

to the nations with news of God's kingdom. Israel's nobility was to be that of a servant whose exaltation was in the sacrifice of suffering. There was a vicarious quality to Israel's call.[46] Israel's practice of sacrifice was therefore radically different from that of other religions in the ancient world, in which sacrifice was a human means for controlling the will of the gods. But for Israel, sacrifice was a two-way street: God approached and graciously provided his people with a means to overcome guilt and live in divine presence. Israel could then approach God in responsive faith. Israel, was not like the nations who sought to control their gods and their own well-being with sacrifice.[47]

Walter Brueggemann advocates for a similar line of thought regarding sacrifice. He reminds us that Israel is essentially a community of worship. Israel's worship mediated Yahweh's real presence and thus gave to Israel a means by which God was available to Israel. Sacrifice provided worship practices by which Israel could interact with Yahweh in order to express Israel's sense of well-being. There was authentic mutuality in relation to God when all seemed well. But sacrifice could also express the need and the means by which amendment and repair could be realized, when Israel's failures, alienation, or hostility required actions of repentance. Regret, resolve, and return to viable relations with Yahweh effected real and actual forgiveness. Sacrifice represents this relationship to which Yahweh is devoted, in which Israel may be restored, and which therefore can serve as a framework for reparations, social and institutional settings for penitence, and effective restoration for relations of well-being.[48]

Martyn emphasizes restoration as rescue or deliverance in Gal 1:4b. He distinguishes with quotation marks the formulaic phrase in Gal 1:4a, *"who gave up his very life for our sins."* He suggests that Paul's opponents reflect the traditional Jewish-Christian interpretation of Jesus' death. Christ-as-sacrifice would then have had a significant place in their understanding.

> Could it also be that the Galatians are even now hearing this formula in the sermons of the Teachers? The possibility of an affirmative answer emerges from Rom 3:25, for there we find a formula worded by a Jewish Christian for use among Jewish Christians ... The Teachers will certainly have had to interpret Jesus' death, even though ... they were far from taking their

---

46. B. Anderson, *Understanding*, 488–500.

47. Anderson, 498. Grimsrud, 20, "... the Old Testament does not present salvation as linked with a will of God for violence ... salvation in the Old Testament emerges from God's mercy ... sacrifice plays the role of providing a way for people to show their commitment to God as a response to God's saving works ..."

48. Brueggemann, *Theology*, 650–3, 666–68.

theological bearings from the cross as such. Toward Jesus' death they may have had a view similar to the one encapsulated in Rom 3:25.[49]

Romans 3:25 may contain a clue for reading Gal 1:4a.[50] The clue is a key word that is variously translated, with roots in Ex 25:17. The Hebrew word in Exodus is *kappōreth* (כפרת), and in LXX, *hilastērion* (ἱλαστήριον). It refers to the *top* or *cover* of the ark of the covenant. Exodus 25 has instructions for the ark of the covenant and its cover, reference to which reappears in Rom 3:25.

Hultgren identifies various meanings for *hilastērion* that have been proposed throughout the history of NT interpretation. Regarding Rom 3:25 this variety includes, (1) *propitiation*, (Vulgate, KJV, ASV, JB, NASV, NKJV, ESV), *appeasing God's wrath*;[51] (2) *expiation*, (RSV, NEB, NAB, REB), *removal of the offense of sin before God*;[52] (3) *mercy seat*, (Luther, Tyndale, NET), a *place of atonement*.[53] Hultgren says,

> The term ἱλαστήριον appears at only one other place in the NT (Heb 9:5). At that place it is typically translated "mercy seat," a clear allusion to the mercy seat ... of the OT (Exod 25:17-22; Lev 16:11-17) ... the lid (or cover) over the ark of the covenant, which was sprinkled with blood for the sin offering on the Day of Atonement.[54]

The institution of the *mercy seat* in Exodus 25:17 includes God's promise to be present, *above the mercy seat* (25:22), that is, near the location of the thing itself. The ark is the footstool of God's throne (1 Chr 28:2; Ps 132:7),

---

49. Martyn, 89; 264-66, Paul knows a Jewish Christian rectification tradition, three important *snippets* of which occur in Rom 3:25; 4:25; 1 Cor 6:11. Martyn, 18, uses the term *Teachers* to signify those who came into Galatia seeking to correct Paul's message. They claimed a significant connection to the Jerusalem church, and they centered their message in the Sinaitic Law. See R. Longenecker, *Christology*, 104-9.

50. The pertinent part in Rom 3:25 is, ὃν προέθετο ὁ θεὸς ἱλαστήριον διὰ πίστεως ἐν τῷ αὐτοῦ αἵματι.

51. KJV: *Whom God hath set forth to be a propitiation through faith in his blood.*

52. NRS: *Whom God put forward as a sacrifice of atonement by his blood.*

53. NET: *God publicly displayed him at his death as the mercy seat accessible through faith.*

54. Hultgren, *Romans*, 663. See Luther's translation: *welchen Gott hat vorgestellt zu einem Gnadenstuhl durch den Glauben in seinem Blut, damit er die Gerechtigkeit, die vor ihm gilt, darbiete in dem, daß er Sünde vergibt, welche bisher geblieben war unter göttlicher Geduld.* For the term, *Gnadenstuhl*, in the *Luther Bibel of 1912* see: Exod. 25:17, 20; 26:34; 30:6; 31:7; 35:12; 37:6, 9; 39:35; 40:20; Lev. 16:2, 13; Num. 7:89; Rom. 3:25; Heb. 4:16; 9:5. BDAG, 474. For *Atonement in Hebrews* see Long.

a place of worship, and a central part of the instructions to Aaron for *the seventh month, on the tenth day of the month* (when) *atonement shall be made* (Lev 16:29–30).[55] Leviticus 16:14–15 details the instructions for the sin offering that Aaron is to perform on behalf of the people, with the use of blood, at the mercy seat.

> He shall take some of the blood of the bull, and sprinkle it with his finger on the front of the *mercy seat*, and before the *mercy seat* he shall sprinkle the blood with his finger seven times. He shall slaughter the goat of the sin offering that is for the people and bring its blood inside the curtain, and do with its blood as he did with the blood of the bull, sprinkling it upon the *mercy seat* and before the *mercy seat*.[56]

Dodd has pursued the verb form of the word, *hilastērion* (*mercy seat*). He notes that the meaning of the verb, *hilaskesthai*, in the LXX can be either, (1) with human subject, *to cleanse from sin or defilement, to expiate*, or (2) with divine subject, *to be gracious, to have mercy, to forgive*. He sees the emphasis in the LXX to be that of *delivering* humankind from sin, with God as *deliverer*, rather than the human action of pacifying God by way of sacrifice. Therefore, the sense of the term that best fits Jewish and Christian thought is, "... the place where God shows mercy ... (as) in the Pentateuchal account the *kapporeth* was the throne of grace, the mercy–seat, the place where the mercy of God was supremely manifested on the Day of Atonement."[57] Manson then also reflects the sense of *locale* in considering Christ crucified as the *hilastērion*, the place of God's supreme mercy in the mission of reconciliation:

> In what sense is it possible to say of Christ crucified that, like the mercy–seat in the Holy of Holies, he was the place where God's mercy was supremely manifested? A provisional answer

---

55. Fretheim, *Exodus*, 275–8, for God's presence and the tabernacle.
56. NRS, emphasis added.
57. Manson,"ἱλαστήριον," 4, referring to Dodd, ΙΛΑΣΚΕΣΘΑΙ, (*hilaskesthai*), 359. BDAG, 473, for the verb. Von Rad, *Theology* 1: 253, is helpful regarding sacrifice: "Sacrifice was so comprehensive that there was always room for thoughts and ideas suggested by the special reason connected with it. It is self-evident of course that this was far from meaning that sacrifice became a prey to every conceivable subjective interpretation: that would have been impossible for a people of antiquity so well versed in cultic matters as ancient Israel. Sacrifice was, and remained, an event which took place in a sphere lying outside of man and his spirituality: man could as it were only give it the external impulse; its actual operation was not subject to the control of his capacity or capabilities: all this rested with Jahweh, who had the power to accept the offering and let it achieve its purpose." Splendid!

can be given in Paul's own words: (*God was in Christ reconciling the world to himself, not counting their trespasses against them.*) But I think it is possible to go further and argue that what is at the back of Paul's mind in Rom iii.25 is the solemn ritual of the Day of Atonement.[58]

Manson's study of Rom 3:25 describes the relation of Paul to the Jewish rite. He says, first, that the verb *proetheto* speaks of *putting forth on display* what had been confined to the Holy of Holies.[59] The mercy-seat is now brought out into the *rough and tumble of the world and set before the eyes of hostile, contemptuous, or indifferent crowds*. Second, the phrase *through faith*, indicates that the benefits from the *hilasterion* are appropriated to believers. Third, the words, *in his blood*, relate to the dying Jesus, Christ crucified, as Paul makes precise the sense in which he speaks of the *hilasterion*. Fourth, *For the demonstration of his righteousness* is in contrast to wrath (Rom 1:18; 3:21). God's saving power, God's will to bring people into the Kingdom, and God's deliverance from the power of sin find manifestation in the *hilasterion*.[60]

Hultgren agrees with this line of thought:

> Here Paul makes a connection between the *mercy seat* of the OT as a *type* and the crucified Christ as the *antitype*. The crucified Christ is the ἱλαστήριον, the *mercy seat*, that God has put forth publicly for an atoning purpose. The crucified Christ is the place at which atonement is made for all of humanity. Furthermore, since God has promised to be present at the mercy seat (Exod 25:22; Lev 16:2; Num 7:89), God has now fulfilled the promise of his presence in effecting atonement. Whoever would look for the presence of God need look no further than to the crucified Christ.[61]

---

58. Manson has the Greek text of 2 Cor 5:19. Büchsel, *TDNT* 3:19–23; Käsemann, *Romans*, 97; Nygren, 158.

59. BDAG, 474, notes the (public) setting forth and/or removal of impediments.

60. Manson, "ἱλαστήριον," 5–6. BDAG, 889.

61. Hultgren, 157; 664, "In . . . Romans 3:25 the term ἱλαστήριον is seen in typological exegesis to have been derived from those passages in the LXX that speak of the *mercy seat*." OT scenes foreshadow Christ's redemptive work; 665, "According to a typological interpretation of Romans 3:25, the crucified Christ is the ἱλαστήριον . . . God has now set forth (προέθετο) this 'mercy seat' publicly, visibly, and out in the open at the cross. According to OT regulations, the mercy seat was to be located in the Holy of Holies, where no one could enter except the high priest once a year on the Day of Atonement. But according to the typological interpretation, in Christ crucified the place of atonement is brought into the midst of his people, and atonement is made once and for all."

Paul proclaims a new center as the focus of God's saving work, appropriated by faith in the Crucified Christ. Manson draws out what amounts to a typological interpretation as he compares the old mercy-seat with the new *place of God's mercy* that is in the crucified Christ.[62]

Grimsrud distinguishes between "sacrificial payment that makes salvation possible," and the "merciful, shalom-oriented story of salvation," regarding the death of Jesus.[63] Sacrificial payment relates to retributive justice that satisfies God's righteousness by punishment for sin. Violence is inherent in this view, and carries with it a justification for the violence by which the punishment is administered.[64] Shalom-oriented salvation relates to the primacy of God's covenant with humankind, involving mercy and peace-making. God's covenant is by God's initiative, not dependent on prior human action or faithfulness. God's covenant is generative of human faithfulness and gratitude for God's saving action.[65] The *merciful, shalom-*

---

62. Manson,"ἱλαστήριον," 6; Büchsel, *TDNT* 3, 322: "For Paul ἱλαστήριον is not something which makes God gracious. This expiation for human sin presupposes the grace of God. For Paul even those who fall victim to the wrath of God are also set under His patience, kindness and long-suffering, R. 2:4." Hultgren, 668, "Paul writes that God has put forth Christ as a ἱλαστήριον to *demonstrate* his righteousness, not to placate it. The clause speaks of (1) God as subject, (2) Christ as object, and (3) a divine action . . . expressed by an aorist verb stating that God put forth his Son for a redemptive purpose (similar forms of expression at Rom 8:3; 8:32; Gal 4:4). Thus the emphasis is totally on divine action." Fitzmyer, 348–50, agrees about *inherited formula* and understands that an *appeasement* "interpretation of *hilastērion* finds no support in the Greek OT or in Pauline usage elsewhere . . . Here it is part of the adopted pre-Pauline formula. Consequently, *hilastērion* is better understood against the background of the LXX usage of the Day of Atonement rite, so it would depict Christ as the new 'mercy seat,' presented or displayed by the Father as a means of expiating or wiping away the sins of humanity, indeed, as the place of the presence of God, of his revelation, and of his expiating power." Black, 69–70: "The startling thing in this verse is that Paul here speaks of the public display of the *hilastērion*; it is no longer simply a piece of Temple furniture hidden behind the Veil to which only the High Priest had access. This divinely appointed *hilastērion*, Christ, in his death (or through his blood) has been brought out into the open, and all (persons) can go, by faith, directly into this Holy of Holies."

63. Grimsrud, 2–4, 7, says of the former, "Jesus satisfies God's retributive justice on our behalf." Of the latter he says, 19, "'restorative' justice rather than retributive justice . . . (issues in) responses to violence that break the cycle, and strive for healing rather than punishment."

64. Calvin, *Institutes* II.xvi.10, Christ has "to undergo the severity of God's vengeance, to appease his wrath and satisfy his just judgment" and, "Christ's body was given as the price of our redemption" as well as the greater suffering in his soul as "a condemned and forsaken man." II.xvi.6: "Therefore, to perform a perfect expiation, he gave his own life as an *Asham*, that is, as an expiatory offering for sin, as the prophet calls it [Isa. 53:10; cf. v. 5], upon which our stain and punishment might somehow be cast, and cease to be imputed to us."

65. Aulén, 2, of Anselm and Abelard: "These two are commonly contrasted as the

oriented story of salvation emphasizes the worldly causes of Jesus' death, de-emphasizes the sacrifice of Jesus' life as a violent divine act, and focuses on the resurrection as the point of victory and atonement.

> The sacrificial necessity that claims Jesus is a sinful mechanism for victimization, whose rationale maintains it is necessary that one innocent person die for the good of the people. The free, loving "necessity" that leads God to be willing to stand in the place of the scapegoat is that this is the way to unmask the sacrificial mechanism, to break its cycles of mythic reproduction, and found human community on a non-sacrificial principle: solidarity with the victim, not unanimity against the victim.[66]

The cycle of sacrifice and violence is broken. Accordingly, Walter Wink has written:

> The death of Jesus was not "necessary" because God needed Jesus killed in order to save the world. Rather, Jesus was killed because the Powers are in rebellion against God and are determined to silence anyone who slips through their barbed-wire perimeter with a message from the sovereign of the universe.[67]

We can summarize this view of the death and resurrection of Christ with four comments.

- Jesus' resurrection vindicates his life as fully faithful to and reflective of God's will.

- Jesus' resurrection rebukes the powers that militate against God's reign as God acts not with retribution but with persevering love.

- Jesus' resurrection calls his followers to a vocation of God's blessing to the world.

- Jesus' resurrection manifests the true nature of reality: God's response to violence and death is reconciling love.[68]

---

authors respectively of the 'objective' and 'subjective' doctrines of the Atonement; the latter term is used to describe a doctrine which explains the Atonement as consisting essentially in a change taking place in men rather than a changed attitude on the part of God." Distinct from these two views, Aulén reviews the classic or dramatic view of atonement, 4–7, ch. VIII, emphasizing God's work in Christ to battle with and triumph over sin.

66. Heim, *Sacrifice*, 114.
67. Wink, 102.
68. Grimsrud, 173, 177, 181, 184.

Jesus freely gave himself. His self-giving encompassed his life and his death. Resurrection affirms the giving and the self-giver as faithful to God's divine intention.[69]

5.2.2. The second phrase in 1:4b, *from the present evil age*, affirms God's solution to the problem of human captivity. *Deliverance* involves transfer from one sphere of power to another, from one lordship to another, from the old aeon to the new creation. The thought of 1:4b echoes that of *dying to the law* (2:19), *crucified with Christ* (2:19), *crucified to the world* (6:14), and Paul's own transfer, *from* zeal for the traditions of his former life *to* the revelation of the Son of God, for the purpose of *evangelizing the nations* (1:14-16). The new aeon to which the believer in Christ is transferred is marked by unity in Christ. The old *kosmos* was marked by the distinction between circumcision and uncircumcision. The new creation (6:15) is all that matters. It is creation in Christ. And yet the *old* continues to exist, and the *new* is not available to obvious display. Thus, analogous to 2:20, where Paul speaks of being at once in the flesh and in faith, it is no ordinary, commonplace, or generic faith. It is, instead, precisely a faith in the *Son of God who loved me and gave himself for me* (2:20). The old order/fallen *kosmos* does not go away: one is delivered *from* it, dies in relation *to* it, just as one has died in relation to the law, in order to live in relation to God (2:19).[70]

Paul speaks in a manner similar to the Letter to the Hebrews, which in typological ways refers to the various events in Israel's long and tumultuous history.[71] The author of Hebrews regards the turning point of the ages, from old to new aeon, as having been initiated by the One who is *pioneer* and *perfecter* of our faith (Heb 12:2; 1:1-2). Luke (9:31) also speaks in a *Paul-like* way, as he reports the transfiguration of Jesus. His companions saw Moses and Elijah conversing with Jesus. The two men *appeared in glory and were speaking of his departure (exodus), which he was about to accomplish at Jerusalem*. We note the word that signifies Jesus' exit/*exodus* from the old and transfer to the new.

But the historical events, circumstances, and persons that played a part in Jesus' *departure* are not matters of which Paul explicitly speaks at any length

---

69. Heim, 160, "There is a sacrificial transaction taking place at the cross, but it is one that humans have organized, not God. And yet God has made this evil transaction the occasion for a better one, one in which scapegoating itself can be overthrown." See his, "The Paradox of the Passion: *Saved by What Shouldn't Happen*."

70. Mußner, 183, sees *in flesh* (ἐν σαρκί) and *in faith* (ἐν πίστει) not opposed as to their existence, but as to reign over human life, a matter of dominion over and allegiance to realms and reigns that are mutually exclusive.

71. Lindars, *Apologetic*; with P. Borgen, "The Place of the Old Testament"; Goppelt, *Typos*; Anderson, "Typology"; Von Rad, *Theologie*, Vol. 2, 375-87; Hagner, *Hebrews*, 158. Attridge, 2266-67.

in his epistles. He asserts that his visit with Peter (Gal 1:18) was not for the purpose of securing historical information that as such would have modified or added to Paul's gospel in any way (2:6–7).[72] And yet, there were unique dynamics of the principalities and powers with which Paul had to deal, and which had been involved in all that led up to the death of Jesus. These would surely have been in Paul's thought as he spoke of *the present evil age*.

Grimsrud points to three sources of antagonism facing Jesus, and establishes the contrast between God's mercy and the resistance mounted by the Powers that were arrayed against him. The Powers that were arrayed against Jesus included, (a) *cultural exclusivism* as centered around the legal system, focused on the issue of law, personified in the Pharisees, and served as an identity marker for its adherents; (b) *religious institutionalism* centered on the temple in Jerusalem, the leadership linked with the temple, and the priests; (c) *political authoritarianism* exercised by the government of the Roman Empire, was constantly and repulsively present in the form of occupying powers, and was represented by the governorship of Pontius Pilate.

> The basic message of salvation throughout is God's unqualified mercy. God's mercy evokes resistance from the Powers, depending as they do upon fearfulness, selfishness, and violence. This resistance, profound and deep, ultimately results in the Powers conspiring to put Jesus to death. They seek retribution for his violation of cultural, religious, and political expectations for humanity subject to the Powers' domination.[73]

Jesus gave himself to a mission that brought confrontation with powers of the *present evil age*. This he did in order to deliver humanity *from* that age and its agents in their cultural, religious, and political forms. The deliverance tradition that supports Paul's view of Jesus' atoning rescue of believers from the *present evil age* is *according to the will of our God and Father*. It is this third clause to which we now turn.

---

72. Büchsel, "ἱστορέω," *TDNT* 3:391–96; Betz, 76; Bruce, 98; Mußner, 93–94. Paul reports that leadership had affirmed his message and mission.

73. Grimsrud, *Atonement*, 94; 21–22, 92, points out that, (1) the OT presents salvation based on God's mercy, anchored in God's covenantal initiative, and eliciting gratitude and faithfulness; sacrifice is an expression of trust; (2) the NT presents Jesus' death due to combined violence of *cultural exclusivity, religious institutionalism,* and *political authoritarianism*; (3) Jesus' death exposes these Powers as rivals to the reign of God; Jesus pioneers anti-idolatry, and distinguishes God's reign of love over evil's rule of violence.

5.3. According to the Will of God, Galatians 1:4c

5.3.1. Galatians 1:4c affirms the origin in God's will of Jesus' self-giving and rescue. The third clause of Gal 1:4, *according to the will of our God and Father* anchors 1:a,b in two assertions of 1:4c. One assertion is implicit: Jesus' God and Father is *our* God and Father.[74] The word, *father*, (πάτερ, *pater*) is the term used by Jesus in his prayer of Mt 6:9. Paul's hearers share in the access to the Father that Jesus himself acknowledged in teaching the Lord's Prayer.[75] Furthermore, "the understanding of χάρις (*charis*, grace) and εἰρήνη (*eirēnē*, peace) depends on the definition of their source . . ."[76] The source is in God the Father and the Lord Jesus Christ.

The other assertion is explicit: Jesus' work of rescue is the fulfillment of the will of God the Father who sent him. In the mission of self-giving and deliverance, "Christ and God are at one."[77] Jesus' faithful obedience to God's sovereign intention ". . . is fundamentally God's act . . . the inversion of the sacrificial system."[78] Thus, Gal 1:4c reflects the theme and content of the whole letter: the fulfillment of God's saving purpose through the work of Christ; the basis for Paul's apostleship, authority, and message; the consequences for the church, especially with respect to issues relating to the law.[79] The anchor for all these facets of Paul's proclamation throughout this epistle is the phrase in 1:4c, *according to the will of our God and Father*.[80]

---

74. Here is an echo of the Jewish *Qaddish* Prayer, Jesus' version of which may have been the *Our Father* that he taught his disciples (Mt 6:9). See Luz, *Matthew*, 3:309–27. BDAG, 787.

75. Luz, *Matthew*, 1:314–15, suggests that πάτερ in the Lord's Prayer "may have corresponded to the Aramaic form of address אבא . . . It is used by small and adult children when speaking to their fathers . . . by addressing God as πάτερ the Lord's Prayer begins with a promise of salvation. It is a prayer of God's children."

76. Ebeling, 37. Mußner, 50, notes that grace and peace "sind Gaben des himmlischen Vaters und des Herrn Jesus Christus . . ." resulting in the eschatological peace between heaven and earth, between Jew and Gentile, between one people and another.

77. Bruce, *Galatians*, 77.

78. Martyn, 91, n. 28: "In the analysis of Hamerton-Kelly Jesus' crucifixion is the act in which, rather than taking vengeance by demanding sacrifice, God himself suffers vengeance (*Violence*, 79)."

79. Bring, 23.

80. Betz, 43; διὰ θελήματος θεοῦ (*according to the will of God*) occurs in Rom. 15:32; 1 Co. 1:1; 2 Co. 1:1; 8:5; (Eph. 1:1; Col. 1:1; 2 Tim. 1:1), usually with respect to Paul's apostleship. But Gal 1:4 is unique in Paul, as a reference to Christ's self-giving and deliverance: "It underscores that the salvation through Christ did not occur apart from, but in complete harmony with the will of God."

5.3.2. *The will of God* has to do with the Father's intention, its fulfillment in Christ, and believers' active faith in Christ's fulfillment of God's intention.[81]

5.3.2.1. Regarding the NT, God's will is a powerful unity, not a set of individual legal directions. It is, therefore, expressed in the singular. This attests that God's will is not a list of separable regulations for given occasions. It is a power field that serves and supports God's redemptive purpose.

5.3.2.2. Regarding Christ as Doer of God's will, the Lord's Prayer says, *your will be done, as in heaven so also on earth.* This expresses submission and consent to a comprehensive fulfillment of God's will, the hallowing of God's name, and the coming of God's kingdom. It shows agreement with Jesus' petition in Gethsemane (Mt. 26:42), and attests that in him all the promises of God, for reconciliation, wholeness, and new creation, find their *yes.*

5.3.2.3. Regarding salvation, the will of God is the basis and purpose of salvation, usually presented with reference to God's will *to save.* Matthew consistently links it to the title, *Father.*

5.3.2.4. Regarding Paul's message, the human will is in need of what only the divine will can accomplish. God's will involves God's resolve for action, as over against merely remaining in the sphere of thought. God's will alone, and nothing human, can provide salvation.[82]

5.3.2.5. Regarding believers, the true test of the will of God is nonconformity to this aeon and readiness for the renewal of the *mind.* Jesus gave himself for others, so that rescue, not sacrifice, defines atonement. God's will in Jesus enables believers' conformity to God's will, freedom from the present evil age, and reconciliation to God through Christ.[83]

The three clauses of Gal 1:4 explicate God's redemptive purpose in Christ. That purpose encompasses Christ's self-giving, believers' deliverance, and the Father's will. The thought of Christ's self-giving has roots in early Jewish Christianity and its struggle to comprehend the death of Christ. A connection to sacrifice could be traced even further back, to pre-Christian

---

81. Schrenk, "θέλημα."

82. Luther, *Bondage,* 107: "with regard to God, and in all that bears on salvation or damnation, (one) has no free-will, but is a captive, a prisoner and bond-slave, either to the will of God, or to the will of Satan." Romans 7.

83 Schrenk, 54–55; 56, ". . . the will of God as the basis and purpose of salvation" with only one exception, is how the NT specifies God's will to save; "the redemption of Christ which frees the community, corresponds to the will of the Father." The submission of Jesus to the will of the Father, 55, is the "attitude demanded of the followers of Jesus because Jesus Himself is wholly rooted and lives in the divine will." BDAG, 447. Bruce, 76–77. Mußner, 52, notes a similarity in Qumran literature of *will of God* statements, that here announce the sovereign power of God over against the evil age in language spelling that aeon's end. Bring, 25; Schlatter, *Galater,* 11.

Jewish lament and liturgy, and to the cries for justice. Martyn's quotation marks at 1:4a indicate Paul's correction of the inherited tradition with the *deliverance* clause of 1:4b.[84] His modification of the traditional interpretation reflects his preference for the singular word, *sin*, signifying a power that holds humanity in bondage, requiring deliverance. Deliverance brings the end of the sacrificial system, rather than its perpetuation. *Atonement as deliverance* anticipates Paul's argument throughout Galatians regarding the death-bringing character of the law (Gal 2:19); the annulment of believer's relation to the world (6:14); imprisonment of all things under the power of sin (3:22–3); his resolve not to *glory* or *boast* (*kauchasthai*) in anything except the cross; the cross as the act of salvation in Christ that brings new creation (6:15); faith in Christ, as a sign of the new creation, over against the old or sinful *kosmos*.[85]

Galatians 1:4b completes the means-to-an-end statement that began in 1:4a. Paul echoes the liberation theme of Exodus 3:7–8, using its same verb, *deliver* (*exelētai*). Deliverance in Christ means transfer from one sphere of power to another, from sinful *kosmos* to *new creation*.

And yet it was sinful *kosmos* that put Christ to death. The powers of death, in the forms of cultural exclusivism, religious institutionalism, and political authoratarianism were the human or institutional faces of sinful *kosmos*, ruling in the present evil age. Paul identifies deliverance through Christ with the will of God, 1:4c. The liberation that is in Christ *is* the will of God by which and to which believers have been delivered, just as Christ had given up his own self to God's will to prevail over the powers of the present age.

---

84. Cousar, *Theology*, 10–11, cites Käsemann, who "consistently draws a distinction between the texts that Paul inherits from the liturgical tradition of the early church and those that emanate from Paul himself . . . he begins with the passages emphasizing 'the scandal of the cross,' because crucifixion language (not appearing in the texts from the received tradition) represents a distinctively Pauline contribution . . . The message of a crucified Messiah was so radical that it became for Jews a stumbling block and for Greeks folly (1 Cor 1:23) . . ." Green, 25, also indicates that the NT posits no single line of understanding of Jesus' death.

85. Cousar, 8, n. 17, "Luz proposes three marks of a true 'theology of the cross.' (1) It understands the cross as the exclusive ground of salvation, with the result that all other saving events (such as the resurrection and the *parousia*) are considered in relation to it and all current understandings are critiqued by it. (2) It understands the cross as the starting point of theology, in the sense that it is not merely an isolated component of theology, but theology itself pure and simple, in the light of which all issues are at stake. (3) It understands the cross as the hub of theology, in the sense that from it statements of anthropology, views of history, ecclesiology, ethics, etc., radiate. Luz lists only Paul and Mark among New Testament witnesses as theologians of the cross in this exclusive sense ('*Theologia crucis*,' 116)."

Jesus' death had meaning for salvation, then, primarily (1) as a public demonstration of the Powers' true character in their fallen state; (2) as a witness to Jesus' own freedom from the Powers' domination; and, (3) when God vindicated Jesus on Easter, as a testimony to God's endorsement of Jesus' way as true faithfulness.[86]

Paul's reference to *hilasterion* in Rom 3:25 is best understood as pointing to the crucified Christ as the place where God meets humankind. There, in Christ, God offers mercy beyond the boundaries of the Holy of Holies, and allows its availability to any who will have faith in God's redemptive act, the cruciform shape of which is seen in the self-giving of Christ.

Luther reflects on Christ's self-giving as Paul speaks of it in Galatians 1:4a:

> *He does not say, "Who has received our works from us" or*
> *"Who has received the sacrifices required by the law of Moses . . ."*
> *Instead he says: "Who has given . . ." Has given what?*
> *Neither gold nor silver nor cattle nor Passover lambs nor an angel,*
> *but "Himself."*[87]

---

86. Grimsrud, 111–12.

87. Luther, *LW* 26:32. Hultgren, *Romans*, 668, "Paul writes that God has put forth Christ as a ἱλαστήριον to *demonstrate* his righteousness, not to placate it. The clause speaks of (1) God as subject, (2) Christ as object, and (3) a divine action, and the action is . . . that God put forth his Son for a redemptive purpose (cf. similar forms . . . at Rom 8:3; 8:32; and Gal 4:4). Thus the emphasis is totally on divine action." Forde, *God*, 30–31; *Law*, 49–68.

Conclusion

WE HAVE FOUND THAT the saying in Gal 2:19, *I through the law died to the law*, may best be understood as asserting that death with Christ occurred when Christ died on the cross. Law is the bringer, or agent, of this death. This is true for the believer, as it was true for Paul, as it was true for Christ himself. It is death in a particular relationship, namely, in relation to the law itself. Several elements of Paul's argument in Galatians support this understanding.

1. What motivated Paul's argument in the first place was the commitment by opponents of Paul's gospel in Galatia to impose conditions of the law on Gentile converts to faith in Christ. These conditions include circumcision, table rules, and calendar piety. But Paul generalizes from these specific conditions, or works of the law, to argue against the whole law or the law as such. The issue relates directly to the daily life of the believer and to the life of the church. Under what condition can the life of faith be lived? That is, on what grounds is one justified in relation to God? Or, what is it that defines the identity of the person of faith, and what characterizes the essence of the church? Paul's answer: *Not works of law, but faith in Jesus Christ*! That is the tension.

2. Paul identifies being under law with being under curse. Christ died an accursed death, as he became a curse for us. Law cannot grant life. The redemptive death of Christ grants life. His death under the curse of law is the result of the law's work. Paul omits the phrase, *by God*, from the Deut 21:23 quotation. The omission distances God from the cursing power of law, and lays the power to curse, and the resulting death, on the law itself.

3. Paul connects this sense of law as curse-bringer and as death-bringer with the idea of slavery under the elements of the world to speak of the inclusive situation of all people. He connects the situation of all people (in need of redemption) with the birth of Jesus under the law. As there was the purpose statement regarding Christ's becoming a curse *so that* the blessing might come upon the Gentiles, so also there is a purposive statement

(redemption) attached to the significance of Christ's birth under law *so that he might save those who are under law*. The same christological structure governs both the statement about death under curse and birth under law.

4. As we turned to the prescript of the epistle (1:1–5), and to Gal 1:4, in particular, we found the implicit tension in the Apostle's understanding of the early, inherited tradition of the self-giving Christ. This servant-like theme has played into a Christian interpretation of the atonement, bringing nuances of sacrifice or martyrdom. But in 1:4 Paul brings his interpretation to the early Christian tradition. He does not speak of sacrifice, but rather redefines the tradition of the self-giving of Christ in terms of *deliverance*, rescue, or liberation.[1] Galatians 1:4 manifests Paul's progress beyond the early tradition. He expands the message of Christ's self-giving, so to make possible the proclamation of the cross as a redemptive event. Indeed, Paul proclaims the cross as *the* redemptive event in the faithful mission of Christ who gave himself for us, granting not just forgiveness for sins, but freedom from the power of sin itself.

5. Paul does not make law simply an agent of sin in Galatians, as he does in Romans. In Galatians the law produces transgressions. The law in Galatians is related in a somewhat reverse way to sin, in contrast to Romans. In Romans death is the effect of which sin is the cause, and law is in the service of the power of sin. In Galatians sin is the effect of which law is the cause. The same is true of death in Galatians: it is caused by the law. Christ's death under law is the paradigm for death to and through the law, for Paul and for every believer who is crucified with Christ.

Paul placards before us the cross of Christ as God's sufficient act of redemption. The crucified Christ has done what the law could not do, what all conditions of which law is a representative could not accomplish, and what any force or standard by which it might be thought that life is granted and defined is found wanting. "The new does not appear from a collection of the elements of the old which are still alive . . . The new is created not out of the old, not out of the best of the old, but out of the *death* of the old."[2] New life in the new age, Paul would have us know, comes only through participation and inclusion in the cross of Christ. Christ's life, death, and faithfulness are the turning point of the ages. He is the paradigm of Christian existence. One who lived four centuries after Jesus and Paul knew this faith, and prayed to the God who suffers and saves through the cross:

> O God of the crosses that are at hand, Come to the aid of your servant.[3]

1. Martyn, *Galatians*, 90, speaks of 1:4b as a *correction* of 1:4a.
2. Tillich, "Behold, I Am Doing a New Thing," 181–82.
3. Moulton and Milligan, 586. Fourth century Christian prayer, P Oxy VII. 10582.

Bibliography

Aageson, James. *Written Also for Our Sake*. Louisville: Westminster, 1993.
Abbott-Smith, G. *Manual Greek Lexicon of the New Testament*. 3rd ed. Edinburgh: T. & T. Clark, 1960.
Aland, Kurt. *Vollständige Konkordanz zum griechischen Neuen Testament*. Berlin: Walter DeGruyter, 1978.
Allegro, J. M. "Fragments of a Qumran Scroll of Eschatological Midrašîm." *JBL* 77 (1958): 350-54.
Alt, Albrecht. *Essays on Old Testament History and Religion*. Translated by R. A. Wilson. Garden City: Doubleday, 1967.
Althaus, Paul. *Der Brief an die Römer*. Göttingen: Vandenhoeck & Ruprecht, 1954.
Anderson, Bernhard W. *Understanding the Old Testament*. Englewood Cliffs: Prentice-Hall, 1986.
———, and Walter Harrelson. *Israel's Prophetic Heritage*. New York: Harpers, 1962.
Anderson, George. "Exodus Typology in Second Isaiah." 177-95, in *Israel's Prophetic Heritage*.
Andresen, Carl, and Günter Klein. *Theologia Crucis—Signum Crucis*. Tübingen: J. C. B. Mohr (Paul Siebeck), 1979.
Aquinas, St. Thomas. *Galatians*. Translated by F. R. Larcher. Albany: Magi Books, 1966.
Aristotle. *Metaphysics I:986a*. Loeb Classical Library. Harvard: 1933.
Attridge, Harold. "The Letter to the Hebrews," 2250-68. In *HarperCollins Study Bible*, Wayne Meeks, General Editor. New York: HarperCollins, 1993.
Aulén, Gustaf. *Christus Victor*. Translated by A. G. Hebert. New York: Macmillan, 1961.
Badenas, Robert. *Christ the End of the Law*. Sheffield: JSOT, 1985.
Bailey, John W. "Gospel for Mankind." *Interpretation* 7 (1953) 163-74.
Bammel, Ernst. *The Trial of Jesus*. Naperville: R. Allenson, 1970.
Barclay, John. *Obeying the Truth*. Minneapolis: Fortress, 1988.
Barr, James. *The Semantics of Biblical Language*. Oxford: Oxford University Press, 1961.
Barrett, C. K. "The Allegory of Abraham, Sarah, and Hagar in the Argument of Galatians." In *Rechtfertigung*, 1-16. Reprinted in *Essays on Paul*, 154-70.
———. "Christianity at Corinth." In *Essays on Paul*, 1-27.
———. *Essays on Paul*. Philadelphia: Westminster, 1982.
———. *The First Epistle to the Corinthians*. New York: Harper & Row, 1968.
———. *Freedom and Obligation*. London: SPCK, 1985.
———. "Paul and the 'Pillar' Apostles." In *Studia Paulina*, 1-19.
———. "Paul's Opponents in II Corinthians." In *Essays on Paul*, 60-86.

———. *The Second Epistle to the Corinthians*. New York: Harper & Row, 1973.

———. *The Signs of an Apostle*. Philadelphia: Fortress, 1972.

———. "ΨΕΥΔΑΠΟΣΤΟΛΟΙ (2 Cor 11:13)." In *Essays on Paul*, 87–107.

Barth, Karl. *Epistle to the Philippians*. Translated by James Leitch. Richmond: John Knox, 1962.

———. *Epistle to the Romans*. Translated by Edwyn C. Hoskyns. Oxford: Oxford University Press, 1933.

———. *Resurrection of the Dead*. Translated by H. J. Stenning. New York: Revell, 1933.

———. *A Shorter Commentary on Romans*. Translated by D. H. van Daalen. London: SCM, 1959.

Barth, Markus. "A Chapter on the Church: the Body of Christ." *Interpretation* 12 (1958) 131–56.

———. *Ephesians*. New York: Doubleday, 1974.

Baasland, Ernst. "Persecution: A Neglected Feature in the Letter to the Galatians." *ST* 38 (1984) 135–50.

Bassler, Jouette. *Pauline Theology, Vol I*. Minneapolis: Fortress, 1991.

Bauer, Walter. *A Greek–English Lexicon of the New Testament and Other Early Christian Literature*, 3rd ed., rev. and ed. Frederick W. Danker; previously with W. F. Arndt and F. W. Gingrich. Chicago: University of Chicago Press, 2000.

Behm, Johannes. "κυρόω." *TDNT* 3:1098–99.

———. "προσανατίθημι." *TDNT* 1:353–56.

Beker, J. Christiaan. *Heirs of Paul*. Minneapolis: Fortress, 1991.

———. *Paul the Apostle*. Philadelphia: Fortress, 1980.

———. *Paul's Apocalyptic Gospel*. Philadelphia: Fortress, 1982.

———. *The Triumph of God*. Minneapolis: Fortress, 1990.

Benoit, Pierre. "The Law and the Cross according to St. Paul." Translated by Benet Weatherhead. In *Jesus and the Gospel*, 2:11–39. London: Darton, Longman & Todd, 1974.

Bertram, Georg. "ἔργον." *TDNT* 2:635–54.

———. "μωρός." *TDNT* 4:832–47.

———. "νήπιος." *TDNT* 4:912–23.

———. "παιδεύω." *TDNT* 5:596–625.

Best, Ernest. *The Letter of Paul to the Romans*. Cambridge: Cambridge University Press, 1967.

———, and R. McL. Wilson. *Text and Interpretation*. Cambridge: Cambridge University Press, 1979.

Betz, Hans Dieter. *Galatians*. Philadelphia: Fortress, 1979.

———. Editor, *Religion in Geschichte und Gegenwart*, 4th ed. Tübingen: J. C. B. Mohr [Paul Siebeck], 1998—.

Billman, Kathleen, and Daniel Migliore. *Rachel's Cry: Prayer of Lament and Rebirth of Hope*. Cleveland: United Church, 1999.

Black, Matthew. "The Christological Use of the Old Testament in the New Testament." *NTS* 18 (1972) 1–14.

———. *Romans*. London: Marshall, Morgan & Scott, 1973.

Blank, Josef. *Paulus und Jesus*. München: Kösel, 1968.

———. "Warum sagt Paulus: 'Aus Werken des Gesetzes wird niemand gerecht'?" *Evangelisch-katholischer Kommentar* 1:79–95. Neukirchener, 1969.

Blass, F., and Debrunner, A. *A Greek Grammar of the New Testament*. Translated and edited by Robert W. Funk. Chicago: University of Chicago Press, 1961.
Bligh, John. *Galatians: A Discussion of St. Paul's Epistle*. London: St. Paul, 1969.
Bonnard, Pierre. *L' Épître de Saint Paul aux Galates*. Neuchâtel: Delachaux & Niestlé, 1972.
Bonsirven, Joseph. *Exégèse Rabbinique et Exégèse Paulinienne*. Paris: Beauchesne et Fils, 1939.
Borgen, Peder. *Bread From Heaven*. Leiden: E. J. Brill, 1965.
———. "The Cross-National Church for Jews and Greeks." In *The Many and the One*, 225–43.
———. *The Many and the One*. Trondheim: Tapir, 1985.
———. "Observations on the Theme 'Paul and Philo.'" In *Die Paulinische Literatur und Theologie*, 85–102.
———. "Paul Preaches Circumcision and Pleases Men." In *Paul and Paulinism*, 37–46.
Bornkamm, Günther. "Gesetz und Natur (Röm 2:14–16)." In *Studien zu Antike und Urchristentum*, 93–118. München: Chr. Kaiser, 1959.
———. *Paul*. Translated by D. M. G. Stalker. New York: Harper & Row, 1971.
Borse, Udo. *Der Brief an die Galater*. Regensburg: Friedrich Pustet, 1984.
———. *Der Standort des Galaterbriefes*. Bonn: Hanstein, 1972.
Botterweck, G. Johannes, and Helmer Ringgren. *TDOT*. Translated by John T. Willis. Grand Rapids: Eerdmans, 1974.
Bousset, Wilhelm. "Der Brief an die Galater." In *SNT* 2:28–72. Göttingen: Vandenhoeck & Ruprecht, 1908.
Bouttier, Michel. *En Christ*. Presses Universitaires de France, 1962.
Brichto, Herbert Chanan. *The Problem of "Curse" in the Hebrew Bible*. Philadelphia: Society of Biblical Literature, 1963.
Bright, John. *The Kingdom of God*. New York: Abingdon, 1953.
Brinsmead, Bernard. *Galatians—Dialogical Response to Opponents*. Missoula: Scholars, 1982.
Brock, Rita Nakashima. "The Cross of Resurrection and Communal Redemption." *Cross Examinations*. 241–51.
Brown, Francis. *Hebrew and English Lexicon: The New Brown, Driver, Briggs, Gesenius*. LaFayette: Associated Publishers and Authors, 1978.
Brownlee, William H. *The Midrash Pesher of Habakkuk*. Missoula: Scholars, 1979.
———. *The Text of Habakkuk in the Ancient Commentary from Qumran*. Philadelphia: Society of Biblical Literature, 1959.
Bruce, F. F. "'Called to Freedom': A Study in Galatians." In *The New Testament Age*, 1:61–72.
———. *Commentary on Galatians*. Grand Rapids: Eerdmans, 1982.
———. "The Curse of the Law." In *Paul and Paulinism*, 27–36.
———. "Further Thoughts on Paul's Autobiography (Galatians 1:11—2:14)." In *Jesus und Paulus*, 21–9.
———. *Paul, Apostle of the Free Spirit*. Exeter, 1980.
———. "Paul and the Law of Moses." *BJRL* 57 (1975) 259–79.
———. "Paul and the Law in Recent Research." In *Law and Religion*, 115–25.
———. *Philippians*. San Francisco: Harper & Row, 1983.
Brueggemann, Walter. *Genesis*. Atlanta: John Knox, 1982.
———. *Theology of the Old Testament*. Minneapolis: Fortress, 1997.

Büchsel, Friedrich. "ἀγοράζω." *TDNT* 1:124–28.
———. "ἱστορέω." *TDNT* 3:391–396.
———. "ἱλάσκομαι." *TDNT* 3:314–318.
———. "ἱλαστήριον, ἱλασμός." *TDNT* 3:319–323.
———. "λύω." *TDNT* 4:335–36.
Bultmann, Rudolf. *Faith and Understanding*. Translated by Louise P. Smith. London: SCM, 1969.
———. *History and Eschatology*. New York: Harper & Brothers, 1957.
———. *Jesus and the Word*. Translated by Lousie P. Smith. New York: Scribner's Sons, 1958.
———. "New Testament and Mythology." In *Kerygma and Myth*. Translated by Reginald H. Fuller. Edited by Hans Werner Bartsch. London: SPCK, 1953.
———. *The Second Letter to the Corinthians*. Translated by Roy A. Harrisville. Minneapolis: Augsburg, 1985.
———. *Theology of the New Testament*. Translated by Kendrick Grobel. New York: Scribners, 1951.
———. "ἀγαλλιάομαι." *TDNT* 1:19–21.
———. "ζάω." *TDNT* 2:855–75.
———. "θάνατος." *TDNT* 3:7–25.
———. "καυχάομαι." *TDNT* 3:645–54.
———. "πιστεύω." *TDNT* 6:174–82, 197–228.
Buttrick, George. *Interpreter's Dictionary of the Bible*. Nashville: Abingdon, 1962.
Burkert, Walter. *Greek Religion*. Translated by John Raffan. Cambridge: Harvard University Press, 1985.
Burton, Ernest De Witt. *The Epistle to the Galatians*. Edinburgh: T. & T. Clark, 1921.
Callan, Terrance. "Pauline Midrash: The Exegetical Background of Gal 3:19b." *JBL* 99 (1980) 549–67.
Calvin, John. *The Epistles of Paul the Apostle to the Galatians, Ephesians, Philippians and Colossians*. Translated by T. H. L. Parker. Oliver & Boyd, 1965.
———. *Institutes of the Christian Religion*. Edited by John McNeill. Translated by Ford Battles. Philadelphia: Westminster, 1960.
Campbell, K. M. "Covenant or Testament?" *EQ* 44 (1972) 107–11.
Carlson, Richard. *Baptism and Apocalyptic in Paul*. Ann Arbor: University Microfilms International, 1983.
Carr, Wesley. *Angels and Principalities*. Cambridge: Cambridge University Press, 1981.
Catchpole, David. "Paul, James and the Apostolic Decree." *NTS* 23 (1977) 428–44.
Cavallin, H. C. "The Righteous Shall Live by Faith." *ST* 32 (1978) 33–43.
Chadwick, Henry. "All Things to all Men." *NTS* 1 (1954–5) 261–75.
Childs, Brevard. *The New Testament as Canon: An Introduction*. Philadelphia: Fortress, 1984.
Clements, Ronald. *Abraham and David*. London: SCM, 1967.
———. *God's Chosen People*. London: SCM, 1968.
Conzelmann, Hans. *1 Corinthians*. Translated by James W. Leitch. Philadelphia: Fortress, 1975.
———. *An Outline of the Theology of the New Testament*. Translated by John Bowden. New York: Harper & Row, 1969.
———. "χάρις." *TDNT* 9:387–415.

Corsani, Bruno. "ΕΚ ΠΙΣΤΕΟΣ in the Letters of Paul." In *The New Testament Age*, 1:87–94.
Cousar, Charles. *Galatians*. Atlanta: John Knox, 1982.
———. *A Theology of the Cross*. Minneapolis: Fortress, 1990.
———. "Paul and the Death of Jesus."*Interpretation*, 51 (1997) 38–52.
Cranfield, C. E. B. "St. Paul and the Law." *SJT* 17 (1964) 43–68.
———. *The Epistle to the Romans*. Edinburgh: T. & T. Clark, 1975.
Cullmann, Oscar. *The Christology of the New Testament*. Translated by Shirley C. Guthrie and Charles A. M. Hall. London: SCM, 1959.
———. "The Plurality of the Gospels as a Theological Problem in Antiquity." In *The Early Church*, 39–58. London: SCM, 1956.
Dahl, Nils Alstrup. "The Atonement—An Adequate Reward for the Akedah?" In *The Crucified Messiah*, 146–60.
———. "Contradictions in Scripture." In *Studies in Paul*, 159–77.
———. *The Crucified Messiah*. Minneapolis: Augsburg, 1974.
———. "The Doctrine of Justification: Its Social Function and Implications." In *Studies in Paul*, 95–120.
———. "Eschatology and History in Light of the Qumran Texts." In *The Crucified Messiah*, 129–45.
———. "The Messiahship of Jesus in Paul." In *The Crucified Messiah*, 37–47.
———. "The Particularity of the Pauline Epistles as a Problem in the Ancient Church." In *Neotestamentica Et Patristica*, 261–71.
———. "Paul and the Church at Corinth." In *Studies in Paul*, 40–61.
———. "Promise and Fulfillment." In *Studies in Paul*, 121–36.
———. *Studies in Paul*. Minneapolis: Augsburg, 1977.
Dana, H. E., and Mantey, Julius R. *A Mannual Grammar of the Greek New Testament*. New York: MacMillan, 1927.
Daube, David. *The New Testament and Rabbinic Judaism*. London: Althone, 1956.
Davies, Donald M. "Free from the Law." *Interpretation* 7 (1953) 156–62.
Davies, W. D. *Jewish and Pauline Studies*. Philadelphia: Fortress, 1984.
———. "Law in First Century Judaism." *IDB* 3:89–95.
———. "Law in the New Testament." *IDB* 3:95–102.
———. "Paul and the Law: Reflections on Pitfalls in Interpretation." In *Paul and Paulinism*, 4–16.
———. *Paul and Rabbinic Judaism*. London: SPCK, 1948.
———. *Torah in the Messianic Age and/or the Age to Come*. Philadelphia: Society of Biblical Literature, 1952.
Delling, Gerhard. "ἀργός." *TDNT* 1:452–54.
———. "στοιχέω." *TDNT* 7:666–87.
———. "τάσσω." *TDNT* 8:27–48.
Dibelius, Martin. *James*. Translated by Michael A. Williams. Revised by Heinrich Greeven. Philadelphia: Fortress, 1976.
———, and Werner Kümmel. *Paul*. Translated by Frank Clark. Phildelphia: Westminster, 1975.
Dietzfelbinger, Christian. *Die Berufung des Paulus als Ursprung seiner Theologie*. Neukirchener, 1985.
Dodd, C. H. *According to the Scriptures*. London: Nisbet, 1952.
———. *The Epistle of Paul to the Romans*. London: Hodder and Stoughton, 1932.

———. ΙΛΑΣΚΕΣΘΑΙ. *JTS* 32(1931), 352–60, reprinted as "Atonement," in *The Bible and the Greeks*, 82–95. London: Hodder & Stoughton, 1935.
Donaldson, T. L. "The 'Curse of the Law' and the Inclusion of the Gentiles: Galatians 3:13–14." *NTS* 32 (1986) 94–112.
Douglas, Mary. *Leviticus As Literature*. Oxford: Oxford University Press, 1999.
Driver, S. R. *Deuteronomy*. New York: Scribner's Sons, 1903.
Duncan, George S. *The Epistle of Paul to the Galatians*. London: Hodder and Stoughton, 1934.
Dunn, James. "The Incident at Antioch." *JSNT* 18 (1983) 3–57.
———. *Jesus, Paul and the Law*. Louisville: Westminster, 1990.
———. "The New Perspective on Paul." *BJRL* 65 (1983) 95–122.
———. "The Relationship between Paul and Jerusalem according to Galatians 1 and 2." *NTS* 28 (1982) 461–78.
———. "Works of the Law and the Curse of the Law (Galatians 3:10–14)." *NTS* 31 (1985) 523–42.
Ebeling, Gerhard. *The Truth of the Gospel*. Translated by David Green. Tübingen: J. C. B. Mohr (Paul Siebeck), 1981.
Eichholz, Georg. *Die Theologie des Paulus im Umriss*. Neukirchener, 1972.
Elliot, Neil. *The Arrogance of Nations*. Minneapolis: Fortress, 2010.
Ellis, E. Earl. *Paul's Use of the Old Testament*. Edinburgh and London: Oliver and Boyd, 1957.
———. *Prophecy and Hermeneutic*. Tübingen: J. C. B. Mohr (Paul Siebeck), 1978.
———, and Erich Gräßer. *Jesus und Paulus*. Göttingen: Vandenhoeck & Ruprecht, 1975.
Ellis, Peter. *Seven Pauline Letters*. Collegeville: Liturgical Press, 1982.
Esler, Philip F. *Conflict and Identity in Romans: The Social Setting of Paul's Letter*. Minneapolis: Fortress, 2003.
Feldman, L. H. "Flavius Josephus Revisited: the Man, His Writings, and His Significance." In *Aufstieg und Niedergang der Römischen Welt* II.21.2:763–862.
Fensham, F. Charles. "Malediction and Benediction in Ancient Near Eastern Vassal-Treaties and the Old Testament." *ZAW* 74 (1962) 1–9.
Fitzmyer, Joseph A. *To Advance the Gospel*. New York: Crossroad, 1981.
———. "Aramaic *Kephā* and Peter's Name in the New Testament." *To Advance the Gospel*, 112–24.
———. "Crucifixion in Ancient Palestine, Qumran Literature, and the New Testament." *CBQ* 40 (1978) 493–513. Reprint in *To Advance the Gospel*, 125–46.
———. *Essays on the Semitic Background of the New Testament*. London: Geoffrey Chapman, 1971.
———. "The Gospel in the Theology of Paul." In *To Advance the Gospel*, 149–61.
———. "Habakkuk 2:3–4 and the New Testament." In *To Advance the Gospel*, 236–46.
———. *An Introductory Bibliography for the Study of Scripture*. Rome: Biblical Institute, 1981.
———. "The Letter to the Galatians." In *JBC*, 236–46. London: Geoffrey Chapman, 1968.
———. *Paul and His Theology*. Englewood Cliffs: Prentice Hall, 1989.
———. "Paul and the Law." In *To Advance the Gospel*, 186–201.
———. *Romans*. New Haven: Yale University Press, 2008.

———. "The Use of Explicit Old Testament Quotations in Qumran Literature and in the New Testament." In *Essays on the Semitic Background of the New Testament*, 3-58.
Foerster, Werner. "κλῆρος." *TDNT* 3:758-85.
———. "κύριος." *TDNT* 3:1039-98.
Forde, Gerhard. *The Law-Gospel Debate*. Minneapolis: Augsburg, 1969.
———. *Where God Meets Man*. Minneapolis: Augsburg, 1972.
Fretheim, Terrence. "Because the Whole Earth is Mine." *Interpretation* 50 (1996) 229-39.
———. *Exodus*. Louisville: John Knox, 1991.
Fridrichsen, Anton, and other members of Uppsala University. *The Root of the Vine*. Westminster: Dacre, 1953.
Friedrich, Wolfgang, W. Pöhlmann, and Peter Stuhlmacher. 1-16. *Rechtfertigung*. Tübingen: J. C. B. Mohr (Paul Siebeck), 1976.
Friedrich, Gehard. "εὐαγγελίζομαι." *TDNT* 2:707-37.
———. "κῆρυξ." *TDNT* 3:683-718.
Fuller, R. H. *The Foundations of New Testament Christology*. Glasgow: William Collins & Sons, 1979.
Funk, Robert. *Language, Hermeneutic, and Word of God*. New York: Harper & Row, 1966.
Furnish, Victor. *II Corinthians*. New Haven: Yale University Press, 2005.
———. *Theology and Ethics in Paul*. Nashville: Abingdon, 1982.
Gager, John. *Reinventing Paul*. New York: Oxford University Press, 2000.
Gardner, Percy. *The Religious Experience of Saint Paul*. London: Williams and Norgate, 1911.
Gaster, T. H. "Azazel," in *IDB* 1:325-26.
———. *The Dead Sea Scriptures*. New York: Doubleday, 1956.
Gaston, Lloyd. "Paul and the Law in Galatians 2-3." In *Anti-Judaism in Early Christianity*.
Gaventa, Beverly Roberts. "Comparing Paul and Judaism, Rethinking Our Methods." *BTB* X (1980) 37-44.
———. *From Darkness to Light*. Philadelphia: Fortress, 1986.
Georgi, Dieter. *Die Geschichte der Kollekte des Paulus für Jerusalem*. Hamburg: Bergstedt, 1965.
———. *The Opponents of Paul in Second Corinthians*. English Translation from *Die Gegner des Paulus im 2. Korintherbrief*. Philadelphia: Fortress, 1986.
———. *Remembering The Poor*. Nashville: Abingdon, 1992.
Gibb, Helmut O. *"Torheit" und "Rätsel" im Neuen Testament*. Stuttgart: Kohlhammer, 1941.
Giallanza. "When I Am Weak, Then I Am Strong." *The Bible Today*, March 1978, 1572-77.
Glasswell, Mark E. and Fasholé-Luke, Edward W. *New Testament Christianity for Africa and the World*. London: SPCK, 1974.
Gnilka, Joachim. *Neues Testament und Kirche*. Freiburg, Basel, Wien: Herder, 1974.
Goppelt, Leonhard. *The Theology of the New Testament*. Translated by John Alsup. Grand Rapids: Eerdmans, 1981.
———. *Typos*. Translated by Donald H. Madvig. Grand Rapids: Eerdmans, 1982.
Gordon, T. David. "The Problem at Galatia." *Interpretation* 41 (1987) 32-43.

Gormanm, Michael. *Cruciformity.* Grand Rapids: Eerdmans, 2001.
Grant, Robert M. *A Historical Introduction to the New Testament.* New York: Harper & Row, 1963.
Guthrie, Donald. *Galatians.* Grand Rapids, London: Eerdmans/ Marshall, Morgan, and Scott, 1973.
Green, Joel. "The Death of Jesus and the Ways of God." *Interpretation,* 52 (1998) 24–37.
Grimsrud, Ted. *Instead of Atonement.* Eugene: Cascade, 2013.
Grundmann, Walter. "δεξιός." *TDNT* 2:37–40.
Gunton, Colin. Review of *Jesus: An Experiment in Christology,* by Edward Schillebeeckx. *SJT* 33 (1980) 173–75.
Gutbrod, Walter. "Ἰουδαῖος." *TDNT* 3:369–91.
Gyllenberg, Rafael. *Rechtfertigung und Altes Testament bei Paulus.* Stuttgart, Berlin, Köln, Mainz: Kohlhammer, 1973.
Haenchen, Ernst. *Die Apostelgeschichte.* Göttingen: Vandenhoeck & Ruprecht, 1959.
The Acts of the Apostles. Translated by R. McL. Wilson. Philadelphia: Westminster, 1971.
Hagner, Donald A. *Encountering the Book of Hebrews.* Grand Rapids: Baker, 2002.
———, and Murray J Harris. *Pauline Studies.* Grand Rapids: Eerdmans, 1980.
Hahn, Ferdinand. "Genesis 15:6 im Neuen Testament." In *Probleme Biblischer Theologie,* 90–107.
———. *The Titles of Jesus in Christology.* Translated by Harold Knight and George Ogg. New York: World, 1969.
Hamerton-Kelly, R. G. *Sacred Violence: Paul's Hermeneutic of the Cross.* Minneapolis: Fortress, 1992.
Hanson, A. T. *The Paradox of the Cross in the Thought of St. Paul.* Sheffield: JSOT, 1987.
———. *Studies in Paul's Technique and Theology.* London: 1974.
Harnack, Adolf von. *The Expansion of Christianity in the First Three Centuries.* Translated and edited by James Moffatt. New York: Putnam's Sons: 1904.
———. *What is Christianity?* Translated by Thomas Bailey Saunders. New York: Harper, 1957.
Harrelson, J. W. "Law in the Old Testament." *IDB* 3:77–89.
Harrisville, Roy A. *Romans.* Minneapolis: Augsburg, 1980.
Harvey, A. E. *Jesus and the Constraints of History.* Philadelphia: Westminster, 1982.
Hatch, Edwin, and Henry Redpath. *A Concordance to The Septuagint and the Other Greek Versions of the Old Testament.* 2 Volumes. Grand Rapids: Baker,1987.
Hauck, Friedrich. "καρπός." *TDNT* 3:614–16.
Hawthorne, Gerald F. *Philippians.* Waco: Word, 1983.
Hays, Richard. "Christology and Ethics in Galatians: The Law of Christ." *CBQ* 49 (1987) 268–90.
———. *The Conversion of the Imagination.* Grand Rapids: Eerdmans, 2005.
———. *Echoes Of Scripture In The Letters Of Paul.* New Haven: Yale University Press, 1989.
———. *The Faith of Jesus Christ.* Missoula: Scholars.
———. *First Corinthians.* Atlanta: John Knox, 2011.
Heidland, H. W. "λογίζομαι." *TDNT* 4:284–92.
Heim, S. Mark. "Saved by What Shouldn't Happen." *Cross Examinations,* 211–24.
———. *Saved From Sacrifice.* Grand Rapids: Eerdmans, 2006.
Hengel, Martin. *The Atonement.* Translated by John Bowden. London: SCM, 1981.

———. *Between Jesus and Paul*. Eugene: Wipf & Stock, 2003.
———. *Crucifixion*. Translated by John Bowden. Philadelphia: Fortress, 1977.
Herrmann, Johannes. "ἱλαστήριον." *TDNT* 3:318–19.
Herntrich, Volkmar. "κρίνω." *TDNT* 3:921–33.
Hewitt, J. W. "The Use of Nails in the Crucifixion." *HTR* 25 (1932) 29–46.
Hoad, John. "Some New Testament References to Isaiah 53." *ET* 58 (1956) 254–55.
Hock, Ronald. "Paul's Tentmaking and the Problem of his Social Class." *JBL* 97 (1978) 555–64.
Holmberg, Bengt. *Paul and Power*. Phildelphia: Fortress, 1978.
Hooker, Morna. "Beyond the Things that are Written? St. Paul's Use of Scripture." *NTS* 27 (1981) 295–309.
———. "Interchange in Christ." *JTS* 22 (1971) 349–61.
———. *Jesus and the Servant*. Eugene: Wipf and Stock, 2010.
———. *Not Ashamed of the Gospel*. Grand Rapids: Eerdmans, 1995.
———. "ΠΙΣΤΙΣ ΧΡΙΣΤΟΥ." *NTS* 35 (1989) 321–42.
———, and S. G. Wilson. *Paul and Paulinism*. London: SPCK, 1982.
Horsley, Richard. *Paul and the Roman Imperial Order*. Harrisburg: Trinity, 2004.
———. "Wisdom of Words and Words of Wisdom in Corinth." *CBQ* 39 (1977) 224–39.
———, and Neil Silberman. *The Message and the Kingdom*. Minneapolis: Fortress, 1997.
Howard, George. *Crisis in Galatia*. Cambridge: Cambridge University Press, 1979.
Hübner, Hans. *Law in Paul's Thought*. Translated by James Greig. Edinburgh: T. & T. Clark, 1984.
Hultgren, Arland. *Paul's Letter to the Romans*. Grand Rapids: Eerdmans, 2011.
———. "Paul's Pre-Christian Persecutions of the Church: Their Purpose, Locale, and Nature." *JBL* 95 (1976) 95–111.
———. "The *Pistis Christou* Formulation in Paul." *NT* 22 (1980) 248–63.
Hurd, John C. "Chronology, Pauline." *IDB*, Supp., 166–67. Nashville/ New York: Abingdon, 1976.
———. *The Origin of 1 Corinthians*. London: SPCK, 1965.
Jepsen, Alfred. "אמה." *TDOT* 1:318–19.
Jeremias, Joachim. *The Eucharistic Words of Jesus*. Translated by Norman Perrin. London: SCM, 1966.
———. "μωυσῆς." *TDNT* 4:848–73.
———. "παῖς θεοῦ." *TDNT* 5:677–717.
———. "Paulus als Hillelit." *Neotestamentica et Semitica*, 88–94. Edited by E. E. Ellis and M. Wilcox. Edinburgh: T. & T. Clark, 1969.
Jewett, Robert. "The Agitators and the Galatian Congregation." *NTS* 17 (1971) 198–212.
———. *A Chronology of Paul's Life*. Philadelphia: Fortress, 1979.
———. *Paul's Anthropological Terms*. Leiden: E. J. Brill, 1971.
Josephus, Flavius. *Antiquities* XIII:379–83; XV:136. Loeb Classics Library.
Juel, Donald. *Messianic Exegesis*. Philadelphia: Fortress, 1988.
Käsemann, Ernst. "A Critical Analysis of Philippians 2:5–11." Translated by Alice F. Carse. *JTC* 5:45–88. New York: Harper, 1968.
———. *Essays on New Testament Themes*. Translated by W. J. Montagne. London: SCM, 1965.
———. *Exegetische Versuche und Besinnungen*. Göttingen: Vandenhoeck & Ruprecht, 1964.

———. "The Faith of Abraham." In *Perspectives on Paul*, 79–101.
———. *Jesus Means Freedom*. Translated by Frank Clarke. Philadelphia: Fortress, 1977.
———. *New Testament Questions of Today*. Translated by W. J. Montagne and Wilfred F. Bunge. Philadelphia: Fortress, 1979.
———. "Paul and Early Catholicism." In *New Testament Questions of Today*, 236–51. Translated by Wilfred F. Bunge.
———. *Perspectives on Paul*. Translated by Margaret Kohl. Phildelphia: Fortress, 1971.
———. *Romans*. Translated by Geoffrey Bromiley. Grand Rapids: Eerdmans, 1980.
———. "The Saving Significance of the Death of Jesus." In *Perspectives on Paul*, 32–59.
———. "On the Subject of Primitive Christian Apocalyptic." In *New Testament Questions of Today*, 108–37. Translated by W. J. Montagne.
Kaym, James. "The Word of the Cross at the Turn of the Ages." *Interpretation*, 53 (1999) 44–56.
Keck, Leander. Editor, *The New Interpreter's Bible*. 12 vols. Nashville: Abingdon, 1994–2004.
———. "Paul and Apocalyptic Theology." *Interpretation* 38 (1984) 229–41.
———. *Paul and His Letters*. Philadelphia: Fortress, 1979.
———. "The Post-Pauline Interpretation of Jesus' Death in Rom 5:6–7." In *Theologia Crucis—Signum Crucis*, 237–48.
Kee, H. C. "Who Were the Super Apostles of 2 Corinthians 10–13?" *RQ* 1980 65–76.
Kertelge, Karl. "Apokalypsis Jesou Christou (Gal 1:12)." In *NTK*, 261–81.
———. "Das Apostleamt des Paulus, sein Ursprung und seine Bedeutung." *Biblische Zeitschrift* 14 (1970) 161–81.
———. "Autorität des Gesetzes und Autorität Jesu bei Paulus." SNTS Paulusseminar: Trondheim, 1985.
———. "Zur Deutung des Rechtfertigungsbegriffs im Galaterbrief." *BZ* 12 (1968) 211–22.
———. "Gesetz und Freiheit im Galaterbrief." *NTS* 30 (1984) 382–94.
———. *"Rechtfertigung" bei Paulus*. Münster: Aschendorff, 1967.
Kilpatrick, G. D. "Gal 2.14, ὀρθοποδοῦσιν." *Neutestamentliche Studien für R. Bultmann*, 269–74. Edited by W. Eltester. Berlin: Töpelmann, 1957.
Kilunen, Jarmo, Vilho Riekkinen, and Heikki Räisänen. *Glaube und Gerechtigkeit*. Helsinki: 1983.
Kim, Seyoon. *The Origin of Paul's Gospel*. Tübingen: J. C. B. Mohr (Paul Siebeck), 1981.
Kirk, J. Andrew. "Apostleship Since Rengstorf." *NTS* 21 (1975) 249–64.
Kirk, G. S., and Raven, J. E. *The Presocratic Philosophers*. Cambridge: Cambridge University Press, 1962.
Kittel, Gerhard. *TDNT*. Translated by Geoffrey Bromiley. Grand Rapids: Eerdmans, 1964–76.
Klausner, Joseph. *From Jesus to Paul*. Translated by William F. Stinespring. Boston: Beacon, 1961.
Koester, Helmut. *Introduction to the New Testament, Volume One: History, Culture, and Religion of the Hellenistic Age*. Philadelphia: Fortress, 1982.
———. "φύσις." *TDNT* 9:251–77.
Kramer, Werner. *Christ, Lord, Son of God*. Translated by Brian Hardy. Chatham: SCM, 1966.
Kubo, Sakae. *A Readers' Greek-English Lexicon of the New Testament*. Grand Rapids: Zondervan, 1979.

Kuhn, Heinz-Wolfgang. "Jesus als Gekreuzigter in der fruhchristlichen Verkündigung bis zur Mitte des 2. Jahrhunderts." *ZTK* 72 (1975) 1-46. Tübingen: J. C. B. Mohr (Paul Siebeck).

Kuhn, Karl Georg. "προσήλυτος." *TDNT* 6:727-44.

Kümmel, Werner Georg. *Introduction to the New Testament*. Translated by Howard C. Kee. Nashville: Abingdon, 1975.

Kuss, Otto. *Der Römerbrief übersetzt und erklärt*. Regensburg: Friedrich Pustet, 1959.

Lagrange, M. J. *Saint Paul, Épître aux Galates*. Paris: Librairie Lecoffre, 1942.

Lake, Kirsopp. *The Beginnings of Christianity*. London: MacMillan, 1920-33.

Lambrecht, Jan. "The Line of Thought in Gal 2:14b-21." *NTS* 24 (1978) 484-95.

Lewy, Immanuel. "The Puzzle of Dt. XXVII: Blessing Announced, But Curses Noted." *VT* XII (1962) 207-11.

Liddell, Henry G. and Robert Scott. *A Greek-English Lexicon*. Revised by Henry S. Jones. Oxford: Clarendon, 1968.

Lightfoot, J. B. *The Epistle of St. Paul to the Galatians*. Grand Rapids: Zondervan, 1976.

———. *The Epistle of St. Paul to the Philippians*. Grand Rapids: Zondervan, 1953.

Linton, Olof. "Paulus och Juridiken." *STK* 21(1945) 173-92.

———. "The Third Aspect." *ST* III (1949) 79-95.

Lindars, Barnabas. *Law and Religion*, 115-25. Worcester: Billing & Sons, 1988.

———. *New Testament Apologetic*. Philadelphia: Westminster, 1961.

———, and P. Borgen. "The Place of the Old Testament in the Formation of New Testament Theology: Prolegomena and Response," *NTS* 23:59-75.

Loh, I-Jin, and Nida, Eugene A. *A Translators Handbook on Paul's Letter to the Philippians*. Stuttgart: United Bible Societies, 1977.

Lohse, Eduard. *Colossians and Philemon*. Translated by Robert J. Karris. Philadelphia: Fortress, 1971.

———. *The Formation of the New Testament Canon*. Translated by M. Eugene Boring. Nashville: Abingdon, 1981.

———. "χείρ." *TDNT* 9:424-37.

Long, Thomas G. "Bold in the Presence of God, *Atonement in Hebrews*." Interpretation 52 (1998) 53-69.

Longenecker, Bruce. *Narrative Dynamics in Paul*. Louisville: Westminster John Knox, 2002.

Longenecker, Richard. *The Christology of Early Jewish Christianity*. Grand Rapids: Baker, 1970.

———. *Paul, Apostle of Liberty*. Grand Rapids: Baker, 1976.

Louw, Johannes, and Eugene A. Nida. *Greek-English Lexicon of the New Testament Based on Semantic Domains*, 2d ed. New York: United Bible Societies, 1989.

Lüdemann, Gerd. *Opposition to Paul In Jewish Christianity*. Minneapolis: Fortress, 1989.

———. *Paul, Apostle to the Gentiles*. Translated by F. Stanley Jones. Philadelphia: Fortress, 1984.

Lührmann, Dieter. "Abendmahlsgemeinschaft?" In *Kirche*, 271-86.

———. *Der Brief an die Galater*. Zürich: Theologischer Verlag, 1978.

———. *Das Offenbarungsverständnis bei Paulus und in paulinischen Gemeinden*. Neukirchener, 1965.

———, and Georg Strecker. *Kirche*. Tübingen: J. C. B. Mohr (Paul Siebeck), 1980.

Luther, Martin. *The Bondage of the Will*. Translated by J. I. Packer and O. R. Johnston. Westwood: Revell, 1957.

———. *Lectures on Galatians 1519, 1535*. Translated by Richard Jungkuntz. St. Louis: Concordia, 1964.

———. *Lectures on Galatians 1535*. Translated by Jaroslav Pelikan. St. Louis: Concordia, 1963.

———. *Lectures on Isaiah: Chapters 40–66; Luther's Works, Vol. 17*. Edited by J. J. Pelikan, H. C. Oswald & H. T. Lehmann. Libronix Digital Library System. Fortress; Concordia: 1999, 1972.

———. *Luther's Works*. Edited by Jaroslav Pelikan and Helmut T. Lehmann, et al., 55 vols. St. Louis: Concordia; Philadelphia: Muhlenberg, 1955–76.

Luz, Ulrich. *Das Geschichtsverständnis des Paulus*. München: Christian Kaiser, 1968.

———. *Matthew*. Translated by James Crouch. Edited by Helmut Koester. Minneapolis: Fortress, 2001, 2005, 2007.

———. "Theologia Crucis als Mitte der Theologie im Neuen Testaments." *ET* 34 (1974) 116–40.

Manson, T. W. "ἱλαστήριον." *JTS*, 46 (1945) 1–10.

———. "Jesus, Paul, and the Law." In *Judaism and Christianity*, 3:125–41. London: Sheldon, 1938.

———. *On Paul and John*. Naperville: Allenson, 1963.

Marcus, Joel. "The Evil Inclination in the Epistle of James." *CBQ* 44 (1982) 606–21.

Martyn, J. L. "Apocalyptic Antinomies in Paul's Letter to the Galatians." *NTS* 31 (1985) 410–24.

———. *Galatians*. New York: Doubleday, 1997.

———. "A Law-observant Mission to Gentiles: the Background of Galatians." *SJT* 38 (1985) 307–24.

Marshall, I. Howard. "Pauline Theology in the Thessalonian Correspondence." In *Paul and Paulinism*, 173–83.

Maurer, Christian. "σχίζω." *TDNT* 7:959–964.

———. "τίθημι." *TDNT* 8:152–68.

Marxsen, W. *Introduction to the New Testament*. Translated by G. Buswell. Philadelphia: Fortress, 1968.

Mayes, A. D. H. *Deuteronomy*. London: Marshall, Morgan & Scott, 1979.

McKane, William. *Prophets and Wise Men*. London: SCM, 1965.

McKenzie, John L. *Second Isaiah*. Garden City: Doubleday, 1968.

Meeks, Wayne A. *The First Urban Christians*. New Haven and London: Yale University Press, 1983.

———. *The HarperCollins Study Bible*. New York: HarperCollins, 1993.

———. "The Image of the Androgyne: Some Uses of a Symbol in Earliest Christianity." *HR* 13: 165–208.

———, and Wilken, Robert L. *Jews and Christians in Antioch in the First Four Centuries of the Common Era*. Missoula: Scholars, 1978.

Mendenhall, George E. "Covenant." *IDB* 1:714–23.

Menoud, Philippe H. *Law and Covenant in Israel and the Ancient Near East*. Pittsburg: The Biblical Colloquium, 1955.

———. "Revelation and Tradition (The Influence of Paul's Conversion on His Theology)." *Interpretation* 7 (1953) 131–41.

Metzger, Bruce M. "The Formulas Introducing Quotations of Scripture in the New Testament and Mishnah." *JBL* 70 (1951) 297–307.
Meyer, Paul W. "The Holy Spirit in the Pauline Letters." *Interpretation* 33 (1979) 3–18.
Michael, J. Hugh. *The Epistle of Paul to the Philippians*. New York and London: Harper & Row, 1927.
Michaelis, Wilhelm. "ὁπάω." *TDNT* 5:315–82.
Michel, Otto. *Der Brief an die Römer*. Göttingen: Vandenhoeck, 1955.
———. *Paulus und seine Bibel*. Gütersloh, 1929.
———. "συγκλείω." *TDNT* 7:744–47.
Minear, Paul Sevier. "The Crucified World: The Enigma of Galatians 6:14." In *Theologia Crucis- Signum Crucis*, 395–407.
Mitton, C. L. "Atonement," *IDB* 1:309–13.
Moe, Olaf. *The Apostle Paul, His Life and Work*. Translated by L. A. Vigness. Minneapolis: Augsburg, 1950, 1954.
Mol, Hans J. *Identity and the Sacred*. New York: Free, 1977.
Moltmann, Jürgen. "The Crucified God Yesterday and Today: 1972–2002." *Cross Examinations*, 127–38. Translated by Margaret Kohl.
Montefiore, C. G., and H. A. Loewe. *A Rabbinic Anthology*. New York: Schocken, 1974.
Moore, George F. *Judaism in the First Centuries of the Christian Era*. Cambridge: Harvard University Press, 1962.
Morgenthaler, Robert. *Statistik des neutestamentlichen Wortschatzes*. Zürich: Gotthelf, 1958.
Morris, Leon. *The Apostolic Preaching of the Cross*. Grand Rapids: Eerdmans, 1955.
———. *The Cross in the New Testament*. Grand Rapids: Eerdmans, 1965.
Morton, A. Q., and James McLeman. *Paul, the Man and the Myth*. New York: Harper and Row, 1966.
Moule, C. F. D. "Death 'to Sin', 'to Law', and 'to the World': A Note on Certain Datives." In *Mélanges Bibliques*, 367–75. Gembloux, 1970.
———. "Interpreting Paul by Paul." In *New Testament Christianity for Africa and the World*, 78–90. London: SPCK, 1974.
———. *The Origin of Christology*. London: Cambridge University Press, 1977.
Moulton, W. F., and A. S. Geden. *A Concordance to the Greek Testament*. Edinburgh: T. & T. Clark, 1978.
Moulton, James Hope, and George Milligan. *The Vocabulary of the Greek Testament*. London: Hodder and Stoughton, 1952.
Mowinckel, Sigmund. *He That Cometh*. Translated by G. W. Anderson. Nashville: Abingdon, 1954.
Moxnes, Halvor. *Theology in Conflict*. Leiden: E. J. Brill, 1980.
Muilenburg, James. *The Way of Israel*. New York: Harper, 1961.
Munck, Johannes. *Paul and the Salvation of Mankind*. Translated by Frank Clarke. Atlanta: John Knox, 1977.
Mußner, Franz. *Der Galaterbrief*. Freiburg, Basel, Wien: Herder, 1974.
Nanos, Mark. *The Irony Of Galatians*. Minneapolis: Fortress, 2002.
Nelson, Richard D. "He Offered Himself." *Interpretation* 57 (2003) 251–65.
Neusner, Jacob. *From Politics to Piety*. Englewood Cliffs: Prentice-Hall, 1973.
———. *Judaism in the Beginning of Christianity*. Philadelphia: Fortress, 1984.
———. *Judaism in the Matrix of Christianity*. Philadelphia: Fortress, 1986.
———. *The Rabbinic Traditions about the Pharisees before 70*. Leiden: E. J. Brill, 1971.

———. Review of E. P. Sanders' *Paul and Palestinian Judaism*. In *History of Religions* 18 (1978) 177–91.
Neyrey, Jerome. "Bewitched in Galatia: Paul and Cultural Anthropology." *CBQ* 50 (1988) 72–100.
Nygren, Anders. *Romans*. Translated by Carl C. Rasmussen. Philadelphia: Muhlenberg, 1949.
Oepke, Albrecht. *Der Brief des Paulus an die Galater*. Berlin: Evangelische Verlagsanstalt, 1973.
———. "διά." *TDNT* 2:65–70.
———. "καλύπτω." *TDNT* 3:556–92.
———. "μεσίτης." *TDNT* 4:598–624.
O'Neill, J. C. *The Recovery of Paul's Letter to the Galatians*. London: SPCK, 1972.
Park, David M. "Paul's *Skolops tae Sarki*: Thorn or Stake?" *NT* XXII (1980) 179–83.
Pederson, Sigfred. *Die Paulinische Literatur und Theologie*. Århus: Forlaget Aros; Göttingen: Vandenhoeck & Ruprecht, 1980.
Phillips, Anthony. *Deuteronomy*. Cambridge: Cambridge University Press, 1973.
Philo. *De Abrahamo*. Translated by F. H. Colson and G. H. Whitaker. *Loeb Classical Library* VI:2–135. Cambridge: Harvard University Press, 1964.
———. *On Flight and Finding*. Translated by F. H. Colson and G. H. Whitaker. *Loeb Classical Library* V:10–125. Cambridge: Harvard University Press, 1958.
———. *Questions and Answers on Exodus*. Translated by Ralph Marcus. *Loeb Classical Library*, Supp. II:2–176. Cambridge: Harvard University Press, 1953.
———. *Who is the Heir?* Translated by F. H. Colson. *Loeb Classical Library* IV:284–447. Cambridge: Harvard University Press, 1958.
Plato. *Apology*. Translated by B. Jowett. New York: Tudor.
Plummer, Alfred. *Second Epistle of St. Paul to the Corinthians*. Edinburgh: T. & T. Clark, 1978.
Porter, Stanley. *Paul, Luke and the Graeco-Roman World*, Essays in Honor of Alexander J. M. Wedderburn. London: Sheffield, 2002.
Preisker, Herbert. "ὀρθός." *TDNT* 5:449–51.
Proudfoot, C. Merrill. "Imitation or Realistic Participation?" *Interpretation* 17 (1963) 140–60.
Quell, Gottfried, and Johannes Behm, "διαθήκη." *TDNT* 2:106–34.
———, and Siegfried Schulz. "σπέρμα." *TDNT* 7:536–47.
Räisänen, Heikki. "Galatians 2:16 and Paul's Break with Judaism." *NTS* 31 (1985) 543–53.
———. "Das ‚Gesetz des Glaubens' (Röm 3:27) und das ‚Gesetz des Geistes' (Röm 8:2)." *NTS* 26 (1980) 101–17.
———. "The 'Hellenists'—a Bridge between Jesus and Paul?" In *The Torah and Christ*, 202–306.
———. "Legalism and Salvation by the Law." In *Die paulinische Literatur und Theologie*, 63–83. Edited by S. Pederson. Göttingen: Vandenhoeck & Ruprecht, 1980.
———. *Paul and the Law*. Tübingen: J. C. B. Mohr (Paul Siebeck), 1983.
———. "Paul's Conversion and the Development of His View of the Law." *NTS* 33 (1987) 404–19.
———. "Paul's Theological Difficulties with the Law." *SB* 1978, III:301–20. Sheffield: *JSNT*, 1980.

———. "Sprachliches zum Spiel des Paulus mit *nomos*." In *Glaube und Gerechtigkeit*, 131–54.

———. *The Torah and Christ*. Helsinki: Finnish Exegetical Society, 1986.

Reicke, Bo. "Der Geschichtliche Hintergrund des Apostelkonzils und der Antiochia-Episode, Gal 2:1–14." In *Studia Paulina*, 172–87.

———. "Law and This World according to Paul: Some Thoughts concerning Gal 4:1–11." *JBL* 70 (1951) 259–76.

———. *The New Testament Era*. Translated by David E. Green. Philadelphia: Fortress, 1968.

———. "A Synopsis of Early Christian Preaching." In *The Root of the Vine. Essays in Biblical Theology*, 128–60. Westminster: Dacre, 1953.

Rengstorf, Karl Heinrich. "ἀποστέλλω." *TDNT* 1:394–447.

———. "δοῦλος." *TDNT* 2:261–80.

Richardson, Peter. *Israel in the Apostolic Church*. London: Cambridge University Press, 1969.

———, and John C. Hurd. *From Jesus to Paul*. Waterloo: Wilfrid Laurier University Press, 1984.

———, and David Granskou. *Anti-Judaism in Early Christianity*. Waterloo: Wilfrid Laurier University Press, 1986.

Riesenfeld, Harald. "The Misinterpreted Mediator in Gal 3.19–20." In *The New Testament Age*, 405–12.

———. "ὑπέρ." *TDNT* 8:507–16.

Rivkin, Ellis. *What Crucified Jesus?* Nashville: Abingdon, 1984.

Robertson, A. T., and W. Hersey Davis. *A New Short Grammar of the Greek Testament*. New York: Harper & Brothers, 1933.

Robertson, Archibald, and Alfred Plummer. *The First Epistle of St. Paul to the Corinthians*. Edinburgh: T. & T. Clark, 1914.

Robinson, John A. T. *The Body*. Philadelphia: Westminster, 1952.

Rochford, Dennis. "The Theological Hermeneutics of Edward Schillebeeckx." *TS* 63 (2002) 251–67.

Roetzel, Calvin. *The Letters of Paul*. 4th ed. Louisville: Westminster John Knox, 1998.

Ross, W. D., Editor. *Aristotle's Metaphysics*. Oxford: Clarendon, 1924.

Russell, Bertrand. *A History of Western Philosophy*. New York: Simon and Schuster, 1945.

Rylaarsdam, J. C. "Atonement, Day of." *IDB* 1:313–16.

Sahlin, Harald. "The New Exodus of Salvation according to St. Paul." *The Root of the Vine*, 81–95. Westminster: Dacre, 1953.

Sakenfeld, Katharine Doob, ed. *The New Interpreter's Dictionary of the Bible*, 5 vols. Nashville: Abingdon, 2006–.

Sanday, William and Arthur C. Headlam. *The Epistle to the Romans*. Edinburgh: T. & T. Clark, 1980.

Sanders, E. P. "Patterns of Religion in Paul and Rabbinic Judaism: A Holistic Method of Comparison," *HTR* 66 (1973) 455–78

———. *Paul*. Oxford: 1991.

———. *Paul, the Law, and the Jewish People*. Philadelphia: Fortress, 1983.

———. *Paul and Palestinian Judaism*. London: SCM, 1977.

Sanders, J. A. "Habakkuk in Qumran, Paul, and the Old Testament." *JR* XXXIX (1959) 232–44.

Sasse, Hermann. "κοσμέω." *TDNT* 3:867-98.
Scharbert, Josef. "ארר." *TDOT* 1:405-18.
Schlatter, Adolf von. *Die Briefe an die Galater, Epheser, Kolosser und Philemon*. Stuttgart: Calwer, 1963.
———. *Gottes Gerechtigkeit: Ein Kommentar zum Römerbrief*. Stuttgart: Calwer, 1952.
———. *Romans: The Righteousness of God*. Translated by Siegfried Sschatzmann. Peabody: Hendrickson, 1995.
———. *Die korinthische Theologie*. In *Beiträge zur Förderung christlicher Theologie* 18, 2. Gütersloh: 1914.
Schlier, Heinrich. *Der Brief an die Galater*. Göttingen: Vandenhoeck & Ruprecht, 1965.
———. *Der Römerbrief*. Freiburg, Basel, Wien: Herder, 1977.
Schillebeeckx, Edward. *Jesus: An Experiment in Christology*. New York: Crossroad, 1981.
Schmidt, Karl Ludwig. "ἔθνος." *TDNT* 2:364-72.
Schmithals, Walter. *Paul and James*. Translated by Dorthea M. Barton. Naperville: Allenson, 1965.
Schnackenburg, Rudolf. *Baptism in the Thought of St. Paul*. Translated by G. R. Beasley-Murray. Oxford: Blackwell, 1964.
Schneider, Johannes. "παραβαίνω." *TDNT* 5:737-40.
———. "σταυρός." *TDNT* 7:572-84.
Schoeps, H. J. *Paul*. Translated by Harold Knight. London: Lutterworth, 1961.
Schrenk, Gottlob. "γράφω." *TDNT* 1:742-73.
———. "θέλημα." *TDNT* 3:44-62.
Schweitzer, Albert. *The Mysticism of Paul the Apostle*. Translated by William Montgomery. New York: MacMillan, 1960.
Schweizer, Eduard. "Dying and Rising with Christ." *NTS* 14 (1968) 1-14.
———. "Slaves of the Elements and Worshipers of Angels: Gal 4:3, 9 and Col 2:8, 18, 20." *JBL* 107(1988) 455-68.
———. "Versöhnung des Alls." In *Jesus Christus in Historie und Theologie*, 487-502. Reprint in *Neues Testament und Christologie im Werden*, 164-78. Göttingen: Vandenhoeck & Ruprecht, 1982.
———. "υἱός." *TDNT* 8:363-92.
———. "πνεῦμα." *TDNT* 6:332-455.
———. "σῶμα." *TDNT* 7:1024-94.
Sevenster, J. N. and W. C. van Unnik. *Studia Paulina*. Haarlem, 1953.
Stählin, Gustav. "σκάνδαλον." *TDNT* 7:339-58.
Stanley, David Michael. *Christ's Resurrection in Pauline Soteriology*. Romae: E Pontificio Instituto Biblico, 1961.
Stauffer, Ethelbert. "εἷς." *TDNT* 2:434-42.
———. *New Testament Theology*. Translated by John Marsh. New York: MacMillan, 1955.
Stendahl, Krister. *Paul Among Jews and Gentiles*. Philadelphia: Fortress, 1976.
———. *The Scrolls and the New Testament*. London: 1958.
Stewart, James S. *A Man in Christ*. Grand Rapids: Baker, 1975.
Strack, Hermann L., and Paul Billerbeck. *Kommentar zum Neuen Testament aus Talmud und Midrasch*. München: C. H. Beck'sche, 1926.
Strecker, Georg. *Jesus Christus in Historie und Theologie*. Tübingen: J. C. B. Mohr (Paul Siebeck), 1975.

Stuhlmacher, Peter. "The End of the Law." Translated by Everett R. Kalin. In *Reconciliation, Law, and Righteousness*, 134–54.
———. *Das Paulus Evangelium. I: Vorgeschichte*. Göttingen: Vandenhoeck & Ruprecht, 1968.
———. "Recent Exegesis on Romans 3:24–26." *Reconciliation, Law, and Righteousness*, 94–105.
———. *Reconciliation, Law, & Righteousness*. Philadelphia: Fortress, 1986.
Suhl, *Paulus und seine Briefe*. Gütersloh: Gerd Mohn, 1975.
Sykes, J. B. (Editor). *Oxford Concise Dictionary*. Oxford: Oxford University Press, 1984.
Szeles, Maria Eszenyei. *Wrath and Mercy*. Translated by George F. Knight. Grand Rapids: Eerdmans, 1987.
Tannehill, Robert. *Dying and Rising with Christ*. Berlin: Alfred Töpelmann, 1967.
———. *Dying and Rising with Christ*. PhD diss., Yale University, 1963.
Taylor, Greer M. "The Function of ΠΙΣΤΙΣ ΧΡΙΣΤΟΥ in Galatians." *JBL* 75 (1966) 58–76.
———. "Soteriologische Symbolik in den paulinischen Schriften." *KD* 20 (1974) 282–304.
Theißen, Gerd. *Psychological Aspects of Pauline Theology*. Translated by John P. Galvin. Philadelphia: Fortress, 1987.
Thiselton, Anthony. "Realized Eschatology at Corinth." *NTS* 24 (1978) 510–26.
Thrall, Margaret. *I and II Corinthians*. Cambridge: Cambridge University Press, 1965.
———. "Super Apostles, Servants of Christ, Servants of Satan." *JSNT* 6 (1980) 42–57.
Tiede, David. *The Charismatic Figure as Miracle Worker*. Missoula: SBL, 1972.
———. *Prophecy and History in Luke/Acts*. Philadelphia: Fortress, 1980.
Tillich, Paul. "Behold, I Am Doing a New Thing." In *The Shaking of the Foundations*, 173–86. New York: Scribner's Sons, 1948.
Tomson, Peter. *Paul and the Jewish Law*. Minneapolis: Fortress, 1990.
Trelstad, Marit. *Cross Examinations*. Minneapolis: Augsburg Fortress, 2006.
———. "Lavish Love." In *Cross Examinations*. 109–24.
Van Unnik, W. C. *Neotestamentica Et Patristica*. Leiden: E. J. Brill, 1962.
Vielhauer, Philipp. "Gesetzesdienst und Stoicheiadienst im Galaterbrief." *Rechtfertigung*, 543–56.
Vincent, Marvin R. *Epistles to the Philippians and to Philemon*. New York: Scribner's Sons, 1911.
Von Rad, Gerhard. *Deuteronomy*. Translated by Dorothea Barton. Philadelphia: Westminster, 1966.
———. *Old Testament Theology*. Translated by D. M. Stalker. New York: Harper & Row, 1957.
Wall, Robert. *1 & 2 Timothy and Titus*. Grand Rapids: Eerdmans, 2012.
Watson, Francis. *Paul, Judaism and the Gentiles*. Cambridge: Cambridge University Press, 1986.
Weber, Hans-Ruedi. *The Cross*. Translated by Elke Jessett. London: SPCK, 1979.
Wedderburn, A. J. M. *Baptism and Resurrection*. Tübingen: J. C. B. Mohr (Paul Siebeck), 1987.
———. "The Body of Christ and Related Concepts in 1 Corinthians." *SJT* 24 (1971) 74–96.
———. "Paul and Jesus: Similarity and Continuity." *NTS* 34 (1988) 161–82.
———. "Some Recent Pauline Chronologies." *The Expository Times* 92 (1981) 103–8.

Weder, Hans. *Das Kreuz Jesu bei Paulus*. Göttingen: Vandenhoeck & Ruprecht, 1981.
Weinrich, William. *The New Testament Age*. Macon: Mercer, 1984.
Weiß, Johannes. *Der erste Korintherbrief*. Göttingen: Vandenhoeck & Ruprecht, 1925.
———. *The History of Primitive Christianity*. Translated by Arthur Forster, Paul Kramer, Sherman Johnson, Frederick Grant. London: MacMillan, 1937.
Wengst, Klaus. *Humility: Solidarity of the Humiliated*. Translated by John Bowden. Philadelphia: Fortress, 1988.
Westerholm, Stephen. *Israel's Law and the Church's Faith*. Grand Rapids: Eerdmans, 1988.
Westermann, Claus. *Isaiah 40–66*. Translated by David Stalker. Philadelphia: Westminster, 1969.
Westhelle, Vítor. *The Scandalous God*. Minneapolis: Fortress, 2006.
Wilckens, Ulrich. "Statements on the Development of Paul's View of the Law." In *Paul and Paulinism*, 17–26.
———. "Was heisst bei Paulus: ‚Aus Werken des Gesetzes wird kein Mensch gerecht?'" In *Rechtfertigung als Freiheit*, 77–109. Neukirchener, 1974.
———. "σοφία." *TDNT* 7:465–528.
———. "στῦλος." *TDNT* 7:732–36.
Wilcox, Max. "On Investigating the Use of the Old Testament in the New Testament." In *Text and Interpretation*, 231–43.
———. "'Upon the Tree'—Deut 21:22–23 in the New Testament." *JBL* 96 (1977) 85–99.
———. "The Promise of the 'Seed' in the New Testament and the Targumim." *JSNT* 5 2–20.
Williams, S. K. "Again *Pistis Christou*." *CBQ* 49 (1987) 431–37.
Wink, Walter. *The Human Being: Jesus and the Enigma of the Son of Man*. Minneapolis: Fortress, 2002.
Winter, Paul. *On the Trial of Jesus*. Berlin: Walter de Gruyter & Co., 1961.
Wilson, S. G. *Luke and the Law*. Cambridge: Cambridge University Press, 1983.
Wolff, Hans Walter. *Probleme Biblischer Theologie*. Christian Kaiser, 1971.
Wolfson, Harry Austryn. *Philo*. Cambridge: Harvard University Press, 1948.
Wrede, W. *Paul*. Translated by Edward Lummis. London: Philip Green, 1907.
Wright, N. T. *The Climax of the Covenant*. Minneapolis: Fortress, 1992.
———. *Paul*. Minneapolis: Fortress, 2005.
———. *Romans*. In *The New Interpreters Bible*, ed. Leander E. Keck, 12 vols. Nashville: Abingdon Press, 1994–2004), 10:395–770.
Wuellner, Wilhelm. "Haggadic Homily Genre in 1 Corinthians 1–3." *JBL* 89 (1970) 199–204.
Yadin, Yigael. "Pesher Nahum (4QpNahum) Reconsidered." *IEJ* 21 (1971) 1–12.
———. *The Temple Scroll*. New York: Random House, 1985.
Ziesler, J. A. *The Meaning of Righteousness in Paul*. Cambridge: Cambridge University Press, 1972.
———. *Pauline Christianity*. Oxford: 1992.
———. *Paul's Letter to the Romans*. Philadelphia: Trinity International, 1989.

Subject Index

Note to reader: words in *italics* represent specific words and phrases discussed in the text.

Abraham. *See also* Genesis
  language used to describe, 99nn187–188
  obedience as prototype for justification by faith, 94, 94n162, 96n171, 123
  role in Galatians, 96
Abraham, God's covenant with
  contrast with Horeb-Sinai covenant, 115
  as everlasting, extending through time, 95, 114n258, 115n264
  as foreknowledge of the gospel, 94–95
  Paul's interpretation/references to, 15, 90, 91n142, 92, 96n170, 99, 113–14, 118–19
  traditional interpretations/Jewish view, 92–93, 99n186, 114
according to flesh, 16, 68–69, 139n76, 140, 152
Acts
  background conditions, 76–77n74
  "corrected" version of Paul in, 74n61, 75, 75n66, 115n268, 157n49
  discussion of circumcision and Jerusalem accord, 24–25, 65n10, 73–77, 77n76
  and Jewish resistance to Christ as a Messiah, 106n223
adoption, historical context, 133n43
Agrippa, Paul's defense before, 154n41
Akedah tradition, 112n250
Alexander Jannaeus, 105
Amos, concepts of good and evil, 138
Anderson, Bernhard W., 115n264, 155–56
angels. *See also* old aeon
  as demonic, 118n288
  as *elemental spirits*, 143
  in Galatians, 118–19n289
  as mediators/bringers of the law, 113n257, 116n273, 118n283
animal sacrifice, 108n236
Anselm and Abelard contrast, 160–61n65
antinomy. See opposites, paired
Antioch
  "Christian" as a title, 77–78n81
  conflicts between Jews and Gentiles, 78n84
  Gentile converts, 77–79, 78n81
  Jewish population, 77n79
  Paul as church delegate from, 65n10
Antioch incident. *See also* table-fellowship
  dating of, 65n8, 84

Antioch incident (continued)
  discussion of in Galatians, xxv, 77n77
  and issue of church unity, 79n86
  and Jerusalem decision on circumcision, 76
  and table-fellowship, 81–85
  works of the law in relation to, 84, 86
apocalyptic theology, 43, 69, 141–42, 141n87, 141n89, 142n90
Aquila and Priscilla, Paul's description of in Romans, 152
Aristotle, 136–37
atonement. *See also* redemption
  and the Anselm and Abelard contrast, 160–61n65
  as deliverance, 159–160, 166
  Judaic *mercy-seat* (*hilastērion*) traditions, xxii, 102, 157–60, 159–160nn61–62
  and sin-offerings, 107, 111–12
Aulén, Gustaf, 161n65

Badenas, Robert, 121n305
baptism
  baptismal interpretation of epistles, 41nn44–47
  in Galatians, 122
  as participation in Christ's death, 38, 40–42, 59
  Paul's doctrine of, 42n51
  relationship to crucifixion, 42n48, 57, 58n123
  relationship to faith and justification, 42
Barabbas, Jesus' exchange for, 153
Barnabas, 65, 65n9, 73, 78n84
Barr, James, xxivn13
Barrett, C. K., 2n6, 28n120, 71n44, 108n234
Barth, Karl, 7n37, 31n132, 58–59
Barth, Markus, 6n33
bearing fruit, 54, 54n101
because of transgressions, 26, 117
Beker, J. Christiaan, 5n28, 18n81, 29, 98n181, 141
belief. *See* faith/belief
Benoit, Pierre, 46

Bertram, Georg, 63n3, 127n4
Betz, Hans Dieter
  on Christ's *humanity*, 132n32
  on *did not know God*, 128n11
  disagreement about Akedah tradition, 112n250
  on discussion of circumcision in Galatians, 10–11n51
  on *flesh*, 11n53
  on *freedom*, 46n66, 88–89n132
  on Galatians 3:16, 114n259
  on *grace and peace*, 144n2
  on identification of apostles, 69n33
  on the Jerusalem agreement, 73n54
  on Jewish view of Christ's death, 152m33
  on Jewish view of law as eternal, 117n281
  on language of doxology, 144n1
  on law and change, 113n254
  on mentions of baptism, 41n47
  on Paul's Christology, 68n28
  on Paul's relationship with Peter and the Jerusalem leaders, 33n1, 64n7, 70n40, 71n44, 74, 77n77
  on Paul's writing style and language choices, 124n324, 154n39
  on Paul's view of apostolic task, 66n15
  on Paul's views on justification, 33–34n5
  on *those of faith*, 94n162
  on *through the law*, 44n62
  on Titus' circumcision, 72nn50–51
  on Torah observances as *works of the law*, 64n4
Black, Matthew, 160n62
Blank, Josef, 53n94
blessing. *See also* Abraham, God's covenant with; faith; redemption; salvation
  contrast with *law* and *curse*, 13, 15, 24, 113b253, 124n324
  with *faith*, as keyword, 93, 120
Bligh, John, 77n77
boast, 5n27, 12, 141n87
body of Christ, 53–54, 57–58, 60
body of sin, 54n98

SUBJECT INDEX

bondage. *See* slavery/bondage
Bonsirven, Joseph, 99n191
Borgen, Peder, 10–11n51
born of woman, 132n32
Bornkamm, Günther, 97n173
Borse, Udo, 49, 49–50
Bousset, Wilhelm, 21n100
Brichto, Herbert Chanan, 104n217
Bring, xxx, 144–45n3, 146n9
Brinsmead, Bernard, 95–96, 95–96n168, 96n170, 96n172
Bruce, F. F.
   on Christ's becoming a *curse*, 107n232
   on *circumcision* and *shame*, 7n37
   on cohesion in Paul's theology, 22
   on faith coming from what is heard, 90n140
   on Gentiles and the curse of law, 21n94
   on Paul's revelatory experience, 22n105, 52
   on Paul's relationship with Peter, 33–34n5
   on Paul's relationship with Jerusalem leaders, 71n44
   on Paul's use of familiar words and phrases, 154n39
   on signs of the new aeon, 90n141
Brueggemann, Walter, 154n42, 156
Bultmann, Rudolf, 7n37, 38, 38n29
Burton, Ernest De Witt
   on Christ as the Crucified One, 10n48
   contrast of *elements* with revelation, 128, 131n23, 135n52
   and Paul's revelatory experience, 65n15
   on Paul's relationship with Peter, 33n1
   on Paul's understanding of the law, 52n91

calendar observance/calendar piety, 21, 26, 130, 168
Carr, Wesley, 131n23
causative function of the law, 46
Cephas. *See* Peter (Cephas)

Childs, Brevard, 30–31n129
Christ. *See also* Christ crucified; self-sacrifice; the Son, *sonship*
   as agent of sin, 34–35
   authority of, extension to the Old Testament, 91nn145–146
   and birth and death under the law, 53, 133n45, 169
   humanity of, 132, 132n26, 132n29
   opponents view of as secondary to the law, 76
   self-giving as act of faith, 145–46, 153–55
   sources of antagonism against, 163
   teachings on cleanliness, 80n96
   virginal conception, 132n26
Christ crucified. *See also dying with* or *through Christ*; the *law*; self-sacrifice
   and becoming a curse to bless us, 61–62, 95, 105–6, 110, 143
   as the Crucified One, 10n48
   crucifixion in weakness, 5
   death *under the law for us*, 61
   dying with meanings, 37n24
   early church struggles to interpret, 103n207, 146, 146n8, 151n31, 152n35
   and the end of law, 51–52, 97, 117, 169
   as God's means of overthrowing scapegoating, 162n69
   as God's means of suffering vengeance, 164n78
   as God's sacrifice, 150n26, 165n83, 167n87
   as the Messiah, Jewish rejection of, 103–4, 166n84
   participation of believers in, 46–-47
   as proclamation, 90
   as purposive/necessary, bringing deliverance/redemption/blessings, xiii–xiv, 146–47, 149–150, 153, 161, 165, 168–69
   as voluntary sacrifice, 59n127, 59n129, 147–48, 161–62
with Christ vs. in Christ, 40–41n43

Christ-event
  centrality to Paul's apostolic mission, 22, 30, 66n15, 68n30, 69, 127, 142, 143
  the cross as shorthand for, 29
Christ-faith, 34n5, 101n200
Christian theology, early development
  Jewish contributions to, 146n10
  new doctrinal practices, 71–72
  pagan views of, 3–4
  and Paul's views before and after revelation, 104n211
circumcision. *See also* Jerusalem conference
  among early Christians, 12n55
  as confirmation of God's covenant with Abraham, 96n171, 115n264
  as cultic observance, 21, 76n71, 136
  and exclusion crucifixion, 135–36
  focus on, in Galatians, 7–8, 11–12, 24, 64, 88–89, 136n58
  and Jewish identity, 86–87
  as justification/salvation, Paul's rejection of, 72, 76, 76–77, 89n135, 141
  negating of, as negating the whole law, 23, 26, 84
  pairing with uncircumcision, 126, 136, 139
  references to in Acts, 24–25, 65n10, 73–77, 77n76
  references to in Philippians, 7–8, 7n37
  of Timothy, by Paul, 74n63
  Titus's, as a test case, 65n9, 72n51
  as traumatic, 89
coherence, in Paul's message, 30
Colossians
  absence of discussion of *law* in, 14
  cross/crucify in, 6
  elements of the world in, 128, 131n23
  theme of reconciliation, 8
contingency, in Paul's message, 30–31
the contraries (pairing of opposites), 136–37. *See also* opposites, paired
conversion, by Jews, need for, 87–88n131

Conzelmann, Hans, 2n5, 4n22, 18n84, 57
Corinth, people of
  Paul's preaching the *word of the cross* to, 2–3
  Paul's visits to/work among, 2–3
  situation of, and Paul's message, 3n14, 4n22
1 Corinthians
  body as community, 57
  cross vs. *wisdom* in, 3–4, 3n13, 26–27, 27, 27n118
  Dahl's analysis on, xxiii
  elemental spirits of the world vs. Spirit from God, 4
  emphasis on prophetic texts, 92n152
  equating of *law* with *sin*, 15
  law, positive aspects, 14–15, 14n67
  and Paul's apostolic mission, 2n6, 11n52, 14–15
  Paul's authorship, 6n33
  references to crucifixion/cross in, 1–3, 8, 10
  righteousness terminology in, 27
  scriptural references/arguments, 11, 92n149
  use of *revealed* in, 28n121
  use of *stumbling block* (*scandal*) in, 10–11
2 Corinthians
  absence of word *law* in, 6, 14
  citing of Old Testament, 110
  comparison with Galatians, 5–6, 60
  cross/crucify in, 1, 59–60
  for God, 36
  and Paul's apostolic mission, 11n52
  Paul's authorship, 6n33
  references to crucifixion/cross in, 4
  strength in weakness paradox, 4–5
  two-aeon perspective in, 59–60
Cornelius episode, Luke's view, 82n107
covenant/promise, God's. *See also* Abraham, God's covenant with; *nomism*, covenantal
  law juxtaposed with, 113n253, 114–15nn260–262, 115–17, 115n265, 118, 119–21, 120n300

SUBJECT INDEX 193

Paul's association with *inheritance*,
  Christ's *sonship*, 113–14, 133–34
theological *vs.* legal view of,
  113n256
as unconditional, 115n264
Cranfield, C. E. B., 31n132, 54n101
crucifixion/cross. *See also* Christ
  crucified; *curse*; *dying through
  the law/to the law*; the law; new
  aeon; wisdom
as action on behalf of all humanity,
  59–61, 135n54
association with faith, blessing,
  deliverance and redemption, 9,
  13–14, 27n118, 29, 59–60, 76,
  88–89n132, 139–140n76, 160,
  162, 166
baptism vs., 42n48
and being *put to death*, 57–58, 60
and the *body of Christ*, 57
centrality of in Paul's message, xxi,
  1–13, 15–16, 22–23, 26–27,
  30–31, 134–35
and Christ's actions as humanity's
  representative, 59–61, 59n127,
  59n129, 135n54
conflation with resurrection, 29–30,
  88–89n132, 166n85
crucified-with Christ, xxv, 6n32, 9,
  38, 52, 162
crucifixion of the world, 134–36,
  135n52, 143
and the crucifixion of Jews under
  the Romans, 105
and *dying to/dying with*, 36, 38–39,
  42–43
early Christian struggles to
  understand, 103n207, 146,
  146n8, 151n31, 152n35
John's *vs.* Paul's view of, 5n28
juxtaposition with *wisdom/
  foolishness*, 2, 11, 27, 29
Paul's perception of, Martyn's
  perspective, 38n33, 39–40n37
as proclamation, implications for
  faith in Galatians, 90
relationship to *curse*, accursedness,
  103–4, 104n214, 106–9

relationship with the *law*/rule of
  law, xxi, xxvi, 11–12, 29, 31–32,
  42–43, 48, 60n131
as *scandal*, 4n16, 10–11, 89
and the transition to the new aeon,
  30
theology of the cross, 166n85
use of in Galatians, 6, 8–13, 15,
  22–23, 27, 29–30, 59, 76, 142
use of in Romans, 6, 6n30, 8, 11,
  15–16, 47, 57–58
Cullmann, Oscar, 110n245
cultural exclusivism, 163, 166
curse
  association with *law*, xxv, 15, 64,
    94, 100–101, 108–12, 121n301,
    168–69
  Christ's becoming, as basis for
    redemption, 61–62, 104n214,
    109n239, 110, 133, 143
  Christ's becoming, scholarly
    interpretations, 107–8nn232–
    233, 108nn233–234
  crucifixion as, 103–4, 104n214,
    106–9
  in Deuteronomy *vs.* Galatians, 100,
    106–9, 106n224, 109n238
  juxtaposition with *blessing*, 13, 15,
    24, 113b253, 124n324
  overcoming/triumphing over, 107–
    8nn232–233
Cyrus, 138–39

Dahl, N. A., xxiii, xxiii–xxiivn11,
  112n250
Damascus-road experience, 9, 22n105,
  43, 52–53
datives, types of in Paul's epistles, 35n17,
  36, 36n17
David, King, association of Abraham
  with, 96n170
Davies, W. D., 136n56
Day of Atonement rituals, 158–59,
  159–160nn61–62
death. *See also* crucifixion, cross; *dying
  through the law/to the law*
association with *law*, 46, 61,
  118n286

death (continued)
  association with *sin*, 50–51
  dying for us, 35n14, 110–11, 110–11n245, 151, 153
  and *dying to/dying with*, 36, 38–39, 42–43
  dying to/living to, 35, 43, 60
deliverance. See also redemption; salvation
  deliverance from the present evil age, 154–55, 162–63
  as major theme of Galatians, xiii, 145, 154n39
  and the *mercy-seat* tradition, 159
  Old Testament terms for, 154n41
  as purpose Christ's self-giving death, 149, 151–54, 169
  and servanthood to Yahweh, 155–56
Deuteronomy
  angels attending the giving of Mosaic law, 118
  conditional Horeb-Sinai covenant in, 115
  curse in, 100, 106n224, 109
  influence on Peter's description of Christ, 110n245
  and Jewish arguments against Christ as the Messiah, 48
  Paul's citing and interpretations of, 11, 13–14, 48, 100, 103–6, 109, 123–24n323, 123n321
  use of for Christian arguments, 106n222
developmental interpretations, 18n84
did not know God, 128n11
dietary laws. See also table-fellowship
  as definitive of Jewish identity, 86–87
  as reflection of cultic side of law, 21
  religious and social meanings, 79–80, 79n88
  and table-fellowship, 78–79
  variability in observance, 80, 83–84
Dodd, C. H., 54–55n102, 100n191, 158
Dodecalogue, Paul's reinterpretation, 100–101
Donaldson, T. L., 13n66

the doxology
  function during worship, 145n4
  in Galatians, unique elements, 144–45
  language associated with, 144n1
  in Philippians, 12n56
Duncan, George S., 6n32, 41n46, 118n286, 126n2, 132n32
Dunn, James, 5n27, 72n52, 81n104, 82, 82–83
dying for us
  and the exchange of Jesus for Barabbas, 153
  Paul's use of, 35n14, 151
  Scriptural origins, 110–11, 110–11n245
dying through the law/to the law
  and the absence of existence, 51
  and *crucifixion of the world*, 134–36, 135n52, 143
  and law as curse-bringer, xxv, 15, 64, 94, 100–101, 108–12, 121n301, 100–101, 168–69
  and law as reason for Christ's death, 43–46, 52–54, 60–61
  as past event, vs. *dying to Christ*, 37
  Paul's arguments using, 9–10, 35–37, 40, 42, 46, 53, 86n125, 124–25, 162
  relationship to *dying (being crucified) with Christ*, 37
  relationship to *dying through the body of Christ*, 37, 37n24, 39, 41n47, 53n95, 56–57, 60
  relationship with *dying to/through sin*, 46–47, 54, 54n100, 151
  and severing of relationships with the past, 36–38, 40, 55–56, 88
dying to/dying with, 36, 38–39, 42–43
dying-to/living-to
  in Galatians and Romans, 35, 60
  psychological/personalized interpretations, 43

Ebeling, Gerhard, 48–49, 85n118, 91n142
Eichholz, Georg, 25n111

SUBJECT INDEX

elemental spirits of the world, the
elements (*stoicheia*)
   Aristotle's references to, 137
   association with *angels*, 143
   association with demons, 129n14, 130n21
   equating with the old aeon, 127–130
   as term in the New Testament, 128, 128n10
   enslavement by, 128nn12–13
   Paul's association with imperfect/dogmatic teaching systems, 131n23
   Paul's equating of law with, 127n5
Elliott, Neil, 66n13
Ellis, E. Earl, 91n146, 99n191
enslave (kurieuo), 54n99, 108n236. *See also* slavery
Ephesians
   cross/crucify in, 6
   law, abolition of, 15
   Paul's authorship, 6n33
epistles, Paul's. *See also* Paul the Apostle; Scripture *and specific epistles*
   absence of figurative language, 36–37
   arguments based on Scripture, characteristic format, 91
   authenticity discussions of, 6n33, 1n2
   contextual interpretations, 18n84
   conversation partners, response patterns, xxiii–xxiv
   derivative *vs.* original material in, 166n84
   focus of messages on specific audiences, xxii–xxiii, 30–31, 34, 134, 145
   and generalizing tendency, xxivn11
   inconsistencies in, accepting, 116n273
   internal logic of, 18, 19
   introductory formulae, 91n144
   it is written in, 91n144
   literature associated with, xxiv
   order of, 8–9, 8n42, 8n44
   overlapping of Scripture and law in, 121n303
   psychological/personalized interpretations, 43
   reference to *sin* in the singular, 151n30
   reflections of Jewish Christian rectification tradition in, 157n49
   as responses to specific audiences/problems, xxiii
   scriptural arguments in, 92n149, 92n151
   specificity of meaning and intent, xxv–xxvi
   stating of conclusions first, 124n324
   tracing development of thought in, 9n44
   uniform intent, xxv–xxvi
   unique elements in Galatians, 144–45
   use of language familiar to readers, 112n250
   use of oppositional pairs, 136
   viewing as independent of other Pauline writings, xxiii
   vocabulary/language used in, as starting point for scholarship, xxiii, 9n46, 27, 36–37
eschatology/eschatological, defined, 41m45
exclusivism, x, 163n73
exelētai (set free) terminology, 154–55
existentialist interpretations, 18n84
Exodus
   liberation theme, Paul's echoing of, 154, 166
   mercy seat in, 157–58
   move from servitude to Pharaoh to service to Yahweh, 154n42
experience, personal, as basis for Paul's arguments against the law, 88–90, 112n253
faith. See also justification by faith
   Christ's crucifixion as consequence of, 149
   Christ-faith, 34n5
   as coming from what is heard, 90n140
   by faith, interpretations, 97n174, 98–100

faith (continued)
  in Habakkuk 2:4, 99–100n191
  as key element of the divine-human relationship, 101n199
  references to in 1 Corinthians, 27
  references to in Galatians, 95, 98
  and the two-aeon paradigm, 29, 121–22, 133–34, 140–41
father (*pater*), Jesus's, 164. *See also* the Son, *sonship*
figurative language in Paul's epistles, 36–37
Fitzmyer, Joseph A.
  categories of Paul's references to the law, 16–17
  interpretation of *body of sin*, 54n98
  interpretations of *dying to sin* and *rising to life*, 54n100
  on Paul's arguments against rival Christian missionaries, 35n10
  on Paul's introductory formulae, 91n144
  on Paul's use of *place of God's mercy* for *mercy seat*, 160n62
  on primary *vs.* secondary causes for Christ's death, 48
  on Scriptural argument in Galatians, 91n142
  on stages of Paul's salvation history, 17–18n80
  on treatment of law in Galatians *vs.* Romans, 17–18
flesh. See also circumcision; *curse*
  alignment of *law* with, 142
  and circumcision, 89
  contrast with *cross*/faith, 89
  pairing against Spirit, 11–12, 24, 55n105, 139–140, 139n76
Foerster, Werner, 54n99
food laws. *See* dietary laws; Judaism/Jewish tradition
foolishness/folly
  and Greek view of a crucified Messiah, 166
  identification of cross with, 27
  as opposite of wisdom, 3–4, 3–4nn15–16, 27

forgiveness. See also redemption; self-sacrifice
  as the end result of Jesus' self-giving, 151–52
  Paul's limited use of, 154n43
for us phrase in preaching and hymnic texts, 112n250
freedom/liberation though faith. *See also deliverance*; new aeon; redemption; salvation; *slavery/bondage*
  and acceptance of Christ's Sonship, 127n4
  and freedom from the law, 51–52, 53, 55n105
  language associated with, 142–43
  as purpose of Christ's death and resurrection, 23, 127, 88–89n132, 133, 153
  as theme in Galatian, xiii, 17–18
  as theme in Romans, 14, 16, 37, 47, 54–55
Fretheim, Terrence, 154n42

Gager, John, 18n81, 82–83n109
Galatia, Paul's opponents in
  acceptance of circumcision, as basis for justification, 7–8, 11–12, 15, 24, 24–25, 72n51, 76–77
  accusations against Paul, 74, 115
  efforts to identify, 28n120
  efforts to impose *works of the law*, 49
  Jewish and Gentile Christians, 28n120
  observance of Mosaic laws and church membership, 11–12, 21n100, 35, 49, 83n109, 88
  past paganism, 128, 128n11
  Paul's arguments against, 101–2, 102n203, 123–24, 123–24n323, 168
  traditional interpretation of Jesus' death, 156–57
  use of Old Testament texts, 102
  view of Paul as evangelist rather than Apostle, 75–76, 75n67
  willingness to accept circumcision, 136n58

SUBJECT INDEX

Galatia, people of
  familiarity with pairing of opposites
    (*the contraries*), 136
  incomplete adherence to Judaic law,
    61, 86n124
  unique conditions faced by, Paul's
    addressing of, 31
Galatians. *See also* circumcision; the
    law; Paul the Apostle; two-aeon
    paradigm *and specific words,
    phrases and concepts*
  acceptance of Scriptural
    contradiction, 98n180
  apocalyptic interpretation, 43
  arguments based on experience,
    88–90
  arguments based on Scripture, 11,
    88, 91–124, 92n149, 106n224,
    109n238
  association of faith, justification,
    deliverance, and salvation, 10,
    27–28, 34–35, 89–90, 93–94, 98,
    142, 162, 164–67
  baptism reference, 41n47, 42–43,
    122
  baptismal interpretations, 40–42
  canonical significance, 30–31n129
  comparisons with 2 Corinthians,
    5–6, 60
  comparisons with Romans, 16–18,
    18n81, 31–32, 31n133, 53–59
  concept of *inheritance* in, 113n256
  concept of *freedom*/liberty in, xiii
  context and unique elements, 144
  crucifixion/cross references, 6, 8–13,
    15, 22–23, 27, 29–30, 59, 76, 142
  datives of respect, 36n17
  discussion of sinfulness in, 34nn6–7
  doxology in, as unique, 145n4
  dying *through the law*, 44–53
  dying to vs. *dying with* phrasing,
    9–10, 35–37, 40, 53, 60, 162
  eschatological orientation,
    perspectives on, 38n33
  exposition of justification in, 87n130
  justification through circumcision,
    opposition to, 7–8, 11–12, 15,
    24–25, 72n51, 76–77
  justification through observance of
    Mosaic law, arguments against,
    11–12, 21n100, 35
  guardian/trustee analogy, 126
  interrelationships within, 124–25,
    131–32, 143
  keywords and changing analogies,
    126–27
  language of theophany in, 28–29
  like a Jew/like a Gentile, 82–86
  logic of, 37
  paired opposites in, 136
  and Paul's apostolic mission, 9,
    11n52, 118n288, 123–24,
    126–27, 134
  Paul's authorship, 6n33
  and Paul's experience of Judaism,
    xxi, 34–35
  and Paul's reference to Christ
    becoming a curse *for us*, 110–12
  Paul's references to Jesus, the Son of
    God, 67–68
  position regarding the law,
    comparison with Romans,
    31–32
  primacy of the gospel in, 25n111
  psychological interpretations, 45n63
  reading independently from Paul's
    other epistles, 31
  reference to Jewish disputes about
    Jesus as Messiah, 48
  references to Abraham story in, 15,
    90
  relationship of *seed/offspring* with
    covenant in, 113
  relationship with leaders from
    Jerusalem, 33n1, 34, 74–75,
    77–79
  salutation, 144, 145n5
  self-giving, Christ's, and obedience
    to the will of God, 145–46, 153,
    164, 164n80
  scholarly perspectives on, xxv, 36,
    116n273 123–24
  table-fellowship discussion, 33n1,
    77–79
  theme of *new creation*, 7–8
  timing of, 34

SUBJECT INDEX

Galatians (continued)
    unique salvation history in, 13, 96n170
    use of legal language to support theological arguments, 112–123
Gaster, T. H., 99n189
Gaventa, Beverly Roberts, xxi–xxiv
Genesis. *See also* Abraham
    and God's covenant with Abraham, 113–14, 115
    and Akedah tradition, 112n250
    opposite pairings in, 138
    Paul's citing of in Galatians, 101–2, 114n258, 123, 123n320
    Philo's comments on, 137–38
genitives, use of in Galatians, 33–34n5
Gentile Christians
    conditions and laws required of, reports of in Acts, 74–75
    conflicts with Jewish Christians, 77n78
    controversies with Jews, eruption of at Antioch, 78n84
    entrance requirements for church membership, 22n103
    and experience of minority, 127
    inclusion under curse of law, 21n94
    inconsistent observance of law, 80–81, 86n124
    and justified by faith, not law, 97–98
    as Paul's audience, 18n81
    Paul's call to preach to, 27–28
    Paul's suppositions related to, 34–35
    pre-Christian experience, 128–131
Georgi, Dieter, 72n50
glory. See doxology
from God, Paul's removal of *from God* from Deuteronomy 21:23 quote in Galatians 3:13, 109
God. *See also* Abraham; covenant; deliverance; new aeon; redemption; salvation; the Son, *sonship*
    as *foolish*, contrast with worldly wisdom, 3, 27
    gift of law to Jewish people, 85–86n121
    new creative act, xiii–xiv, 67–68, 141, 147–48, 164–65
    Spirit of, *vs.* spirit of the world, 4
    use of as *word crochet* in Galatians 3, 95–96
God-fearers, 80–81
good and evil, 137–39
good news, bases for, 76
Goppelt, Leonhard, 92n148
gospel. *See also* Paul the Apostle
    circumcision viewed in opposition to, 24
    divine origin, 28–29
    juxtaposition with law, 25n111, 27–28, 85, 85n118, 118
    Paul's, unity of, 72–73n53, 118n288
    and Paul's use of Scripture-based arguments, 91–124, 92n148
grace and peace, 164n76
    contrast with *law* in Romans, 55
    in Galatians *vs.* other epistles, 144–45
Grant, Robert M., 9n46
Green, Joel, 147m15, 151n31
Grimsrud, Ted, 156n47, 160, 160n63, 163
Gyllenberg, Rafael, 46n66

Habakkuk 2:4, 97–100, 99–100nn189–191
Haenchen, Ernst, 106n223
Hagar bondage, 96n172, 134n47
Hagar-Sarah contrast, 134n47
Hamerton-Kelly, R. G., 164n78
hanging following execution, 13–14, 104, 106–8
Harnack, Adolf von, 77–78n81, 78n84
Harvey, A. E., 48n74
Hawthorne, Gerald F., 7n37
hearing with faith, 89–90, 139n76
Hebrews (epistle), 162
Heim, S. Mark, 162n69
Hellenists
    Hellenistic law, 113nn255–256, 120n299
    Paul's relationship with, 45
    as source of Paul's practice, 29n123
    and use of Scripture by, 94–95

Hengel, Martin, 4n16
Heraclitus, 137–38
hilastērion (*mercy seat*) reference, 157, 158–59, 159, 160n62, 167
Hoad, John, 110
Hooker, Morna, 102n203, 110n244, 133n45, 148n19
Horeb-Sinai covenant, 115. *See also* Abraham, God's covenant with
Howard, George, 72n52
Hübner, Hans
  on *angels* as demons, 25n112, 113n257, 118n288, 130n21
  on Jewish view of law as pre-existing, 114n260, 116n271, 117n275
  on law as angel-mediated, 116n273
  on meaning of *law of faith*, 23n107
Hultgren, Arland
  on God's redemptive purpose, 167n87
  interpretation of *body of sin*, 54n98
  on Paul's reasons for prosecuting Christians, 104n211
  on Paul's use of the *mercy seat* in Romans, 159, 159n61
  on Paul's use of *place of God's mercy* for *mercy seat*, 160n62
  on self-definition by Jewish Christians, 33n5
  on union with Christ during life, 54n99
humanity
  Christ's actions on behalf of 59–61, 59n127, 59n129, 135n54
  Christ's personal experience of, 132, 132n26, 132n29
hyper (for, on behalf of), Paul's use of, 152
hyper hêmôn, 110n242

infancy, minority. *See also* freedom; old aeon; the Son, *sonship*
  contrasts with *heir, sonship*, 127n4, 131
  as keyword for old aeon, 126–27, 127n4, 142–43
  as subjugation/slavery, 125, 131n23

inheritance, heir. *See also* freedom; new aeon; the Son, *sonship*
  and acceptance of sonship, 123, 125, 133–34
  comparison with status of the redeemed slave, 131n24
  as keyword for new aeon, 95–96, 95n167, 113, 113n256, 126–27
  and thematic unities in Galatians, Isaac-Christ typology, 114n259
Isaiah
  impact on early Christian theology, 150n25
  as proof text for Paul's Christology, 14, 110–11, 110–11n245
  the *Suffering Servant* in, 147n12, 149n22, 149n24, 150
Israel. *See also* Judaism, Jewish tradition; Mosaic law
  as centered on Mosaic law, 20
  and Hagar-bondage, 96n172
  Israel of God vs. Israel of Judaism, 136
  and salvation history, 96n172

James
  Paul's interactions with, 70n39, 70n40
  relationship with the Jerusalem church, 73, 73n55
James, letter of
  as example of wisdom teaching, 140
  letter of, view of Abraham in, 93, 93n159, 96n171
James, men from
  purpose in Antioch, 80n96, 84n112
  reactions to threats against Jewish identity, 81n104
  and table-fellowship issues, 81–84
  Weiß's interpretation, 24n109
Jepsen, Alfred, 99n190
Jeremiah, reference to in Romans, 63n3
Jerusalem church
  as authority, Paul's response, 69–73
  James' relationship with, 73, 73n55
  Paul's distancing self from, 28–29, 68

SUBJECT INDEX

Jerusalem church (continued)
   Paul's relationship with leaders of, 33n1, 64n7, 70, 73, 70n40, 71n44, 74, 77n77
   Paul's visits to, 64–65, 64n7, 70n39, 71
   recognition of Paul's authority, 73
Jerusalem conference/agreement. *See also* circumcision
   Antioch incident as sequel to, 84
   and the background conditions in Acts, 76–77n74
   and circumcision requirement, 77–79
   implications, Paul's need to clarify in Antioch and Galatia, 78n84
   Paul's recounting *vs.* Acts version, 73–74
   works of the law in relation to, 86
Jewett, Robert, 9n45, 89n135
Jewish Christians
   controversies with Gentiles, 77n78, 78n84
   and *death to law*, 55n107
   experience of minority, 127
   need for conversion, 87–88n131
   nonadherence to Mosaic law, as separating factor, 20–21
   pre-Christian experience under the law, 128–131
   reconciliation with Gentile Christians, as theme, 7–8
   rectification tradition, 157n49
   self-definition, 33–35, 33–34n5
   variability in adherence to Judaism among, 80–81
   use of Scripture, 93n155, 94–95, 100, 100n193
Jews
   in Antioch, numbers, 77n79
   crucifixion of by Romans, 105
Job, and good and evil, 138
John, Apostle, as a pillar of the church, 73
John, Gospel of, 5n28
Judaism/Jewish tradition. *See also* Mosaic law; Pharisaic Judaism; Torah
   and combining of *law* with God's *promise*, 114
   covenantal nomism, xxii
   cultish vs. moral aspects, 21–22
   Day of Atonement rituals, 158–59, 159–160nn61–62
   and development of early Christian theology, 146n10
   importance of circumcision and dietary laws, 10–11n51, 86–87
   interpretations of the Abraham story, 92–93, 99n186, 114
   literature associated with, xxiv
   mercy-seat (hilastērion) tradition, 157–160, 159–160nn61–62
   and *obedience* to the law, 20–21, 24n109, 63, 74–75, 80–81, 85–86n121, 87n128, 96, 98, 121n301
   as the old aeon, xxi, 5, 26
   rabbis as personification of Scripture, 94n163
   religious and national identity, 81n104
   resistance to adopting cross as symbol for suffering, 105
   resistance to concept of a crucified Messiah, 13n63, 27–28, 103–6, 150n27, 166n84
   ritual observances, Pharisees vs. laypeople, 80n96
   and sacrifice and servanthood to Yahweh, 155–56
   salvation history, 17–18n80, 96
   view of law as pre-existing/eternal and salvatory, 116n271, 117, 117n275, 117n281
Judaizers. *See also like a Jew/like a Gentile* phrases
   imposition of *works of the law* by, 49
   Martyn's term "Teachers" for, 75n69
   struggles with Paul, 10n51, 74–75n64, 75–76, 98, 135n52
justification by faith
   Habakkuk as authority for, 97–98
   justification through circumcision *vs.*, 89, 89n135

SUBJECT INDEX 201

justification through the law *vs.*,
  22n103, 24, 24–25, 61, 87n128,
  168
Paul's arguments for, 27, 34–35, 87,
  87n130, 89–90, 102–3n203
and the sharing of Abraham's
  blessing, 93–94, 97–98, 123
as sole basis for church membership,
  19n89, 96, 168

kappōeth (throne of grace), 157–58. *See
  also* mercy-seat
Käsemann, Ernst
  on catholicizing of Paul, 6n33
  on Christ as the slain Paschal lamb,
    149n21
  on derivative *vs.* original material in
    Paul's writings, 166n84
  on Paul's Christology, 38n29
  on Paul's doctrine of baptism, 42n51
  on Paul's use of the term *forgiveness*,
    154n43
  on primitive Christian apocalyptic,
    141n89
  on viewing salvation as "chain of
    events," 111n248
Keck, Leander, 6n30, 22n103, 141–42
Kertelge, Karl, 19n89, 41n46
Kilpatrick, G. D., 70n40
Kittel, Gerhard, 144n1
Koester, Helmut, 128n13
kosmos (old world). *See also* old aeon
  as the old aeon, 162, 166
  composite profile of in Galatians
    6:11-16, 135–36
  identification of with old aeon, 96,
    128, 162
  possible meanings, 135n52
Kümmel, Werner Georg, 7n37

Lambrecht, Jan, 34n6, 34n7
laments, pre-Christian, 146
the *law*, 117–18. *See also* Mosaic law
  absence of from 2 Corinthians, 6
  as basis for justification, Paul's
    arguments against, 31, 34–35,
    117

applicability to both Jewish and
  Gentile Christians, 15, 20–21,
  128–130
association with death, 9–10, 36–37,
  46–53, 61–62, 87n127, 97,
  109n241, 118n286, 142, 166,
  168–69
association with *slavery/bondage/
  infancy*, xiv, 23, 37, 127, 132n29
association with *sin/flesh*, 15–16, 26,
  34–35, 50, 52, 54–55, 55nn102–
  103, 96n170, 102–103, 142
Christ's birth under, implications,
  132–33
contrast with crucifixion, xxi, xxvi,
  10
dying to, Paul's personal experience,
  43, 45
ending of/failure of, 25, 36n18, 37,
  43, 101n200, 109–10, 120, 122,
  127, 141, 141n83
experiential arguments against,
  88–90, 112n253
as inadequate pathway to
  justification, 24, 34–35, 87, 168
as indivisible, whole, 16, 23, 26,
  35n13, 64, 64n6, 82–83, 86n124
as instruction, 87n127
and judicial practice, 113n254
juxtaposition with blessing/faith/
  deliverance, xiv, 12, 15, 21n94,
  24, 25n111, 27–28, 31n132,, 43,
  51n85, 53, 55, 55n105, 68, 84,
  92–93, 97, 108–12, 108nn235–
  236, 23113n253, 123–24, 133,
  168–69
law of Christ, 23, 23n107, 75–76
moral bankruptcy of, 21n100, 49
multiple senses of in Paul's writings,
  xxiii, 8, 14, 16, 18–19, 22–23,
  22n102, 52n91, 61–62
positive references to, 14n67, 15
as powerless manifestation of old
  aeon, 4, 16–18, 22–23, 22n105,
  24, 29, 39, 42–43, 44n60, 46,
  45–46n66, 49n80, 50, 52, 65–67,
  77n75, 84–85, 117n274, 126–27,
  127n5, 141

the *law* (continued)
   as principle, 16
   psychological interpretations, 29n123
   purpose, 115–16
   as rational for silence and subordination of women, 14–15
   Scriptural arguments against, 16, 112–13n253, 121n303
law, Mosaic. *See* Mosaic law
law of faith, *law of the Spirit* (Romans), 23n107
under the law, 132n33
legalism, 87
letters, Paul's. *See* epistles, Paul's
Leviticus, Book of, 98
liberation. *See* freedom; faith; new aeon
Lietzmann, xxx, 45–46n66
Lightfoot, J. B., 49n80
like a Jew/like a Gentile, 82–86, 84n115, 85–86n121
Linton, Olof
   on corrections of Paul in Acts, 115n268
   on dating the material in Acts, 70n39
   on the end of law as a consequence of its death-bringing character, 51–52
   on inconsistent observance of law in Galatia, 86n124
   on Judaizers' view of Paul as subordinate to Apostles at Jerusalem, 74–75n64
   on Paul's uncompromising views on circumcision, 72n51
   on role of Acts in enhancing Paul's authority, 74n61, 75n66
living to/belonging to, 35–36, 55–56
logizomai (count, reckoning), 101–2n202
Loh, I-Jin, 7n37
Lohse, Eduard, 2n4
Lord's Prayer, 164–65, 164n75
Lührmann, Dieter
   on death-bringing aspect of law, 51
   equivalence of law and the elements, 127n5
   on failure of law to deliver righteousness, 121n301
   on Hellenistic traditions of inheritance, 126n2
   on Paul's connection of *Son of God* to his Gospel, 68n28
   on Paul's status at time of visit to Jerusalem, 70n40
   pedagogues in Paul's world, 122n311
   on redemption from slavery, 131n24
Luke, Gospel of, 76–77n74, 115
Luther, Martin, xiii, xiin1, 44n61, 157n54
Luz, Ulrich, 8n41, 153n37, 166n85
LXX. *See* Septuagint (LXX)

the Maccabees, 79n88
Manson, T. W., 19n86, 26n117, 158–59, r
marriage analogy (Romans), 54n101, 55–56
Marshall, I. Howard, 9n44
Martyn, J. L., 42n48
   on angel-generated law *vs.* Gods *promise*, 120n300
   on Christ as a *curse*, 108n233
   on Christ's *humanity*, 132n31
   on circumcision as a commandment, 76n71
   on divorcing of God's covenant from the law, 114–15n261-262
   on early efforts to interpret Jesus' death, 103n207, 146n8, 156–57
   on enslavement by the elements, 128n12
   on false teachers in Galatia, 157n49
   on function of doxology in Christian worship, 145n4
   Paul's opponents in Galatia, 28n120, 75n68
   on new creational community of new aeon, 134n49
   on Paul's perception of Christ's crucifixion, 38n33, 39–40n37
   on Paul's perception of himself, 40n41
   and Paul's rejection of Jewish tradition of sacrifice, 165–66

on Paul's selective quoting from
  Genesis, 114n258
on Paul's varying of the prescript to
  Galatians, 145n5
on possible meaning for *element of
  the world*, 128n10
on sin of following law instead of
  Christ, 35n12
on *through the law*, 44n62
translation of Galatians 1:3-5,
  145–46n7
translation of *works of the law*, 63n2
on use of early Christian hymns
  in Galatians and Romans,
  145–46n7
on use of term *adoption*, 133n43
on use of the term *sons*, 133–34n46
on use of early Christian hymns
  in Galatians and Romans,
  145–46n7
use of term "Teachers" for Paul's
  opponents, 75n69
on voice of law *vs.* voice of God,
  108nn235–236
martyrdom. *See also* self-sacrifice
  as mark of prophet in Jewish
    tradition, 147
martyr-servant concept, 149–51
view of Jesus' death as, 152m33
Masorete Text (MT)
  comparison of Deuteronomy 21:23
    and 27:26, 106–8, 106n224
  curse in Deuteronomy, word used
    for, 100, 106n224
Matthew (gospel), 153n37
McLeman, James, 6n33
Meeks, Wayne A., 78n81, 78n84
mercy-seat (*hilastērion*) tradition, 157–
  160, 159–160nn61–62, 167. *See
  also* atonement; self-sacrifice
Messiah, Christ as, Jewish polemic
  against, 13n63, 27–28, 103–6,
  150n27, 166n84
Michael, J. Hugh, 7n37
Michel, Otto, 91n147
Minear, Paul Sevier, 135n52
minors, minority. *See infancy, minority*
Morton, A. Q., 6n33

Mosaic law. *See also* Abraham, God's
  covenant with; Judaism/Jewish
  tradition; *the law*
abandonment by Christian converts,
  34–35, 69
as angel-mediated and inferior,
  97n173, 113n257, 116n273, 118,
  120n300
complete break with in Galatians,
  27–28
cultic obedience to, 24n109, 63,
  74–75
cultish vs. moral aspects, 21–22
dietary laws, religious significance,
  78–79, 79–80
divorcing of from *God's promises/
  testament/covenant*, 114–
  15nn260–262
Galatian Christian adherence to, 8,
  75, 75n68, 76
as God-given, 20n93, 25, 25n113,
  47n72, 51–52, 67, 69, 83n109,
  114, 118, 118n288
inconsistencies in references to,
  19–20
and Jewish identity, 81, 85–86n121
juxtaposition to Christ's dominion,
  35n12
Noachic laws, 80n100
obedience to, as basis for
  justification, 22n103, 24, 24–25,
  61, 87n128, 168
Paul's personal experiences under,
  19, 45
Paul's references to in epistles, 17, 23
and Paul's use of *nomos* for, 23–
  24n107
as preexisting, eternal, 113n257,
  117n275, 117n281
and righteousness associated with
  observance, 63n3
validity for Jews, Paul's acceptance
  of, 83n109
variable adherence to, by early
  Christians, 80, 82–83
Moses
  association with Adam in Romans,
  96n170

Moses (continued)
   and God's announcement of deliverance, 154
   as mediator of the law, 119, 119n292, 119n294
   Paul's assignment to the old aeon, 5
   Philo's views on, 138
   as symbol for slavery 4, 96
   view of as divine by Hellenistic Jews, 120n299
motifs, comparison of, as scholarly approach to understanding Paul-Judaism relationship, xxii
Moule, C. F. D., 36n17
Mowinckel, Sigmund, 150n27
Moxnes, Halvor, 98n181
MT. *See* Masorete Text (MT)
Mußner, Franz
   on *grace and peace*, 164n76
   on observance and curse, 51n85
   on Paul's apostolic mission, 73n54
   thematic unities related to *inheritance*, 95n167
   on *under the law*, 132n33
   on *will of God* references in the Qumran, 165n83
mystery religions, 2n4

Neusner, Jacob, 80n96
new aeon, new age. *See also* deliverance; the *law*; old aeon; redemption; two-aeon paradigm
   communicating, as Paul's mission, 65n15
   divine origin, through the Son of God, 29, 59–60, 67–69, 133–34, 140
   faith as basis for, 34n5, 97, 121n22, 140, 166
   inheritance as keyword for, 95–96, 95n167, 113, 113n256, 126–27
   and new relationships/pairings associated with, 122n315, 123n318, 139
   as new-creational community, 15, 102, 134n49
   and obliteration of the old aeon and the law, 41n45, 43, 135–36, 155n43, 169
   and promise of deliverance/new beginning, xiii–xiv, 41, 65n12, 87–88, 131, 162
   signs of, 90n141
   spirit as signifier of, 139n76
   as timeless, extending back in time, 117–18, 131n23, 136n56
Neyrey, Jerome, 89n134
Nida, Eugene A., 7n37
Noah
   God's covenant with, as everlasting, 115n264
   Noachic laws, 80–81, 80n100, 83–84
nomism, covenantal, xxii, 20, 20n93, 79n88, 87, 87n128, 114–15nn260–262, 116n273
not by works of law, 22n103, 23n106, 24–25
numbers (Aristotle), 137

Oepke, Albrecht, 38n33, 46, 48n76
old aeon, old dominion. *See also* new aeon, new dominion
   assignment of Judaism to, 5
   association with infancy/minority, 126, 127n4, 142–43
   association with slavery, 142–43
   break from, divine direction, 41n45, 67
   Christ's crucifixion as overturning of, 8–9, 39, 43, 87
   as concept in Galatians, 134
   kosmos/elemental spirits as, 96, 127, 130, 141, 162
   law as manifestation of, 4, 16–18, 22–23, 22n105, 24, 29, 39, 42–43, 44n60, 46, 45–46n66, 49n80, 50, 52, 65–67, 77n75, 84–85, 117n274, 121–22, 126–27, 127n5, 141
   total destruction of, by new aeon, 65n12, 139
Old Testament. *See also* Scripture *and specific books and writings*
   atonement and, 102
   contrast between Abraham covenant and Horeb-Sinai covenant, 115
   emphasis on opposites, pairings in, 138

SUBJECT INDEX

extension of Jesus' authority to, 91nn145–146, 147n12
as gospel, 92n148
law-keeping texts, Paul's reinterpretation of to lay aside law and law-keeping, 101
mercy seat and atonement in, 159n61
Paul's references to/use of in arguments, 17, 91n142, 91n144, 92, 95–98, 110
sacrifice, self-sacrifice in, 152n35
salvation as way of showing commitment to God, 156n47
opposites, paired (*the contraries, antinomy*)
as building blocks of universe and human nature, 136–38
circumcision-uncircumcision, 126, 139
and the Galatian view of the cosmos, 120n300, 122
listing of, 137n63
in Pythagorean theory, 137n62
tensions associated with, 137n64

paganism among pre-Christian Galatians, 128–29, 129n14, 130n21
participationist eschatology, xxii
Paschal lamb, Jesus as, 149n21
Paul and Palestinian Judaism (Sanders), xxi–xxiii
Paul the Apostle. *See also* circumcision; epistles, Paul's; Galatian opponents; two-aeon paradigm *and, specific epistles and concepts*
arguments against the law, 16–18, 45, 47n72, 77n75, 82–83, 83n109, 115, 117–19, 118n283, 120, 121n301
canonical *vs.* historical views of, 151n30
on Christianity as new community discontinuous with the past, 51, 93, 104n211, 117n274, 141
Christocentric theology, development of, xxi–xxii, 13, 8–10, 8n41, 9, 19n86, 19n88, 38–39, 38n33, 39–40n37, 96–97, 98n180, 110
conversion/experience of primacy of faith over law, 9, 22n105, 28, 43, 49–50, 52–53, 52n91, 53n94, 65n15, 69–71, 84–85, 112
development of ideas, 19n88, 95, 139, 152, 154n39
divine authority for apostolic mission, xiv, 5, 13n62, 28–29, 59n127, 59n129, 65–66, 66n17, 67n20, 69–72, 71n44, 132, 144–45n3
doctrine of baptism, 42n51
epistles, as specific to their audiences, xxii–xxiii, 30–31, 34, 134, 145
experience, arguments based on, 29n123, 65n15, 88–90, 96n170
gospel/apostolic mission, xxv–xxvi, 2–3, 2n5, 10, 11n52, 65–66, 68, 73n54, 83n109, 118n288, 134, 141–42, 142n90
kerygma, 4, 8, 10, 27n118, 30, 31n129, 38, 48, 150n25
legal terms, use of, 14, 112–123
meaning of *freedom*, 88–89n132
portrayal in Acts, 69n37, 74n61, 73–75, 75n66, 115n268, 157n49
psychological interpretations, 45n63
relationship with leaders from Jerusalem, 33n1, 34, 65n10, 69–70, 71n42, 71n44, 74–75, 77–79, 78n84
responses to contemporary critics, 40n41, 70n39, 75–76, 87n128, 93
scriptural language, arguments based on, 7, 13, 88, 92n149, 93, 99–100, 105–6, 109, 109n238, 128n11, 128n13, 149n24
visits to Jerusalem, 64–65, 71n42
Paul the persecutor
Pharisee training, experience of Jewish traditions, xxi–xxiii, 19, 21–22, 27–28, 49, 80n96, 120–21

Paul the persecutor (continued)
   references to life as, 52, 103, 106
   reasons for prosecuting Christians, 104n211
   views about law, 112
peace and grace, 146n9
pedagogues (false teachers), 122, 122n311, 127
perfect tense, meanings of, 40, 40n41
persecution, Paul's use of with *cross* in Galatians, as unique, 12
Peter (Cephas)
   apostolic mission, 73n54
   failed orthodoxy, 85, 85n118
   importance of covenant-keeping/ritual purity to, 77, 83–84
   life as Christian in Antioch, 82n107
   Paul's rebukes to, 3–4, 33n1, 35, 64, 70–73, 70n39, 70n40, 71n42, 77n7, 85–86, 163
   and Paul's relationship with the Jerusalem church, 70, 73
   teachings regarding circumcision, 72n52
Pharisaic Judaism, Pharisees. *See also* Judaism/Jewish tradition
   Paul's separation from, 15, 26
   and Paul's rabbinic training, xxi–xxiii, 19, 21–22, 27–28, 49, 80n96, 120–21
   strict observance of ritual practices, 79–80s, 80n96
Philemon, 1, 6n33
Philippians (epistle), 6, 12, 15
Philo of Alexandria, 93, 137–38
Pilate, Pontius, release of Barabbas, 153
placarded, 89
Plato, 71n44
Plummer, Alfred, o Christ's death as turning point, 60n131
plurality of angels, 119–120
political authoritarianism, x, 163, 163n73, 166
Pontius Pilate, 163
post-*parousia* with Christ, in Galatians 2:19, 40–42
preaching the gospel, and the cross as the source of power for, 2n6
pre-Christian laments, 146

preparatory function of the law, 45–46
promise. *See* Abraham, God's covenant with; covenant/promise, God's; *nomism*, covenantal
proselytes (full converts), 80
Pythagorean theory, contraries/opposites in, 137, 137n62, 138

Quaddish Prayer, 164n74
Qumran
   covenant community, 100, 100n193
   use of Habakkuk 2:4 in, 99n191
   will of God references, 165n83
   works of the law concept in, 63n3

Räisänen, Heikki
   on contradictions in Paul's writings, 18–20, 121n301
   on *dying through the law*, 44–50, 45–46n66
   on need for conversion by Jews, 87–88n131
   on Paul's adaptation of Jewish traditions, 119n289
   on Paul's metaphorical uses of *law*, 23–24n107
   on Paul's opponents in Galatia, 28n120
   on Paul's personal power, 18n84
   psychological interpretation of Paul's writings, 45n64, 45nn63–64
   on Romans 5:20, 114n260
   on *telos*, 44n60
   on universalistic vs. peculiarist view of law, 21n97
   on view that Mosaic laws were unfulfillable, 101n200
redemption/redemptive purpose. *See also* deliverance; salvation; self-sacrifice
   as Christ's crucifixion as embodiment of law as curse, 108–12, 133
   as consistent theme in Paul's epistles, 8
   and God as a unity, 165
   and moving from *infancy* to *sonship*, 131
   as purpose Christ's death, xiii–xiv

as purpose of Christ's self-giving death, 169
as purpose of God's sacrifice of the Son, 167n87
through Christ, as Paul's central theme, 8–9, 23
view of law as preparatory for, 45–46
Reicke, Bo, 55n105
religious institutionalism, x, 163, 163n73, 166
resident aliens, Gentiles as, 80
resurrection. *See also* crucifixion, cross; *dying*; new aeon, new age; redemption; salvation; self-sacrifice
and the *Christ-event*, 29–30
crucified as code word for, 88–89n132
Grimsrud's view, 161
mentions in 1 Corinthians, 4n22
mentions in Galatians, 41
mentions in 1 Thessalonians, 2–3n10, 37n24
role in "theology of the cross," 166n85
and time-independent nature of salvation, 111n248, 117–18
Wink's view, 161–62
revelation
contrast with *elements*, 128, 131n23, 135n52
impact on Paul's views of Christianity, 104
mentions of in First Corinthians, 28n121
Paul's personal experience of, 28–29, 64–67, 66n17
and Paul's rejection of law as standard of faith, 87
traditional language for, Paul's use of, 3n13, 53, 67n25
Riesenfeld, Harald, 110n245, 152n35
righteousness
and Abraham's faith, 92, 102n202
and adherence to Jewish laws, 63
and Christ's redemption from curse under the law, 55, 133
equating with *faith* and *life*, 97–99, 98n181
in Habakkuk 2:4, 99–100n191
juxtaposition with law, 51, 94, 112
use of epistles, 27
rising to life, 54n100
Robinson, John A., 57
Rochford, Dennis, 147n12
Romans (epistle)
acceptance of Paul's authorship, 6n33
baptismal interpretations, 42–43
Christ's *body* in, 57–59
comparisons with Galatians, 16–18, 18n81, 31–32, 31n133, 46–48, 53–59, 60
cross/crucify/crucifixion in, 6, 6n30, 8, 11, 15–16, 47, 57–58
description of Aquila and Priscilla, 152
dying to in, 35, 42, 56–59
faith/by faith in, 15, 98
flesh reference, 11
the *law, works of the law* in, 15–18, 17n76, 31–32, 31n133, 50, 56–59, 64n5
and liberation from law/slavery/bondage, 14, 16, 37, 47, 54–55
logizomai in (count, reckoning), 102n202
marriage analogy, 55–56
mercy seat in, 156–57, 159
redemption/salvation in, 42n51, 110, 165n82
psychological interpretations, 45n63
resurrection theme, 41n47
salvation history in, 96n170
telos, end in, 44n60

sacrifice. *See* self-sacrifice, self-giving
salutation in Galatians, unique elements, 144–45
salvation. *See also deliverance*; faith; the *law*; new aeon; redemption
and centrality of cross in arguments related to, 13, 27
as "chain of events," Käsemann's cautions, 111n248

salvation (continued)
  and Christ's obedience to God the
    Father, 164–67, 164n80, 165n83
  as coming from God alone, 165n82
  Paul's emphasis on, 27, 42n51, 110,
    165n82
  shalom-oriented approach, contrast
    with sacrificial payment,
    159–160
  through Christ's redemptive death,
    xxv, 29–30, 89–90, 149–150,
    153–55, 160, 164–65, 165, 169
Sanders, E. P.
  analysis of Galatians 3, 123–24
  on arguments related to angels,
    118n289
  on cohesion in Paul's theology, 22
  on equating of *righteousness* with
    life, 98n181
  on *by faith*, 97n174
  on the indivisibility of law, 124n324
  on Jesus' conviction under the law,
    48n74
  on law as agent of death, 47–48
  on *not by works of law*, 14n67,
    22n103
  pattern comparison analytic
    approach, xxi–xxiii
  on Paul's Galatian opponents as
    Christians, 28n120, 102n203
  on Paul's use of scriptural texts,
    92n153, 123n320, 123n321
  on treatment of law in Galatians vs.
    Romans, 16
Sanders, J. A., 99n191
Sasse, Hermann, 135n52
Schillebeeckx, Edward, 146n10, 147n12
Schlatter, Adolf von, 3n14, 59n127,
  86n125
Schlier, Heinrich, 41n46, 58n123, 72–
  73n53, 77n77, 132n29
Schnackenburg, Rudolf, 41n46
Schoeps, H. J., 19n88
Schweizer, Eduard, 40–41, 41nn44–46,
  57, 130n19, 132n32, 139n76
Scripture. *See also* Abraham, God's
  covenant with; Old Testament
  and specific books and writings

arguments against the law based on,
  88, 91–123, 91n142, 92n149,
  92n151. 100, 110–11, 112–
  13n253, 121n303
contradictory texts, Paul's
  acceptance of, 98n180
format of arguments using, 91
and the juxtaposition of law and
  faith, 97–98
as proof texts for Christology, 110–
  11, 110–11n245
prophetic texts, 92n152
rabbis as personification of, 94n163
relationship with Christ's death,
  early Christian understandings,
  103n207
as source of knowledge of opposites,
  137–38
use of counter opponents'
  arguments, 101–2, 91–124,
  92n153, 123n320, 123n321
seed/offspring, 96n172, 113–14,
  114n258. *See inheritance*; the
  Son, *sonship*
self-sacrifice, self-giving. *See also* the
  mercy-seat
  Christ's, as voluntary act of faith,
    59n127, 59n129, 147–49, 154–
    55, 161–62
  Christ's, as obedience to the will
    of God, 164–67, 164n80, 165,
    165nn82–83
  deliverance as purpose of, xxv,
    29–30, 89–90, 149–151, 153–55,
    160, 164–65, 165, 169
  expiatory, Jewish view of Christ's
    death as, 152m33
  in Jewish tradition, 156, 165–66
  and the message of the cross, 149
  multiple meanings, 155n45
  and *the one who gave* (giving,
    didomi), xxv, 148, 148n18,
    149n24
  Paul's terms for, 152
  ultimate meanings, 161–62
  understandings of in ancient world,
    155–56, 158n57
Septuagint (LXX)

SUBJECT INDEX 209

comparison of Deuteronomy 21:23
with 27:26, 104–5, 106–8,
106n224
curse in Deuteronomy, words used
for, 100, 106n224
in faith in, 98–99
role in development of Paul's
theology, 113n255
tradition of angels attending the
giving of the law to Moses, 118
servant/serving (*doulos/douleuo*),
54n99, 149. *See also* self-
sacrifice; will of God
Shechemite Dodecalogue, 100, 106
sin, sinfulness. *See also* slavery
association with death, 50–51
association with *flesh*, 15–16, 26, 52,
54–55, 102–103, 142
association with the *law*, 15–16, 26,
34–35, 50, 52, 54–55, 55nn102–
103, 96n170, 102–103, 142
Christians as sinners, 34n6
and *dying to sin*, 46–47, 54–55,
153–55, 160n64
as imprisonment, 166
Jewish traditions related to, 34n6,
34n7, 108n236
Paul's references to in the singular,
151n30, 155
and Paul's view of his former life, 52
as transferable to others, 108n236
sin-offering, 107, 108n236, 110n244,
111. *See also* atonement; *mercy-
seat*
slavery, enslavement, bondage
association with infancy/minority,
xiv, 23, 37, 125, 127, 131n23,
132n29, 125
association with old aeon, 142–43
Moses as symbol for, 4, 96
and law, faith as path of redemption
from, 15, 27–28, 34–35, 53–55,
64, 68, 87, 87n130, 122, 127,
131n24, 133, 142–43, 154
juxtaposition with *sonship*, 96
liberation from, in Romans, 14, 16,
37, 47, 54–55
and pre-Christian experience of
minority, 127–28

and the return to observance by
Gentile Christians, 130–31
the Son, *sonship*. *See also* inheritance,
heir
adoption into, as definition of
liberation, 127n4
association with *inheritance of faith*,
123, 125, 133–34
and Christ's connection with Spirit
and faith, 140–41
and God's mission in sending Christ
to earth, 141, 148
identification of Christ as, 114, 132,
148, 148n17
Son of God, 67–68, 68n28, 133–
34n46
soul, as a mix of good and evil, 137–38
the Spirit, as gift, confluence with faith,
confluence with faith, 89–90
connection with the Son, 139n76,
140–41
juxtaposition with *flesh*, 11–12,
55n105, 139–140, 139n76
juxtaposition with law in Galatians,
11–12, 55n105, 27–28
opposition to law and flesh, in
Romans, 55n105
spirituality, and theological
understanding, 89–90
Stanley, David Michael, 29–30
Stauffer, Ethelbert, 112n250
Stendahl, Krister, 13n62
Stephen, adherents of among Greeks,
78n84
stoicheia (elements), 130n19, 134, 137.
See also elements
strength in weakness paradox, in 2
Corinthians, 4–5
stumbling block (*scandal*), 10–11
suffering. *See also* mercy-seat; self-
sacrifice
Christ's, as necessary for
redemption, 160n64
and personal identification with the
cross, 7
sharing in, as part experiencing
Christ, 5n28
Synoptic Gospels, 148

table-fellowship. *See also* dietary laws
  at Antioch, approaches to
    understanding, 81–85
  discussion of in Galatians, 64, 77–79
  Dunn's views on, 72n52
  as marker of identity, 81
  Paul's focus on, in Galatians, 88
  religious and social functions, 79
  rules governing, Pharisee pre-
    occupation with, 79–80
  and unity of Jewish and Gentile
    Christians, 79n86
  variability in adherence to, 80
Tannehill, Robert, 37n24, 39, 41m45,
  41n44, 54
teachers (pedagogues), 89n134, 157n49
telos in Romans, Räisänen's
  interpretation, 44n60
Ten Commandments. *See* Dodecalogue
Theißen, Gerd, 19n88
theological arguments, use of legal
  language to support, 112–123
theology of the cross, 166n85
theophany, language of, 28–29
Thessalonians, 1, 2–3n10
Thiselton, Anthony, 15n71
through (preposition), categories of
  usage, 46
through the law, 9–10, 44nn61–62, 168–
  69. *See also died to the law*
Timothy, circumcision of, 74n63
Titus
  and the circumcision requirement,
    72n51, 84
  mention of in Galatians, meaning,
    72
  role as test case, 65n9, 72n50
Torah. *See also* Judaism/Jewish tradition
  impossibility of keeping the law,
    101nn199–200
  submission to, as form of bondage,
    130
  Torah piety, Paul's alienation from,
    23–24n107, 26n117, 126
  as tree of life, Paul's contradiction of,
    121n301
  view of as cultic, 21, 112, 130n21
transgression. *See sin, sinfulness*

Trypho, 104
two-aeon paradigm. *See also* the law;
  new aeon, new dominion; old
  aeon, old dominion
  complete discontinuity between old
    and new, 43, 134n47, 141, 169
  in 2 Corinthians, 59–60
  and *deliverance from the present age
    of evil*, 162–63
  and dismissal of circumcision-
    uncircumcision distinction, 126
  emphasis on in Galatians, 5, 39, 166
  elements vs. fullness of time, 131n23
  and faith, 29, 121–22, 133–34,
    140–41
  and the law as manifestation of the
    past, 44n60
  and Paul's apocalyptic theology,
    69, 141–42, 141n87, 141n89,
    142n90
  as fundamental to Paul's preaching,
    xxii–xxiii, 68n30 126, 169
  Watson's dismissal of, 68

in vain/for nothing, in Galatians,
  thematic unity provided by,
  95–96n168
Vincent, Marvin R., 7n37
vocabulary, Paul's, importance of
  understanding, xxiii
Von Rad, Gerhard, 158n57

Watson, Francis, 10–11n51, 68n30
weakness, as aspect of Christ's
  crucifixion, 4–5, 5n28
Weber, Hans-Ruedi, 27n118
Wedderburn, A. J. M., 6n32, 36n17
Weder, Hans, 3n13, 7, 90n139,
  109nn238–39, 109n241
Weiß, Johannes
  interpretation of *from James*, 24n109
  on issue of church unity in Antioch,
    79n86
  on Titus' circumcision, 72n51
  on use of *revealed* in 1 Corinthians,
    28n121
Westhelle, Vitor, 146n10

who gave himself for . . . 146, 149. *See also* self-sacrifice
Wilckens, Ulrich, 58n123, 78n81, 78n84, 101n199
Wilcox, Max, 91n145
will of God
   echoes of Jewish *Qaddish* Prayer, 164n74
   and Mosaic law, 63n3
   Paul's use of, 164–67, 164n80
   in the Qumran, 165n83
   and redemptive salvation, 165, 165nn82–83
will/testament (covenant), Paul's conflation with *inheritance* in Galatians 3, 113
Wilson, S. G., 76–77n74
Wink, Walter, 161
wisdom, wisdom talk (*sophia*)
   cross as antithesis of, 2, 11, 27, 29
   James' letter as example of, 140
   Paul's arguments against, 2–3, 3n13, 3n14, 7, 29

with- construction, compound verbs using, 40–41
women, as subordinate, *law* supporting, 14–15
works of the law. See also the *law*; Mosaic law
   and the Antioch incident, 84, 86
   association with *curse*, 94
   Betz's views on, 64n4
   Borse's interpretation, 49
   examination of, xxv
   in Greek, 63n1
   importance in Jewish tradition, 49, 63, 64n4, 115
   Martyn's translation, 63n2
   as parallel concept to *flesh*, 139n76
   Paul's use of, 23, 63n3, 64, 64n5
   in the Qumran, 63n3
the world, 134–35. *See also kosmos* (old world); old aeon, old dominion
Wuellner, Wilhelm, 92n149

yeser (impulse, evil inclination), 140, 140n79

Index of Scriptural References

Old Testament

Genesis

1:3–5	138
3:16	15
12:2–3	115, 148n17
12:3	92, 92n153, 93, 101, 123n320
12:7	102, 114n258
13:15	102, 114n258
15:6	92, 93, 93n155, 96n171, 97, 98, 99n191, 101, 101n199, 123, 124
15:10	137–38
17:1–8	115
17:1–11	113
17:7	102, 114n258
17:9–14	79
18:18	92n153, 93, 101, 103, 123, 123n320, 124
22:15–18	96n171
22:18	92, 102
24:7	102, 114n258
37:21	154n40

Exodus

3:7–8	154, 154n41, 166
3:8a	154n41
18:4	154n41
18:8	154n41
18:9	154n41
18:10	154n41
25:17	157, 157n54
25:17–22	157
25:20	157n54
25:22	157, 159
26:34	157n54
30:6	157n54
31:7	157n54
34:29	119, 119n294
35:12	157n54
37:6	157n54
37:9	157n54
39:35	157n54

Leviticus

3:17	79n93, 101
7:26–27	79n93
11:1–23	79
16:2	157n54
16:11–17	157

Leviticus (continued)

16:13	157n54
16:29-30	58, 159
17:10-14	79n93
17-18	76-77n74
18:5	92, 95, 97, 98, 102, 112
24:13-16	108n236
24:20-22	108n236

Numbers

7:89	157n54, 159

Deuteronomy

6:4	120n298
6-26	100n196
12:6	79n93
12:23-24	79n93
14:3-21	79
5:23	79n93
21:23	11, 13, 48, 92, 94, 100, 102, 103-4, 104, 104-5, 104n211, 105-6, 106, 106nn222-23, 107, 108, 109, 110n245, 111, 124n323
21:23b	108
27:15-26	111
27:26	92, 94, 94n165, 95, 100, 101, 101-2, 106-7, 107, 108, 109, 123, 123n321, 123-24n323, 124
28:49	14
30:12-14	98
30:15	138
30:20	138
32:17	129n14
32:39	154n40
33:2	118

Joshua

8:29	104

Esther

25:17	157

Job

2:10	138
5:4	154n40
5:19	154n40

Psalms

5:12	8n41
13:1	147
22:1	147
30:2-3	154n40
132:7	157
143:2	92, 92n151

Ecclesiastes

18:7	xiin1

Isaiah

53:10	160n64
28:11-12	14
31:5	154n40
42:1-4	149n22
42:11	138
43:13	154n40
44:24—45:13	138
45:1	138n72
45:7	138
45:56	138
	49:1, 132
	49:1-6, 149n22
49:5	132

50:4–11	149n22	**Daniel**	
52:7	65–66		
52:13—53:12	149n22	1:8–10	79n88
53	110, 110n245, 112, 150n25		
53:1	90n140	**Joel**	
53:9b	110		
53:9b-11	95, 110	2:28	90n141
53:10	110		
53:11	90n139, 110		
53:11–12	110–11n245, 152n35	**Amos**	
53:12	149, 149n22, 152	3:6	138
		5:18–20	138

Jeremiah

Habakkuk

1:5	65–66, 132	2:3–4	100n191
1:7	132	2:4	92, 94, 95, 97, 98, 98n180, 99, 99n189, 100, 101n199, 102, 112
31:33	63n3		

New Testament

Matthew

3:17	148n17	24:9–10	148n18
4:12	148n18	25:14	148n18
5:25	148n18	25:20	148n18
6:9	164, 164n74	25:22	148n18
10:4	148n18	26:2	148n18
10:17	148n18	26:15–16	148n18
10:21	148n18	26:21	148n18
11:27	148n18	26:24ff	148n18
15:2	80n95	26:42	165
15:17	80n96	26:45–46	148n18
15:20	80n96	26:48	148n18
17:21–22	153	27:2ff	148n18
	17:22, 148n18	27:15	153
17:25	153	27:15–26	153
18:34	148n18	27:18	148n18
20:18–19	148n18	27:19	153
21:33–46	148	27:26	148n18
23:23	80n96	27:44	6

Mark

1:11	148n17
1:14	148n18
3:19	148n18
4:29	148n18
7:2–5	80n95
7:13	148n18
7:19	80n96
9:31	148n18
10:33	148n18
12:1–12	148
13:9	148n18
13:11–12	148n18
14:10–11	148n18
14:18	148n18
14:21	148n18
14:24	110n245
14:41–42	148n18
14:44	148n18
15:1	148n18
15:6–15	153
15:10	148n18
15:15	148n18
15:32	6
16:20	46

Luke

1:2	148n18
3:22	148n17
4:6	148n18
9:31	162
9:44	148n18
10:22	148n18
11:38	80n95
12:58	148n18
18:12	80n96
18:32	148n18
20:9–19	148
20:13	148
20:20	148n18
21:12	148n18
21:16,	148n18
22:4	148n18
22:6	148n18
22:19	110n245
22:21–22	148n18
22:48	148n8
23:13–25	153
23:25	148n18
24:7	148n18
24:20	148n18

John

1:29	112n250
3:16	133n44
3:17	133n44
6:64	148n18
6:71	148n18
10:26–27	104
12:4	148n18
13:2	148n18
13:11	148n18
13:31	148n18
18:2	148n18
18:5	148n18
18:30	148n18
18:35–36	148n18
18:40	153
19:11	148n18
19:16	148n18
19:30	148n18
19:32	6
20:25	8
21:20	148n18

Acts

3:13	148n18
5:30	13n65, 106, 106n223
6:5	82
6:14	148n18
7:42	148n18
7:58	74n60
8:1	74n60
8:3	148n18
9:10–19	69n37
9:19–25	74n61

9:26–30	70n39	2–3	54n101
10–11	82	2:6	111
10:39	13n65, 106, 106n223	2–10	15
		2:12	17
11:19	78n84	2:12–16	21n94
11:26	82	2:12–29	20
11:30	82n108	2:13	17
12:4	148n18	2:14d	16, 17
13:29	13n65, 106	2:15	63n3, 64n5
14:26	148n18	3:3	54n98
15	24, 82n108	3:5–8	115
15:1	83	3:9	151n30
15:2	65n10	3:19	121n303
15:11	46	3:19–31	15
15:20	79n92, 79n93	3:19a	17
15:26	148n18	3:19b	17
15:28	74, 74n63, 75	3:20	17, 64n5, 151n30
15:29	79nn92–93, 82	3:21	15, 17, 17n76
15:40	148n18	3:22	46, 102nn202–203
16	74n63	3:24	112n250
16:4	74, 148n18	3:25	46, 156, 157, 157nn49–50, 157n54, 159, 159n61, 167
17	2		
18:13	115		
21:11	148n18		
21:21	115	3:26	102n203
21:24	115	3:27	23n107, 64n5
22:4	148n18	3:27a	16
24:5	115	3:27b	16, 46, 49
24:13	115	3:28	64n5
25:7	115	3:31	54n98
26:12	74n60	3:31b	17, 159
26:18	154n41	4:1–22	92, 92n149
27:1	148n18	4:2	64n5
28:17	148n18	4:3	55n105, 101–2n202
		4:6	64n5

Romans

		4:7	151n30
		4:11–12	16, 49
1:3–6	68n28	4:13	114n261
1:7	68n28, 144n2	4:13–15	115n265
1:9	68n28	4:13–25	15
1:16	102n202	4:14	54n98
1:17	97n174, 98	4:15b	16
1:18—3:9	16, 159	4:16	96n172
1:24	148, 148n18	4:25	112n250, 146, 148n18, 157n49
1:26	148, 148n18		
1:28	148, 148n18	5:5	54n101
		5:6	6

Romans (continued)

Reference	Pages
5:8	152
5:9–10	155n43
5:10	46
5:12	151n30
5:12–21	38n33
5:13	16, 17
5:13–14	17n80
5:17–18	55n105
5:18	55n105
5:20	17, 17n80, 55n103, 114n260, 151n30
6	41n47, 54, 54n101
6:1—7:6	55n103
6:1–14	42
6:2	35, 47, 54, 57
6:2–11	54, 59, 60
6:2–14	41n46
6:3	57
6:3–5	41n44
6:3–11	58n123
6:4	59
6:4–8	41n46
6:5–11	47
6:6	6n30, 8, 11, 15, 29, 42, 54, 54n98, 59, 151n30
6–7	55n106
6:7	58
6:8b	40n43
6:9	54
6:10	47, 151n30
6:10–11	35, 54
6:11	42, 46
6:14	17, 54, 115, 151n30
6:14–15	55
6:14–23	47
6:15	17
6:16	151n30
6:16–23	54
6:17	148n18
6:19	113
6:20	55, 151n30
6:21–22	54
6:22–23	151n30
7	19n88, 45n63
7:1	54, 55–56
7:1–4	46
7:1–6	xxv, 37n24, 54, 54n55, 56, 57, 59
7:1–9	17
7:2	54, 56
7:2–3	54n101, 55
7:4	xxv, 31, 35, 37, 44n62, 47, 53, 53n95, 54, 55, 56, 57, 58, 58n123, 59, 60
7:4–5	54
7:4a	56, 57
7:4b	56
7:4c	56
7:5	54n101, 55n102, 61, 117, 151, 151n30
7:5–6	55n106
7:6	35, 47, 54, 54n101, 58, 59
7:7	151n30
7:7–12	50
7:7–20	14n67, 47
7:8	15, 117
7:8–13	50
7:9	117
7:9–11	16
7:9–13	47
7:10	15, 117
7:11	151n30
7:12	15
7:13	15, 16, 151n30
7:13—8:4	17
7:14	17
7:17	17
7:20	151n30
7:21	16
7:23	151n30
7:23a	16
7:23c	16
7:25	151n30
7:25b	16
8:2	23n107, 151n30, 155n43

8:2a	16	1:10–13	1–2
8:2b	16	1:13	8, 89n132
8:3	16, 18, 133n44, 160n62	1:13–15	2
		1:13–17	41n47
8:3–4	110	1:17	2, 3, 8, 89n132
8:4	110	1:17b	2
8:10	46–47, 151n30	1:17–18	2, 29
8:32	41n44, 112n250, 146, 148n18, 150n26, 152, 160n62, 167n87	1:18	3, 8, 27, 89n132, 164n80
		1:18–20	7
		1:19	1–2, 91, 94n165
9:3	52	1:19—3:23	27
9–11	16	1:19–20	3
9:11	64n5	1:21	27
9–11	96n172, 142	1:23	8, 10, 11, 29, 30, 89n132, 166n84
9:32	64n5		
9:33	10n50	1:24–25	3
10:4	121n305	1:30	27
10:4–5	44n60	1–3	91, 92, 92n149
10:5–8	98	2:1	2
10:9	144n2	2:1–5	3
10:10	102n202	2:2	3, 8, 10, 29, 30, 89n132
10:16	90n139, 90n140		
11:6	64n5	2:6–8	2
11:9	10n50	2:6—3:4	3
11:27	151n30	2:8	4, 8, 29, 89n132
12:5	57, 58	2:9	91
12:19	94n165	2:10	28n121
13:8	15	2:10–13	28n121
13:10	15	2:12	4
14:1–2	82		2:14, 4
14:8–9	41n44	3:1	4
14:11	94n165	3:4	4
14:13	10n50	3:5	27
14:21	10n50	3:15	27
14:23	151n30	3:19	91, 94n165
14:34	17	4:4	27
15:32	164n80	4:7	4
16:4	152	4:15	46
16:17	10n50	4:20	3
16:25	65n11, 65n17	5:5	27, 148n18
		5:7	112n250, 149n21
		6:11	27, 157n49
1 Corinthians		7:16	27
		7:17–20	20
1:3	144n2	7:19	136
1:10—4:21	xxiii	8	82
		8:6	120n298

1 Corinthians (continued)

8–10	79n92
8:13	10n50
9:8–9	14
9:9	17
9:15	14
9:17	27
9:19	14
9:19–23	115
9:20–23	20
9:21	20
9:22	27
9:22–23	14
10:1–22	142
10:17	57
10:33	27
11:2	148n18
11:19	27
11:23	148n18
11:23–24	152
11:24	57, 110n245
12:3	144n2
12:12–13	58
12:13	57
12:27	57
13:3	148n18
13:7	27
14:6	65n17
14:21	14, 17
14:22	27
14:34	14
14:40	14
15:2	27
15:3	148n18, 151, 151n30, 152
15:3–5	150n25
15:8	74n60
15:9	52
15:11	27
15:12	30
15:17	151, 151n30
15:22	38n33
15:24	148n18
15:45–47	38n33
15:56	15, 117, 151n30
28:2	157

2 Corinthians

1:2	144n2
1:4	5
1:8	5
1:12	5n27, 164n80
2:4	5
3:1	6
3:3	6
3:3–13	44n60
3:6	5, 6, 47, 117
3:6–11	5, 6
3:7–18	118n283, 119n294
3:9	6
3:11	6
3:13	5
4:5	30
4:6	19n88
4:7–14	37n24
4:11	41n43, 148n18
4:14	41n43
4.17	5
5:7	49
5:13	36
5:14	39, 59, 135n54
5:14–19	59
5:15	36
5:16	60
5:17	6, 59
5:19	159n58
5:21	108n234, 108n236, 109n239, 110, 110n244, 111, 151n30
6:4	5
7:4	5, 5n27
7:14	5n27
8:2	5
8:5	164n80
8:9	110n244
8:13	5
8:24	5n27
9:2	5n27
10:8	5n27
10–13	7
10:18	5

11:4	5	1:6–9	65, 85n118
11:5	5	1:6–10	96
11:7	151n30	1:7	87
11:10	5n27	1:7–9	87
11:12	5	1:8	71
11:21	5	1:10	28n121, 136
11:29	10n50	1:11	28, 28n121, 65, 65n11, 113
11:30	5, 5n27		
12:1	5n27	1:11–12	70
12:9	37n24	1:12	19, 25, 28, 28n121, 43, 65n11, 65n12, 66, 67, 68, 87, 118, 127, 142
12:9–12	5		
12:9–13	4		
12:11	6		
13	5n27	1:13	103
13:4	4, 37n24, 40n43, 89n132	1:13–14	28, 142
		1:13–17	74n60
17	5n27	1:14–16	162
		1:15	46, 66n15, 132
		1:15–16	13–14, 13n62, 28, 43, 65
## Galatians			
		1:15–20	74
1	74	1:16	19n88, 25, 28, 28n121, 29, 43, 52n91, 65, 65n11, 65n12, 66n15, 67, 68, 69, 87, 127, 142, 150, 153n38
1:1	28, 65n12, 70, 88n132, 136, 145n5		
1:1–5	144, 169		
1:2	145n5		
1:3	144, 145n5	1:16a	87
1:3–5	144	1:16b	87
1:4	xiii, xiv, xxv, 29, 43, 88n132, 103n207, 144, 145, 145n7, 147, 150, 150n26, 151, 151n30, 152, 164, 164n80, 165, 169	1:16c	87
		1:16–17	68n29
		1:17	70
		1:17–18	28
		1:18	64, 65, 70, 163
		1:18–19	87
		1:21	43, 64
1:4a	xiii, xxv, 145, 146, 148, 149, 153, 156, 157, 164, 166	1:22–25	140
		1:23	87
		1–2	82
1:4b	xiii, xxv, 145, 149, 152, 153, 154n39, 156, 162, 164, 166	1–11	142
		2	74
		2:1–10	21, 65n8, 73, 78, 84, 86
1:4c	xxv, 145, 164, 166	2:1–18	23
1:4–5	145n5	2:2	25, 65n11, 65n12, 71
1:5	144, 145		
1:6	28n120, 52, 70, 75n67	2:2b	87
		2:3	68, 72, 83, 84, 86

Galatians (continued)

2:3–5	65n9, 87
2:4	5, 114n260
2:5	65, 65n9
2:6	71, 72
2:6c	87
2:6–7	163
2:7–8	72
2:9	73, 148
2:10	64n5, 82n108
2:11–12	21
2:11–14	64, 77, 78, 84
2:11–15	86
2:11–17	24
2:12	24n109, 68, 77, 79, 83
2:13	xiii
2:14	20–21, 33, 72, 82, 84, 85n119, 136
2:14b	33, 33n1
2:14–15	20, 84, 85
2:15	11, 13, 24, 82, 89
2:15–16	33, 89
2:15–21	33
2:15–24	82
2:15—3:25	131
2:16	17, 24, 27, 34, 35, 39, 46, 49, 64, 64n5, 83, 86, 87, 89, 90, 92, 92n151, 94, 102n203, 115, 120, 133, 136, 153n38
2:16–17	87, 87n130
2:17	27, 34–35, 115, 115n268, 151n30
2:17a	34
2:17a-b	34n7
2:17c	34
2:17–18	34
2:17–19	35n10
2:18	25n115, 34–35, 39, 85
2:18–19	34–35
2:19	xiv, xxi, xxv–xxvi, 6, 8, 9–10, 16, 17, 23, 24, 25n115, 26, 27, 29, 31, 33, 35, 35n13, 36, 37, 38, 39, 40–42, 41n44, 41n46, 42, 43, 44, 44n60, 46, 46–47, 47, 48n76, 49, 49–50, 52, 53, 53n94, 56, 59, 60, 68, 83, 88, 89, 90, 95, 102n203, 106, 117, 124, 135n54, 136, 142, 143, 153n38, 162, 166, 168
2:19–20	8, 37n24
2:19–21	37
2:20	xxv, 29, 41n46, 43, 59, 60, 68, 88n132, 94, 102n203, 128, 146, 148, 148n18, 149, 150n26, 152, 162
2:20b	87
2:21	17, 25, 27, 35, 42, 46, 49, 51, 65, 65n11, 87
2:28	94n162
2–3	51n85
2–10	64
3	15
3:1	9, 88, 89, 90, 108, 141n87
3:1–2	90
3:1–3	10
3:1—4:11	95
3:1–5	10, 27, 76, 88, 90, 95, 96, 112n250, 122, 124
3:2	17, 23, 24, 64n5, 89, 90, 139n76
3:2–4	136
3:2–5	85
3:3	89, 90, 96n168, 136, 139n76
3:3–12	123
3:4	89, 95–96n168

INDEX OF SCRIPTURAL REFERENCES

3:5	10, 17, 23, 24, 64, 64n5, 89, 90, 90n139, 95, 120, 139n76		131n24, 132n32, 133, 133n45, 143
		3:13a	94, 109, 112
		3:13b	94, 109, 112, 132n32
3:6	27, 90, 91n142, 92, 95, 96, 97, 101, 112n253, 120, 123	3:13c	20
		3:13–14	20, 46, 94, 95, 110, 112n250, 124, 133
3:6–9	93, 94, 95		
3:6–12	94	3:14	20, 24, 93, 94, 95, 113, 116, 120, 124, 129, 131n24, 133, 153n38
3:6–14	87n130, 90n139, 95, 97		
3:6–29	88, 91, 91n142, 92, 92n149	3:14a	112
3:7	93, 96, 129	3:14b	90, 112
3:7–14	95	3:15	113, 116
3:8	27, 91, 92, 92n153, 93, 94, 97, 120, 123, 124	3:15b	113
		3:15–17	126n2
		3:15–18	112, 113n253, 115
3:9	93, 120	3:15–29	112
3:10	16, 23, 24, 26, 64, 90, 91, 92, 93, 94n162, 94n165, 100, 101, 101n200, 106, 109, 111, 115, 117, 120, 123n321, 124, 124n324, 143	3:16	25, 92, 95, 102, 113, 114, 114n258, 114n259, 116, 120
		3:17	17, 17n80, 23, 24, 25, 54n98, 113, 114, 114n260, 116, 118n283, 120, 129
3:10a	17	3:17b	113
3:10b	17	3:17–18	24
3:10–12	94, 95, 97, 124	3:17–20	21
3:10–13	10, 37, 124	3:18	17, 24, 95, 113, 113n256, 115, 116, 118, 121, 123, 134
3:10–14	53, 93, 97, 98		
3:11	17, 24, 27, 92, 97, 98, 120, 133		
3:12	17, 24, 92, 98, 120	3:18c	118
3:13	5, 8, 9, 11, 13, 16, 17, 24, 27, 29, 30, 40n337, 42, 44n60, 48, 48–49, 48n76, 51, 52, 53, 61, 64, 88, 88n132, 90, 91n146, 93, 94, 97n173, 100, 103, 103n207, 105, 106, 109, 110n244, 111, 120, 123, 124, 124n323, 131,	3:19	17, 17n80, 23, 24, 25n111, 26, 44n60, 46, 50, 96, 113n257, 116, 117, 118n283, 120, 121, 129, 143
		3:19b	116, 118
		3:19c	116
		3:19d	120
		3:19e	120
		3:19–20	115
		3:19–29	95n167
		3:20	17

Galatians (continued)

3:20a	119, 120
3:20–26	15
3:21	17, 25, 27, 51, 98n181, 101n199, 116, 117, 118, 121
3:21b	118
3:21–22	120
3:21–23	21, 24
3:22	24, 46, 50, 95, 116, 121, 122, 151n30, 154n38
3:22–23	166
3:22–26	142
3:23	17, 17n80, 24, 25, 65n11, 68, 95, 97, 97n173, 121, 127, 127n5, 141, 142
3:23–24	17
3:23–25	44n60, 141n83
3:23–26,	20
3:23–29	121, 121n305
3:23–4:10,	16
3:24	17, 24, 25, 26, 26n117, 27, 42, 44n62, 46, 64, 89, 95, 96, 97, 118, 120, 122, 127, 154n38
3:24–29,	95
3:25	97, 121, 122
3:26	6, 100n196, 121, 122, 131n24
3:26–29	131
3:27	23n107, 41n47, 116, 122
3:27–28	122, 139
3:28	102, 127n4, 130
3:29	xiii, 91n142, 95, 97, 121, 123
3:31	23n107
4	123, 130–31
4:1	127n4
4:1–2	127
4:1–6	91n142
4:1–7	95n167
4:1–11	xxv, 126
4:2	18, 96, 121, 131n23
4:3	96, 121, 127, 127n4, 127n5, 128, 130, 131n23, 137n62, 143
4:4	24, 37, 42, 43, 44n60, 46, 49n80, 53, 61, 68, 96, 97, 110n244, 111, 121, 125, 127, 131, 131n23, 132, 132n32, 133, 133n45, 140, 142, 143, 160n62, 167n87
4:4–5	26, 133
4:5	68, 88n132, 111, 127, 131, 133n43
4:5a	131
4:5b	129, 130, 131
4:5–6	20, 24, 97n173, 129, 131n24, 133, 154n38
4:6	xiii, 68, 96, 129, 133, 133n46, 140
4:7	95, 96, 126n1, 127, 133
4:8	95, 96, 128
4:8–11	95, 96
4:9	96n168, 128, 130, 131n23, 137n62, 143
4:10	86n125, 129, 130
4:11	89n132, 95, 95–96n168, 122, 126n2, 127
4:21	24
4:21–31	96, 96n172, 134n47
4:23	121
4:24	96
4:25	96, 134n47
4:28	96
4:29	139n76
4:31	91n142
5	89

INDEX OF SCRIPTURAL REFERENCES

5:1	xiii, 11, 20, 139n76	6:13–14	136
5:2	11	6:13–16	136, 136n56
5:2–4	139n76	6:14	5n27, 8, 9, 28, 29, 36, 37n24, 39, 41n47, 59, 89n132, 130, 135n52, 141n87, 142, 143, 162, 166
5:2–6	11		
5:2–12	21		
5:3	24, 140, 141		
5:3–4	75, 86, 89		
5:4	11, 24, 27, 54n98, 139n76	6:14a	12, 134
		6:14b	12, 135
5:5	27, 139n76	6:14–15	xxv, 15, 126, 134, 143
5:6	136, 139n76, 143		
5:7	89	6:15	xiii, 6, 7, 59, 134, 162, 166
5:8	89		
5:10	89	6:15a	12, 136, 143
5:11	8, 9, 10–11, 29, 74, 89n132, 139n76	6:15b	134, 136
		6:16	136, 136n56
5:11b	89	6:17	89n132
5:12	26n117, 89		
5:13	24, 89, 139n76		
5:13–14	89	## Ephesians	
5:14	14n67, 24		
5:16–17	89, 139, 139n76, 140	1:3	112n250
		1:6–8	7n34, 112n250
5:16–18	139n76	1:17	65n17, 164n80
5:16–21	89	2:1	151n30
5:16–24	136	2:14–16	7
5:16–26	24	2:15	15
5:17	139, 139n76	2:16	89n132
5:18	12, 24, 139n76, 140	3:3	65n17
		4:3–6	120n298
5:19–23	139n76	4:19	148n18
5:23	16, 23, 115	5:2	148n18
5:24	8, 9, 11–12, 29, 41n47, 59, 89, 89n132	5:25	146, 148n18
		5:29–32	146
5:25	59, 134		
6:2	16, 23, 23–24n107, 23n107, 75	## Philippians	
		1:23	41n43
6–9	94	1:27–29	7
6:11–16	135	1:29	7
6:12	8, 9, 12, 12n55, 28n120, 89n132	2:8	89n132
		2:8b	6, 89n132
6:12–13	135	2:11	144n2
6:12–14	135n52	3:2	15, 26n117
6:13	11, 12, 12n55, 24, 86	3:5–6	74n60, 103

Philippians (continued)

3:5–9	15
3:8	26n117
3:9	102n203
3:18	89n132
3:18–19	7, 12
3:19	12n56
3:20	41n43

Colossians

1:13	8
1:14	151n30, 164n80
1:20	8, 46, 89n132
1:22	46
2:8	128
2:12–13	41n46
2:14	8, 89n132
2:20	128
3:1	41n46
3:4	40n43

1 Thessalonians

1:9–10	2–3n10
2:16	151n30
4:17	40n43
5:1–2	41n44
5:10	41n43

1 Timothy

1:20	148n18
2:6	146
5:22	151n30
5:24	151n30

2 Timothy

1:1	164n80
3:6	151n30

Titus

2:14	146

Hebrews

1:1–12	162
2:2	118n283
4:16	157n54
5:12	128
9:5	157, 157n54
10:38	99
11:17	93n156
12:2	162

James

2:2	93n156
2:21–23	93

1 Peter

1:19	112n250
2:23	148n18
2:24	13n65, 106, 110n245

2 Peter

2:4	148n18
2:21	148n18
3:10	128

1 John

4:9	133n44

Jude

1:3	148n18

Revelation

5:6	112n250

Old Testament Pseudepigrapha

Jubilees

1	118n283
23:10	96n171

Dead Sea Scrolls

Thanksgiving Hymns

6:13–14	120n298

Manual of Discipline

2:1–8	100n193

Pesher Habakkuk

8:1–3	99nn189

Apocryphal/Deuterocanonical Books

Tobit

1:10–13	79n88

Judith

10:5	79n88
12:1–20	79n88

Sirach (Ecclesiasticus)

17:11	98n178
44:19–21	93n156

Baruch

4:1	98n178
57:2	96n171
58:1	96n171

1 Maccabees

1:62–63	79n88, 79n91
2:25	86n123
2:50–52	93n156
2:52	96n171

2 Maccabees

6:1	86n123
6:7	86n123
6:18	86n123

4 Maccabees

5:2	79n92, 86n123
5:27	86n123
8:1	86n123

Prayer of Manasseh

8	96n171

www.ingramcontent.com/pod-product-compliance
Lightning Source LLC
Chambersburg PA
CBHW050851230426
43667CB00012B/2241